ARE
ALL THE
WOMEN
STILL
WHITE?

SUNY SERIES IN FEMINIST CRITICISM AND THEORY

Michelle A. Massé, editor

ARE ALL THE WOMEN STILL WHITE?

RETHINKING RACE, EXPANDING FEMINISMS

Edited by

JANELL HOBSON

STATE UNIVERSITY OF NEW YORK PRESS

Published by
STATE UNIVERSITY OF NEW YORK PRESS, ALBANY

© 2016 STATE UNIVERSITY OF NEW YORK

For information, contact State University of New York Press, Albany, NY
www.sunypress.edu

Production, Laurie D. Searl
Marketing, Michael Campochiaro

Library of Congress Cataloging-in-Publication Data

Are all the women still white? : rethinking race, expanding feminisms / edited
   by Janell Hobson.
       pages cm. — (SUNY series in feminist criticism and theory)
   Includes bibliographical references and index.
   ISBN 978-1-4384-6059-8 (hc : alk. paper)—978-1-4384-6060-4 (pb : alk. paper)
   ISBN 978-1-4384-6061-1 (e-book)
   1. African American women.   2. United States—Race relations.
3. Feminism—United States.   I. Hobson, Janell, 1973– editor.

   E185.86.A74 2016
   305.48'896073—dc23   2015021625

10 9 8 7 6 5 4 3 2 1

Contents

PART ONE

RETHINKING SOLIDARITY, BUILDING COALITION

PART FOUR

RECLAIMING THE PAST,
LIBERATING THE FUTURE

Illustrations

Images

Table

Acknowledgments

Amoo-Adare, Epifania Akosua. "Renegade Architecture." In *Spatial Literacy: Contemporary Asante Women's Place-Making* by Amoo-Adare, 7–9, 15–20, and 128. London: Palgrave Macmillan, 2013. Reproduced with permission of Palgrave Macmillan.

Duncan, Patti. "Hot Commodities, Cheap Labor: Women of Color in the Academy." *Frontiers: A Journal of Women's Studies* 35, no. 3 (2014): 39–63. Reproduced with permission of University of Nebraska Press.

Garza, Alicia. "A Herstory of the #BlackLivesMatter Movement." *The Feminist Wire* (October 7, 2014). Available: http://www.thefeministwire.com/2014/10/blacklivesmatter-2/. Reproduced with permission of *The Feminist Wire*.

Gan, Jessi. "'Still at the Back of the Bus': Sylvia Rivera's Struggle." *Centro Journal* 19, no. 1 (2007): 124–139. Reproduced with permission of *Centro Journal*.

Smith, Andrea. "Heteropatriarchy and the Three Pillars of White Supremacy." In *The Color of Violence: An INCITE Anthology*, edited by INCITE: Women of Color Against Violence, 66–73. Boston: South End Press, 2006. Reproduced with permission of Andrea Smith.

This edited volume could not have been assembled without the inspiration of the original editors of *All the Women Are White, All the Blacks Are Men, But Some of Us Are Brave*, including Barbara Smith (whose conversations with me guided the latter part of this process), Patricia Bell Scott, and Akasha Gloria Hull, as well as an old friend and colleague, Ime A. S. Kerlee, who started this dialogue with me since our time at Emory University. I am also grateful to Tamika Carey, for reviewing early drafts, and the editors of *The Feminist Wire*—Tamura Lomax, Monica

Casper, and Darnell Moore—who recommended and contributed important voices relating to social media and social movements emerging from
#BlackLivesMatter. I am especially thankful to all the contributors who
kept the faith and stayed committed to the fruition of this project.

Introduction

Janell Hobson

More than thirty years have passed since editors Akasha Gloria T. Hull, Patricia Bell Scott, and Barbara Smith published *All the Women Are White, All the Blacks Are Men, but Some of Us Are Brave: Black Women's Studies* through the independent publisher The Feminist Press. This occurred just two years after Barbara Smith cofounded the independent Kitchen Table: Women of Color Press. Realizing back then that neither of the established programs in women's studies and black studies would include the contributions of black women and their intellectual traditions in any meaningful way, black feminist scholar-activists created their own spaces for naming, asserting, and politicizing their radical existence. That such an independent-minded and radical act would be remembered today through this twenty-first-century edited volume and homage—published this time via a university press—is a testament to its tremendous impact on academia and especially on the diverse field of women's and gender studies.

In their introduction to this groundbreaking collection, Hull and Smith argued for the need for analyses that intersected gender, race, and class and asserted a political feminist stance that would reposition black women within academic research, academic curricula, and community engagement. Such analyses, they reasoned, would necessarily transform our knowledge of and resistance to multiple forms of oppression. As they suggest, "Only a feminist, pro-woman perspective that acknowledges the reality of sexual oppression in the lives of Black women, as well as the oppression of race and class, will make Black Women's Studies the transformer of consciousness it needs to be."[1]

Given the growth of women's and gender studies in the last thirty-plus years, this updated and responsive collection will reflect upon this transformation of consciousness through multiracial feminist perspectives. Indeed, the fields of women's and gender studies and other academic disciplines have been critically shaped by intersectional analyses, transnational feminist perspectives, action research and activist development, and the rearticulation of gender and sexuality in queer studies—all critical interventions that such early publications helped foster. Even with such growth and progress, concerns still remain as to how inclusive our feminist theories and practices have become in recognizing and complicating analyses of women and gender across races, ethnicities, nationalities, sexualities, and dis/abilities as well as in dismantling gender binaries and cultural and national borders. Since the initial appearance of *All the Women Are White . . .* , we have experienced considerable shifts in how we talk about race and its relationship to gender.

So why ask the question: Are all the women still white? We do so with the understanding that, as Purvi Shah notes in this volume, "across global topographies and idioms, the category of women is itself mobile and changing: the term refuses to be encompassed in one demarcation." The volume's titular question is a guiding reminder that gender and racial signage must be viewed as inherently questionable and unfixed, ever shifting and destabilized in different contexts, despite efforts to continually "fix" the category of *woman* through narrow frames. Our question also acknowledges the ways that the major shifts in the past thirty-plus years have reflected *superficial* rather than *transformative* change. As Patti Duncan argues in this volume, "In response to the challenges made by women of color, many women's and gender studies programs have shifted to make race and the experiences of women of color more central. However, these gestures are often deeply problematic, relying on additive approaches, occurring with little or no institutional structural framework, and/or shaped by an imperial feminism fraught with assumptions about the labor of women of color." We are still struggling to create transformative theories and practices that dismantle racism and its interlocking effects on hetero/sexism, classism, imperialism and other oppressive ideologies.

Rethinking Race

In their own updated anthology *Still Brave: The Evolution of Black Women's Studies*, editors Stanlie M. James, Frances Smith Foster, and

Beverly Guy-Sheftall described participating in the 2000 University of Wisconsin–Madison Symposium, "Are All the Women Still White? Globalizing Women's Studies." The event—organized by James and the late Nellie Y. McKay—invited questions on the similarities and differences between the concerns addressed in the 1982 edition and the challenges facing twenty-first-century black women's studies. They noted, specifically, "that the theorists, advocates, and practitioners of Black Women's Studies no longer feel compelled to present a united front . . . [hence fostering] lively debates and even tensions that have enriched the field."[2]

Interestingly, such tensions and debates framed a series of conversations with my friend and colleague Ime A. S. Kerlee that began in 2002. We had both completed doctoral work in women's studies, participated at different points in the feminist blogosphere on the Internet, and Kerlee specifically worked in feminist antiviolence nonprofits. In these various spheres of feminism, we were nonetheless disheartened by the ways that women of color were still relegated to the margins through tokenism and segregation—despite the occasional inclusion in college curricula of writers like Audre Lorde and bell hooks, whose words castigated our exclusion.

At the same time, when addressing black feminism in particular, we had grown increasingly wary of reductionist and racially essentialist claims that often posited black feminist studies as merely a *reactionary* response to racially unmarked "mainstream" feminist studies—which, when racialized, became a reductive label termed "white feminism." While such scholars as Kimberly Springer have historically recorded how "black and white feminist ideologies developed on parallel tracks,"[3] there is often the assumption that black feminists and other feminists of color came along at a much later date than their white counterparts to advance a narrow political agenda. Such views tend to ignore the foundational women's liberation work of black feminists Flo Kennedy, Shirley Chisholm, and Pauli Murray, while they also minimize criticisms of racial exclusion from feminist movements. Of course, reactions against racism need not suggest limitations or divisiveness in feminist theory and praxis. As Sara Ahmed notes, "Being against something is also being for something, something that has yet to be articulated or is not yet."[4] Here, Ahmed signifies the work of Audre Lorde, who envisioned anger as a liberatory tool, reminding us, "Every woman has a well-stocked arsenal of anger potentially useful against those oppressions, personal and institutional, which brought that anger into being. Focused with precision it can become a powerful source of energy serving progress and change."[5]

Within these emotions and critical tensions, we see a generative opportunity to consider how these earlier conversations have complicated our theories and practices and can move us forward in expanding feminisms and other social justice movements.

Eventually Kerlee and I issued a call for papers on the subject—Are all the women still white?—with the goal of broadening the subject of black women's studies to encompass a multiracial and transnational apparatus for rearticulating feminisms. As a result, we were hardly surprised but still disappointed by the vast number of responses e-mailed to us that accused us of engaging in an anti-white women project, a militant black women's project, or any other number of assumptions. Such responses, which also included a mix of those who were excited that certain women will be shifted once again "from margin to center," to quote bell hooks, and those who immediately assumed we were playing an age-old game of "divisive" identity politics, illustrated the need to continue investigating the complex interplay between race and gender, especially as it manifests in women's and gender studies and other academic and political arenas.

The question Are all the women still white? is a loaded inquiry, calling attention to a certain ideology of womanhood and questioning a normalizing and essentializing view of woman that implies a particular race, class, nationality, sexuality, ability, age, and, yes, gender. Certainly not everyone is comfortable with these ideologies being called into question. As Suey Park and David Leonard note in this volume, the labeling of "white womanhood" is less about targeting a specific racial demographic of women and more about challenging racial ideologies and positions of privilege and power. As they suggest, "White feminism isn't just a nickname or a descriptor of feminists who are white; it is a term used to group women whose political goals actually harm women of color. . . . That is, white feminism does not exist apart from white supremacy."

Despite these racialized divisions in feminist discourse and movements, multiple efforts were made in the previous century to create a postcolonial, transnational, and gender-variant apparatus that would shape twenty-first-century feminisms. Out of this struggle emerged a multiracial and multifaceted consciousness that has prevailed in our current struggles against various systems of oppression. Hence, when we inquire about race in the context of womanhood, we do so with the aim of dismantling these systems.

In updating these struggles, this volume takes its cue from the late Gloria Anzaldúa, who, in her essay, "now let us shift . . . in the path of conocimiento . . . inner work, public acts," embraces change and the epistemological and cultural shifting that twenty-first-century feminist theorizing and praxis now require. As she observed, "The binaries of colored/white, female/male, mind/body are collapsing. . . . Though these markings are outworn and inaccurate, those in power continue using them to single out and negate those who are 'different' because of color, language, notions of reality, or other diversity."[6]

A complete overhaul of systems based in gender, race, class, sexuality, nationality, and other markers of difference is now needed. Such shifts would collapse the workings of power and reimagine a different world in which we engage each other outside of accepted norms. Indeed, the twenty-first-century world must now *complicate* the binaries, not simply move beyond them as Anzaldúa argues, whether based in the racial binary of black/white, the gender binary of male/female, the cultural binary of the West/the Rest, or even, as Alexis Pauline Gumbs and Julia Roxanne Wallace observe in their essay, "Black Feminist Calculus Meets Nothing to Prove," the computer binary of zeros and ones framing our digital culture.

As Gumbs and Wallace passionately argue in this volume, "The value of our community and the brilliance of the individuals within it exceed the binary. Who we are is not limited to what the system that recognizes or punishes us can understand. We are nothing and everything. We are both zero and one, where zero is the circle that connects us to each other and one is the unity of our profound connection to each other and all life. And we are every other number too." This is the shifting value toward liberation that must now characterize contemporary feminist struggles.

Expanding Feminisms

The critique of racial power, privilege, and meaning, as well as other critical interventions based in cultural, national, gender, and sexual differences, is a mainstay in black feminist praxis. As the Combahee River Collective argued in their "Black Feminist Statement," included in *All the Women Are White* . . . : "If Black Women were free, it would mean that everyone else would have to be free since our freedom would necessitate the destruction of all the systems of oppression."[7] Theorizing from a position of racial, gender, class, and sexual minority status, the Combahee River Collective advances both a future liberation project and a

historical memory of liberation—felt most profoundly in their adapting
the name of Harriet Tubman's military-led raid at Combahee River in
South Carolina, which resulted in the emancipation of 750 slaves during
the Civil War in 1863. In the past, present, and future, black feminist
praxis proffers freedom as the necessary universal outcome for all if those
at the bottom of society attain theirs. Such sentiment also undergirds the
contemporary social movement surrounding #BlackLivesMatter, as its
hashtag cocreator Alicia Garza proclaims in this volume, "When Black
people get free, everybody gets free. This is why we call on Black people
and our allies to take up the call that Black lives matter."

The Combahee River Collective and #BlackLivesMatter activists
both allude to the words of Civil Rights leader Fannie Lou Hamer—
"Nobody's free until everybody's free"[8]—as well as the longer history
of black feminism dating back to Anna Julia Cooper, who asserted in
1892: "Only the BLACK WOMAN can say when and where I enter,
in the quiet, undisputed dignity of my womanhood, without violence
and without suing or special patronage, then and there the whole Negro
race enters with me."[9] Cooper wrote this at a time of intense Western
imperialism, racial violence, and lynching, which would in a few years
be sanctioned by legal race segregation in the United States. These
oppressive forces also merged with a white women's suffrage movement
that increasingly asserted white supremacist arguments to substantiate
"women's rights"[10] while simultaneously contesting the rights of black
men, who had achieved suffrage through the Fifteenth Amendment even
as they were slowly being disenfranchised with the onslaught of Jim
Crow. As such, Cooper recognized a century before Hamer, the Combahee River Collective, and #BlackLivesMatter the same urgent need for
black women's liberation, which would precipitate everyone else's rights.

Writing in the same period, Ida B. Wells also advanced black
women's liberation and highlighted the need for racial justice alongside
gender equality. Her journalistic work bore this out as she raised awareness of lynch law and the convict lease system, "twin evils which flourish
hand in hand"[11] in the criminalization of black communities. Wells specifically recognized how criminalizing blackness impacted *all* community
members, including women and children, despite what Darnell L. Moore
and Hashim Khalil Pipkin observe in this volume as the persistent and
exclusionary practice of organizing "around the needs of and presumed
social ills that impact black men." Consequently, this criminalization,
which arguably began with the penalization of enslaved women and
men who ran away or learned to read and write, would continue in the

forms of federal wiretapping of Civil Rights and Black Panther leaders, "war on drugs" affecting low-income communities of color, and the labeling of Black Lives Matter activists as potential "anti-police terrorists." This racialized history also fuels the twenty-first-century prison-industrial complex, built on a loophole found in the Thirteenth Amendment that allowed for slavery's continuation among incarcerated persons.[12]

In this volume, Julia Chinyere Oparah's essay "Beyond the Prison-Industrial Complex" details the long and arduous work of women of color antiviolence activists and prison abolitionists to intersect state violence with intimate violence for the twenty-first century. Such work necessarily disrupts a paradigm—perpetuated in both real and virtual environments—that is "built upon the entitlement to space and safety of white women," as Park and Leonard further argue in this volume. When situating our present condition in a historical context, we may note how Cooper and Wells laid a theoretical foundation at the turn of the twentieth century on which to analyze these interlocking systems of oppression.

Writing a decade after Cooper and Wells, Native American writer, music composer, and activist Zitkala-Sa also explored these systems of oppression through affirmation of her Sioux heritage and Native American resistance to US imperialism; consequently, in her recognition of these external forces that were "grossly perverting the spirit of my pen,"[13] she subverted her "assimilationist" education from Native American boarding schools. In essence, she resisted what Andrea Smith in this volume terms a "logic of genocide [in which] indigenous peoples must disappear [from national memory]. In fact, they must *always* be disappearing in order to allow nonindigenous peoples' rightful claim over this land" (emphasis in original). Such early examples of women of color accessing education and literacy to solidify their own identity formations, while also fueling an intellectual tradition based in political resistance, would be invaluable to later generations of feminist scholar-activists.

Even in referencing such feminist genealogies, I am indebted to the feminist scholars who emerged during the vibrant women's and black and other racial liberation movements in the 1960s and the 1970s—a period often referred to as "second-wave" feminism—as they began to recover and reclaim these women's writings, histories, and lives from the archives and other artifacts. Encouraged by political developments, feminist scholars repositioned diverse women for rediscovery and reevaluation—from Gerda Lerner's *Black Women in White America* to Angela Y. Davis's *Women, Race, & Class* to Paula Gunn Allen's *The Sacred Hoop* to Alice Walker's literary excavation of Zora Neale Hurston and other black women artists, women she would learn to recover when reading history not "for facts but to find clues."[14] Such methods, approaches, and topics intersecting race, gender, class, nationality, and sexuality transformed the academy at large and the field of women's and gender studies in particular.

Outside of the discipline of women's history, feminist scholars of color would apply similar methods in researching contemporary women and in rethinking resistance strategies in activist, artistic, media, and policy work that impact on the lives of women as well as women-identified and women-allied people, while also crossing national borders, complicating cultural flows, challenging gender binaries, refocusing from reproductive "rights" to reproductive "justice,"[15] and redefining feminist movements beyond ideas of "universal" struggles. As Amrita Basu notes in the arena of global and transnational feminisms, "Recall that some of the earliest and most important critiques of feminist universalism came from African American and Latina women in the United States,"[16] a development she believes reduced tensions in the sphere of international women's movements. Such critical interventions encompass not only the work of *All the Women Are White* . . . but also Gloria Anzaldúa and Cherríe Moraga's edited collection *This Bridge Called My Back: Radical Writings by Women of Color* (published through the Kitchen Table: Women of Color Press), soon to be followed by the contributions of Chandra Mohanty, Gayatri Spivak, Trinh T. Minh-ha, Grewel and Kaplan, and Ella Shohat to "Third World" feminist scholarship (or what Mohanty now champions as women-of-color-majority affirming "Two-Thirds World"[17]).

These global and transnational shifts were not without problems, however, as US-based feminists of color noted their "disappearance," once again, from critical fields of inquiry.[18] Because of these tensions, this volume has done much to interrelate the perspectives of both US-based feminists and feminists abroad—including their nexus at transnational points—whether in the comparative "Othering" of immigrant and overseas women, as Purvi Shah examines in "The Power of Sympathy," in the transnational struggles of Haitian-American Gina Athena Ulysse's *Because When God is Too Busy: Haiti, Me, and the WORLD,* or in the politicizing of urban space that frames the experiences of women of African descent—wherever they may reside in the world—as Epifania Amoo-Adare explores in her essay "Renegade Architecture." Ultimately, these feminist-of-color articulations that launched intersectional and transnational analyses in women's and gender studies assert the similar goal of what Hull and Smith argued about black women's studies: "Every aspect of our fight for freedom, including teaching and writing about ourselves, must in some way further our liberation."

Although *liberation* was an articulated goal in the wake of the radical movements in the 1960s and 1970s, such discourse is rarely utilized in our contemporary moment. Presently, we take for granted what our predecessors fought to proclaim: yes, we are here, and *we* intend to have full participation in democracy and progress. Unfortunately, now that "we"—if only in small numbers—can participate and indeed now occupy high positions of power, the very existence of democracy, social progress, and economic opportunities is under threat.

Even our high positions can be undermined through racial, sexual, and class rhetorics that would question our right and qualifications to occupy these positions—from the peeling back of affirmative action policies to racialized attacks on the leadership of public officials of color to the "presumed incompetence" of women faculty of color in academia.[19] In an era that requires that we all act bravely, not just "Some of Us," we are called upon to strive all the harder in maintaining and radicalizing the goals of liberation in academic fields of study and activist movements. This is especially urgent in order to combat the global spheres of white supremacy, imperialism, and hetero/sexism fueling perpetual warfare, neoliberal capitalism, corporate globalization, digital (mis)information, economic and environmental crises, mass incarcerations, political disenfranchisement, and the professionalization of many of our progressive movements that has diminished the social justice impulse of this work.

On the last point, the professional move from grassroots feminist activism to academic fields, nonprofits, and NGOs (nongovernmental agencies) affects the radicalism of such movements, especially in symbiotic relationships that often include activists who seek educational credentials by pursuing degrees at increasingly corporatized spheres of higher education in such fields as women's and gender studies, which in turn grant degrees to those who eventually work for and direct nonprofits and other community organizations. These major shifts in the last thirty-plus years have shaped how we as academics and activists view myriad complexities and the interrelatedness of race, gender, class, sexuality, and nationality. Yet, we do not always use a litmus test, which as Barbara Smith proposes—borrowing from poet Sonia Sanchez—may require a simple response to a simple question about our theories, methods, and practices: "How do [they] free us?"[20]

It was within this context of freedom that Smith had already asserted a practical definition of feminism: "Feminism is the political theory and practice that struggles to free all women . . . anything less than this vision . . . is not feminism, but merely female self-aggrandizement."[21] Of course, before we can "struggle to free all women," we would first need to *recognize* and *redefine* women (including transgender women and other gender-variant individuals) and then expand feminisms to encompass their struggles and dreams in all their complexities.

An Overview

With these various issues in mind, the essays and poetry in this collection contribute to an interdisciplinary collage in which multiple voices, experiences, theories, practices, and genres paint an intricate and multicolored picture. Such multiple positions dislodge the "all the women are white" question, while also gesturing toward more than mere reactionary exposition that women of color feminisms are expected to convey. Because of this, the different subjects and concerns illuminate the tensions and interventions that now structure rich, vibrant, and diverse feminisms.

Despite my best efforts to include a wide range of works, I would be remiss to overlook the various ways that, within this collection, different silences abound. Due to different restrictions on time, resources, labor, and physical conditions—often impacted by the current economic limitations of global capitalism—as well as the arbitrary academic gatekeeping of whose writing matters, important voices are missing from this volume. Because of such limits, this collection necessitates an ongoing conversation beyond this publication.

Some of the authors in this volume write as scholars, others as artists and activists, and still others embrace all identities in their work. Some operate within the historically constructed and generational "waves" of US-based feminist movements. Conversely, others occupy different times, spaces, and places or disrupt notions of history, myths, scholarship, activism, and poetics. They discuss rage, creativity, teaching, organizing, the prison-industrial complex, global capitalism, urbanization, digitization, wars, intimate partner and sexual violence, situated sexualities, transgender identities, and resistance to legacies of white supremacist capitalist and imperialist heteropatriarchy. In these intricate and complex conversations, the authors included here reformulate concepts of selfhood, community, solidarity, and liberation.

This collection begins with an invocation in the form of a poem by Jamie D. Walker, who pays homage to a tradition of black women writers, a gesture in keeping with this volume's own homage to the work captured in *All the Women Are White, All the Blacks Are Men, But Some of Us Are Brave*. The subsequent works are assembled according to four overarching themes. The first section, "Rethinking Solidarity, Building Coalition," focuses on activism and begins with Alicia Garza's "A Herstory of the #BlackLivesMatter Movement," which traces the development of the viral Twitter hashtag that launched a racial justice movement while Garza also questions the politics of inclusion: be it the raced, classed, gendered, sexualized, and dis/abled differences of "Black Lives," or the solidarity needed for non-blacks to assert the value of these lives. In light of this call, it is only fitting to segue to Brothers Writing to Live writers Moore and Pipkin, who combined their efforts in articulating a black male profeminist rumination on how the question Are all the blacks still men? is as urgent as Are all the women still white?

In the interstices of men of color and white women marginalizing women of color, Oparah's essay describes the different strategies women of color have used in challenging both second-wave antiviolence activists, who work with the state, and prison abolitionists, who have not paid enough attention to the safety concerns of those who have been victimized by intimate partner violence. By providing a comprehensive overview of this more than a decade-long work, Oparah asserts that women of color have transformed our thinking about sexual violence activism that neither serves the interests of a capitalist system invested in the mass incarceration of people of color nor in communities that have not done enough to keep women and transgender persons safe from state and intimate violence. In a similar vein of rethinking solidarity and coalition building, Andrea Smith's essay "Heteropatriarchy and the Three Pillars of White Supremacy" closes out this section as she challenges women of color to recognize the "separate and distinct, but still interrelated logics" of white supremacy, which complicate organizing efforts that must move beyond the limited ideology of "shared victimization" that different communities of color often embrace.

However, some may find this work problematic since Smith has been accused of falsely claiming a Cherokee identity. On the one hand, Smith defends her identity,[22] even though acknowledging that she is

not officially enrolled in the Cherokee nation, while some indigenous
members—including indigenous and Cherokee women scholars and
activists—openly questioned her claims to an indigenous identity since
tribal sovereignty includes official enrollment.[23] On the other hand,
other indigenous scholar-activists, as well as those who are nonindigenous, have vehemently defended Smith's right to self-determination
and assertion of her heritage.[24]

Indeed, Smith's essay in this volume addresses this very concern
over questions about Native identities, which she believes are based on
"US policies of forced assimilation and forced whiteness on American
Indians . . . [that] have become so entrenched that when Native peoples
make political claims, they have been accused of being white." Her essay
grapples with the complexities of white supremacy and goals for antiracist feminism, which makes it an important contribution to this volume.
Nonetheless, given the questions about her identity, reading this work
through this particular lens also invites us to contend with the meanings of indigeneity and strategies for solidarity and coalition building.

These issues are worth exploring as we continue to complicate and
challenge our various identities and locations, as outlined in the next
section, "Situating Identities, Relocating Feminisms." Amoo-Adare's
opening essay, "Renegade Architecture," utilizes a womanist architectural praxis to investigate how the urban built environment impacts on
our identities, lived experiences, and abilities to develop what she calls
"critical spatial literacy." We then move from the subject of designing
from the margins to surviving in the margins, as explored in Jessi Gan's
essay on Sylvia Rivera (1951–2002).

Gan specifically addresses situated identities when historicizing
Rivera's role in the protests at New York City's Stonewall Inn in 1969.
Much like other gender-variant Stonewall "veterans" of color, including
Marsha P. Johnson, Miss Major, and Stormé DeLarverie, Sylvia Rivera's
participation legitimated transgender activism and identity within LGBT
(lesbian, gay, bisexual, and transgender) movements. Rivera's gendered
and sexual identities are mobilized for political purposes while other
markers of difference are marginalized within this political history.

A different analysis of complex, situated sexualities frames the
essay "Theoretical Shifts in the Analysis of Latina Sexuality" by Ana
M. Juarez, Stella Beatríz Kerl-McClain, and Susana L. Gallardo. These
coauthors specifically take issue with scholars and writers who often "universalize" feminisms and position Latina/o and Chicana/o communities
as "more sexually repressed" than Anglo communities, a presupposition

that may not be based in actuality. Similar ethnocentric arguments that label women of color as "more oppressed" than their white and/or Western counterparts are dismantled in Shah's subsequent essay, which closes out this section. Revisiting the post–September 11 climate that gave us the "war on terror," Shah questions what she identifies as a "politics of sympathy," often used as an imperialist pretext that "places undue emphasis on cultural accounts of violence against women," specifically Afghan, Muslim, and immigrant women, and forecloses on transnational feminist movements.

The following section is titled "Redefining Difference, Challenging Racism," alluding to Audre Lorde's powerful call for feminists to relate across our differences.[25] Examining race and racism as they manifest in teaching, online communities, and feminist movements, this section opens with "The Proust Effect," a personal account by Gigi Marie Jasper, who chronicles her struggles as an African American English teacher in an all-white rural high school in the state of Wyoming. Similarly, Duncan's essay, "Hot Commodities, Cheap Labor," explores themes of racial isolation and the problematic discourse of diversity and multiculturalism that curtails her own raced and gendered experiences as an Asian Pacific American woman faculty member who is reduced to both "hot commodity" and "cheap labor" status in the contemporary corporate university.

Duncan's call to decenter whiteness and reposition women of color also undergirds the subsequent essay, "Toxic or Intersectional?" by Park and Leonard, which investigates how online spaces perpetuate the same racial tensions found offline through problematic constructions of *safety* and *toxicity* in feminist discourses via social media. However, writer Joey Lusk engages Bernice Reagon Johnson's "Coalition Politics: Turning the Century" to challenge herself on issues of white privilege, "safe space," and coalition building for feminism. Specifically, in her experimental "Note to Self," Lusk acknowledges, "As a white feminist, you are up against yourself. . . . Your relationship to racial privilege will always be asymptotic."

While these works provide us with theoretical and methodological maps for complicating differences and building toward solidarity, the final section, "Reclaiming the Past, Liberating the Future," offers us glimpses into different practices utilizing the arts to create visions for liberation, both from the past and toward our future. To do this, they draw on myths, religion, performances, personal experiences, poetry, and dreams of an inclusive postdigital future. Opening with the essay, "Mary Magdalene, Our Lady of Lexington," Raquel Z. Rivera articulates what she calls a "liberation mythology." As an agnostic singer-songwriter who has created praise songs for Mary Magdalene, Rivera integrates Caribbean feminist thought, artistic collaboration, and sacred-secular communities to reinterpret and reposition an ancient religious icon for a present-day poetic and mythical praxis. Likewise, Ulysse interweaves Vodou chants, spoken word, and a theory of "alter(ed)native" subjectivity to reflect on personal and historical "rage" as she transcends silences to create the provocative performance *Because When God Is Too Busy: Haiti, Me, and the WORLD*.

A different performance is offered by Praba Pilar, who ruminates on being a Latina performance artist who continually challenges the celebratory framework of tech industries by exposing the insidious side effects of emerging technologies. However, if, as Pilar concludes, such high-tech environments reinforce our disconnectedness, the work of Gumbs and Wallace resists these frameworks by retooling technology for their "Mobile Homecoming" project. This section (and volume) concludes with their important essay "Black Feminist Calculus Meets Nothing to Prove," which documents their journey as historic and prophetic travelers who use their recreational vehicle on a cross-country road trip across the United States in search of different black queer communities while simultaneously connecting them through poetry and "media sharing." In formulating a theory of "black feminist calculus," they seek out the *limits* and *truth values* of solidarity, community, political cartographies, and reclamations.

Conclusion

In many ways, we come full circle to where this collection of works began: with an affirmation of black women's testimonies changing and challenging ideas of feminism and resistance while branching out toward multiracial perspectives. In sum, the essays, poems, and art included in this collection continue to assert that those of us who are not white, who are not men are still brave. And those of us who *are* white, who *are* men, including men of color, and especially those whose existence disrupts these binaries of white/nonwhite and male/female, must also be courageous in accepting and proclaiming our collective humanity across the intersections. In this ever-evolving world of ours, we can consider these new visions and assertions as political, intellectual, ethical, and spiritual incentives for the continued struggle toward liberation.

Notes

1. Gloria Hull and Barbara Smith, "Introduction," in *All the Women Are White, All the Blacks Are Men, but Some of Us Are Brave: Black Women's Studies*, ed. Gloria Hull, Patricia Bell Scott, and Barbara Smith (New York: Feminist Press, 1982), xxi.

2. Stanlie M. James, Frances Smith Foster, and Beverly Guy-Sheftall, eds., *Still Brave: The Evolution of Black Women's Studies* (New York: Feminist Press, 2009), xix.

3. Kimberly Springer, *Living for the Revolution: Black Feminist Organizations, 1968–1980* (Durham: Duke University Press), 4.

4. Sara Ahmed, *The Cultural Politics of Emotion* (New York: Routledge, 2004. 2012), 175.

5. Audre Lorde, *Sister Outsider: Essays & Speeches* (Freedom, CA: Crossing Press, 1984), 127.

6. Gloria E. Anzaldúa, "now let us shift . . . in the path of conocimiento . . . inner work, public acts," in *This Bridge We Call Home: Radical Visions for Transformation*, ed. Gloria E. Anzaldúa and Analouise Keating (New York: Routledge, 2002), 541.

7. The Combahee River Collective, "A Black Feminist Statement," in *All the Women Are White, All the Blacks Are Men, but Some of Us Are Brave: Black Women's Studies*, ed. Gloria Hull, Patricia Bell Scott, and Barbara Smith (New York: Feminist Press, 1982), 18.

8. Maegan Parker Brooks and Davis W. Houck, eds. *The Speeches of Fannie Lou Hamer: To Tell it Like it is* (Jackson: University Press of Mississippi, 2011).

9. Anna Julia Cooper, *A Voice from the South* (New York: Oxford University Press, 1892. 1988).

10. Louise Michele Newman, *White Women's Rights: The Racial Origins of Feminism in the United States* (New York: Oxford University Press, 1999).

11. Robert W. Rydell, ed., *The Reason Why the Colored American Is Not in the World's Columbian Exposition* (Urbana: University of Illinois Press, 1893. 1999), 23.

12. Douglas A. Blackmon, *Slavery by Another Name: The Re-Enslavement of Black Americans from the Civil War to World War II* (New York: Anchor Books, 2009).

13. Zitkala-Sa, "Why I Am a Pagan," *Atlantic Monthly* 90 (1902), 803.

14. Cited in entry on artist Maud Sulter, *Phalia*, accessed February 17, 2014, http://www.art.newhall.cam.ac.uk/kiosk/location/12/artist/227.

15. Kimala Price, "What Is Reproductive Justice? How Women of Color Activists Are Redefining the Pro-Choice Paradigm," *Meridians* 10, no. 2 (2010): 42–65.

16. Amrita Basu, "Globalization of the Local/Localization of the Global: Mapping Transnational Women's Movements," *Meridians* 1, no. 1 (2000): 71.

17. Chandra Mohanty, *Feminism without Borders: Decolonizing Theory, Practicing Solidarity* (Durham, NC: Duke University Press, 2003).

18. Sandra K. Soto, "Where in the Transnational World Are U.S. Women of Color?" In *Women's Studies for the Future: Foundations, Interrogations, Politics,* eds. Elizabeth Lapovsky Kennedy and Agatha Beins, 111–124 (New Brunswick, NJ: Rutgers University Press, 2005).

19. Gabriella Gutiérrez y Muhs, Yolanda Flores Niemann, Carmen G. Gonzalez, and Angela P. Harris, eds., *Presumed Incompetent: The Intersections of Race and Class for Women in Academia* (Boulder: University Press of Colorado, 2012).

20. Barbara Smith, *The Truth That Never Hurts: Writings on Race, Gender, and Freedom* (New Brunswick, NJ: Rutgers University Press, 2002), 172.

21. Barbara Smith, "Racism and Women's Studies," in *All the Women Are White, All the Blacks Are Men, but Some of Us Are Brave: Black Women's Studies,* ed. Gloria Hull, Patricia Bell Scott, and Barbara Smith (New York: Feminist Press, 1982), 4.

22. See Andrea Smith's statement on her blog, accessed August 18, 2015, https://andrea366.wordpress.com/2015/07/09/my-statement-on-the-current-media-controversy.

23. See "Open Letter from Indigenous Women Scholars Regarding Discussions of Andrea Smith," accessed July 10, 2015, http://indiancountrytodaymedianetwork.com/2015/07/07/open-letter-indigenous-women-scholars-regarding-discussions-andrea-smith; also "Cherokee Women Scholars and Activists' Statement on Andrea Smith," accessed July 17, 2015, http://indiancountrytodaymedianetwork.com/2015/07/17/cherokee-women-scholars-and-activists-statement-andrea-smith.

24. A defense of Andrea Smith is available, accessed July 10, 2015, https://againstpoliticsofdisposability.wordpress.com.

25. Audre Lorde, "Age, Race, Class, and Sex: Women Redefining Difference," in *Sister Outsider: Essays & Speeches* (Freedom, CA: Crossing Press, 1984).

References

Against a Politics of Disposability. Accessed July 10, 2015. https://againstpoliticsofdisposability.wordpress.com.

Ahmed, Sara. *The Cultural Politics of Emotion.* New York: Routledge, [2004] 2012.

Anzaldúa, Gloria E. "now let us shift . . . in the path of conocimiento . . . inner work, public acts." In *This Bridge We Call Home: Radical Visions for Transformation,* edited by. Gloria E. Anzaldúa and Analouise Keating, 540–578. New York: Routledge, 2002.

Anzaldúa, Gloria, and Cherríe Moraga, eds. *This Bridge Called My Back: Writings by Radical Women of Color.* New York: Kitchen Table Women of Color Press, 1982.

Basu, Amrita. "Globalization of the Local/Localization of the Global: Mapping Transnational Women's Movements." *Meridians* 1, no. 1 (2000): 68–84.

Blackmon, Douglas A. *Slavery by Another Name: The Re-enslavement of Black Americans from the Civil War to World War II.* New York: Anchor Books, 2009.

Brooks, Maegan Parker, and Davis W. Houck, eds. *The Speeches of Fannie Lou Hamer: To Tell it Like it is.* Jackson: University Press of Mississippi, 2011.

"Cherokee Women Scholars and Activists' Statement on Andrea Smith." Accessed July 17, 2015. http://indiancountrytodaymedianetwork.com/2015/07/17/cherokee-women-scholars-and-activists-statement-andrea-smith.

Combahee River Collective. "A Black Feminist Statement." In *All the Women Are White, All the Blacks Are Men, but Some of Us Are Brave: Black Women's Studies,* edited by Gloria Hull, Patricia Bell Scott, and Barbara Smith, 13–22. New York: Feminist Press, 1982.

Cooper, Anna Julia. *A Voice from the South.* New York: Oxford University Press, [1892] 1988.

Davis, Angela Y. *Women, Race, & Class.* New York: Random House, 1981.

Grewal, Inderpal, and Caren Kaplan. *Scattered Hegemonies: Postmodernity and Transnational Feminist Practice.* Minneapolis: University of Minnesota Press, 1994.

Gutiérrez y Muhs, Gabriella, Yolanda Flores Niemann, Carmen G. Gonzalez, and Angela P. Harris, eds. *Presumed Incompetent: The Intersections of Race and Class for Women in Academia.* Boulder: University Press of Colorado, 2012.

hooks, bell. *Feminist Theory: From Margin to Center.* Boston: South End Press, 1984.

Hull, Gloria, Patricia Bell Scott, and Barbara Smith, eds. *All the Women Are White, All the Blacks Are Men, but Some of Us Are Brave: Black Women's Studies.* New York: Feminist Press, 1982.

James, Stanlie M., Frances Smith Foster, and Beverly Guy-Sheftall, eds. *Still Brave: The Evolution of Black Women's Studies.* New York: Feminist Press, 2009.

Lerner, Gerda. *Black Women in White America: A Documentary History.* New York: Random House, 1973.

Lorde, Audre. *Sister Outsider: Essays & Speeches.* Freedom, CA: Crossing Press, 1984.

Mohanty, Chandra. *Feminism without Borders: Decolonizing Theory, Practicing Solidarity.* Durham: Duke University Press, 2003.

Newman, Louise Michele. *White Women's Rights: The Racial Origins of Feminism in the United States.* New York: Oxford University Press, 1999.

"Open Letter from Indigenous Women Scholars Regarding Discussions of Andrea Smith." Accessed July 10, 2015. http://indiancountrytodaymedianetwork.com/2015/07/07/open-letter-indigenous-women-scholars-regarding-discussions-andrea-smith.

18

Janell Hobson

Janell Hobson

Price, Kimala. "What Is Reproductive Justice? How Women of Color Activists Are Redefining the Pro-Choice Paradigm." Meridians 10, no. 2 (2010): 42–65.
Rydell, Robert W., ed. The Reason Why the Colored American Is Not in the World's Columbian Exposition. Urbana: University of Illinois Press, [1893] 1999.
Shohat, Ella, ed. Talking Visions: Multicultural Feminism in a Transnational Age. Cambridge: Massachusetts Institute of Technology Press, 1998.
Smith, Andrea. "My Statement on the Current Media Controversy" (July 9, 2015). Accessed August 18, 2015. https://andrea366.wordpress.com/2015/07/09/my-statement-on-the-current-media-controversy.
Smith, Barbara. "Racism and Women's Studies." In All the Women Are White, All the Blacks Are Men, but Some of Us Are Brave: Black Women's Studies, edited by Gloria Hull, Patricia Bell Scott, and Barbara Smith, 48–51. New York: Feminist Press, 1982.
———. The Truth That Never Hurts: Writings on Race, Gender, and Freedom. New Brunswick, NJ: Rutgers University Press, 2002.
Soto, Sandra K. "Where in the Transnational World Are U.S. Women of Color?" In Women's Studies for the Future: Foundations, Interrogations, Politics, eds. Elizabeth Lapovsky Kennedy and Agatha Beins, 111–124. New Brunswick, NJ: Rutgers University Press, 2005.
Spivak, Gayatri. "Can the Subaltern Speak?" In Marxism and the Interpretation of Culture, eds. Cary Nelson and Lawrence Grossberg, 271–313. Urbana: University of Illinois Press, 1988.
Springer, Kimberly. Living for the Revolution: Black Feminist Organizations, 1968–1980. Durham, NC: Duke University Press, 2005.
Trinh, T. Minh-ha. Woman, Native, Other: Writing Postcoloniality and Feminism. Bloomington: Indiana University Press, 1990.
Walker, Alice. Cited in Phalia, the Zabat Series by Maud Sulter. 1992. Accessed February 17, 2014. http://www.art.newhall.cam.ac.uk/kiosk/location/12/artist/227.
Zitkala-Sa. "Why I Am a Pagan." Atlantic Monthly 90, 1902, 801–803.

A Poem for Dead Hearts

(for an ignorant mo' fo)

Jamie D. Walker

what does my poem on 'loneliness'
do for the revolution? you might ask.
or, rather, what does it say about *me*?

why don't you ask sanchez about her blues?
or toni morrison about pecola—
a young blk/girl impoverished, raped, and mute?
ask alice about the incest you think is taboo
and tell kincaid her mother's loss means nothing

bury every gwen brooks poem you can find
on motherhood and abortions
and tell nella larsen not to speak
about the consequences of passing

ask angie grimké or, better yet, mrs. dunbar
what she thinks about her 'thwarted' sexuality
at the turn of the century
and seek out zora for an explication
of her (re)pressed, battered wives

allow maya angelou to tell you
why the caged bird still sings

and if you still can't hear us humming
or sighing quiet the dark night
let a true sistah like audre lorde
whisper in your ear:

my brother.

          the blk/woman's testimony

is power/

& the world's greatest joy.

Part One

RETHINKING SOLIDARITY, BUILDING COALITION

A Herstory of the
#BlackLivesMatter Movement

Alicia Garza

I created #BlackLivesMatter with Patrisse Cullors and Opal Tometi, two
of my sisters, as a call to action for Black[1] people after seventeen-year-old
Trayvon Martin was posthumously placed on trial for his own murder and
the killer, George Zimmerman, was not held accountable for the crime
he committed. It was a response to the anti-Black racism that permeates
our society and also, unfortunately, our movements.

Black Lives Matter is an ideological and political intervention in
a world where Black lives are systematically and intentionally targeted
for demise. It is an affirmation of Black folks' contributions to this society, our humanity, and our resilience in the face of deadly oppression.
We were humbled when cultural workers, artists, designers, and techies
offered their labor and love to expand #BlackLivesMatter beyond a social
media hashtag. Opal, Patrisse, and I created the infrastructure for this
movement project—moving the hashtag from social media to the streets.

Our team grew through a very successful Black Lives Matter ride,
led and designed by Patrisse Cullors and Darnell L. Moore. We organized
to support the movement that was growing in St. Louis, Missouri, after
eighteen-year-old Michael Brown was killed at the hands of Ferguson
police officer Darren Wilson. We've hosted national conference calls
focused on issues of critical importance to Black people working hard for
the liberation of our people. We've connected people across the country
working to end the various forms of injustice impacting our people.
We've created space for the celebration and humanization of Black lives.

The Theft of Black Queer Women's Work

As people took the #BlackLivesMatter demand into the streets, the mainstream media and corporations also took up the call. #BlackLives-Matter appeared in an episode of *Law & Order: SVU* in a mash-up containing the Paula Deen racism scandal and the tragedy of the murder of Trayvon Martin. Suddenly, we began to come across varied adaptations of our work—all lives matter, brown lives matter, migrant lives matter, women's lives matter, and on and on. While imitation is said to be the highest form of flattery, I was surprised when an organization called to ask if they could use "Black Lives Matter" in one of their campaigns. We agreed to it, with the caveats that a) as a team, we preferred that they not use the meme to celebrate the imprisonment of any individual and b) it was important to us they acknowledged the genesis of #Black-LivesMatter. I was surprised when they did exactly the opposite and then justified their actions by saying they hadn't used the "exact" slogan and, therefore, they deemed it okay to take our work, use it as their own, fail to credit where it came from, and use it to applaud incarceration.

I was surprised when a community institution wrote asking us to provide materials and action steps for an art show they were curating, titled "Our Lives Matter." When I asked who was involved and why they felt the need to change the very specific call and demand around Black lives to "our lives," I was told the artists decided it needed to be more inclusive of all people of color. I was even more surprised when, in the promotion of their event, one of the artists conducted an interview that completely erased the origins of their work: the labor and love of queer Black women.

Pause.

When you design an event, campaign, etc. based on the work of queer Black women, don't invite them to participate in shaping it but ask them to provide materials and ideas for next steps for said event, that is racism in practice. It's also heteropatriarchal. Straight men, unintention-ally or intentionally, have taken the work of queer Black women and erased our contributions. Perhaps if we were the charismatic Black men many are rallying these days, it would have been a different story, but being Black queer women in this society (and apparently within these movements) tends to equal invisibility and nonrelevancy.

We completely expect those who benefit directly and improperly from white supremacy to try to erase our existence. We fight that every day. But when it happens among our allies, we are baffled, we are saddened, and we are enraged. And it's time to have the political conversation about why that's not okay.

We are grateful to those of our allies who have stepped up to the call that Black lives matter and taken it as an opportunity to not just stand in solidarity with us but investigate the ways in which anti-Black racism is perpetuated in their own communities. We are also grateful to those allies who were willing to engage in critical dialogue with us about this unfortunate and problematic dynamic. And for those who have yet to engage adaptations of the Black Lives Matter call, please consider the following points.

Broadening the Conversation to Include Black Life

Black Lives Matter is a unique contribution that goes beyond extrajudicial killings of Black people by police and vigilantes. It goes beyond the narrow nationalism that can be prevalent within some Black communities, which merely call on Black people to love Black, live Black, and buy Black, keeping straight cis-Black men in the front of the movement while our sisters, queer and trans and disabled folk, take up roles in the background or not at all. Black Lives Matter affirms the lives of Black queer and trans folks, disabled folks, Black undocumented folks, folks with records, women, and all Black lives along the gender spectrum. It centers those that have been marginalized within Black liberation movements. It is a tactic to (re)build the Black liberation movement.

When we say Black Lives Matter, we are talking about the ways in which Black people are deprived of our basic human rights and dignity. It is an acknowledgment that Black poverty and genocide are state violence. It is an acknowledgment that one million Black people locked in cages in this country—one half of all people in prisons or jails—is an act of state violence. It is an acknowledgment that Black women continue to bear the burden of a relentless assault on our children and our families, and that assault is an act of state violence. Black queer and trans folks bearing a unique burden in a heteropatriarchal society that disposes of us like garbage and simultaneously fetishizes us and profits off of us is state violence. The fact that 500,000 Black people in the United States are undocumented immigrants and relegated to the shadows is state violence. The fact that Black girls are used as negotiating chips[2] during times of conflict and war is state violence. Black folks living with disabilities and different abilities who bear the burden of state-sponsored Darwinian experiments that attempt to squeeze us into boxes of normality defined by white supremacy is state violence. And the fact is that Black people—not ALL people—exist within these conditions, the consequences of state violence.

When Black People Get Free, Everybody Gets Free

#BlackLivesMatter doesn't mean your life isn't important—it means that Black lives, which are seen as without value within white supremacy, are important to your liberation. Given the disproportionate impact state violence has on Black lives, we understand that when Black people in this country get free, the benefits will be wide reaching and transformative for society as a whole. When we are able to end the hypercriminalization and -sexualization of Black people and end the poverty, control, and surveillance of Black people, every single person in this world has a better shot at getting and staying free. When Black people get free, everybody gets free. This is why we call on Black people and our allies to take up the call that Black lives matter. We're not saying Black lives are more important than other lives, or that other lives are not criminalized and oppressed in various ways. We remain in active solidarity with all oppressed people who are fighting for their liberation, and we know that our destinies are intertwined.

And, to keep it real—it is appropriate and necessary to have strategy and action centered on Blackness without other, non-Black communities of color, or white folks for that matter, needing to find a place and a way to center themselves within it. It is appropriate and necessary for us to acknowledge the critical role that Black lives and struggles for Black liberation have played in inspiring and anchoring, through practice and theory, social movements for the liberation of all people. The women's movement, the Chicano/a liberation movement, queer movements, and many more have adopted the strategies, tactics, and theory of the Black liberation movement. And if we are committed to a world where all lives matter, we are called to support the very movement that inspired and activated so many more. That means supporting and acknowledging Black lives.

Progressive movements in the United States have made some unfortunate errors when they push for unity at the expense of really understanding the concrete differences in context, experience, and oppression. In other words, some want unity without struggle. As people who have our minds focused on freedom, we can learn to fight anti-Black racism by examining the ways in which we participate in it, even unintentionally. We can avoid the worn-out, sloppy practice of drawing lazy parallels of unity between peoples with vastly different experiences and histories.

When we deploy "All Lives Matter" to correct an intervention specifically created to address anti-Blackness, we lose the ways in which the state apparatus has built a program of genocide and repression mostly on the backs of Black people—beginning with the theft of millions of people for free labor—and then adapted it to control, murder, and profit off of other communities of color and immigrant communities. We perpetuate a level of white supremacist domination when we reproduce the tired trope that we are all the same, rather than acknowledging that non-Black oppressed people in this country are impacted by racism and domination and, simultaneously, *benefit* from anti-Black racism.

When you drop "Black" from the equation of whose lives matter and then fail to acknowledge that it came from somewhere, you further a legacy of erasing Black lives and Black contributions from our movement legacy. And consider that when dropping the Black you are, intentionally or unintentionally, erasing Black folks from the conversation or homogenizing very different experiences. The legacy and prevalence of anti-Black racism and heteropatriarchy is a lynchpin holding together this unsustainable economy. And that's not an accidental analogy.

Currently, heteropatriarchy and anti-Black racism within our movement is real and felt. It's killing us, and it's killing our potential to build power for transformative social change. Adopting the work of queer women of color, not naming or recognizing it, and promoting it as if it had no history of its own is problematic. When I use Assata Shakur's powerful demand[3] in my organizing work, I always begin by sharing where it comes from, sharing about Assata's significance to the Black liberation movement, what its political purpose and message is, and why it's important in our context.

When you adopt Black Lives Matter and transform it into something else (if you feel you really need to do that—see above for the arguments not to), it is appropriate politically to credit the lineage of your adapted work. It is important that we work together to build and acknowledge the legacy of Black contributions to the struggle for human rights. If you adapt Black Lives Matter, use the opportunity to talk about its inception and political framing. Lift up Black lives as an opportunity to connect struggles across race, class, gender, nationality, sexuality, and disability.

And, perhaps more importantly, when we Black people cry out in defense of our lives, which are uniquely, systematically, and savagely targeted by the state, we are asking you, our family, to stand with us in affirming Black lives. Not just all lives. Black lives. Please do not change the conversation by talking about how your life matters too. It does, but we need less watered-down unity and more active solidarities with us, Black people, unwaveringly, in defense of our humanity. Our collective future depends on it.

Notes

1. For the purposes of this chapter, the author departs from the spelling used in the other chapters by deliberately capitalizing "Black" to assert both a political and racial identity.

2. One example is the political and rallying cry surrounding the kidnapping of more than 200 schoolgirls in the Nigerian state of Chibok on April 15, 2014.

3. Accessed July 14, 2015, http://www.liberationink.org/content/assata-unisex.

Are *All* the Blacks Still Men?

Collective Struggle and Black Male Feminism

Darnell L. Moore and Hashim Khalil Pipkin

> *Daily living is a radical act of resistance if you happen to exist in the United States as a suspicious black boy like Trayvon Martin or Emmett Till; a potential threat like any young or old black or brown male living in New York City in the time of rampant "stop and frisk" policies; a black male deviating from restrictive gender binaries like the so-named fag, sissy, or DL brother; as a black boy or man.*[1]

Several months before we wrote this reflection, one of us profeminist black men actually offered these words at a public lecture on black manhood and emancipation. At the time, it seemed profound. And, yet, it is very clear while presently writing this response that it was inadequate. While the statement might be true in part, it is only a fragment of a more expansive narrative of the workings of antiblackness in the lives of black men *and* women, boys *and* girls.

It is easy to willfully forget the particular experiences of black girls and women when much of our narratives of black progress are organized around the needs of and presumed social ills that impact black men. Even the feminist minded among us are sometimes guilty of reinforcing the illogical idea that the collective black struggle for liberation is, chiefly, a fight to first save the black man from an already burning house, leaving all else who are left behind to be consumed by the fires of structural violence. And even if it is an idea that foregrounds presidential initiatives (e.g., President Barack Obama's 2014 My Brother's Keeper initiative for mentoring young men and boys of color), philanthropic efforts (e.g., the Black Male Achievement Project), and masculinist black political agendas, collective liberation cannot be achieved by single-variable politics.

Indeed, it does not help any black person—women and men, boys and girls, queer and straight, cisgender and transgender, with various capitals and without—if the fiction of black male exceptionalism[2] is not continually challenged. Furthermore, it is equally dangerous to perpetuate the pervasive idea that the survival of black men and the survival of black women are mutually exclusive. Yet, the notion that two separate agendas, with two separate discourses, are necessary in order to accomplish black liberation attuned to the specificities of sex, gender, and desire prevails.

Black feminisms have sought to intervene in this fractured notion of progress that imagines black boys and men as in need of saving from white racial supremacy even while black girls and women are daily impacted by "the Man's" system of racial supremacist heteropatriarchy and sexism/misogyny/rape and homo- and transantagonism at the hands of some black men. That is why black feminist theory is vital. It is a multivalent political framework that maps the route to collective liberation. Black feminist theory, therefore, is a project for all of us.

In his historicizing of black feminist theory while articulating an approach to black male feminist criticism, David Ikard invokes Barbara Smith, who "introduced the dominant theme of black feminist criticism and . . . the idea that race, gender, and class are interlocking factors that inform the complex reality of black women's oppression. She showed how white feminists frequently obscured their racial privilege by focusing on gender oppression and, similarly, how black male critics obscured their gender privilege by focusing on racial oppression."[3] The intersectional, locally realized, but globally concerned theoretical thrust of black feminist theory posited by Ikard at the point of its academic emergence has yet to register among those of us men who refuse to engage black feminism because of the gendered adjective in its name. What unfortunately undergirds much of the misrecognition of black feminist theory's investment in the interrogation of multiple markers of identity is the reality that black feminism is the "mirror" that many of us men seek to avoid. Who wants to examine critically and redress the very features that offer him privileges and afford him power? The type of work necessary to undo the asymmetrical power relations that privilege men and marginalize women is work we must all undertake.

Indeed, transforming a black-women-hating-shaming-silencing culture, destroying heteropatriarchy, and combatting more precise forms of
racialized sexism—or, what black feminist scholar Moya Bailey has aptly
named "misogynoir"—require both self-reflexive work on the part of us
men (cis-, trans-, and heterosexual and queer) and collective reckon-
ing on the part of men and women whether black, white, or brown.
We are writers and educators who have realized there is great potential
in profeminist coalitional politics because it can foster the creation of
communities free from the antagonistic energies of male centeredness
and sexism. As such, we write as members of a collective called "Brothers Writing to Live." We individually and collectively use writing as a
pedagogical tool for self- and communal transformation.

Indeed, one of our collective statements begins with the call to
action and politics that foreground our work. It reads:

> We are a collective of black men dedicated to challenging
> the ideas of black masculinity and manhood through the writ-
> ten word. Through our work, we explore the ugliest parts of
> ourselves and our community, in the hope that we can illu-
> minate the beauty that we know exists as well. We challenge
> each other daily to create and be more than what this racist,
> patriarchal society has raised us to be. But simply wanting it
> will not do. It requires tons of hard work, and much of that
> work includes listening to our sisters, black women, who tend
> to bear the brunt of our messiness.[4]

In short, we write to heal and re-form ourselves as black bodies
shaped by and, in many ways, privileged within white racial supremacist
capitalist patriarchy.

Brothers Writing to Live formed by way of an organic coming
together of fellow writers who shared mutual admiration for each other's
work. Darnell Moore and Kiese Laymon had connected through social
media and soon discussed what seemed to be recurrent themes appearing
in their writings. It was clear that themes like self-harm, violence, love,
and lovelessness were more than coincidental despite the differences
that defined two black men, one a heterosexual black man from the
rural south and the other a queer-identified black man from the urban
northeast. They eventually reached out to other black men, including
Mychal Denzel Smith, Wade Davis, Mark Anthony Neal, Marlon Peterson, Hashim Pipkin, Kai Green, and Nyle Fort.

The group, which is composed of black men who have been similarly and differently shaped by the forces of heteropatriarchy and homo- and transantagonism within a culture that taught us how to hate ourselves and our sisters even more, represents a range of black male identities. We are queer, heterosexual, cisgender, and transgender black men who hail from various areas across the country, and, yet, none of us has been exempt from performing deeds that have resulted in the violation or victimization, knowingly or not, of black women. We write, but we also hold each other accountable to *living* the words we write, to addressing the ways heteropatriarchy is violent and has failed (and continues to fail) all of us: black women *and* men.

The work Brothers Writing to Live engages is in conversation with the long history of male feminism, broadly defined. It should be noted, however, that the type of male feminism that energizes Brothers Writing to Live is of a particular orientation, which is decidedly attuned to the complicated histories and intersections of nation, class, sex, and *race*. This iteration of male feminism is better understood as "black male feminism" because of its commitment to intervening in the long tradition of male feminism that too often sidesteps issues of race, its attending violences, and their impact on the bodies of the marginalized.

Whether one chooses to point to Frederick Douglass's attendance at the 1848 Seneca Falls Women's Right Convention or John Stuart Mill's *The Subjection of Women*, there does exist a historical genesis of male intellectual and activist labor allied with the social, economic, and political equality of women. However, in these two examples alone, the mistreatment or altogether absence of treatment regarding the racialization of gender and gender inequity is glaringly apparent. Although Mill argues for the right to vote for all women contingent on their education, his philosophy is undermined by the racist mechanisms of the postbellum period (Jim Crow laws, carpetbaggers) responsible for the variances in educational attainment among black and white women. Thus, a male feminism that is not attuned to the racist iterations of social institutions will ultimately fail in its goal of gender and sex equity.

Similarly, although Douglass's historical moment was one shaped by the forces of chattel slavery, an economic machine fueled by white racial supremacy, his appeal to the voting rights of black *men* over and above suffrage for black and white women is emblematic of the male-centered racial justice politics that centers men and dismisses women. In the example of Douglass and women's suffrage, black male feminism activates a tool of discovery and practice that would acknowledge the

ways antebellum America sustained black illiteracy across sexes and
also remain sensitive to the *particular* ways black female procreative and
industrial slave labor still was not enough to guarantee citizenship. The
impulse to inextricably link social, economic, and political progress to
gender inspires the work that Brothers Writing to Live does such that
the black male narrative of oppression, as Douglass sought to advance,
does not run the risk of serving (inaccurately) as a proxy for *all* black
gendered and sexual oppression.

The ways in which the violence of white supremacist capitalist
patriarchy gets distilled more or less into a product of violence against
black *male* life is too often part and parcel of the method of African
American history proper. In his work *New Black Man*, Mark Anthony
Neal makes clear the consequences of black men corroborating their
participation in black female subjugation with the faulty pass afforded
by the "challenge" of black male life in America. Neal states, "Too often
when I discuss black male privilege with black men, they fall back on
defense mechanisms that highlight the effects of racism and unemploy-
ment in the lives of black men. What many of these young men want
to do is excuse the behavior of black men because of the extenuating
circumstances under which black manhood is lived in our society, suggesting that black male behaviors that oppress women are understand-
able."[5] Neal posits the illogical practice of casting black male victimhood
as an excuse for black male subjugation of black women and girls. This
is undoubtedly an outgrowth of the American ethos of individuality at
the expense of the collective.

Black men have too often appropriated this American rendering
of self at the expense of black women. Oppression can never serve,
regardless of its iteration, as the justification for further oppression. This
interconnected understanding of oppression is especially crucial because,
historically, black oppression has never operated unidirectionally. If one
is sensitive to moments in American history when black survival was
in question, the presence of both black male *and* female marginalization
was operative.

The interconnected, intraracial gender inequities impacting the
lives of black women and men have material consequences in this contemporary moment. Rather recently, sociopolitical discourse has been
imbued with a death-focused interest in black men and, more accurately,
black boys—including the shooting deaths by civilians and police of
teenagers Trayvon Martin in Florida and Michael Brown in Ferguson,
Missouri, respectively. In some ways, this development is a response to

a rupture in a highly classed and highly static American legal system, but as black feminist theory makes clear, class operates in coordination with race and gender. However, this moment of hypervisibility of the black male body furthers the hyperinvisibility of black women and girls.

The case of Trayvon Martin's murder at the hands of self-appointed community watchman George Zimmerman on the night of February 26, 2012—followed by Zimmerman's acquittal of his murder on July 13, 2013—is often understood to be the catapult for the current politically saturated moment of representations of the black male body, for example. But it was also during this trial that Rachel Jeantel's black female self was subjected to racialized, classed, and aestheticized rubrics of femininity, intelligence, and decorum. Just as Trayvon was posthumously on trial for his own murder per his assumed hypermasculinity, criminality, and aggressive nature, his friend Rachel was similarly being prosecuted for her nonadherence to not only antiquated norms of femininity but also violent and altogether imagined norms of American character.

As the only person who spoke with Trayvon while he was being pursued by George Zimmerman, Rachel was understood as the make-or-break witness; her testimony was anticipated as key to either convicting Zimmerman or letting him walk free. Her presence and Trayvon's life were at once bound up with one another. Here is no clearer example of how black men and black women's freedom is entangled in this country. But every media representation of the Zimmerman trial, and specifically of Rachel's presence on the witness stand, dodged how standards of masculinity *and* femininity were working conjunctively and pejoratively in this black context.

Indeed, notions of black manhood are constructed (and constricted) by structural forces as expansive and entrenched within contemporary US society, like white racial supremacy, heteropatriarchy, global capitalism, neoliberalism, prison industrial systems, and rape culture. But so too are notions of black womanhood. Black manhood and womanhood tend to be conceived as a performance in response to the very social and political structures and spaces that limit black subjectivity. No doubt some of those structures and spaces are violent.

Some of us survive. But some of *us*—black women and men—do not. So why do we continue to think that collective struggle for liberation will be obtained through partial uplift, the achievement of black men, when the body count says otherwise? How might we reimagine manhood in such a way that it might also lead us to the undoing of the very forces of sexism, misogyny, rape culture, and heteropatriarchy that harm women *and* men?

We conceptualize an emancipatory black manhood as one that can be realized only after we men begin to theorize gender as a set of hegemonic and socially constructed roles that are conceptualized and performed in response to legacies of heteronomativity and heteropatriarchy, as well as other forms of structural violence like gendered racialization, which has resulted in totalizing forms of marginalization of Blacks in America. If emancipation, or the act of freeing oneself to live, is to be realized in the lives of black men assailed by the state, its laws, its systems, by black men weighed down by expectations to become what Neal calls the figure of the "Strong Black Man," by black men who benefit from the privilege of maleness, by black men who may be guilty of violating black women and girls, men and boys then we must commit to participating in the revolutionary act of living—freeing ourselves to live in loving community with women, children, and other men, as a "generation of pro-feminist, anti-homophobic nurturing black men."[6] We must also commit to the act of undoing the systems of sexism and misogyny that structure so much of our living.

It is essential to remember that the work of reconstructing a black manhood that is nurturing in its engagement with not only men but also women requires self-reflexive analysis and willful self-remaking on the part of black men. This work is important to us, because it is about all of *us*. This work is a matter of life and death for the collective black: men, women, and children. When one of us is pursued by death, we all are. And it just so happens that this nation*hood* usually coordinates black death across the signatures of gender. Thus, any form of black masculinity claiming a stake in black life must confront *this* American fact: the breath that sustains black living can do the job of sustenance only when it is allowed the freedom to dance in the collective space drawn by the strivings of black men *and* black women.

Notes

1. Darnell Moore, "Black Manhood and the Racist Imagination," March 20, 2012, New Black Man (in Exile), http://www.newblackmaninexile.net/2012/03/black-manhood-and-racist-imagination.html?m=1

2. See Paul Butler's insightful article "Black Male Exceptionalism? The Problems and Potential of Black Male Focused Interventions," in *Du Bois Review* 10, no. 2 (2013): 485–511, http://scholarship.law.georgetown.edu/facpub/1314.

3. David Ikard, *Breaking the Silence: Toward a Black Male Feminist Criticism* (Baton Rouge: Louisiana State University Press, 2007), 14.

4. See our statement #BlackPowerIsForBlackMen: Letters from Brothers Writing to Live at http://thefeministwire.com/2013/08/blackpowerisforblackmen.
5. Mark A. Neal, *New Black Man* (New York: Routledge, 2005), 152.
6. Ibid., 151.

References

Ikard, David. *Breaking the Silence: Toward a Black Male Feminist Criticism*. Baton Rouge: Louisiana State University Press, 2007.
Neal, Mark A. *New Black Man*. New York: Routledge, 2005.

Beyond the Prison-Industrial Complex

Women of Color Transforming Antiviolence Work

Julia Chinyere Oparah

Twenty years ago, and a decade after *All the Women Are White, All the Blacks Are Men, but Some of Us Are Brave* was published, I was working as the coordinator of a center for African and Caribbean women in the small, impoverished urban town of Coventry in England. The Hillside neighborhood could have been located in any urban center throughout Europe, the United States, or Canada. It featured high-rise blocks of public housing, graffitied walls, barricaded and overpriced liquor and food stores, and broken families struggling to survive.

Working out of a former storefront, I and the other women who staffed the center witnessed and intervened in everyday acts of violence against women and children, negotiated with small-time drug dealers not to carry out their business too close to our daycare center, cared for children unexpectedly dropped off on our doorstep, dealt with the residue of a broken mental health system, and trained hopeful and undereducated women for the few jobs that had not been downsized or moved offshore. Returning to work on an average Monday, we would hear anecdotes about the weekend's activity: the community bar raided, men beaten, sex workers arrested. Tensions with the police remained from the urban uprisings of the early 1980s, and the bollards blocking egress on key streets were a permanent reminder of the time when the community had been under overt lockdown. While the center in the 1990s prioritized economic development and sustainability for low-income families, it was clear to us that the intimate violence that many women faced prevented them from taking up training and employment opportunities. As a result, we began to organize toward the establishment of a program for black women seeking to escape family violence, which we named "Solace."

Although I didn't think of it in that way at the time, founding Solace provided fascinating lessons in the limitations of second-wave feminism.[1] The existing antiviolence infrastructure in Coventry was governed by white women, with the exception of a shelter run by and for South Asian women. While local white feminists were supportive of a shelter for South Asian women, who they saw as having a different and incompatible culture and language and therefore needing to be catered to separately, our attempts to build an autonomous organization for African and Caribbean women met significant resistance.

Black women infrequently used the mainstream shelter system, citing racism from staff and residents, a reluctance to move to the predominantly white areas of town where the shelters were located, and fear of racial violence and isolation as reasons. They argued that the counseling they received from these shelters assumed that leaving the family was the best and safest option for them and their children and overlooked the ways in which family and community were for these women a necessary bulwark against racial hostility and tensions. They were also anxious about what they saw as a close relationship between the mainstream shelters and the police and cognizant of the excessive and sometimes fatal violence inflicted on black men by the police and the militarized policing that would be summoned by a 999 (911) call. Despite these concerns, white feminists were reluctant to admit that black women were not well served by the existing shelter system or to support funding of a separate facility for black women.

My experience of working within and writing about the antiviolence and antiprison movements in the United States and Canada has been informed by my early experiences of community-based organizing alongside and sometimes in conflict with second-wave white feminists. Much of the strife we experienced in Britain was mirrored by the experiences of black women and women of color in the United States, Canada, and elsewhere.[2] These interracial collisions were not simply a matter of white racism or a desire by white feminists to exclude black women and other women of color. Rather they signaled deep-rooted political and theoretical differences between white women and women of color.

Second-wave feminism developed core concepts in relation to gendered violence based on a dualistic approach, which viewed oppression only or primarily through the lens of patriarchal control. This understanding positioned women as victims/survivors and men as perpetrators of violence and thus overlooked forms of gendered, racial, and economic violence that both women and men of color experienced, particularly at the hands of the state but also by non–state actors. This conceptualization of violence left second-wave feminists particularly vulnerable to state cooption, as the state positioned itself as protector of vulnerable women and partner to antiviolence organizations. By working with the state in this way, many antiviolence activists contributed to the legitimation, consolidation, and expansion of a prison-industrial complex, which has been particularly enormous and devastating in the United States but has also had significant impact on communities of color in other industrialized countries as well as the global South.[3]

This chapter explores the fundamental challenges that women of color antiprison and antiviolence activists and scholars in the United States have posed to feminist understandings of violence and safety. By raising the visibility of criminalized women, in particular black, Latina, and Native American women, and asking what their lives and experiences tell us, women of color have initiated a paradigm shift. Instead of viewing the state as protector and partner, women of color have demonstrated the multifaceted nature of state and state-sanctioned violence in the lives of women and transgender people of color. Rather than reproducing the dyadic conceptualization of (female) victim versus (male) perpetrator/offender, we have identified a continuum of victimization and criminalization in the lives of women, men, and transgender people of color.

We have generated new explanations for women's victimization that utilize an intersectional and transnational framework and explore the impact of interlocking systems of dominance. And we have begun to generate new community accountability mechanisms that reduce our reliance on the state to resolve conflict and work toward building communities that manifest the world we are seeking to create. Finally, women of color and our allies have challenged the often invisible violence of the gender binary by exploring the commonalities between women, gender variant, and transgender people of color.

Against Complicity: Confronting State Violence

From the 1970s onward, the United States engaged in an aggressive project of prison, jail, and detention center construction, increasing the country's imprisoned population by 700 percent to over two million and positioning the United States as the world leader in incarceration.[4] This prison-building boom is the direct result of the ascendance of a law-and-order agenda, fueled by the racialized fear of crime and manifested in tough on crime policies, including mandatory minimum sentencing, three strikes, and zero tolerance policing. It has resulted in the emergence and consolidation of a "prison-industrial complex," a symbiotic web of corporate and state interests that uses mass incarceration as a solution to the complex social problems generated by advanced capitalism.[5] Rather than investing in schools and youth programs, addiction treatment and mental health programs, or job creation and training initiatives, governments have withdrawn resources from community infrastructure, in part to fund costly law enforcement and prison budgets. As a result, low-income communities of color, in particular racialized, queer, and transgender youth, people with addictions and mental illness, and those living with poverty and homelessness have been swept up by the criminal justice system and transformed into raw materials for the prison-industrial complex.

The ascendance of the law-and-order agenda coincided with the institutionalization and solidification of the second-wave feminist movement. While early feminist organizations in the 1970s were grassroots and countercultural and operated on minimal funding, by the 1980s and 1990s, feminist agendas had begun to penetrate the corridors of power, with "women's issues," such as domestic violence, sexual assault, and child abuse, coming out of the shadows and into public policy discussions. For antiviolence activists, this appeared to represent an important achievement.[6] No longer would police treat women who called emergency services patronizingly while implicitly supporting the violent partner; no longer would survivors of sexual assault be interrogated about their alleged complicity in the assault through immodest dress or being in the wrong place; instead, police and courts would aggressively pursue perpetrators of violence against women with the same vigor that they brought to other criminal cases.

Many antiviolence activists embraced new initiatives that promoted greater criminal justice involvement, including mandatory arrest laws, more funding for law enforcement (often attached to the establishment of police domestic violence units), and tougher sentences for those convicted of battering and sexual assault.[7] In so doing, they provided legitimacy for the exponential growth in police, court, and prison/jail budgets and thus unwittingly supported the transfer of public resources from community-based services—many of which offered alternatives to women escaping violence with the attendant homelessness, poverty, trauma, and addiction—to the criminal justice system. The passage of the Violence Against Women Act in 1994 reinforced the symbiotic relationship between the antiviolence movement and the criminal justice system by providing state resources for domestic violence shelters and sexual assault centers, ensuring that these organizations would work closely with the police and courts and rely on state funding.[8] The state had successfully positioned itself as protector and defender of (female) survivors, prosecutor and rehabilitator of (male) perpetrators, and provider and partner of feminist organizations. There was little space in this configuration for second-wave feminists to make visible and confront state violence against women or men of color.

The antiviolence movement's reliance on criminal justice responses to violence against women has failed women of color, especially poor, immigrant, queer, and indigenous women, leaving them more vulnerable to violence. It has not reduced violence against women or the numbers of women murdered by people with whom they are intimate.[9] By supporting initiatives designed to enforce more stringent policing of violence against women without taking into consideration entrenched racial and economic bias within law enforcement agencies, antiviolence activists failed to anticipate their potentially negative impact on women of color. For example, mandatory arrest laws, which require the police to make an arrest where there is probable cause without taking into consideration the wishes of the victim, have led to numerous incidents where the woman being battered has been arrested alongside her violent partner.[10] Racialized stereotypes of black women as aggressive, Latinas as "hot tempered," or indigenous women as "savage" make these women more vulnerable to arrest in situations where physical force may have been used as a form of self-defense. For immigrant women, mandatory arrest laws have also resulted in cases of sexual assault or domestic violence escalating to become the basis for deportation proceedings, for either the woman or her male partner.[11]

The antiviolence movement's complicity with the proliferation of prisons and jails has had a particularly harsh impact on women of color. Since the mid-1980s, the number of women behind bars has increased over 400 percent to over 200,000. African American women represent a disproportionate 30 percent of that number, and Latinas a further sixteen percent.[12] A large proportion of these women are survivors of violence who come into contact with the criminal justice system because of trauma-related drug and alcohol use, survival crimes related to poverty and homelessness, or assault or murder charges related to actions taken against a violent partner.

While incarcerated, women and girls of color experience horrific and retraumatizing forms of state violence, including strip and cavity searches, sometimes fatal medical neglect, rape and harassment, and the forced removal and loss of custody of children, and they are more likely to engage in self-harm or suicide as a result.[13] In supporting a criminal justice response to these women, antiviolence organizations failed to identify that the primary orientation of the criminal punishment industry toward women of color is that of prosecutor, not protector. Women of color who are survivors are more likely to experience criminalization, prosecution, and the violence of incarceration than to encounter the caring, protecting guise of the state.[14] As Miller notes in relation to mandatory arrest laws: "An arrest policy intended to protect battered women as victims is being misapplied and used against them. *Battered women have become female offenders.*"[15]

As a result of the contradictions and conflicts involved in working within antiviolence organizations led by white women, many women of color left the antiviolence movement and found alternate spaces to do radical work against all forms of violence, including the antiprison, police accountability, economic justice, indigenous sovereignty, and anti-racist movements. In 2000, a group of women of color activists from a cross section of movements convened a conference and strategy session in Santa Cruz, California titled *"The Color of Violence."*[16] Attended by two thousand women, the conference was an extraordinary event marked by remarkably honest storytelling by survivors and radical analyses of state and intimate violence.

The conference shifted understandings of violence against women and exploded the mainstream movement's narrow focus on domestic violence and sexual assault by highlighting the many forms of violence experienced by women of color. Speakers elucidated the violence of conquest and ongoing colonization, border enforcement and immigration raids, law enforcement brutality, mass incarceration, reproductive violence, economic injustice, ableism, militarism, and the occupation of Palestine, among other topics. They demonstrated the need to address state and intimate violence simultaneously and moved toward articulating a new approach to confronting violence against women and communities of color.

The powerful energy generated by the conference was harnessed in the creation of a national organization of radical women of color called INCITE! Women of Color Against Violence.[17] INCITE! has been instrumental in shifting the conversation on violence against women to include state and institutional violence and in encouraging mainstream antiviolence activists and organizations to become accountable for the consequences of their relationships with the criminal punishment industry. The publication of the *INCITE! Anthology* has provided women's studies and ethnic studies classrooms with an important resource, which foregrounds the intersections of state and intimate violence and places women of color at the center of theorization about gender violence.

In addition, the Critical Resistance-INCITE! Statement, a collaboration between the country's leading prison abolition organization and INCITE!, generated a blueprint for activist work that simultaneously works to dismantle oppressive systems of law enforcement and incarceration and to end all forms of gender violence. Finally, INCITE! has carried out important participatory action research into the violence experienced by women and transgender people of color at the hands of law enforcement agencies.[18] By making visible the violence routinely carried out by local and state police, immigration enforcement (such as, ICE [the US Immigration and Customs Enforcement], the US Border Patrol, and customs and drug enforcement agents), the FBI, private security agents, and military forces, INCITE! interrupts the symbiotic relationship between the antiviolence movement and the "state as protector" in order to unveil and confront the reality of the "state as perpetrator" in the lives of many women of color.

From Crime and Punishment to the Victimization-Criminalization Continuum

What was my crime, why 5 years in prison?
Less than $2,000 of welfare fraud
What was my crime?
Being a survivor of molestation and rape
What was my crime?
Being addicted to alcohol and drugs
What was my crime?
Being a survivor of domestic violence
What was my crime?
Being an American Indian woman.[19]

Most second-wave feminists ascribed to a dualistic understanding of oppression and resistance, which posited patriarchy as the primary (or sometimes only) system of dominance and identified the male/female binary as the most important division within society. One well-documented result of this binary analysis was that women of color, who live on the intersections of multiple systems of oppression, were frequently viewed as lacking an adequate feminist analysis. This was due in part to our tendency to make alliances with men of color in the fight against racism and colonialism and our willingness to align ourselves with antiracist and sovereignty movements while sometimes rejecting feminism as "white," "colonial," or "bourgeois."[20] A less frequently discussed consequence of this dualistic thinking is that it produced an analysis of violence against women that was equally dichotomized, with women positioned as victims/survivors and men as perpetrators. As the feminist antiviolence agenda was coopted by state agencies in the 1980s and 1990s, this dyad mapped neatly onto the existing victim/offender dyad, which is at the basis of retributive forms of justice.[21]

This dyad has dangerous ramifications for women of color, particularly poor, immigrant, queer, and indigenous women. In the context of the historical racialization of crime, which labeled black people as intrinsically dishonest and aggressive; criminalized indigenous people's social, economic, and governance systems; and constructed immigrants as variously treasonous, uncivilized, and polluting Anglo normalcy, women of color are automatically considered suspect. In order to fit into the category of victim, women of color must have no characteristics that would tip them into the criminal category, for this would locate them in the other half of the dyad.[22] The criminal punishment industry has little room for ambiguity, border crossing, or simultaneity. As a result, women of color who deploy everyday strategies to survive are considered criminals and are dealt with by the state through policing, arrest, prosecution, and incarceration rather than treated as being in need of protection, healing, or support.[23]

Stormy Ogden's autobiographical story of "the little girl who grew up to be a convict" uproots this dualistic paradigm.[24] I got to know Stormy through her involvement in antiprison organizing in the San Francisco Bay Area and invited her to share her story as part of an anthology that I put together in order to spark a conversation about the links between race, gender, globalization, and the prison-industrial complex. The survivor of a family devastated by colonial racism, alcoholism, and domestic violence, Stormy experienced continuous sexual exploitation at the hands of family members, racial abuse from her white mother, and rape by schoolmates. Running away from home numerous times, she was apprehended and incarcerated in the juvenile justice system before being released as a teenager to a life of sexual exploitation, rape, and addiction.

As she puts it, "There were too many men, too many empty bottles, and too many suicide attempts."[25] The state's response to the persistent violence in Stormy's life is an outgrowth of the colonial roots of the prison-industrial complex. Built on ancestral indigenous lands, California prisons and jails continue the removal of indigenous people while erasing sovereign identities by placing Native American prisoners into the racial category "other." The racialized labor exploitation that began with the enslavement of African and native peoples is mirrored today in the meager wages paid to workers in UNICOR (the California prison industry). This simultaneous relocation, erasure, and exploitation are part of a project of ongoing colonization.[26]

In order to understand the experiences of women of color survivors like Stormy who are incarcerated for nonviolent property or drug offenses, women of color scholars and activists have rejected gender-only analyses that fail to account for racial, colonial, and economic dynamics. Instead, we have demonstrated that women of color experience what Beth Richie calls the "gendered entrapment of battered [black] women," a complex web of cultural norms, colonial legacies, racial exclusion, economic marginalization, and gender violence that compels women of color to engage in criminalized activities in order to survive.[27] The survival strategies that women of color and poor women adopt, from using drugs and alcohol to numb the effects of sexual abuse and childhood trauma to welfare fraud, petty theft, or dealing in drugs in order to supplement inadequate incomes, are closely related to the racialized feminization of poverty and cutbacks in services and economic supports for women and children promoted by neoliberal economic restructuring.[28] The state's response to these strategies is to punish these women as offenders rather than constructively addressing their safety, economic, and health concerns as victims/survivors. Their lives represent a continuum of victimization and criminalization that results in an ongoing cycle of intimate and state violence, poverty, social marginalization, surveillance, and imprisonment.

While women are more likely to be imprisoned for nonviolent acts than men, approximately one third of women in prison are convicted of a violent act.[29] The lives of women who are both victims and perpetrators of violence confound the dualistic paradigm of the mainstream antiviolence movement. These women's lives remind us that battered women of color are more likely to be found in a prison cell than in a women's shelter. Women of color antiprison activists, working in multiracial and multigender organizations, such as Free Battered Women, California Coalition for Women Prisoners, Legal Services for Prisoners with Children, the Habeas Project, Justice Now, and the National Network for Women in Prison, have demonstrated the need for a more flexible understanding of violence. By making visible the lives of women like Flozelle Woodmore, who was locked up for two decades for killing her abusive estranged boyfriend, these organizations reveal the ways in which intimate, institutional, and self-protective violence are intricately bound together.[30] Additionally, by placing their work within an abolitionist framework that resists the brutality of incarceration as it affects all prisoners, these activists push the mainstream antiviolence movement to interrogate and eventually abandon its reliance on the criminal punishment system. In so doing, they conceptualize and promote an alternative vision of safety in "a world without prisons, a world where all people have access to the material, educational, emotional, and spiritual resources necessary to be safe and thrive in our communities."[31]

Removing the Cop in our Hearts: Toward Community Accountability

Another way that women of color have interrogated the victim/perpetrator binary is through advancing a more complex understanding of violence by men of color. During the 1970s and 1980s, women of color frequently found themselves forced to pick between two untenable positions on violence by men of color. On the one hand, white feminists argued that men of color who committed intimate violence were motivated by misogynist attitudes toward women that were universally shared by all men within patriarchy. On the other, racial justice movements, in particular nationalist movements, viewed efforts to confront violence by men of color, particularly men who were viewed as progressive, as a divisive tool of white supremacy that aimed, like COINTELPRO (the FBI's Counter Intelligence Program) and other counterrevolutionary forces, to undermine movements for racial justice.

Many women of color chose to remain silent about abuse and harassment by men of color in both intimate relationships and activist spaces in order to be "loyal" to their race and to avoid subjecting their men to excessive and potentially fatal police responses. At the same time, some women of color developed an analysis of male violence as a natural response to the displacement of men of color under white supremacy from their rightful leadership positions in their families and community. Rather than standing up for women violated by men of color, these nationalist women sought to prop up subordinated racial masculinities as a solution to male violence.

The emergence of the women of color antiviolence movement has created a space for a different understanding of violence by men of color and appropriate actions to address it. In this conceptualization, intimate violence by men of color is understood within a broader context of racial, economic, and colonial oppression. However, this contextualization does not permit or legitimate the violence. Instead, women of color have worked to create systems and practices that hold people who commit harm accountable for their actions, keep women as safe as possible, and bring about change in the community relations and power dynamics that supported the violence. A key aspect of these "community accountability" practices is a commitment to recognize the humanity of everyone involved in order to break the cycle of racialized and gender violation in communities of color.[32] As women of color activists from the Seattle-based Communities Against Rape and Abuse (CARA) explain:

> It is very easy to slip into a perpetual rage that wants the aggressor to suffer. . . . And why not? We are talking about rape after all, and rage is a perfectly natural and good response. However, though we should make an intentional space to honor rage, it's important for the purposes of an accountability process to have a vision for specific steps the aggressor needs to take in order to give [him] a chance for redemption. Remember the community we are working to build is not one where a person is forever stigmatized as a "monster."

By engendering accountability while honoring the humanity of men of color who harm women, CARA disrupts the controlling images promoted in media accounts of male offenders as animalistic "superpredators"—monsters who are beyond rehabilitation and can only be incapacitated through long mandatory sentences.[33] Instead, they push against retributive approaches to violence, arguing that people who harm others are defined by more than the violent act or acts and using collective pressure and engagement to transform, but not sever, the relationship between the person who has committed violence and their community.

The move toward community accountability is in part a response to the inadequacies of prison-industrial complex abolition. In 2001, members of INCITE! Women of Color Against Violence came together with members of Critical Resistance to debate and dialogue about the intersections of gender violence and the prison-industrial complex. The result of that weekend was the "*Critical Resistance-INCITE! Statement on Gender Violence and the Prison-Industrial Complex.*" The statement included a vigorous critique of both the antiviolence and the antiprison movements and pointed out the inadequate attention paid in abolitionist circles to the impact of demands for an end to policing and imprisonment on the safety of women, transgender, and queer communities.

The statement made four important observations with regard to women's safety. First, it pointed out that the antiprison movement had rejected criminalization as a solution for violence, without developing alternative strategies for addressing intimate and state violence against women of color. Second, the movement had not worked to build alliances with and learn from the antiviolence movement. Third, the antiprison movement, while correctly identifying that rapists and serial killers are a tiny part of the prison population, had failed to address the question of how these egregious forms of violence should be addressed. And finally, the movement has supported the development of alternatives to incarceration that rely on romanticized notions of community and do not provide adequate protection for survivors of domestic and sexual violence. As a result of these blind spots, the statement argued, the antiprison movement was interpreted by antiviolence activists as lacking real concern for the safety of women.

Women of color are rooted in both antiviolence and antiprison movements and thus have particular insights into the weaknesses of both and the contributions and lessons that each have to offer the other. Because women of color experience extensive violations by both individuals and by the criminal punishment system, we have a particular stake in creating genuine ways to deal with perpetrators of harm that do not fuel or legitimate prison expansion. In so doing, we work alongside and learn from the efforts of white women and progressive men doing similar work.

Innovative strategies developed by Creative Interventions, Sista II Sista, Generation Five, Philly Stands Up, CARA, Critical Resistance and the Southern Coalition for Social Justice demonstrate that it is possible to empower communities to create effective responses to harm, to dismantle flawed beliefs that it is possible to "fix" violence with more vio-

lence, and to release our attachment to retributive justice.[34] By envisioning and creating community accountability strategies, women of color
are at the forefront of building a world without prisons, not in some
distant utopia but in our everyday lives and within the limitations of the
communities we inhabit. In this sense, community accountability work
is part of "living abolition," enabling us to decouple our imaginations
from the prison-industrial complex and to put our creativity to work.[35]

Crossing Borders:
Building Transnational Feminist Prison Praxis

In the past decade, antiprison organizers and activist scholars in the
United States have used the phrase "a world without prisons" as a way
to explore what abolition would look like in practice. For example,
the Building a World without Prisons campaign, coordinated by Justice Now—an Oakland-based organization that seeks to end violence
against women and end their imprisonment—uses popular education,
training, theater, music, art, and community organizing to create a collective vision based on the lives and testimonies of people in women's
prisons.[36] The concept of a world without prisons evokes the possibility of an abolitionist vision that reaches beyond the limitations of US
borders. As such, it heralds a shift from the US-centrism that has been
a feature of much progressive organizing. Women of color scholar activists have been at the forefront of pushing antiprison and gender justice
advocates in the United States to make visible and then look beyond
the limits of the nation-state. By bringing together the insights of transnational feminist praxis with antiprison work, we have illuminated the
complex connections between globalization, US imperialism, militarism,
and women's criminalization and incarceration.[37]

Women of color activist scholars have played a critical role in
bringing the antiprison and gender justice movements into conversation
with the insights of global justice advocates. When the antiglobalization
movement exploded into popular consciousness with the mass protests
against the G8 summit in Cologne, Germany in June 1999 and the
World Trade Organization in Seattle in November 1999, the global rise
in mass incarceration was not on the movement's agenda. Although
the antiglobalization movement brought together a range of social justice causes, including resistance to neoliberalism, free trade, growing
economic disparities, militarism, environmental abuses, dispossession of

indigenous peoples, and homelessness, movement intellectuals failed to interrogate how these same processes had fueled an unprecedented prison build-up during the prior two decades. Angela Y. Davis's analysis of the cycle of impoverishment, criminalization, and incarceration generated by the globalization of capital laid the groundwork for examining the connections between globalization and mass incarceration: "In fleeing organized labor in the US to avoid paying higher wages and benefits, [corporations] leave entire communities in shambles, consigning huge numbers of people to joblessness, leaving them prey to the drug trade, destroying the economic base of these communities, thus affecting the education system, social welfare—and turning the people who live in these communities into perfect candidates for prison."[38]

Davis, along with anti-imperialist political prisoner Linda Evans, disseminated important information about the role of multinational corporations in financing, building, equipping, and operating prisons and revealed their symbiotic relationship with politicians, thus enabling the antiprison movement to identify and target those who profit from and promote mass incarceration.[39]

Davis's analysis is elaborated on by Ruth Wilson Gilmore, whose analysis of the emergence and consolidation of a "golden gulag" in California demonstrates that prison expansion was a response to political and economic restructuring driven by the globalization of capital and attempts by the state to deal with the surpluses of land and labor it engendered.[40] While analyzing such immense global structures could lead to a sense of inevitability and powerlessness, Gilmore's discussion of Mothers Reclaiming Our Children, a multiracial group of women fighting prison construction in Los Angeles, shows that resistance to "globalization from above" is possible and comes in the form of strategic actions that target the localized impacts of neoliberal structural adjustments.[41]

My own work in this area made two contributions. First, it called for a move beyond US-centric and unidimensional analyses of women's imprisonment that failed to explore the transnational links between mass incarceration in diverse locales and the rise of neoliberal political and economic regimes. Second, it created conversations among scholars, activists, and prisoners globally about the importance of engaging in what I labeled "transnational feminist prison praxis."[42] This work builds on the scholarship of women of color who have articulated transnational feminism as a form of theorizing and praxis that makes visible the impact of transnational economic and social factors on women's lives. Transnational feminists have elucidated the gendered impacts of multinational corporations, structural adjustment policies, neoliberalism, free trade agreements, processing zones, and outsourcing practices, redefining these as women's issues.

We have also debunked "global feminisms," which tend to view women globally as universally suffering from patriarchal oppression as defined by Western women. Instead of this unitary vision of women's experiences, we have revealed how women's lives are shaped by the intersections of race, class, gender, sexuality, and nation, as these systems of dominance interact with political and economic forces that are both local and transnational in nature. By asking what these insights meant for the lives of women of color prisoners in the global South and the postindustrial North, we brought attention to the criminalization of the strategies that women of color and women from the global South use to survive the impacts of global capital and neoliberal restructuring.

In this conceptualization, women's acts in crossing borders illegally, transporting drugs from the Caribbean and Latin America to the United States and Europe, welfare fraud, and petty theft are all faces of the crisis engendered by the new global economic order and demand solutions rooted in a vision of global economic justice. The testimonies of incarcerated women of color are central to this work. These women, often represented by pseudonyms and thus unrecognized for their contributions as thinkers and analysts, have nevertheless transformed our understanding of women's victimization, criminalization, and resistance.[43]

These interventions by women of color have made a significant impact on the contemporary antiprison and global justice movements.[44] Increasingly, US-based antiprison activists are determined to engage with global justice issues and to explore the links between criminalization and globalization. The efforts of organizations like Grassroots Global Justice to involve more activists of color in setting the agenda for the US antiglobalization movement have also resulted in the participation of activists of color from the antiprison movement participating in the World Social Forum and the US Social Forum.

As a result, prisons, policing, and surveillance have increasingly become integrated into the global justice agenda of US-based activists. For example, abolitionist workshops were visible at the 2010 US Social Forum, and participants at a People's Movement Assembly on prisons drafted a resolution on ending the global prison-industrial complex.[45] In addition, US-based antiprison organizations have participated in the past four International Conferences on Prison Abolition (ICOPA) in Canada, Nigeria, London, and Ireland. Perhaps even more significant, books like *Global Lockdown* and *Are Prisons Obsolete?* have become classic texts used in classrooms in ethnic studies, women's studies, American studies, and other disciplines.

From Women Prisoners to People in Women's Prisons: Challenging the Gender Binary

During the past decades, women of color activists and scholars have generated important theoretical advances that have greatly enhanced efforts to end violence against women of color and to challenge the exponential increase in women's imprisonment. However, there have also been limitations to this work. In particular, the writings and political organizing of many women of color prior to the turn of the twenty-first century—including my own early work—have unquestioningly adopted and followed a binary gender system that forcefully corrals all humanity into two distinct categories and demands a convergence between biological designation at birth and current gender identity. In so doing, we have been complicit with the repression of the gender fluidity and complexity that exists in our communities as well as within both men's and women's prisons, jails, juvenile halls, and detention centers. That is, we have often failed to think critically about how the gender binary that underpins penal regimes is produced and maintained through forms of gender policing that have a particularly marginalizing and brutal impact on people of color who do not conform to dominant expectations relating to gender identity and performance.[46]

In the past few years, organizations that focus on abolition and advocacy for women in prison, such as the California Coalition for Women Prisoners (CCWP), Critical Resistance, and Justice Now, have shifted the language they use to describe their constituencies. For example, while Justice Now's mission statement refers to ending "violence against women and stop[ping] their imprisonment," materials produced by the organization more recently demonstrate a shift in thinking. In an invitation to a strategy session on gender and prison expansion, the term "violence against women" was revised to read "harm against female-bodied and women-identified people."[47] This shift represents a deliberate process of moving from a "born women only"–oriented feminist analysis to a broader "gender justice" platform that recognizes a range of experiences of gender oppression.[48] Similarly, these organizations have adopted new language to describe those held in women's prisons. For example,

CCWP, which was founded in 1995, now uniformly uses the language "people in women's prisons" rather than the term "women prisoners," which it used when it was established.

This shift has occurred as a result of advocacy by transgender and genderqueer antiprison activists, who have raised awareness about the experiences of transgender people of color.[49] For example, writing in the Fire Inside's special edition on transgender prisoners, Shawnna D. demonstrates the link between transphobia and criminalization: "The two-gender system is used to regulate gender expression. For those of us who fail to follow these two rigid options for gender expression—female or male, we are forced to the fringes of every segment of society. Transgender youth are routinely kicked out of their families of origin, drop out of school, are denied housing and medical care, and a majority find it almost impossible to obtain employment. Consequently, many resort to illegal economies to support themselves leading to the high rates of imprisonment in transgender communities."[50]

This observation was supported at the Transforming Justice conference coordinated in San Francisco in 2007 by a coalition of transgender and antiprison organizations, where formerly incarcerated transwomen screened video journals of their lives featuring a collage of photographs, documents, and memories from early childhood through adult experiences with the criminal justice system.[51] The women's narratives illustrated a continuum of racialized gender violence and policing, beginning in the family; continuing in difficulties with education, housing, and employment; and later appearing in encounters with the police, courts, jails, and prisons. As veteran antiprison activist Miss Major summarizes: "We can be beaten, attacked and killed and its OK 'Oh well, who gives a shit about that mother****r, he's confused.' You are already a convict for just how you express yourself and you might start living a lifestyle of a person that is living outside of the law. Because you can't get a legitimate job, you can't get a chance in school, you can't get a chance to function and survive as a part of mainstream society."[52]

Drawing on the work of Beth Richie in relation to battered black women, I labeled this process "racialized (trans)gender entrapment" because it often propels transgender people, in particular low-income people of color, to "choose" survival strategies that lead to criminalization and imprisonment.[53] Once in prison or jail, these individuals experience institutionally sanctioned gender policing and violence.[54] On release the cycle continues as "postincarceration sentences," which deny many former prisoners access to welfare, housing, educational grants, employment, and voting and reinforce social and economic marginality. The stigma of a criminal record interacts with existing social stigmas related to race, class, and gender nonconformity to lead back to "the merry-go-round of recidivism."[55]

Transgender advocacy organizations like the Sylvia Rivera Law Center and TGIJP (Transgender, Gender Variant, and Intersex Justice Project) have played a key role in empowering transgender women of color to speak out and take action on the cycle of violence and criminalization they experience. In addition, INCITE! has played a key role in shifting feminist consciousness as the leading radical voice in women of color antiviolence work by advocating a "transgender solidarity model" that uses a gender justice analysis and seeks to dismantle the gender binary as well as other systems of dominance.[56] Through their national project to document law enforcement violence, INCITE! has made visible to the feminist movement the particularly harsh treatment of transgender people of color. By theorizing the connections between the policing of race, gender, and gender nonconformity, INCITE! insists that the experiences of transgender people of color are central rather than peripheral to any political work that aims to end intimate and state violence.

Conclusions

In a little over a decade, women of color involved in the antiprison and antiviolence movements in the United States have radically transformed our understanding of violence against women and the most effective ways to combat it. First, we have greatly expanded the range of harmful acts that are included within the concept violence against women. Where second-wave white feminists constructed an antiviolence movement around intimate harms committed by individual men against women and girls, women of color pointed out that these acts were only a fraction of the violence experienced by women and transgender people of color. In so doing, we redefined the concept violence against women to include state violence, such as rape and harassment by police officers or immigration control agents; institutional violence, such as strip searching in jail intake rooms and the emotional violence associated with being housed as a transwoman in a men's prison; and systemic violence, such as the violence of poverty, addiction, and neglect.

Second, we learned from the lives of women and transgender people of color in order to develop a new understanding of the processes that lead to criminalization and incarceration. Listening to Stormy and other women and transgender people of color led some of us to theorize the existence of a continuum of victimization and criminalization that leads to the (trans)gender entrapment of women and transpeople of color who have experienced violence and social exclusion. This conceptualization allowed us to foreground the role of structural forces, while simultaneously acknowledging the power that intimate relationships have in the lives of women and transgender people. It also enabled us to conceive of a more nuanced understanding of victimization and harm that recognized the porosity of the positionalities of victim/perpetrator or victim/offender. This enhanced our ability to recognize and challenge the criminalization of women and transgender people of color who are criminalized and imprisoned for the strategies they use to survive colonial legacies, intimate violence, and the racialized feminization of poverty under neoliberal globalization.

Third, we developed an important critique of the strategies developed by the feminist movement to address harms experienced by women and to create safety. We demonstrated that using the criminal punishment system to address violence has not made women and transgender people of color safer. Instead it has contributed to the build-up of an enormous prison-industrial complex that has drained resources from supports that might enable women to leave violent situations and create safer environments. In addition, it has contributed to the increased criminalization and imprisonment of women and transgender people of color, who are incarcerated in violent and violating environments and in ever-greater numbers.

And finally, women of color have generated "community accountability" practices as alternatives to a reliance on the criminal punishment system to address situations where intimate violence has occurred. Rather than removing communities from accountability processes, as occurs with the legal system, these strategies build on the creativity and resourcefulness of communities; rather than treating the perpetrator as irredeemable and monstrous, they seek to heal all parties involved while prioritizing safety and accountability.

Women and transgender people of color have played a significant role in the emergence and consolidation of the contemporary prison-industrial complex abolition and women of color antiviolence movements. From those radical collective spaces, activists and scholars have launched critiques, analyses, and praxes that have led to significant advances in feminist consciousness and organizing. It is to be hoped that these advances will continue to infuse women's studies, ethnic studies, and queer studies classrooms as well as inform the activist and advocacy work of organizations working against racial and gender injustice in all its forms.

Notes

1. For further discussion on the relationship between black and white feminists in Britain, see Julia Sudbury, *Other Kinds of Dreams: Black Women's Organisations and the Politics of Transformation* (London: Routledge, 1999), 199–220; Hazel Carby, "White Woman Listen: Black Feminism and the Boundaries of Sisterhood," in *The Empire Strikes Back: Race and Racism in 70s Britain*, ed. Centre for Contemporary Cultural Studies, University of Birmingham (London: Hutchinson, 1982), 212–235. Reprinted in *Cultures in Babylon: Black Britain and African America* (London: Verso, 1999), 67–92.

2. Gloria Joseph and Jill Lewis, *Common Differences: Conflicts in Black and White Feminist Perspectives* (Boston: South End Press, 1999).

3. For an extensive discussion of this history, see Beth Richie, *Arrested Justice: Black Women, Violence, and America's Prison Nation* (New York: New York University Press, 2012).

4. Public Safety Performance Project, *Public Safety, Public Spending: Forecasting America's Prison Population 2007–2011* (New York: Pew Charitable Trusts, 2003), ii, accessed January 27, 2012, http://www.pewtrusts.org/uploadedFiles/wwwpewtrustsorg/Reports/State-based_policy/PSPP_prison_projections_0207.pdf. The Sentencing Project, *U.S. Prison Populations—Trends and Implications* (Washington, DC: The Sentencing Project, 2003), 1, accessed January 27, 2012, http://www.prisonpolicy.org/scans/sp/1044.pdf.

5. Julia Sudbury, "A World without Prisons: Resisting Militarism, Globalized Punishment, and Empire," *Social Justice* 31, nos. 1/2 (2004): 9–30, 11–17.

6. Richie, *Arrested Justice*.

7. Andrea Smith, *Conquest: Sexual Violence and American Indian Genocide* (Boston: South End Press, 2005), 139.

8. Richie, *Arrested Justice*.

9. Critical Resistance and INCITE!, "Critical Resistance-INCITE! Statement on Gender Violence and the Prison-Industrial Complex," *Social Justice* 30, no. 3 (2003): 141–150, 141. Short version accessed January 31, 2012, http://www.incite-national.org/index.php?s=92.

10. Susan Miller, "The Paradox of Women Arrested for Domestic Violence: Criminal Justice Service Providers Respond," *Violence Against Women* 7, no. 12 (2001): 1339–1374.

11. Critical Resistance and INCITE!, "Statement on Gender Violence," 142.

12. The Sentencing Project, *Women in the Criminal Justice System* (Washington, DC: The Sentencing Project, 2007), 1, accessed January 26, 2012, http://www.sentencingproject.org/doc/publications/womenincj_total.pdf.

13. Amnesty USA, "*Not Part of My Sentence: Violations of the Human Rights of Women in Custody*," 1999, accessed January 26, 2012, http://www.amnesty.org/en/library/asset/AMR51/019/1999/en/7588269a-e33d-11dd-808b-bfd8d459a3de/amr510191999en.pdf.

14. Beth Richie, *Compelled to Crime: The Gender Entrapment of Battered Black Women* (New York: Routledge, 1999); Juanita Díaz-Cotto, *Chicana Lives and Criminal Justice: Voices from El Barrio* (Austin: University of Texas Press, 2006); Luana Ross, *Inventing the Savage: The Social Construction of Native American* Criminality (Austin: University of Texas Press, 1998).

15. Miller, "The Paradox of Women," 1369. Italics added.

16. Andrea Smith, "The Color of Violence: Violence against Women of Color," *Meridians: Feminism, Race, Transnationalism* 1, no. 2 (2001): 65–72.

17. "INCITE! is a national activist organization of radical feminists of color advancing a movement to end violence against women of color and our communities through direct action, critical dialogue, and grassroots organizing." INCITE! Women of Color Against Violence, accessed January 12, 2012, http://www.incite-national.org/.

18. INCITE! Women of Color Against Violence, "*Law Enforcement Violence against Women of Color and Trans People of Color: A Critical Intersection of Gender Violence and State Violence*," http://www.incite-national.org/sites/default/files/incite_files/resource_docs/3696_toolkit-final.pdf.

19. Stormy Ogden, "The Prison-Industrial Complex in Indigenous California," in *Global Lockdown: Race, Gender and the Prison-Industrial Complex*, ed. Julia Sudbury (New York: Routledge, 2005), 64–65.

20. Annette M. Jaimes and Theresa Halsey, "American Indian Women: At the Center of Indigenous Resistance in North America," in *The State of Native America*, ed. M. A. Jaimes (Boston: South End Press, 1992), 311–344

21. This is in contrast to transformative justice, which conceptualizes both the person who has been harmed and the person who commits violence as part of a collective that needs healing and recognizes that "sooner or later, we are all both victims and offenders." Ruth Morris, *Stories of Transformative Justice* (Toronto, Canada: Canadian Scholars Press), 3.

22. For a discussion of this dilemma, see Julia Sudbury, "Rethinking Antiviolence Strategies: Lessons from the Black Women's Movement in Britain," in *Color of Violence: The INCITE! Anthology*, ed. INCITE! Women of Color Against Violence (Cambridge, MA: South End Press, 2006), 13–24.

23. Julia Sudbury, ed., *Global Lockdown: Race, Gender and the Prison-Industrial Complex* (New York: Routledge, 2005), 3–102.

24. Ogden, "The Prison-Industrial Complex," 59.

25. Ibid., 61.

26. Ibid., 63.

27. Richie, *Compelled to Crime*.

28. Julia Sudbury, "Unpacking the Crisis: Women of Color, Globalization and the Prison-Industrial Complex," in *Interrupted Life: Experiences of Incarcerated Women in the U.S.*, ed. Rickie Solinger, Paula C. Johnson, and Martha L. Raimon (Berkeley: University of California Press, 2010), 11–25.

29. The Sentencing Project, *Criminal Justice System*, 3.

30. In 1986 Flozelle Woodmore shot and killed her estranged boyfriend in response to escalating violence toward her and her two-year-old son. Imprisoned at Central California Women's Facility in Chowchilla for two decades, Flozelle's successful appeals before the state parole board were overruled by governors Davis and Schwarzenegger five times. Her case was taken up by Free Battered Women and the California Habeas Project, and she was paroled in 2007. Flozelle, "Free at Last," http://articles.sfgate.com/2007-08-03/opinion/17258921_1_parole-board-flozelle-woodmore-governor-s-veto; "A Prisoner of Politics," http://articles.sfgate.com/2007-04-08/opinion/17238284_1_parole-board-flozelle-woodmore-latest-parole.

31. "Free Battered Women, Our Vision and Guiding Principles," accessed January 12, 2012, http://www.freebatteredwomen.org/aboutus.html.

32. I borrow this concept from Paula X. Rojas, "Are the Cops in Our Heads and Hearts?" in *The Revolution Will Not Be Funded: Beyond the Non-Profit Industrial Complex*, ed. INCITE! Women of Color Against Violence (Boston: South End Press, 2007): 197–214.

33. For a discussion of the emergence and impact of the "superpredator" label, see Barry Krisberg, *Juvenile Justice: Redeeming Our Children* (Thousand Oaks, CA: Sage, 2004), 1–7.

34. Harm Free Zone Project, "General Framework," accessed January 31, 2012, http://harmfreezone.org/framework.pdf; Mimi Kim, "Moving Beyond Critique: Creative Interventions and Reconstructions of Community Accountability," *Social Justice* 4, no. 37 (2011/2012):14–35; Sista II Sista, "Sistas Making Moves: Collective Leadership for Personal Transformation and Social Justice," in *Color of Violence*, ed. INCITE! Color of Violence (Boston: South End Press, 2006); CARA, "Taking Risks: Implementing Grassroots Community Accountability Strategies," in *Color of Violence*; Esteban Lance Kelly, "Philly Stands Up: Inside the Politics and Poetics of Transformative Justice and Community Accountability in Sexual Assault Situations," *Social Justice* 4, no. 37 (2011/2012):44–57.

35. Julia C. Oparah, "After the Juggernaut Crashes," *Social Justice* 4, no. 37 (2011/2012):133–138.

36. Justice Now, *The We That Sets Us Free: Building a World without Prisons* (Oakland, CA: AK Press, 2008), CD.

37. Sudbury, *Global Lockdown*; Juanita Díaz-Cotto, "Latinas and the War on Drugs in the United States, Latin America and Europe," in *Global Lockdown*,

ed. Sudbury; Kum-Kum Bhavnani and Angela Y. Davis, "Women in Prison: Researching Race in Three National Contexts," in *Racing Research, Researching Race: Methodological Dilemmas in Critical Race Studies*, ed. France Winddance Twine and Jonathan Warren (New York: New York University Press, 2000), 207–218.

38. Angela Y. Davis, "Race and Criminalization: Black Americans and the Punishment Industry," in *The Angela Y. Davis Reader*, ed. Joy James (Malden, MA: Blackwell, 1998), 67.

39. Angela Y. Davis, *Are Prisons Obsolete* (New York: Seven Stories Press, 2003).

40. Ruth Wilson Gilmore, *Golden Gulag: Prisons, Surplus, Crisis, and Opposition in Globalizing California* (Berkeley: University of California Press, 2007).

41. Ruth Wilson Gilmore, "Pierce the Future for Hope: Mothers and Prisoners in the Post-Keynesian Landscape," in Sudbury, *Global Lockdown*, 231–254.

42. Sudbury, *Global Lockdown*; "Celling Black Bodies: Black Women in the Global Prison Industrial Complex," *Feminist Review* 70 (2002): 57–74.

43. For a discussion of the ethical dilemmas of using the testimonies of women prisoners for antiprison scholarship, see Julia Sudbury, "Challenging Penal Dependency: Activist Scholars and the Antiprison Movement," in *Activist Scholarship: Antiracism, Feminism and Social Change*, ed. Julia Sudbury and Margo Okazawa-Rey (Boulder, CO: Paradigm, 2009); Asale Angel-Ajani, "Expert Witness: Notes toward Revisiting the Politics of Listening," in *Engaged Observer: Anthropology, Advocacy and Activism*, ed. Victoria Sanford and Asale Angel-Ajani (New Brunswick, NJ: Rutgers University Press, 2006): 77–89.

44. Julia Sudbury, "Rethinking Global Justice: Black Women Resist the Transnational Prison-Industrial Complex," *SOULS: A Critical Journal of Black Politics, Culture & Society* 10, no. 4 (2008): 344–360.

45. Anti-Prison People's Movement Assembly, "Draft Resolution," accessed January 31, 2012, http://peoplesmovementassembly.org/node/165.

46. For a comprehensive discussion, see Julia Sudbury, "From Women Prisoners to People in Women's Prisons: Challenging the Gender Binary in Antiprison Work," in *Razor Wire Women*, ed. Jodie Lawston (New York: SUNY Press, 2011).

47. Personal e-mail communication, March 3, 2008.

48. For an extensive discussion of the debates on these concepts within feminist organizing, see Julia C. Oparah, "Feminism and the (Trans)Gender Entrapment of Gender Nonconforming Prisoners," *UCLA Women's Law Journal* 18, no. 2 (2012), http://escholarship.org/uc/item/3sp664r9.

49. Julia Sudbury, "Maroon Abolitionists: Black Gender-Oppressed Activists in the Antiprison Movement in the U.S. and Canada," *Meridians: Feminism, Race, Transnationalism* 9, no. 1 (2009): 1–29.

50. Shawnna D., "Race, Class and Transgender," *The Fire Inside* 35 (2007), accessed January 26, 2012, http://www.womenprisoners.org/fire/000687.html.

51. Transforming Justice, "*Transforming Justice Conference Report*," November 29, 2007, accessed May 27, 2009, http://www.transformingjustice.org/summary.html.

52. Jayden Donahue, "Making It Happen, Mama: A Conversation with Miss Major," in *Captive Genders: Trans Embodiment and the Prison Industrial Complex*, ed. Eric A. Stanley and Nat Smith (Oakland, CA: AK Press, 2011), 267–280, 277.

53. Oparah, "(Trans)Gender Entrapment."

54. Lori Girshnick, "Out of Compliance: Masculine-Identified People in Women's Prisons," in *Captive Genders: Trans Embodiment and the Prison Industrial Complex*, ed. Eric A. Stanley and Nat Smith (Oakland, CA: AK Press, 2011), 189–208; Alex Lee, "Gendered Crime and Punishment: Strategies to Protect Transgender, Gender Variant and Intersex People in America's Prisons," *GIC TIP Journal* 4, no. 3 (2004): 1–16.

55. Miss Major interviewed in Donahue, 275; Oparah, "(Trans)Gender Entrapment."

56. INCITE!, n.d.

Heteropatriarchy and the
Three Pillars of White Supremacy

Rethinking Women of Color Organizing

Andrea Smith

Scenario #1

A group of women of color come together to organize. An argument ensues about whether or not Arab women should be included. Some argue that Arab women are white since they have been classified as such in the US census. Another argument erupts over whether or not Latinas qualify as women of color, since some may be classified as white in their Latin American countries of origin and/or "pass" as white in the United States.

Scenario #2

In a discussion on racism, some people argue that Native peoples suffer from less racism than other people of color because they generally do not reside in segregated neighborhoods within the United States. In addition, some argue that since tribes now have gaming, Native peoples are no longer oppressed.

Scenario #3

A multiracial campaign develops involving diverse communities of color in which some participants charge that we must stop the black/white binary and end black hegemony over people of color politics to develop a more multicultural framework. However, this campaign continues to rely on strategies and cultural motifs developed by the Black Civil Rights struggle in the United States.

These incidents, which happen quite frequently among women of color or people of color political organizing struggles, are often explained as a consequence of "Oppression Olympics." That is to say, one problem we have is that we are too busy fighting over who is more oppressed. In this chapter, I want to argue that these incidents are not so much the result of Oppression Olympics as they are about how we have inadvertently framed women of color or people of color politics. That is, the premise behind much women of color organizing is that women from communities victimized by white supremacy should unite together around their shared oppression. This framework might be represented by five circles, each marked Native women, Black women, Arab/Muslim women, Latinas, and Asian American women, which overlap like a Venn diagram.

This framework has proven to be limited for women of color and people of color organizing. First, it tends to presume that our communities have been impacted by white supremacy in the same way. Consequently, we often assume that all of our communities will share similar strategies for liberation. In fact, however, our strategies often run into conflict. For example, one strategy that many people in US-born communities of color adopt, in order to advance economically out of impoverished communities, is to join the military. We then become complicit in oppressing and colonizing communities from other countries. Meanwhile, people from other countries often adopt the strategy of moving to the United States to advance economically, without considering their complicity in settling on the lands of indigenous peoples that are being colonized by the United States.

Consequently, it may be more helpful to adopt an alternative framework for women of color and people of color organizing. I call one such framework the "three pillars of white supremacy." This framework does not assume that racism and white supremacy is enacted in a singular fashion; rather, white supremacy is constituted by separate and distinct, but still interrelated, logics. Envision three pillars, one labeled slavery/capitalism, another labeled genocide/colonialism, and the last labeled Orientalism/war, as well as arrows connecting each of the pillars.

Slavery/Capitalism

One pillar of white supremacy is the logic of slavery. As Sora Han, Jared Sexton, and Angela P. Harris note, this logic renders black people as inherently slaveable—as nothing more than property.[1] That is, in this logic of white supremacy, blackness becomes equated with slaveability. The forms of slavery may change—whether it is through the formal system of slavery, sharecropping, or the current prison-industrial complex—but the logic itself has remained consistent.

This logic is the anchor of capitalism. That is, the capitalist system ultimately commodifies all workers—one's own person becomes a commodity that one must sell in the labor market while the profits of one's work are taken by someone else. To keep this capitalist system in place—which ultimately commodifies most people—the logic of slavery applies a racial hierarchy to this system. This racial hierarchy tells people that as long as you are not black, you have the opportunity to escape the commodification of capitalism. This helps people who are not black to accept their lot in life, because they can feel that at least they are not at the very bottom of the racial hierarchy—at least they are not property; at least they are not slaveable.

The logic of slavery can be seen clearly in the current prison-industrial complex. While the prison-industrial complex generally incarcerates communities of color, it seems to be structured primarily on antiblack racism. That is, prior to the Civil War, most people in prison were white. However, after the Thirteenth Amendment was passed—which banned slavery, except for those in prison—black people previously enslaved through the slavery system were reenslaved through the prison system. Black people who had been the property of slave owners became state property, through the convict-leasing system. Thus, we can actually look at the criminalization of blackness as a logical extension of blackness as property.

Genocide/Colonialism

A second pillar of white supremacy is the logic of genocide. This logic holds that indigenous peoples must disappear. In fact, they must *always* be disappearing in order to allow non-Indigenous peoples' rightful claim over this land. Through this logic of genocide, non-Native peoples then become the rightful inheritors of all that was indigenous—land, resources, and indigenous spirituality and culture. As Kate Shanley notes, Native peoples are a permanent "present absence" in the US colonial imagination, an absence that reinforces, at every turn, the conviction that Native peoples are indeed vanishing and that the conquest of Native lands is justified. Ella Shohat and Robert Stam describe this absence as "an ambivalently repressive mechanism [which] dispels the anxiety in the face of the Indian, whose very presence is a reminder of the initially precarious grounding of the American nation-state itself. . . . In a temporal paradox, living Indians were induced to 'play dead,' as it were, in order to perform a narrative of manifest destiny in which their role, ultimately, was to disappear."[2]

Rayna Green further elaborates that the current Indian "wannabe" phenomenon is based on a logic of genocide: non-Native peoples imagine themselves as the rightful inheritors of all that previously belonged to "vanished" Indians, thus entitling them to ownership of this land. "This living performance of 'playing Indian' by non-Indian peoples depends upon the physical and psychological removal, even the death of real Indians. In that sense, the performance, purportedly often done out of a stated and implicit love for Indians, is really the obverse of another well-known cultural phenomenon, 'Indian hating,' as most often expressed in another, deadly performance genre called 'genocide.'"[3] After all, why would non-Native peoples need to play Indian—which often includes acts of spiritual appropriation and land theft—if they thought Indians were still alive and perfectly capable of being Indian themselves? The pillar of genocide serves as the anchor for colonialism—it is what allows non-Native peoples to feel they can rightfully own indigenous peoples' land. It is okay to take land from indigenous peoples, because indigenous peoples have disappeared.

Orientalism/War

A third pillar of white supremacy is the logic of Orientalism. Orientalism was defined by Edward Said as the process of the West defining itself as a superior civilization by constructing itself in opposition to an "exotic" but inferior "Orient." (Here I am using the term "Orientalism" more broadly than to solely signify what has been historically named the Orient or Asia.) The logic of Orientalism marks certain peoples or nations as inferior and as posing a constant threat to the well-being of empire. These peoples are still seen as civilizations—they are not property or "disappeared"—however, they will always be imaged as permanent foreign threats to empire. This logic is evident in the anti-immigration movements within the United States that target immigrants of color. It does not matter how long immigrants of color reside in the United States; they generally become targeted as foreign threats, particularly during wartime. Consequently, Orientalism serves as the anchor for war, because it allows the United States to justify being in a constant state of war to protect itself from its enemies.

For example, the United States feels entitled to use Orientalist logic to justify racial profiling of Arab Americans so that it can be strong enough to fight the "War on Terror." Orientalism also allows the United States to defend the logics of slavery and genocide, as these practices enable the United States to stay "strong enough" to fight these constant wars. What becomes clear then is what Sora Han states: the United States is not at war; the United States *is* war.[4] For the system of white supremacy to stay in place, the United States must always be at war.

Because we are situated within different logics of white supremacy, we may misunderstand a racial dynamic if we simplistically try to explain one logic of white supremacy with another logic. For instance, think about the first scenario that opens this chapter: if we simply dismiss Latino/as or Arab peoples as white, we fail to understand how a racial logic of Orientalism is in operation. That is, Latino/as and Arabs are often situated in a racial hierarchy that privileges them over black people. However, while Orientalist logic may bestow on them some racial privilege, they are still cast as inferior yet threatening "civilizations" in the United States. Their privilege is not a signal that they will be assimilated but that they will be marked as perpetual foreign threats to the US world order.

Organizing Implications

Under the old but still potent and dominant model, people of color organizing was based on the notion of organizing around shared victimhood. In this model, however, we see that we are victims of white supremacy but complicit in it as well. Our survival strategies and resistance to white supremacy are set by the system of white supremacy itself. What keeps us trapped within our particular pillars of white supremacy is that we are seduced with the prospect of being able to participate in the other pillars. For example, all non-Native peoples are promised the ability to join in the colonial project of settling indigenous lands. All nonblack peoples are promised that if they comply, they will not be at the bottom of the racial hierarchy. And black, Native, Latino, and Asian peoples are promised that they will economically and politically advance if they join US wars to spread "democracy." Thus, people of color organizing must be premised on making strategic alliances with each other, based on where we are situated within the larger political economy. Thus, for example, Native peoples who are organizing against the colonial and genocidal practices committed by the US government will be more effective in their struggle if they also organize against US militarism, particularly the military recruitment of indigenous peoples to support US imperial wars. If we try to end US colonial practices at home but support US empire by joining the military, we are strengthening the state's ability to carry out genocidal policies against people of color here and all over the world.

This way, our alliances would not be solely based on shared victimization but where we are complicit in the victimization of others. These approaches might help us to develop resistance strategies that do not inadvertently keep the system in place for all of us and keep all of us accountable. In all of these cases, we would check our aspirations against the aspirations of other communities to ensure that our model of liberation does not become the model of oppression for others.

These practices require us to be more vigilant in how we may have internalized some of these logics in our organizing practice. For instance, much racial justice organizing within the United States has rested on a civil rights framework that fights for equality under the law. An assumption behind this organizing is that the United States is a democracy with some flaws but is otherwise admirable. Despite the fact that it rendered slaves three fifths of a person, the US Constitution is presented as the model document from which to build a flourishing democracy. However, as Luana Ross notes, it has never been against US law to commit genocide against indigenous peoples—in fact, genocide *is* the law of the country. The United States could not exist without it. In the United States, democracy is actually the alibi for genocide—it is the practice that covers up US colonial control over indigenous lands.

Our organizing can also reflect antiblack racism. Recently, with the outgrowth of "multiculturalism" there have been calls to "go beyond the black/white binary" and include other communities of color in our analysis, as presented in the third scenario. There are a number of flaws with this analysis. First, it replaces an analysis of white supremacy with a politics of multicultural representation; if we just *include* more people, then our practice will be less racist. Not true. This model does not address the nuanced structure of white supremacy, as do distinct logics of slavery, genocide, and Orientalism. Second, it obscures the centrality of the slavery logic in the system of white supremacy, which is *based on a black/white binary*. The black/white binary is not the *only* binary that characterizes white supremacy, but it is still a central one that we cannot "go beyond" in our racial justice organizing efforts.

If we do not look at how the logic of slaveability inflects our society and our thinking, it will be evident in our work as well. For example, other communities of color appropriate the cultural work and organizing strategies of African American civil rights or Black Power movements without corresponding assumptions that we should also be in solidarity with black communities. We assume that this work is the common "property" of all oppressed groups, and we can appropriate it without being accountable.

Angela P. Harris and Juan Perea debate the usefulness of the black/white binary in the book *Critical Race Theory*. Perea complains that the black/white binary fails to *include* the experiences of other people of color. However, he fails to identify alternative racializing logics to the black/white paradigm.[5] Meanwhile, Angela P. Harris argues that "the story of 'race' itself is that of the construction of Blackness and whiteness. In this story, Indians, Asian Americans, and Latinos/as do exist. But their roles are subsidiary to the fundamental binary national drama. As a political claim, Black exceptionalism exposes the deep mistrust and tensions among American ethnic groups racialized as nonwhite."[6]

Let's examine these statements in conversation with each other. Simply saying we need to move beyond the black/white binary (or perhaps, the "black/nonblack" binary) in US racism obfuscates the racializing logic of slavery and prevents us from seeing that this binary constitutes blackness as the bottom of a color hierarchy. However, this is not the *only* binary that fundamentally constitutes white supremacy. There is also an indigenous/settler binary, where Native genocide is central to the logic of white supremacy and other non-Indigenous people of color also form a subsidiary role. We also face another Orientalist logic that fundamentally constitutes Asians, Arabs, and Latino/as as foreign threats, requiring the United States to be at permanent war with these peoples. In this construction, black and Native peoples play subsidiary roles.

Clearly the black/white binary is central to racial and political thought and practice in the United States, and any understanding of white supremacy must take it into consideration. However, if we look at only this binary, we may misread the dynamics of white supremacy in different contexts. For example, critical theorist Cheryl Harris's analysis of whiteness as property reveals this weakness. In *Critical Race Theory*, Harris contends that whites have a property interest in the preservation of whiteness and seek to deprive those who are "tainted" by black or Indian blood of these same white property interests. Harris simply assumes that the positions of African Americans and American Indians are the same, failing to consider US policies of forced assimilation and forced whiteness on American Indians. These policies have become so entrenched that when Native peoples make political claims, they have been accused of being white. When Andrew Jackson removed the Cherokee along the Trail of Tears, he argued that those who did not want removal were really white.[7] In contemporary times, when I was a nonviolent witness for the Chippewa spear fishers in the late 1980s, one of the more frequent slurs whites hurled when the Chippewa attempted to exercise their treaty-protected right to fish was that they had white parents or they were really white.

Status differences between blacks and Natives are informed by the different economic positions African Americans and American Indians have in US society. African Americans have been traditionally valued for their labor; hence it is in the interest of the dominant society to have as many people marked "black" as possible, thereby maintaining a cheap labor pool. By contrast, American Indians have been valued for the land base they occupy, so it is in the interest of the dominant society to have as few people marked "Indian" as possible, facilitating access to Native lands. Whiteness operates differently under a logic of genocide than it does from a logic of slavery.

Another failure of US-based people of color organizing is that we often fall back on a US-centrism, believing that what is happening "over there" is less important than what is happening here. We fail to see how the United States maintains the system of oppression here precisely by tying our allegiances to the interests of US empire "over there."

Heteropatriarchy and White Supremacy

Heteropatriarchy is the building block of US empire. In fact, it is the building block of the nation-state form of governance. Christian Right authors make these links in their analysis of imperialism and empire. For example, Christian Right activist and founder of Prison Fellowship Charles Colson makes the connection between homosexuality and the nation-state in his analysis of the War on Terror, explaining that one of the causes of terrorism is same-sex marriage:

> Marriage is the traditional building block of human society, intended both to unite couples and bring children into

the world. . . . There is a natural moral order for the family . . . the family, led by a married mother and father, is the best available structure for both childrearing and cultural health. Marriage is not a private institution designed solely for the individual gratification of its participants. If we fail to enact a Federal Marriage Amendment, we can expect not just more family breakdown, but also more criminals behind bars and more chaos in our streets.[8]

Colson is linking the well-being of US empire to the well-being of the heteropatriarchal family. He continues: "When radical Islamists see American women abusing Muslim men, as they did in the Abu Ghraib prison, and when they see news coverage of same-sex couples being 'married' in US towns, we make this kind of freedom abhorrent—the kind they see as a blot on Allah's creation. We must preserve traditional marriage in order to protect the United States from those who would use our depravity to destroy us."[9]

As Ann Burlein argues in *Lift High the Cross*, it may be a mistake to argue that the goal of Christian Right politics is to create a theocracy in the United States. Rather, Christian Right politics work through the private family (which is coded as white, patriarchal, and middle class) to create a "Christian America." She notes that the investment in the private family makes it difficult for people to invest in more public forms of social connection. In addition, investment in the suburban private family serves to mask the public disinvestment in urban areas that makes the suburban lifestyle possible. The social decay in urban areas that results from this disinvestment is then construed as the result of deviance from the Christian family ideal rather than as the result of political and economic forces. As former head of the Christian Coalition, Ralph Reed, states, "The only true solution to crime is to restore the family,"[10] and "Family break-up causes poverty."[11] Concludes Burlein, " 'The family' is no mere metaphor but a crucial technology by which modern power is produced and exercised."[12]

As I have argued elsewhere, in order to colonize peoples whose societies are not based on social hierarchy, colonizers must first naturalize hierarchy through instituting patriarchy.[13] In turn, patriarchy rests on a gender binary system in which only two genders exist, one dominating the other. Consequently, Charles Colton *is* correct when he says that the colonial world order depends on heteronormativity. Just as the patriarchs rule the family, the elites of the nation-state rule their citizens. Any liberation struggle that does not challenge heteronormativity cannot substantially challenge colonialism or white supremacy. Rather, as Cathy Cohen contends, such struggles will maintain colonialism based on a politics of secondary marginalization where the most elite class of these groups will further their aspirations on the backs of those most marginalized within the community.[14]

Through this process of secondary marginalization, the national or racial justice struggle takes on either implicitly or explicitly a nation-state model as the end point of its struggle—a model of governance in which the elites govern the rest through violence and domination and exclude those who are not members of "the nation." Thus, national liberation politics become less vulnerable to being coopted by the Right when we base them on a model of liberation that fundamentally challenges right-wing conceptions of the nation. We need a model based on community relationships and on mutual respect.

Conclusion

Women of color–centered organizing points to the centrality of gender politics within antiracist, anticolonial struggles. Unfortunately, in our efforts to organize against white, Christian America, racial justice struggles often articulate an equally heteropatriarchal racial nationalism. This model of organizing hopes either to assimilate into white America or to replicate it within an equally hierarchical and oppressive racial nationalism in which the elites of the community rule everyone else. Such struggles often call on the importance of preserving the "black family" or the "Native family" as the bulwark of this nationalist project, the family being conceived of in capitalist and heteropatriarchal terms. The response is often increased homophobia, with lesbian and gay community members construed as threats to the family. But, perhaps we should challenge the concept of the family itself. Perhaps, instead, we can reconstitute alternative ways of living together in which families are not seen as islands on their own. Certainly, indigenous communities were not ordered on the basis of a nuclear family structure. This type of family is the result of colonialism, not the antidote to it.

In proposing this model, I am speaking from my particular position in indigenous struggles. Other peoples might flesh out these logics more fully from different vantage points. Others might also argue that there are other logics of white supremacy that are missing. Still others might complicate how they relate to each other. But I see this as a starting point for women of color organizers that will allow us to reenvision a politics of solidarity that goes beyond multiculturalism and develop more complicated strategies that can really transform the political and economic status quo.

Notes

1. Angela P. Harris, "Embracing the Tar-Baby: LatCrit Theory and the Sticky Mess of Race," in *Critical Race Theory*, ed. Richard Delgado and Jean Stefancic, 2nd ed. (Philadelphia: Temple University Press, 2000), 440–447. I also thank Sora Han and Jared Sexton for their illuminating analysis of blackness.

2. Ella Shohat and Robert Stam, *Unthinking Eurocentrism* (London: Routledge, 1994), 118–119.

3. Rayna Green, "The Tribe Called Wannabee," *Folklore* 99, no. 1 (1988): 30–55.

4. Sora Han, "Bonds of Representation: Vision, Race and Law in Post-Civil Rights America" (PhD diss., University of California, Santa Cruz, 2006).

5. Juan Perea, "The Black/White Binary Paradigm of Race," in Delgado and Stefancic, *Critical Race Theory*.

6. Harris, "Embracing the Tar-Baby."

7. William McLoughlin, *Cherokees and Missionaries, 1789–1839* (Norman: University of Oklahoma Press, 1995).

8. Charles Colson, "Societal Suicide," *Christianity Today* 48, no. 6 (2004): 72.

9. Charles Colson and Anne Morse, "The Moral Home Front," *Christianity Today* 48, no. 10 (2004): 152.

10. Ralph Reed, *After the Revolution* (Dallas, TX: Word, 1990).

11. Ibid.

12. Ann Burlein, *Lift High the Cross* (Raleigh, NC: Duke University Press, 2002).

13. Andrea Smith, *Conquest: Sexual Violence and American Indian Genocide* (Cambridge, MA: South End Press, 2005).

14. Cathy Cohen, *The Boundaries of Blackness* (Chicago: University of Chicago Press, 1999).

Part Two

SITUATING IDENTITIES, RELOCATING FEMINISMS

Renegade Architecture

Epifania Amoo-Adare

I am an Asante woman who was born in London, raised in Nairobi and Accra, studied in Cape Coast, London, and Los Angeles, and now works in Bonn, Germany, after employment stints in Doha, Kabul, Herat, and the South Caucasus (based out of Tbilisi). For these and many other reasons, I suffer a contradictory crisis of being placeless and yet simultaneously filled with knowledge and ownership of different languages of urban space. It might be said that my life is subject to the increased mobility associated with today's world citizens.[1] This may well account for my obsession with deciphering the politics of urban space and what my role—as an African woman—is in that place of quintessential social struggle. This is also reflected in the urban geohistorical landscapes that shape the experiences of women like me when it comes to tensions between the global pull away from the local push of "traditional" cultural practices, which are fast becoming nostalgic memories. Nowadays, we live in diasporic conditions even when ensconced in our homelands.

As an Asante woman who has lived in several cities, including Accra, Ghana, my personal migratory experience provides a ground from which theoretical understandings have been made of Asante women's conceptions of contemporary urban space and their structural circumstances in Ghana's capital.[2] My interest in studying Asante women's spatial experiences is tied to a desire to engage in the coconstruction of critical and transformative feminist counternarratives about our spatial conditions, practices, identities, and literacies. It is also rooted in a womanist positionality—to invoke Alice Walker—which recognizes that critical consciousness must incorporate racial, cultural, national, economic, political, and sexual issues into a philosophy that is committed, with love, to the survival and wholeness of an entire people.[3]

I have always lived in urban centers and found that my understanding, negotiation, manipulation, and ownership of space (real and imagined) is often predetermined and confined by the prescribed, colonized, gendered, racialized, and/or class-based social relations of global capitalism. As a woman and as a minority, I am particularly disadvantaged within the politics of space. I have been privy to a minority and female experience of discrimination by design of a predominantly Western "manmade" built environment.[4] Ironically, I experience this disadvantage despite my access to a privileged professional and academic architectural discourse through six years of architectural training. Albeit restrictive, each discriminatory circumstance has often been mediated by my very specific combination of gender, ethnicity, class position, able-bodied heterosexuality, and architectural privilege, which, thus, consequently varies in nuance and degree from situation to situation and location to location. It is from these relational liminal spaces that I began developing my own and arguing for *critical spatial literacy*—in particular, an understanding of the dominant ideologies that inform Western urban architecture, which then enables my imagining of alternative sociophysical spaces.

During my preliminary architectural training (from 1987 to 1990) I found that my personal experience of alternative household configurations, namely my Asante grandmother's communal matrikin house, provided me with concrete examples that contested the Eurocentric and hegemonic spatial conceptions about which we were being taught, for example, the belief that nuclear house spatial configurations and women's roles in those "private" spaces was a universal norm. Within my grandmother's Asante courtyard house located in Fante New Town,[5] Kumase, there were very different gender sociocultural practices and self-perceptions. It was a place where, for example, a woman's ability to share her childrearing responsibilities with her *abusua* (matrilineal family)—rather than bear the urban financial burden of childcare—gave her a different conception of what work she could do outside of the family home.

My grandmother's household contrasted sharply with the one that my mother had created both in Accra and the Diaspora. I grew up in a nuclear household that intermittently accommodated my mother's relatives, who came to help her with her childrearing responsibilities and to improve their education or employment opportunities. My mother's more rigid notions of eternal marriages and the husband as the head of the household, derived from staunch Catholicism, pulled taut against the perceived fluidity of my grandmother's three sequential marriages and female-dominated compound house. This all, consequently, created in me a paradoxical conception of what my role—as an Asante woman— must be, should be, and could be. It was this amorphous reality that jarred against the prescribed tidy Western definitions of what constituted a "normal" family house design.

This example of the tension between my grandmother's house and my mother's was just one reason for a renegade architectural stance[6] that was sown in me during the final two years (from 1992 to 1994) of my six-year architectural training in London. In that time, I developed a critical literacy of space as an academic survival mechanism and to decipher the political ideologies that were hidden in architects', planners', and developers' building practices and thus inscribed in their spatial constructions. By looking for architectural ideas and concepts that seriously addressed specific socioeconomic, spatiotemporal, geohistorical, cultural, and political needs, I resisted the predominant architectural theorizing and practice that reproduced spatial representations of Western technology and a global economy: monuments for the sake of monumentality, the universal adoption of International Style, and the self-glorified architect. This period of obtaining my postgraduate diploma in architecture became a crucial time for my exploration of a philosophical and political standpoint for producing architectural design. In so doing, I looked at how architecture could embody relevant sustainable, radical, and ecologically sound ideologies and physical elements: architecture that would satisfy people's many vulnerabilities. This drew me to regionalist architecture, in particular, the work of Hassan Fathy and Charles Correa.[7]

Inspired by the politics of political regionalist ideals and the exemplars of Fathy's collaborative design and production of the village in New Gourna, Egypt, and Correa's similar efforts for the Belapur Housing scheme in India, I began to conceive the possibility of designing buildings that make contextualized political statements and so developed my design ideas accordingly. One example of this was my design of a birthing center in order to subvert dominant Western medicine's ideological position and architectural manifestations of spaces for birthing (see Figure 1). Through research on the history of Western medicine, existing maternity wards, and their adverse effects on the mother and child's ability to own the birthing process,[8] I came to the conclusion that the usual design of maternity wards should change and that smaller birthing spaces that can

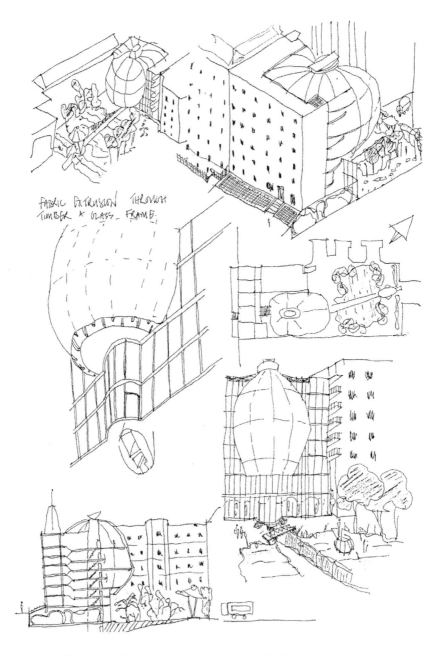

Figure 1. Blueprint of Birthing Center. Sketch by Epifania Akosua Amoo-Adare. Used with permission of the artist.

be shared by individuals locally should be promoted.[9] There also had to be a plurality of birthing spaces such as these rather than the existing large centralized points that do not cater to the deep personal needs of individual women and their families. Any design of such places had to be accessible and familiar to the community, as opposed to the sterile "mysterious" hospitals that prevail.

In designing architecture that attempted to address some of the hegemonic issues in a capitalist manmade spatiality, I realized that my singular understandings and/or actions were insignificant in the spatiopolitical makeup of things and that perhaps substantial sociospatial justice would be enabled if more than just the members of the building profession understood, reinvented, and owned the vocabulary of the built environment. I began to question how a postmodern spatiopolitical language could be encouraged and nurtured in the general public, especially among those who were the most spatially disadvantaged. Simultaneously and most importantly, I also questioned and began to investigate what my role, as a woman architect of African descent, should encompass. Should I serve society as an "expert" with architectural designs that sought to transform the dominant status quo, or would a sociospatial justice agenda be better enacted by my facilitating and enabling critical spatial literacy in the general public? As much as I was drawn to following the community-oriented, collaborative, feminist architectural praxis of the likes of Matrix,[10] I began to believe that a Black[11] woman architect like me would better contribute to her communities by creating arenas for their own critical readings of the built environment, which may lead them to finding ways to change it for themselves by themselves.

Consequently, I began investigations into the lay of the UK architectural profession and institutes of higher education, in particular identifying and familiarizing myself with the work of feminists and women of African descent in architectural education and its practice. This was in order to better understand the challenges and possibilities in the field. For example, in the United Kingdom there was the work of Matrix, Teriwa Okoro, Elsie Owusu, and Ann de Graft Johnson. There were also the writings of Matrix, Christiane Erlemann, Jos Boys, Lynne Walker, Shaheen Haque, Elizabeth Wilson, Janie Grote, the Society of Black Architects, and, later, Doreen Massey.[12] I also researched the architectural writings of feminists in the United States, such as Nunzia Rondanini, Leslie Kanes Weisman, Karen A. Franck, Denise Scott Brown, Sherry Ahrentzen and Linda N. Groat, Carole Després and Denise Piché, and Elizabeth Grosz to name a few.[13] Plus, the writings of Rosemary Aku Mills-Tettey and Madhavi Desai and Ismet Khambatta provided examples of scarce print resources on "Third World" feminist discussions about architecture.[14]

It became clear that those academic pursuits and my self-reflectivity necessitated that I conduct research into what it meant in spatial terms to be a black woman living in London at that time. Through a small-scale research study that I conducted in 1994 with ten women of African descent (with ages ranging from twenty-five to fifty-five), I developed an analytical understanding of the self-perceptions of those women as a consequence of living in urban London. For the women, the city paradoxically represented entrapment due to gendered racism and yet emancipation from their traditional cultural contexts. In addition, the city for them was about a forced anonymity and yet a suitable release from some of the constraining cultural norms of their African or Caribbean societies.

It was through analyzing these women's concerns and experiences that I better understood my own struggles with London's urban built environment and subsequently developed a critical awareness of its politics of space. More specifically, I understood that my previous London housing problems were not just an individual case of misfortune but rather an example of how endemic racism denies many black women access to decent and affordable housing. At that time, I had lived in London for ten years, of which seven had been spent living on my own, and yet I had already moved house ten times, mainly living in a series of single rooms in houses that often did not have living or dining rooms because the homeowners chose to rent out all rooms that could be occupied.

It is only when I began to comprehend the politics of space in London through my architectural training and other black women's experiences that I also realized that the way to affordable housing for a single, black female migrant like me—who was often invisibly homeless[15]—was by negotiating the murky waters of the social housing sector. This knowledge led to my successful entry into Shepherd House Project's (SHP's) temporary housing in 1992, after a string of failed applications to other housing organizations. This was a significant coup because temporary housing always led to permanent affordable housing with a local council or a housing project.

Although SHP ordinarily catered to single, homeless ex-offenders, they had opened their books to other single populations, who are often placed very low on the housing need totem pole set by local government housing policy. SHP's offer of temporary housing did lead to my getting a one-bedroom council flat, but not before a very difficult three years spent living in Hackney. Here I shared a house with women who were mainly ex-offenders and markedly all black.

In that time, I became privy to other black women's lives that were even worse than mine as they fought against (and often ceded to) the law, drug abuse, alcohol, petty theft, abusive partners, and a whole string of other activities that were at first shocking to my so called middle-class black existence. As these women's struggles and private lives became more commonplace to me, I also began to experience symptoms of depression[16] as a result of the stresses of living with what was often too much "sick and tired of being sick and tired"[17]—a strong sentiment that I expressed in my journal writing from that time. My depression was also the result of trying to live off of a very low income, while studying in an architectural program that demanded high expenditure for success, plus a one-year delay in getting my permanent housing because of a technicality and its subsequent bureaucratic blocks.

This period of time in Hackney was my rudest encounter with uneven development of space and a shocking realization that my frustrations were only the tip of the proverbial urban housing issues iceberg. Paradoxically, it was the same critical literacy of space that got me into this predicament that sustained me through it.[18] It is critical spatial literacy that made me imagine alternative sociophysical spaces; that made me design architecture that attempted to address hegemonic issues in capitalist spatiality; that made me question and investigate my role as a woman architect of African descent; and that urged me to join SHP's management committee in order to have some control over my housing destiny. It is all these experiences, among others,[19] that led to my academic transition into the field of education and my interest in developing an understanding of the empowerment possibilities of enabling pedagogies in critical spatial literacy.

Therefore, as an Asante woman and an architect and from my autobiographical relationship with the urban built environment, I argue for the development of critical spatial literacy. I take as my founding assumption that the built environment has a pedagogical nature that either induces individuals to conform to established organization of mainstream society or provides a resource for the successful empowerment of individuals (and most importantly collectives) against that society. A critical literacy of space is an important project. It is the development of a critical understanding of the politics of space, for example, determining and documenting what kinds of social insights are encoded in the built environment, how the built form may reproduce and/or contest dominant ideologies, and (in the latter case) how this contestation requires an ability to "critically read the world."[20]

In describing the importance of the act of reading, Freire tells us how his first act of reading was of the sociophysical world, that is, the "average Recife house," where he was born, "encircled by trees." This world presented for him his first reading of texts, words, and letters that were "incarnated in a series of things, objects, and signs." He perceived this spatial world by using his immediate spatial environment in relationship to his family; through the language of his elders' beliefs, tastes, fears, and values; and through a, then unknown, link between his world and wider contexts. Freire further tells us that in learning to improve his perception and understanding of that spatial world, by reading it, he became familiar with it and also managed to diminish certain fears he had of it.[21] It is to this end that I make an argument for a critical spatial literacy project, especially for women of African descent, to critically read the urban spatiotemporal world and to contribute to a transnational feminist political agenda for radical social change.

For this reason, I argue that research into women of African descent and their families' spatiotemporal experiences cannot simply be a theoretical and/or empirical endeavor. Instead, it must be a womanist spatial research agenda with a pedagogical praxis that is informed by a critical literacy of gender, race, and space[22] to begin with. In other words, it must be an endeavor to develop critical spatial literacy. I define this literacy as a praxis that is essentially rooted in a critical understanding of the dynamics of the social construction of postmodern urban space and the spatial construction of social life, its practices, and its identities. This definition reinforces the centrality of critical consciousness in a womanist positionality. For us, I envisage a critical literacy of space as a theorizing practice with which to understand the local grounded theories that emerge out of our particular sociospatial identities, urban spatiotemporal experiences, and spatiopolitical struggles.

In my vision of how this can take place, I see our academic roles as that of initiating and capturing conversations with black women about how they critically read the spatiopolitical language of space in order to claim it as their own—just as I did with Asante women living in Accra, Ghana.[23] Then, I envisage disseminating the results of such thought collections through print, documentary film, radio, electronic, and word-of-mouth media in order to move these conversations beyond the initial participants. In the process of dissemination as suggested, the idea is to spread the lessons learned to other women of African descent (in Africa and the Diaspora), who may be able to use them to comprehend and transform their own lived circumstances. In this way, there begins to be a role for education within the politics of space, thus making architecture renegade by redefining what it means to be an architect from design and construction to enabling critical literacies of space. Such an endeavor should not be seen as contrary to existing collaborative and transformative feminist architectural practices but rather as a complement to them in our bid to develop what Ahrentzen calls "a new culture of architecture," which imagines and constructs radical architectural counternarratives in contemporary space.[24]

Moreover, place can be viewed as particular unique moments in networks of social relations and spatial understandings. As such, women of African descent must explore their own interpretations and conceptualizations of existing dominant forms of architectural practice and spatial ideology. This requires black women's spatial empowerment and involvement in the redefinition and ownership of the contemporary spaces that they inhabit and influence, which are often experienced as culture shocks by migrant women and worse still as impositions by indigenous women. Unlike their counterparts in rural or "traditional" urban conglomerations, female inhabitants of rapidly changing landscapes must first decipher the ideologies embedded in the existing built environment before they can identify their textual effects and subsequently redefine and own them.

Notes

1. John Urry, *Mobilities* (Cambridge, UK: Polity Press, 2007), 3–6.
2. Epifania Amoo-Adare, "*Akwantu, Anibuei ne Sikasɛm*: Asante Women's Critical Literacy of Contemporary Space" (PhD diss., University of California, Los Angeles, 2006); *Spatial Literacy: Contemporary Asante Women's Place-Making* (New York: Palgrave, 2013).
3. Chikwenye O. Ogunyemi, "Womanism: The Dynamics of the Contemporary Black Female Novel in English," *Signs: Journal of Women in Culture and Society* 11, no. 1 (1985): 64. Alice Walker, *In Search of Our Mother's Garden: A Womanist Prose* (San Diego, CA: Harcourt Brace, 1983), xi.
4. Marion Roberts, *Living in a Man-Made World: Gender Assumptions in Modern Housing Design* (London: Routledge, 1991). Leslie K. Weisman, *Discrimination by Design: A Feminist Critique of the Man-made Environment* (Urbana: University of Illinois Press, 1994).

5. Fante New Town is a neighborhood in Kumase, which is the capital of the Asante region.

6. By this I refer to my subsequent transition into the field of education in order to redefine my architectural role in the politics of space. It is the boundaries or edge conditions of architecture (and being an architect) that I am interested in shifting, rather than just inhabiting their marginality as I did while studying and working in architecture. I enact this already dreamed of spatial imaginary of my diasporic, African, female, architectural permutation mainly within the praxis of critical social and feminist theory as informed by critical pedagogy, postmodern geography, postcolonial theory, and womanism. My agenda is to facilitate arenas for developing critical spatial literacy outside the confines of institutionalized architecture for the purpose of doing what I call "renegade architecture."

7. Hassan Fathy, *Architecture for the Poor: An Experiment in Rural Egypt* (Chicago: University of Chicago Press, 1973). Charles Correa, *The New Landscape: Urbanisation in the Third World* (Singapore/Malaysia: Mimar Books/ Butterworth Architecture, 1989).

8. Arthur Janov, *Imprints: The Lifelong Effects of the Birth Experience* (New York: Coward-McCann, 1983). Michel Odent, *Birth Reborn* (New York: Pantheon Books, 1984); Michel Odent, "Man, the Womb, and the Sea," *Eco Design: Journal of Ecological Design Association* 1, no. 4 (1993): 6–9.

9. Feminist architects Jan Bishop and Barbara Marks discuss the benefits of birthing centers in contrast to hospital delivery services in their article "A Place of Birth: The Changing Structure of Obstetrical Care," *Heresies II* 3, no. 3 (1981): 48–50. They also describe the threat that its institutional counterpart, the organized medical profession, poses to the proliferation of the innovative architectural expression that birthing centers characterize.

10. Matrix was a multiracial, feminist, architectural cooperative and research network established in 1980. Their organizational structure was that of a worker's cooperative in which each employee was both an employee and a director of the company who earned equal pay and had an equal say in its running. Matrix worked collaboratively and intimately with women's groups in London to design and construct buildings that met their clients' specific needs, e.g., projects such as the Jagonari Education Resource Centre and the Harlow Women's Refuge Centre. Whenever working with their female clients, Matrix's main objective was to always empower them to take control of the design and development of their own environments.

11. Here, the capitalized word "Black" is used to denote the political construct "Black" versus the descriptive term "black."

12. Matrix, *Making Space: Women and the Manmade Environment* (London: Pluto Press, 1984); *Building for Childcare: Making Better Buildings for the under-5s* (London: Matrix/ Greater London Council Women's Committee, 1986). Christiane Erlemann, "What Is Feminist Architecture?" in *Feminist Aesthetics*, ed. Gisela Ecker (London: Women's Press, 1985), 125–134. Jos Boys, "Design

for Living," *Architect* 125 (1979): 35–38; "Architect," in *Resource Book on Women Working in Design*, ed. Tag Gronberg and Judith Attfield (London: London Institute Central School of Art and Design, 1986), 11–13. Lynne Walker, "Architect," in Gronberg and Attfield, *Resource Book*, 6–10. Shaheen Haque, "The Politics of Space: The Experience of a Black Woman Architect," in *Charting the Journey: Writings by Black and Third World Women*, ed. Shabnam Grewal, Jackie Kay, Liliane Landor, Gail Lewis, and Pratibha Parmar (London: Sheba Feminist, 1988), 34–39. Elizabeth Wilson, *The Sphinx in the City* (London: Virago Press, 1991). Janie Grote, "Matrix: A Radical Approach to Architecture," *The Journal of Architectural and Planning Research* 9, no. 2 (1992): 158–168. M. Cox, "Designing for Black Communities," *Society of Black Architects Newsletter* 5, no. 1 (1993). Doreen Massey, *Space, Place and Gender* (Cambridge, UK: Polity Press, 1994).

13. Nunzia Rondanini, "Architecture and Social Change. Making Room: Women in Architecture" *Heresies II*, special issue (1981): 3–5. Weisman, *Discrimination by Design*. Karen A. Franck. "A Feminist Approach to Architecture: Acknowledging Women's Ways of Knowing," in *Architecture: A Place for Women*, ed. Ellen P. Berkeley and Matilda McQuaid (Washington, DC: Smithsonian Institution Press, 1989). Denise S. Brown. "Room at the Top? Sexism and the Star System in Architecture," *Architectural Design* 60 (1990): 1–2. Sherry Ahrentzen and Linda N. Groat. "Rethinking Architectural Education: Patriarchal Conventions & Alternative Visions from the Perspectives of Women Faculty," *The Journal of Architectural Planning Research* 9, no. 2 (1992): 95–111. Carole Després and Denise Piché, "Revisiting Knowledge and Practice: Women's Voices in Architecture and Urban Planning," *The Journal of Architectural and Planning Research* 9, no. 2 (1992): 91–94. Elizabeth Grosz, "Bodies-Cities," in *Sexuality & Space*, ed. Beatriz Colomina (Princeton, NJ: Princeton Architectural Press, 1992), 241–253.

14. Rosemary A. Mills-Tettey, "The Creation of Space in African Housing: A Study of Women's Involvement," *International Journal for Housing Science and its Application* 16, no. 3 (1992): 213–221. Madhavi Desai and Ismet Khambatta, "Education and Women: Towards a Non-oppressive Environment," *Journal of the Indian Institute of Architects* 58, no. 3 (1993): 23–26.

15. Invisible homelessness refers to populations in the United Kingdom who would not be considered priority homeless by law because they are not sleeping rough in the streets. These populations, however, do not have permanent homes and rely on the kindness of relatives and friends who are themselves living in overcrowded situations but allow them to sleep in their living rooms or to share their bedrooms.

16. In particular, what I experienced at that time was a persistent feeling of sadness and emptiness; a reduced interest in activities that I used to enjoy; a lack of desire to get up in the morning, to bathe, or even to dress up; a feeling of worthlessness; and a constant preoccupation with suicide without making any attempts at it. All of these symptoms are aspects of depression as defined in

the American Psychiatric Association, *Diagnostic and Statistical Manual of Mental Disorders*, 4th ed. (Washington, DC: American Psychiatric Association, 1994).

17. Angela Y. Davis, *Women, Culture and Politics* (London: Women's Press, 1990), 53–65.

18. This is not to belittle the emotional support from my black friends, who were often in similar circumstances. My mother, who was still in Ghana at that time, and my maternal aunt in Leeds had no inkling of my circumstances due to a stubborn pride and desire to make it on my own in London. I also do not wish to negate the healing power of the visualization techniques, prayers, and journal writing that I was advised to do and did.

19. The other experiences were, namely, knowledge gained by joining SHP's housing committee as well as by working as an administrator for a successful housing cooperative.

20. Paulo Freire, "The Importance of the Act of Reading," trans. Loretta Slover, in *Rewriting Literacy: Culture and the Discourse of the Other*, eds. Candace Mitchell and Kathleen Weiler (New York: Bergin & Garvey, [1983] 1991), 5–11; Paulo Freire, *Pedagogy of the Oppressed*, trans. Myra B. Ramos (London: Penguin Books, [1970] 1996), 68–105.

21. Freire, "Act of Reading," 6–7.

22. Craig Callendar states that time is routinely depicted as another dimension of space, thus creating what he terms "a unified spacetime." See Callendar, "Physics: Is Time an Illusion?" *Scientific American: Special Collector's Edition* 21, no. 1 (2012), 17. For the purposes of this research agenda, however, I am particularly interested in space as its own concept but with a recognition that it works rather intimately over, through, and in time.

23. Amoo-Adare, "*Akwantu, Anibuei ne Sikasɛm*"; *Spatial Literacy*.

24. Sherry Ahrentzen, "The F Word in Architecture: Feminist Analyses in/of/for Architecture," in *Reconstructing Architecture: Critical Discourses and Social Practices*, ed. Thomas Dutton and Lian Hurst Mann (Minneapolis: University of Minnesota Press, 1996), 105–109.

References

Ahrentzen, Sherry. "The F Word in Architecture: Feminist Analyses in/of/for Architecture." In *Reconstructing Architecture: Critical Discourses and Social Practices*, edited by Thomas Dutton and Lian Hurst Mann, 71–118. Minneapolis: University of Minnesota Press, 1996.

Ahrentzen, Sherry, and Linda N. Groat. "Rethinking Architectural Education: Patriarchal Conventions & Alternative Visions from the Perspectives of Women Faculty." *The Journal of Architectural Planning Research* 9, no. 2 (1992): 95–111.

American Psychiatric Association. *Diagnostic and Statistical Manual of Mental Disorders*, 4th ed. Washington, DC: American Psychiatric Association, 1994.

Amoo-Adare, Epifania. "*Akwantu, Anibuei ne Sikasem*: Asante Women's Critical Literacy of Contemporary Space." PhD diss., University of California, Los Angeles, 2006.

Amoo-Adare, Epifania A. *Spatial Literacy: Contemporary Asante Women's Place-Making*. New York: Palgrave Macmillan, 2013.

Bishop, Jan, and Barbara Marks. "A Place of Birth: The Changing Structure of Obstetrical Care." *Heresies II* 3, no. 3 (1981): 48–50.

Boys, Jos. "Architect." In *Resource Book on Women Working in Design*, edited by Tag Gronberg and Judith Attfield, 11–13. London: London Institute Central School of Art and Design, 1986.

Boys, Jos. "Design for Living." *Architect* 125 (1979): 35–38.

Brown, Denise S. "Room at the Top? Sexism and the Star System in Architecture." *Architectural Design* 60 (1990): 1–2.

Callender, Craig. "Physics: Is Time an Illusion?" *Scientific American: Special Collector's Edition* 21, no. 1 (2012): 15–20.

Correa, Charles. *The New Landscape: Urbanisation in the Third World*. Singapore/Malaysia: Mimar Books/Butterworth Architecture, 1989.

Cox, M. "Designing for Black Communities." *Society of Black Architects Newsletter* 5, no. 1 (1993).

Davis, Angela Y. *Women, Culture and Politics*. London: Women's Press, 1990.

Desai, Madhavi, and Ismet Khambatta. "Education and Women: Towards a Non-oppressive Environment." *Journal of the Indian Institute of Architects* 58, no. 3 (1993): 23–26.

Després, Carole, and Denise Piché. "Revisiting Knowledge and Practice: Women's Voices in Architecture and Urban Planning. *The Journal of Architectural and Planning Research* 9, no. 2 (1992): 91–94.

Erlemann, Christiane. "What Is Feminist Architecture?" In *Feminist Aesthetics*, edited by Gisela Ecker, 125–134. London: Women's Press, 1985.

Fathy, Hassan. *Architecture for the Poor: An Experiment in Rural Egypt*. Chicago: University of Chicago Press, 1973.

Franck, Karen A. "A Feminist Approach to Architecture: Acknowledging Women's Ways of Knowing." In *Architecture: A Place for Women*, edited by Ellen P. Berkeley and Matilda McQuaid, 201–216. Washington, DC: Smithsonian Institution Press, 1989.

Freire, Paulo. "The Importance of the Act of Reading," translated by Loretta Slover. In *Rewriting Literacy: Culture and the Discourse of the Other*, edited by Candace Mitchell and Kathleen Weiler, 139–145. New York: Bergin & Garvey, [1983] 1991.

Freire, Paulo. *Pedagogy of the Oppressed*. Translated by Myra B. Ramos. London: Penguin Books, [1970] 1996.

Grosz, Elizabeth. "Bodies-Cities." In *Sexuality & Space*, edited by Beatriz Colomina, 241–253. Princeton, NJ: Princeton Architectural Press, 1992.

Grote, Janie. "Matrix: A Radical Approach to Architecture." *The Journal of Architectural and Planning Research* 9, no. 2 (1992): 158–168.

Haque, Shaheen. "The Politics of Space: The Experience of a Black Woman Architect." In *Charting the Journey: Writings by Black and Third World Women*, edited by Shabnam Grewal, Jackie Kay, Liliane Landor, Gail Lewis, and Pratibha Parmar, 34–39. London: Sheba Feminist, 1988.

Janov, Arthur. *Imprints: The Lifelong Effects of the Birth Experience*. New York: Coward-McCann, 1983.

Massey, Doreen. *Space, Place and Gender*. Cambridge, UK: Polity Press, 1994.

Matrix. *Building for Childcare: Making Better Buildings for the under-5s*. London: Matrix/Greater London Council Women's Committee, 1986.

Matrix. *Making Space: Women and the Manmade Environment*. London: Pluto Press, 1984.

Mills-Tettey, Rosemary A. "The Creation of Space in African Housing: A Study of Women's Involvement." *International Journal for Housing Science and its Application* 16, no. 3 (1992): 213–221.

Odent, Michel. *Birth Reborn*. New York: Pantheon Books, 1984.

Odent, Michel. "Man, the Womb, and the Sea." *Eco Design: Journal of Ecological Design Association* 1 no. 4 (1993): 6–9.

Ogunyemi, Chikwenye O. "Womanism: The Dynamics of the Contemporary Black Female Novel in English." *Signs: Journal of Women in Culture and Society* 11, no. 1 (1985): 63–80.

Roberts, Marion. *Living in a Man-Made World: Gender Assumptions in Modern Housing Design*. London: Routledge, 1991.

Rondanini, Nunzia. "Architecture and Social Change. Making Room: Women in Architecture." *Heresies II*, special issue (1981): 3–5.

Urry, John. *Mobilities*. Cambridge, UK: Polity Press, 2007.

Walker, Alice. *In Search of Our Mother's Gardens: Womanist Prose*. San Diego, CA: Harcourt Brace, 1983.

Walker, Lynne. "Architect." In *Resource Book on Women Working in Design*, edited by Tag Gronberg and Judith Attfield, 6–10. London: London Institute Central School of Art and Design, 1986.

Weisman, Leslie K. *Discrimination by Design: A Feminist Critique of the Man-made Environment*. Urbana, IL: University of Illinois Press, 1994.

Wilson, Elizabeth. *The Sphinx in the City*. London: Virago Press, 1991.

"Still at the Back of the Bus"

Sylvia Rivera's Struggle

Jessi Gan

In New York City, the Sylvia Rivera Law Project is named in her honor, as is Sylvia Rivera Way in the West Village.[1] The history of Rivera, the Puerto Rican and Venezuelan drag queen and transgender activist who lived between 1951 and 2002, is rarely mentioned in Latin@ studies. But since the mid-1990s, she has become increasingly invoked in transgender politics. In part, this is because Rivera was a combatant at the 1969 Stonewall Inn riots in New York, which in dominant accounts of US history are said to have ignited the contemporary lesbian and gay rights movement. Because the post-1969 movement allegedly used more visible and militant tactics than its assimilationist predecessor, the homophile movement, Stonewall bridges the two periods in progressive narratives of gay history in which lesbians and gays, previously forced to occupy the private "closet," move toward a trajectory of "coming out" into the public sphere.[2] In the same way that Rosa Parks and the bus boycott in Montgomery, Alabama became a symbol of black struggle against segregation, gays claimed Stonewall as a symbol of progress, pride, and resistance. "Today," wrote gay historian Martin Duberman, "the word resonates with images of insurgency and self-realization and occupies a central place in the iconography of modern gay awareness."[3] From the Stonewall Democrats and the Stonewall Chorale to June pride marches, the mythology of Stonewall has become integral to how many gay communities see themselves.[4]

Yet, though the iconography of Stonewall enabled middle-class white gays and lesbians to view themselves as resistant and transgressive, Stonewall narratives, in depicting the agents of the riots as "gay," elided the central role of poor gender-variant people of color in that night's acts of resistance against New York City police.[5] It was not until historian Duberman interviewed Rivera for a 1993 book called *Stonewall* that her role in the riots became widely known. She had left gay activism in 1973 and then been forgotten, sidelined in dominant accounts of queer politics.[6] Duberman's telling of Rivera's story, however, enabled transgender activists to write themselves into the heart of US gay history and queer resistance as, during the 1990s, transgender activism itself took a more militant turn and transgender people fought more visibly to be included in gay institutions.[7] They could argue that since they had paid their dues at Stonewall, the names of "gay" organizations should be "lesbian, gay, bisexual, and transgender."[8] With historical authority, they could contend that the largest US gay rights group, Human Rights Campaign, should include transgender people in its mission statement, an argument to which it finally acquiesced in 2001 after years of lobbying.[9]

But just as "gay" had excluded "transgender" in the Stonewall imaginary, the claim that "transgender people were at Stonewall too" enacted its own omissions of difference and hierarchy within the term "transgender." Rivera was poor and Latina, while some transgender activists making political claims on the basis of her history were white and middle-class. She was being praised for becoming visible as transgender while her racial and class visibility were being simultaneously concealed. Juana María Rodríguez has pointed out that making oneself politically legible in the face of hegemonic culture will necessarily gloss over complexity and difference. "It is the experience of having to define one's sense of self in opposition to dominant culture that forces the creation of an ethnic/national identity that is then readable by the larger society," she wrote, "The imposed necessity for 'strategic essentialism,' reducing identity categories to the most readily decipherable marker around which to mobilize, serves as a double-edged sword, cutting at hegemonic culture as it reinscribes nation/gender/race myths."[10] The myth that all gay people were equally oppressed and equally resistant at Stonewall was replaced by a new myth after Rivera's historical "coming out": that all transgender people were *most* oppressed and *most* resistant at Stonewall (and still are today). This myth could be circulated and consumed when, in the service of a liberal multicultural logic of recognition,[11] Rivera's complexly situated subjectivity as a working-class Puerto Rican/Venezuelan drag queen became reduced to that of "transgender Stonewall combatant."[12]

Some recovery projects lubricated by Rivera's memory—in their simultaneous forgetting of the white supremacist and capitalist logics that had constructed her raced and classed otherness—served to unify transgender politics along a gendered axis.[13] The elisions enabled transgender activist Leslie Feinberg, in her[14] book *Trans Liberation*, to invoke a broad coalition of people united solely by a political desire to take gender "beyond pink or blue."[15] This pluralistic approach celebrated Rivera's struggle as one "face" in a sea of "trans movement" faces.[16] The anthology *GenderQueer: Voices from beyond the Sexual Binary*, similarly, called for a "gender movement" that would ensure "full equality for all Americans regardless of gender."[17] The inclusion of Rivera's life story in the largely white *GenderQueer* lent a multicultural "diversity" and historical authenticity to the young, racially unmarked coalitional identity "genderqueer" that had emerged out of middle-class college settings.[18] But the elision of intersectionality in the name of coalitional mythmaking served to reinscribe other myths. The myth of equal transgender oppression left capitalism and white supremacy unchallenged, often foreclosing coalitional alignments unmoored from gender analysis, while enabling transgender people to avoid considering their complicity in the maintenance of simultaneous and interlocking systems of oppression.[19]

It is clear that Rivera's history and memory have been put to a variety of political uses, and not just by others. In the years before her death Rivera consciously used her symbolic power as a Stonewall veteran to raise public awareness of anti-transgender oppression, according to observers.[20] But the contours of her life and her personal statements, I will argue, reveal a figure at once complexly situated and fluid, whose inclusive political affinities resist attempts to reduce her to appropriated symbol. Her life illustrates the limits of dominant theories of queer visibility, while her political commitments challenge us to continually bypass statically reductive visions of identity and community. Rivera is, moreover, profoundly important in a Latin@, transgender, and queer historiography where histories of transgender people of color are few and far between. In the following pages, I reconstruct her life and the context of the Stonewall riot by drawing upon interviews, speeches, essays, and newspapers. With competing claims over Rivera's historical significance having intensified since her death, I have chosen to emphasize her own statements. Believing that Rivera's praxis is inextricably linked to her life experience,[21] I foreground the motivations behind her political stakes through an extended narrative.

The Life

Born male, as assigned at birth, Sylvia Rivera showed early signs of femininity as well as sexual precociousness. She started wearing makeup to school in the fourth grade and would try on her grandmother's clothes when she wasn't home. By age seven, as Rivera described of her sexual history, she had already had sex with her fourteen-year-old male cousin; by age ten she was having sex with her fifth-grade teacher, a married man.[22] That year, she began turning tricks on the streets with her uncle because "we didn't have much money and I wanted things my grandmother couldn't buy."[23] In addition to being poor, Rivera's homelife was emotionally precarious. Her birth father José Rivera had disappeared, and then neglected to send child support. Her mother's second husband, a drug dealer, showed a lack of interest in the children. When Sylvia was three years old, her mother committed suicide by ingesting rat poison and attempted to kill Sylvia along with her, but she did not succeed. Rivera's Venezuelan grandmother, Viejita,[24] who was a pieceworker in a factory, was left to raise the children by herself. She called Rivera a "troublemaker," beat her frequently, and told her she did not really want her.[25] According to Rivera, one reason for her grandmother's pique was that she had wanted a "white child." Prejudiced against darker-skinned people, she carried a grudge against Sylvia because Sylvia's father was a dark-skinned Puerto Rican. "I guess in her own strict way my grandmother loved me," Rivera related, but "I basically grew up without love."[26]

Viejita fretted about Rivera's femininity and blooming sexuality. As a preteen, Sylvia shaved her eyebrows; wore mascara, eyeliner, and tight pants; and had sex with boys and men. "My grandmother used to come home and it smelled like a French whorehouse, but that didn't stop me," Rivera said. "I got many ass-whippings from her."[27] The neighbors, evincing heterosexist beliefs, had teased Viejita about Rivera's expressed femininity, warning that she would become a despicable street-hustling maricón. Viejita took those criticisms, combined with her own homophobia, to heart. When Rivera came home one night with hickeys on her neck, Viejita beat her, screaming, "Next thing I know you'll be hanging out with the rest of the maricones on 42nd Street!"[28] Later, when a neighbor reported sighting Rivera on 42nd Street, Viejita threatened her more vehemently. Rivera attempted suicide and spent two months in a hospital. Viejita, believing Rivera was going to die, tried to remove a cross hanging from around her neck, but Rivera would not let go of it.[29] Recalling her childhood, Rivera expressed frustration with a community that labeled her a gay *maricón* while foreclosing other sexual and social options. "As I've grown up, I've realized that I do have a certain attraction to men. But I believe that growing up the way I did, I was basically pushed into this role. In Spanish cultures, if you're effeminate, you're automatically a fag; you're a gay boy. I mean, you start off as a young child and you don't have an option—especially back then. You were either a fag or a dyke. There was no in-between."[30]

Unhappy with her grandmother and the neighborhood, Rivera left home at age ten to seek a new one on 42nd Street in Times Square.[31] That was where the drag queens and the boy hustlers performed sex work. Although literally homeless and estranged from her birth family, she was able to find a new site of community and kinship. She was excited to find so many drag queens, some of whom adopted her and helped her out,[32] and elated that on her very first night on the street, a man offered her ten dollars for sex. "Ten dollars?! Wow! Ten dollars of my own! Great! Let's go!" she recalled.[33] It was expected that all of the street queens would give themselves new names, and so Ray Rivera became Sylvia Lee Rivera in a ceremony. Fifty street queens, most of them Latin@ and black, attended the celebration, which, Rivera said, felt "just like being reborn."[34]

But such life-affirming joys were rare; street life was hard. Some of the queens Rivera met at the drag balls downtown and in Harlem were affluent, but the street queens turned tricks because they had to. Prostitution was an economic necessity because many of them had left home or been kicked out as children and because of transphobic, homophobic, and racist employment discrimination. "It just wasn't feasible to be working if you wanted to wear your makeup and do your thing," as Rivera put it.[35] Most abused drugs and alcohol. "You must remember, everyone was doing drugs back then," she said. "Everybody was selling drugs, and everybody was buying drugs to take to other bars, like myself. I was no angel."[36] Near the bottom of the social hierarchy, the street queens risked violence at the hands of each other, their customers, and the police—and the threat of arrest and prison time always loomed.[37] "Back then we were beat up by the police, by everybody," recalled Rivera. "When drag queens were arrested, what degradation there was. . . . We always felt that the police were the real enemy. We expected nothing better than to be treated like we were animals—and we were. We were stuck in a bullpen like a bunch of freaks. We were disrespected. A lot of us were beaten up and raped. When I ended up going to jail, to do 90 days, they tried to rape me. I very nicely beat the shit out of a man."[38] In an environment full of dangers induced by poverty, drugs, and state violence, the presence of true friends could be lifesaving. Early in her life on the streets, Rivera met a black street queen named Marsha P. Johnson who became her best friend for the next decade. Like a big sister, Johnson looked out for her, taught her how to apply makeup, and gave her good advice, like "Show a happy face all the time, not to give a fuck about nothing, not to let nothing stop you. . . . Don't mess with anyone's lover; don't rip off anyone's dope or money."[39] When, because of a police crackdown on "vice," Sylvia ended up in prison at Rikers Island in the cellblock reserved for "gay crimes," she met a black queen friend named Bambi Lamour. In jail, the two developed a reputation for being "crazy, abnormal bitches"; according to Rivera, "Nobody ever fucked with us."[40]

On the night of June 27, 1969, Sylvia was only seventeen years old. It was a hot and muggy evening, and she headed to the Stonewall Inn to go dancing. Stonewall was not a drag queen bar. In fact, it allowed few drag queens inside because the owners felt gender-nonconforming people would attract trouble from the police. Racism was central to the story of Stonewall; Rivera characterized the Stonewall Inn as "a white male bar for middle-class males to pick up young boys of different races."[41] But she had connections inside the bar, so she could get in. Then, all of a sudden, police were walking through, ordering the patrons to line up and present identification. There was a New York law requiring people to wear at least three pieces of clothing "appropriate" to their birth-assigned gender, and usually in these raids, only people dressed in clothes of a different gender, people without IDs, and employees of the bar would be arrested. Everyone else would be released.[42] Transgender and gender-variant people were separated from lesbians and gays, according to Rivera: "Routine was, 'Faggots over here, dykes over here, and freaks over there,' referring to my side of the community."[43] She elaborated, "The queens and the real butch dykes were the freaks."[44] But on this night, a confrontation occurred. Who initiated the confrontation has become politically important to transgender people who wish to estab-lish historical authenticity within queer movements. One of historian Martin Duberman's interviewees said it was "a dyke dressed in men's clothing" who resisted as the police put hir into the paddy wagon.[45] Rivera told transgender activist Leslie Feinberg, "It was street gay people from the Village out front—homeless people who lived in the park in Sheridan Square outside the bar—and then drag queens behind them and everybody behind us."[46] She said to Latino Gay Men of New York that "street queens of that era" initiated the Stonewall riots by throwing pocket change at the police.[47] She seemed aware of her role in the historical narratives of Stonewall as she joked with the Latino Gay Men audience: "I have been given the credit for throwing the first Molotov cocktail by many historians but I always like to correct it; I threw the second one, I did not throw the first one!"[48]

Though the riot took place at a bar with a largely white, normatively gendered clientele, it was the street youth and gender-variant people nearby—many of them working class and of color—who were on the front lines of the confrontation. Those who had most been targets of police harassment, those who were most socially and economically marginalized, fought most fiercely. Seymour Pine, the deputy inspector in charge of public morals at the New York Police Department, was the lead police officer on the scene. He recalled on a 1989 National Public Radio program: "One drag queen, as we put her in the car, opened the door on the other side and jumped out. At which time we had to chase that person and he was caught, put back into the car, he made another attempt to get out the same door, the other door, and at that point we had to handcuff the person."[49] A bystander said, "I remember looking back from 10th Street, and there on Waverly Street there was . . . a cop and he is on his stomach in his tactical uniform and his helmet and everything else, with a drag queen straddling him. She was beating the hell out of him with her shoe."[50] Rivera described seeing one drag queen who got beat by the police "into a bloody pulp," and "a couple of dykes they took out and threw in a car."[51] In his historical reexamination of Stonewall, David Carter wrote, "It seems irrefutable that a highly disproportionate amount of the physical courage displayed during the riots came from the more effeminate men in the crowd" and from the street youth.[52] According to Rivera, "Many radical straight men and women" living in Greenwich Village also joined the riot.[53]

Few sources specifically denote race or ethnicity in describing the frontline Stonewall combatants. However, Duberman believes it was mostly street people and drag queens who started the fighting.[54] Because many of the street queens Rivera described working with were black and Latin@, I assume that people of color played pivotal roles.[55] This view is supported by sources' occasionally racialized depictions of the riot's early moments. One recalled a "big, hunky, nice-looking Puerto Rican guy" throwing a milk carton at police near the beginning of the confrontation. According to another account, "a young Puerto Rican taunted the gays, asking why they put up with being shoved around by cops."[56] One of David Carter's interviewees said that Gino, a working-class Puerto Rican gay man, was so enraged at the sight of police mistreating a butch female that he yelled at officers to "let her go!" Others in the crowd chimed in; then Gino threw a heavy cobblestone onto the trunk of a police car, "scaring the shit" out of them.[57] It is also important to note that the Stonewall combatants' resistant acts drew inspiration from contemporaneous movements for racial justice. Uprisings against racist police brutality had accelerated during the late 1960s, and as the confrontation with police intensified that night at Stonewall, the crowd's chants of "Gay power!" and "We're the pink panthers!" referred to Black Power and the Black Panther Party.[58] Rivera confirmed, "I don't know how many other patrons in the bar were activists, but many of the people were involved in some struggle. I had been doing work in the civil rights movement, against the war in Vietnam, and for the women's movement."[59]

Published news accounts, for mainstream as well as gay publications, generally elided the roles of gender-variant people and people of color at Stonewall, while subsuming them under the term "gay." For instance, the headline of a September 1969 article in the *Advocate* magazine, originally written for the *New York Mattachine Newsletter*, was "Police Raid on N.Y. Club Sets Off First Gay Riot."[60] This formulation—that the Stonewall uprising was a "gay riot"—consolidated gender-nonconforming people, poor people, and people of color under the identity category of "gay." But it could not explain why police targeted some "gay" people for harsher treatment. It also couldn't explain why some older, wealthier, white gays turned their noses up at news of the uprising, even if later they were to claim they had supported it. According to Martin Duberman, "Many wealthier gays, sunning at Fire Island or in the Hamptons for the weekend, either heard about the rioting and ignored it . . . or caught up with the news belatedly." They spoke of Stonewall as " 'regrettable,' as the demented carryings-on of 'stoned, tacky queens'—precisely those elements in the gay world from whom they had long since dissociated themselves."

Some of these gay people even praised the police for showing "restraint" with the combatants.[61] The body of the *Advocate* article followed the lead of its headline, describing the rioters as "homosexuals," "gay," and "boys," while generally leaving their ethnicities unmarked.[62]

But the racialized and gendered dynamics of the confrontation, and the classed and raced semiotics of the queens' otherness, occasionally break through nonetheless. At one point the article reads: "A cop grabbed a wild Puerto Rican queen and lifted his arm to bring a club down on 'her.' In his best Maria Montez voice, the queen challenged, 'How'd you like a big Spanish dick up your little Irish ass?'"

Though the more conservative gays may not have wished it, the national political climate did shift in the uprising's wake. Drawing from the energies of the Third World liberation, civil rights, and feminist movements, two gay political groups, Gay Liberation Front (GLF) and Gay Activists Alliance (GAA), formed in the New York area.[63] Fresh from the empowering actions at Stonewall, Rivera started attending the groups' meetings with high hopes. "I thought that night in 1969 was going to be our unity for the rest of our lives," she told Martin Duberman.[64] But the appearance of political unity soon fractured as Rivera found herself shunned on the basis of her race, class, and gender expression. A founder of GAA, Arthur Bell, reported that "the general membership is frightened of Sylvia and thinks she's a troublemaker. They're frightened by street people." At GAA, wrote Duberman, "if someone was not shunning her darker skin or sniggering at her passionate, fractured English, they were deploring her rude anarchism as inimical to order or denouncing her sashaying ways as offensive to womanhood." Despite feeling marginalized in the groups, Rivera had found purpose in the activism. She kept coming to meetings, where she would loudly speak her mind, and fervently engaged in all of their political actions. But some women in the groups had mixed feelings about her femininity. Events came to a head during the 1973 gay pride rally in Washington Square Park, when Jean O'Leary of GAA publicly denounced Rivera for "parodying" womanhood. Lesbian Feminist Liberation passed out flyers opposing the "female impersonators," seeking to keep queens off the stage.[65] "Being that the women felt that we were offensive, the drag queens Tiffany and Billy were not allowed to perform," Rivera recalled. "I had to fight my way up on that stage and literally, people that I called my comrades in the movement, literally beat the shit out of me."[66] Rivera took the 1973 incident hard. She responded by attempting suicide and dropping out of the movement.[67] According to friend Bob Kohler, "Sylvia left the movement because after the first three or four years, she was denied a right to speak."[68]

Rivera was not only involved in GLF and GAA. Sometimes she marched with the Young Lords and the Black Panthers, and she recalled a meeting with Huey Newton as transformative. She dreamed of enacting a very grounded kind of social change: creating a home for "the young-sters," the underage street queens who, like her, had begun working on the streets at age ten and who not long afterward ended up dead. Rivera and her friend and fellow Stonewall participant Marsha P. Johnson called their group "Street Transvestites Action Revolutionaries." They found their refuge for the young street queens first in the back of an abandoned trailer truck and then in a building at 213 East Second Street that they called STAR House and quickly proceeded to fix up.

Though Sylvia tried to enlist the help of GLF and GAA members with her endeavor, they showed little interest. But she and her "STAR House kids" threw a benefit dance to raise money. Rivera set up an altar with incense and candles where the residents of STAR House would pray to the saints, particularly to Saint Barbara (reputed to be the patron saint of queer Latinos) before they went out hustling. And she began to cook elaborate dinners each night for "the children." But this situation was not to last. They were eventually evicted for nonpayment of rent. Before they left, they removed the refrigerator and destroyed the work they had done on the building. Rivera explained, "That's the type of people we are: You fuck us over, we fuck you over right back."[69]

The Legacy

Some formulations of queer and transgender politics assert the signal importance of visibility. They celebrate the Stonewall riots as a turning point in which queer and trans people spoke up to straight society and then found freedom, kinship, and community in their ensuing political vocality. They advocate a similar personal trajectory for gay and trans people: at some point, one must opt to break the silence, come out of the sexual/gender closet, or refuse to pass as normative in order to chal-lenge the hegemony of hetero and gender normativity.

The disjunction between this narrative and Rivera's experience illustrates its hidden assumptions of power and privilege. As a child, Rivera involuntarily became visible to neighbors and to her grandmother as a feminine Puerto Rican boy. Poverty and discrimination, rather than pure choice, pushed her into the sex trade. Her queer visibility resulted in estrangement and sexual/gendered surveillance from her birth family and from a homophobic community. Her classed, gendered, and raced visibility as a Puerto Rican street queen resulted in incarceration and unrelenting harassment by police.

Though Rivera agitated politically at the Stonewall riots and in GAA and GLF meetings, the gay communities that had "come out" together were not supportive spaces but stifling and unwelcoming. It was only in communities of poor street queens of color, it seemed, that she felt more at home. Rivera's life shows that queer/trans visibility is not a simple binary; multiple kinds of visibilities, differentially situated in relation to power, intersect and overlap in people's lives. The consequences and voluntariness of visibility are determined in part by social location and by the systems of power that write gendered and racialized meanings onto bodies. The space "outside" the closet that one comes out to may fail to correspond to romanticized or reductive visions of identity and community.

Political scientist Cathy Cohen has suggested that queer politics has failed to live up to its early promise of radically transforming society. Rather than upend systems of oppression, Cohen says, the queer agenda has sought assimilation and integration into the dominant institutions that perpetuate those systems. In clinging to a single-oppression model that divides the world into "straight" and "queer" and insists that straights oppress while queers are oppressed, queer politics has neglected to examine how "power informs and constitutes privileged and marginalized subjects on both sides of this dichotomy." For instance, it has looked the other way while the state continues to regulate the reproductive capacities of people of color through incarceration. Cohen suggests this is because the theoretical framework of queer politics is tethered to rigid, reductive identity categories that don't allow the possibility of exclusions and marginalizations *within* the categories. Also dismissed is the possibility that the categories themselves might be tools of domination in need of destabilization and reconceptualization.[70]

Rivera's tense relations with mainstream gay and lesbian politics affirm Cohen's analysis.[71] In 1970 she worked hard on a campaign to pass a New York City gay rights bill that included protections for gender-variant people. A few years later, gay activists and politicians agreed in a backroom deal to raise its chances of passage by removing gender protections from the bill. "The deal was, 'You take them out, we'll pass the bill,'" Rivera bitterly recalled.[72] After dropping out of a movement that had begun "to really silence us,"[73] she spent some years homeless on Manhattan's West Side before being asked in 1994 to lead the twenty-fifth anniversary Stonewall march. Yet, the New York City Lesbian and Gay Community Center formally banned her from its premises after she vehemently demanded that they take care of homeless trans and queer youth.[74]

Mainstream gay politics' narrow, single-identity agenda situated
Rivera on its margins and viewed her and her memory as both manipu-
lable and dispensable. By contrast, Rivera's own political affinities, while
fiercely resisting cooptation, remained inclusive, mobile, and contex-
tual. Her political practice, informed by a complexly situated life, built
bridges between movements, prioritizing the project of justice above
arbitrary political boundaries. Her personal identifications, similarly,
eschewed categorization and resisted reductive definition. Press narratives pegged her as "gay," neighbors had called her a *maricón*, transgender
and genderqueer activists narrated her as transgender and genderqueer,
and Jean O'Leary asserted that she "parodied" womanhood. But she told
Martin Duberman: "I came to the conclusion . . . that I don't want to
be a woman. I just want to be me. I want to be Sylvia Rivera. I like
pretending. I like to have the role. I like to dress up and pretend, and
let the world think about what I am. Is he, or isn't he? That's what
I enjoy."[75] Rivera elaborated, "People now want to call me a lesbian
because I'm with [life partner] Julia [Murray], and I say, 'No, I'm just
me. I'm not a lesbian.' I'm tired of being labeled. I don't even like the
label transgender. . . . I just want to be who I am. . . . I'm living the
way Sylvia wants to live. I'm not living in the straight world; I'm not
living in the gay world; I'm just living in my own world with Julia and
my friends."[76]

Juana María Rodríguez has written that political affinities based
on identity categories have "become highly contested sites . . . based
on more precise, yet still problematic, categories of identification and
concomitant modes of definition. Identity politics' seeming desire to
cling to explicative postures, unified subjecthood, or facile social identifications has often resulted in repression, self-censorship, and exclusionary practices that continue to trouble organizing efforts and work
against the interests of full human rights, creative individual expression,
and meaningful social transformation."[77] To some extent Rivera's history
confirms this view. Her distance from a valued Puerto Rican/Venezuelan
male subjectivity characterized by whiteness and hegemonic masculinity resulted in much pain. Her distance from middle-class white gay
maleness resulted in the condemnation of O'Leary, other feminists, and
GAA and GLF members. Narratives of gay history that viewed Stonewall
as a "gay" event prevented recognition of raced, classed, and gendered
hierarchies at Stonewall. And viewing Rivera as a "gay man" makes her
relationship to her life partner Julia Murray incomprehensible.[78]

However, Rivera's statements also support a strategic, contingent mobilization of identity categories. Speaking to gay Latinos, she said of the legacy of Stonewall: "*You* have acquired your liberation, your freedom, from that night. Myself, I've got shit, just like I had back then. But I still struggle, I still continue the struggle. I will struggle til the day I die and my main struggle right now is that my community will seek the rights that are justly ours."[79] "My community," Rivera clarified, the "our" that she was referring to was the "transgender community"; she was sick of seeing transgender political needs continually sold "down the river" in favor of gays.[80] "After all these years, the trans community is still at the back of the bus," she wrote.[81] In this moment, identity labels usefully help Rivera describe her disgust with gay dominance and transgender marginality. She can verbally scold the segment of the lesbian and gay community that wants "mainstreaming, normality, being normal"—to adopt children, to get married, to wear properly gendered clothes—and she can express her political distance from those assimilationist dreams.[82]

Yet, when Rivera says to Latino Gay Men of New York, "I am tired of seeing my children—I call everybody including yous [sic] in the room, you are all my children—I am tired of seeing homeless transgender children; young, gay, youth children," it becomes apparent that her visions of community are suffused with far more complexity and fluidity than a mere denunciation of certain people and a celebrating of others.[83] In that moment, Rivera's articulations of kinship, family, and community exceed models of kinship built upon heterosexual reproduction and models of community that rely upon an identity politics that Rodríguez called "exclusionary" and "repressive." We begin to see in that sentence that her visions of kinship, family, and community are both inclusive and dynamic. Like her lifelong attempts at building "home," they are unpredictable, impatient but generous, provisional yet welcoming. They parallel the ways in which STAR House enacted a limber physical mobility but a steadfast commitment to justice, as circumstance buffeted it.

In encompassing her life partner Julia, young trans sex workers, Bambi Lamour, Marsha P. Johnson, and all those in Latino Gay Men of New York, they engage in what José Esteban Muñoz has called "queer world-making."[84] Even though Rivera "grew up without love," attempts to circumscribe her personal and political positionings are challenged by her abiding ethic of love for all her children: young and old; gay, bisexual, and transgender; normatively gendered and gender variant; in the room and outside it.

Acknowledgments

Many thanks to Emma Garrett, Larry La Fountain-Stokes, Nadine Naber, and reviewers for *CENTRO Journal* for their comments on this essay. Thanks also to Matthew M. Andrews, Maria Cotera, Joelle Ruby Ryan, Amy Sueyoshi, and Xavier Totti.

Notes

1. Sylvia Rivera Law Project, http://www.srlp.org; James Withers, "Remembering Sylvia Rivera: Though a Divisive Figure, Trans Activist and Stonewall Rioter Gets Honored with Street Sign," *New York Blade*, November 25, 2005, http://www.newyorkblade.com/2005/11-25/news/localnews/rivera.cfm.

2. The contention that Stonewall singlehandedly turned the national gay and lesbian tide is refuted by Victor Silverman and Susan Stryker's film *Screaming Queens: The Riot at Compton's Cafeteria. Screaming Queens* uses interviews and archival research to show that San Francisco transgender prostitutes fought police in 1966, three years before Stonewall. The homophile-to-Stonewall narrative of gay history as "coming out" into liberation also ignores the lives of queer street sex workers such as Rivera. Less able to pass as "normal" than white middle-class gender-normative gays, they were more vulnerable to state violence because of their public gendered, racial, and class visibility.

3. Martin Duberman, *Stonewall* (New York: Dutton, 1993), xv.

4. See, for example, John D'Emilio, "Stonewall: Myth and Meaning," in *The World Turned: Essays on Gay History, Politics, and Culture* (Durham, NC: Duke University Press, 2002), 147.

5. I use "gender-variant" provisionally. Because "transgender" is a relatively recent term, there is no seamless transhistorical connection between people in the late 1960s who I am describing as "gender-variant," and those today who we might call "transgender." But this essay contends that in 1969, people whose expressed genders were distant from hegemonic norms were subject to greater discrimination than those closer to norms.

6. Duberman, *Stonewall*, 282; Benjamin Shepard, "Sylvia and Sylvia's Children: A Battle for a Queer Public Space," in *That's Revolting!: Queer Strategies for Resisting Assimilation*, ed. Mattilda, aka Matt Bernstein Sycamore (Brooklyn, NY: Soft Skull Press, 2004), 101.

7. See Patrick Califia, *Sex Changes: Transgender Politics*, 2nd ed. (San Francisco: Cleis Press, [1997] 2003), 227.

8. See, for example, Andy Humm, "Transgender Rights," *Gotham Gazette*, July 2001, http://www.gothamgazette.com/article//20010701/3/183 and Michael Bronski, "Sylvia Rivera: 1951–2002," *Z Magazine*, April 2002, http://www.zmag.org/Zmag/articles/april02bronski.htm.

9. Southern Voice, "'T' Time at the Human Rights Campaign," National Transgender Advocacy Coalition, March 29, 2001, http://www.ntac.org/news/01/04/08southern.html.

10. Juana María Rodríguez, *Queer Latinidad: Identity Practices, Discursive Spaces* (New York: New York University Press, 2003), 10–11.

11. Elizabeth A. Povinelli, *The Cunning of Recognition: Indigenous Alterities and the Making of Australian Multiculturalism* (Durham, NC: Duke University Press, 2002).

12. As I point out later, Rivera herself often strategically made use of this mobilization.

13. Not all recovery projects have done so. The Sylvia Rivera Law Project's mission statement importantly prioritizes those affected by "multiple vectors of state and institutional violence" and emphasizes participation in "a multi-issue movement for justice and self-determination of all people" in order to address root causes of violence. Also significant are the connections made by TransJustice, "Trans Day of Action for Social and Economic Justice," in *Color of Violence: The INCITE! Anthology*, ed. INCITE! Women of Color Against Violence (Cambridge, MA: South End Press, 2006), 228–229. I do not mean to suggest that the projects I scrutinize intentionally sought to elide vectors of power. Rather, I foreground my interpretations of their unintended effects in the hopes of helping to "reenvision a politics of solidarity that goes beyond multiculturalism." Andrea Smith, "Heteropatriarchy and the Three Pillars of White Supremacy: Rethinking Women of Color Organizing," in *Color of Violence*, ed. INCITE!, 73.

14. A gender-neutral pronoun.

15. Leslie Feinberg noted, "We are a movement of masculine females and feminine males, cross-dressers, transsexual men and women, intersexuals born on the anatomical sweep between female and male, gender-blenders, many other sex and gender-variant people, and our significant others." Feinberg, *Trans Liberation: Beyond Pink or Blue* (Boston: Beacon Press, 1998), 5.

16. Ibid., 106.

17. Riki Wilchins, "Gender Rights Are Human Rights," in *GenderQueer: Voices from beyond the Sexual Binary*, ed. Joan Nestle, Clare Howell, and Riki Wilchins (Los Angeles: Alyson Books, 2002), 297.

18. See Wilchins, "Queerer Bodies," in *GenderQueer*, ed. Nestle, Howell, and Wilchins, 37. For the academic origins of "queer," see Cathy J. Cohen, "Punks, Bulldaggers, and Welfare Queens: The Radical Potential of Queer Politics?" in *Sexual Identities, Queer Politics*, ed. Mark Blasius (Princeton: Princeton University Press, 2001), 201.

19. Smith, "Heteropatriarchy," 67.

20. Benjamin Shepard, "History or Myth? Writing Stonewall," *Lambda Book Report* (August/September 2004), 14.

21. Patricia Hill Collins, "Defining Black Feminist Thought," in *The Second Wave: A Reader in Feminist Theory*, ed. Linda Nicholson (New York: Routledge, 1997), 246.

22. Duberman, *Stonewall*, 23; Sylvia Rivera, "Queens in Exile, the Forgotten Ones," in *GenderQueer*, ed. Nestle, Howell, and Wilchins, 68–69.

23. Rivera, "Queens in Exile," 69.

24. In my sources, Rivera only refers to her grandmother as "my grandmother." However, Martin Duberman in *Stonewall* refers to her as "Viejita." I assume that this usage came from Rivera because Duberman interviewed her extensively for his book. Therefore, I have used Viejita as an alternate way to refer to Rivera's grandmother.

25. Duberman, *Stonewall*, 21–22; Rivera, "Queens in Exile," 68.

26. Rivera, "Queens in Exile," 68.

27. Ibid., 69.

28. Duberman, *Stonewall*, 23.

29. Ibid., 66.

30. Rivera, "Queens in Exile," 69.

31. Duberman, *Stonewall*, 24; Rivera, "Queens in Exile," 70.

32. Rivera, "Queens in Exile," 70.

33. Duberman, *Stonewall*, 66.

34. Ibid., 67.

35. Rivera, "Queens in Exile," 70–71. Gender presentation and class were intertwined. The street queens had to hustle, and the affluent queens did not, partly because the street queens were more gender nonconforming. See Rivera, "Queens in Exile," 71 and David Carter, *Stonewall: The Riots That Sparked the Gay Revolution* (New York: St. Martin's Press, 2004), 61.

36. "Sylvia Rivera Talk at LGMNY" (manuscript, June 2001), transcribed by Lauren Galarza and Larry La Fountain-Stokes, 2. See also Rivera, "Queens in Exile," 71; Duberman, *Stonewall*, 66, 70.

37. Rivera, "Queens in Exile," 70–71; Duberman, *Stonewall*, 68–71; Eric Marcus, *Making History: The Struggle for Gay and Lesbian Equal Rights, 1945–1990: An Oral History* (New York: HarperPerennial, 1992), 189–190.

38. Feinberg, *Trans Liberation*, 106.

39. Duberman, *Stonewall*, 68.

40. Ibid., 123–124.

41. Rivera, "Queens in Exile," 78. She also notes, "Even back then we had our racist little clubs. There were the white gay bars and then there were the very few third world bars and drag queen bars" ("Sylvia Rivera Talk," 2). Rivera's depiction of the Stonewall Inn's clientele as being mostly white, middle-class, male, and gender normative is partly corroborated and partly contested by David Carter's sources. Carter, *Riots*, 73–77.

42. Duberman, *Stonewall*, 192; Rivera, "Queens in Exile," 77–78.

43. "Sylvia Rivera Talk," 3.

44. Rivera, "Queens in Exile," 78. New York Police Department Deputy Inspector Seymour Pine has confirmed that in these raids, police singled out gender-variant people for extra harassment and physical "examination" in the

bathroom. It's unclear what happened during this examination. Carter, *Riots*, 140–141.

45. Duberman, *Stonewall*, 196. For more on this butch person, see Carter, *Riots*, 150–151.

46. Feinberg, *Trans Liberation*, 107.

47. "Sylvia Rivera Talk," 3.

48. Ibid., 4. Rivera's role in the Stonewall riots has been questioned by David Carter. See Shepard, "History or Myth?" 12–14.

49. David Isay with Michael Schirker, producers, "Remembering Stonewall," *Weekend All Things Considered*, National Public Radio, July 1, 1989, http://www.soundportraits.org/on-air/remembering_stonewall/.

50. Ibid.

51. Marcus, *Making History*, 192.

52. Carter, *Riots*, 192, 162–163. Carter concludes that combatants were most often young, poor or working class, and gender variant and also notes the participation of middle-class college graduates. Carter, *Riots*, 163, 262.

53. "Sylvia Rivera Talk," 5.

54. Martin Duberman, "Stonewall Place" in *About Time: Exploring the Gay Past*, ed. Duberman, rev. and expanded ed. (New York: Meridian, [1986] 1991), 425.

55. In a speech, Rivera named Marsha P. Johnson, an African American, and fellow street queens as frontline combatants. "[The confrontation] was started by the street queens of that era, which I was part of, Marsha P. Johnson, and many others that are not here." "Sylvia Rivera Talk," 3–4. However, David Carter has asserted that "of those on the rebellion's front lines, most were Caucasian; few were Latino." Carter, *Riots*, 262.

56. Carter, *Riots*, 161.

57. Ibid., 152.

58. Ibid., 164–165; Duberman, *Stonewall*, 197, 203.

59. Rivera, "Queens in Exile," 77. See also Feinberg, *Trans Liberation*, 107.

60. Dick Leitsch, "Police Raid on N.Y. Club Sets Off First Gay Riot," in *Witness to Revolution: The Advocate Reports on Gay and Lesbian Politics, 1967–1999* (Los Angeles: Alyson Books, 1999), 11.

61. Duberman, *Stonewall*, 206.

62. Leitsch, "Police Raid," 11–13.

63. Though inspired by racial justice movements, the groups generally excluded people of color. Duberman, *Stonewall*, 233–234.

64. Ibid., 246.

65. Ibid., 235–236, 238; Shepard, "Sylvia and Sylvia's Children," 99–100.

66. "Sylvia Rivera Talk," 8–9.

67. Duberman, *Stonewall*, 236; "Sylvia Rivera Talk," 9; Shepard, "Sylvia and Sylvia's Children," 100

68. Shepard, "Sylvia and Sylvia's Children," 100.

69. Duberman, *Stonewall*, 251–255.

70. Cohen, "Punks," 200–201, 203, 219–221, 223.

71. In her essay, Cohen is specifically addressing queer, rather than gay and lesbian, politics. However, the politics share similar logics.

72. "Sylvia Rivera Talk," 7; Shepard, "Sylvia and Sylvia's Children," 99.

73. "Sylvia Rivera Talk," 9.

74. Shepard, "Sylvia and Sylvia's Children," 101; "Sylvia Rivera Talk," 6; Bronski, "Sylvia Rivera: 1951–2002."

75. Duberman, *Stonewall*, 125.

76. Rivera, "Queens in Exile," 77.

77. Rodríguez, *Queer Latinidad*, 41.

78. Soundportraits.org, "Sylvia Rivera," June 27, 1999, *New York Times Magazine*, http://www.soundportraits.org/in-print/magazine_articles/sylvia_rivera/.

79. "Sylvia Rivera Talk," 6.

80. Ibid., 7.

81. Rivera, "Queens in Exile," 80.

82. "Sylvia Rivera Talk," 7, 10.

83. Ibid., 6.

84. José Esteban Muñoz, *Disidentification: Queers of Color and the Performance of Politics* (Minneapolis: University of Minnesota Press, 1999).

Theoretical Shifts in the Analysis of Latina Sexuality

Ethnocentrism, Essentialism, and the Right (White) Way to be Sexual

Ana M. Juárez, Stella Beatríz Kerl-McClain, and Susana L. Gallardo

An analysis of "sexual difference" in the form of a cross-culturally singular, monolithic notion of patriarchy or male dominance leads to the construction of a similarly reductive and homogenous notion of what I call the "Third World difference"—that stable, ahistorical something that apparently oppresses most if not all the women in these countries. And it is in the production of this Third World difference that Western feminisms appropriate and colonize the constitutive complexities that characterize the lives of women in these countries. It is in this process of discursive homogenization and systematization of the oppression of women in the Third World that power is exercised in much of recent Western feminist discourse, and this power needs to be defined and named.

—Chandra Talpade Mohanty[1]

Thirty years after the publication of groundbreaking books such as *This Bridge Called My Back*[2] and *All the Women Are White, All the Blacks Are Men, But Some of Us Are Brave*,[3] the literature related to Latina sexuality has gone from being largely ethnocentric, essentialist, and white/Western dominant to increasingly globalized.[4] Recent analyses of Latina women's sexuality reveal "tensions, contradictions, and fluidity that allow women to have sexual agency and pleasure but also to be exposed to forms of control and danger."[5] Still, since much of the history of scholarly and activist literature has reproduced the assumption that feminisms and women's liberation look basically like Western forms of feminisms, those of us writing about Latina sexuality have had to persistently challenge these powerful foundations. Pfaelzer et al. point out, "Problems arise when 'feminism' appears as a universalized concept identified with certain stereotypical North American assumptions about individualism, personal liberty, family, and the state,"[6] and Ferguson argues that researchers from the North "ignore their own non-universal starting points of knowledge and their own vested interests."[7] Our chapter lays out the problematic assumptions that have shaped scholarly and popular understandings of Latina sexuality, the attempts at reclamation of voice by Latina scholars that nevertheless perpetuated the dominant assumptions, and recent progression toward writings informed by global and transnational feminist perspectives. We look at historical and continuing tensions between and about feminisms and women of color, focusing specifically on Latina sexuality and agreeing that we as persons of color must be diligent in preventing our own collusion in the reproduction of essentialized and ethnocentric analyses.[8]

For several decades now, Latinas/os in both the social sciences and humanities have been "talking back" to scholars, researchers, and creators of popular culture.[9] They have questioned previous interpretations of our cultures, lives, and communities, including the politics and unequal relations of power embedded in studies and representations that were normalized, simplistic, and ethnocentric.[10] They have further critiqued and extended early works in Chicana/o and Latina/o studies, and many now emphasize subjects (in all senses of the word) that were previously silenced or excluded as well as the multiple, contradictory, and discontinuous spaces of history and culture.[11] Although Chicana/Latina feminist voices have, at first minimally and then with increasing perseverance, reshaped dominant perspectives,[12] the field of Latina sexuality has had to continually challenge a pervasive foundation based on ethnocentric and essentialized assumptions.

Early on, Domínguez suggested that gender "typifications" could be considered "hegemonic forms of oppression."[13] Our review extends her idea to studies of sexuality. In following the gradual change and development in the understanding of Latina sexuality, we have seen that even

prominent Latina/Chicana scholars situated their analyses within ethnocentric and essentialized frameworks. We argue that these dominant
typifications set up a foundation that narrowly portrayed our sexuality
as inherently negative and/or dichotomized it: Latinas were (and still
are, in many places) categorized as either being traditional and sexually
repressed or being acculturated and sexually liberated.[14]

Dealing almost exclusively with heterosexuality, even Chicana and
Latina interpretations were shaped by these foundations and thus were
characterized by ethnocentric and essentialized understandings of both
Latina/o culture *and* human sexuality. Many authors assumed that modern white sexuality was progressively more liberated and was the healthy,
right way to be sexual. Our critical gaze then looks at these literary and
academic predecessors. While some examined sexuality in more complex
and diverse ways, others normalized Latina cultural practices of sexuality
in a way that we call "negative sex" (attitudes that view sex as injuri-
ous, shameful, distasteful, or otherwise unpleasant). As Bettina Flores
asserted in her popular book, "Sex is still referred to by many Latinas
as 'you know what.' Latinas are naïve about sex. They see it as a duty
and, therefore, don't fake headaches too often."[15]

In addition to pointing out how early and some recent important
work in Latina sexuality colluded with the dominant perspective, we
recognize that there has been a persistent and increasingly prevalent
challenge to the dominant perspective by other Latina writers. Some of
the first voices challenging the white/dominant ideology were primarily
lesbians writing popular literature or working in the humanities,[16] but
recently even perspectives of straight/heterosexual sexuality is increasingly contesting the ethnocentric and essentialized models found in
popular culture and the social sciences.[17] Going beyond the many calls—
often still unheeded—to analyze race, class, and gender as inherently
interconnected, scholars such as Yvonne Yarbro-Bejarano have even
noted the importance of making sexuality central to *all* social analyses.[18]

Within the field of humanities, unfortunately, this work is often
marginalized (e.g., it is published in alternative presses rather than in
mainstream journals) and is rarely cited by mainstream social scientists. Nonetheless, it is critical for both popular writers and scholars to
recognize that Latina sexuality is complex, diverse, and always locally
and historically situated. Recognizing the ethnocentrism and essentialism
inherent in popular and scholarly foundational paradigms, and paying
attention to the persistent and ever-growing perspectives that take more
nuanced and globalized approaches, will lead to better understandings of

Latina and other sexualities. Like many other women of color, Latinas may have unique ways of expressing sexualities, but, as more and more of us are saying, we are neither as repressed nor as oppressed as many have painted us to be.

Ignoring Contradictions: Ethnocentrism, Acculturation, and Traditional Cultures

Ethnocentrism refers to the assumption that one's own culture or ethnic group is better, natural, or unmarked and/or to judging other cultures in terms of one's own cultural perspective. In much of the foundational scholarly work about Latina sexuality, this notion was evident in the assumption that *less* acculturated Latinas are *more* repressed—and that acculturation toward the "natural," (normalized) white American way was the answer. This kind of thinking was evident when scholars described the negative attitudes, submissiveness, and passivity of "traditional" Latina sexuality; they blamed Latina/o culture for Latinas' sexual oppression. However, when this same phenomenon described white American women, that is, when they experienced submissiveness, passivity, discomfort, or shame regarding their sexuality, these scholars did not suggest that American culture was sexually repressive.[19] If Latina/o culture was responsible for keeping Latinas repressed (and if this is purportedly resolved when traditional Latinas acculturated), what was given as the explanation when the same experiences occurred in white women? There was no explanation given: white women were/are not seen as being simply a product of their culture.

Espín, an eminent Latina feminist psychologist who wrote extensively about the intersections of gender, ethnicity, and sexuality, clearly assumed that traditional Latino cultures were/are more repressive: "For many immigrant women, emphasis on self-renunciation and maintaining sexual purity is a primary determinant of their sexuality. Many of them still deem shunning sexual pleasure to be virtuous . . . they regard sexual behavior exclusively as an unwelcome obligation toward their husbands and a necessary evil to create children. Some immigrant women express pride at their own lack of sexual pleasure or desire."[20] Her work has set a particularly powerful and influential foundation for other scholars, especially in the field of psychology. Her work explicitly linked sexual liberation with acculturation: "For parents and young women alike, acculturation and sexuality are closely connected. In many immigrant communities, to be 'Americanized' is seen as almost synonymous with being sexually promiscuous."[21] Although Espín tied traditional cultures to sexual control and repression, is there not "promiscuity" in traditional cultures? What if one were looking at a community that had not migrated—would Espín still tie acculturation with promiscuity or sexual liberation? In fact, as Boyd points out, "Espín's model seems dependent on the United States as a liberating environment."[22]

According to Espín, acculturation is the process of growth and development that takes immigrants out of a repressed state and into an (implied) healthier state.[23] Instead of challenging dominant models of acculturation, as some scholars have,[24] her work reproduced the dominant models, dichotomizing traditional culture as repressive and US culture as liberating. Unfortunately, although she hinted at the possibility of immigrant dynamics actually creating a more repressive environment, she failed to consider the significance of political and structural factors. For example, she acknowledged that "policing women's bodies and sexual behavior becomes for immigrant communities the main means of asserting moral superiority over the host culture."[25] In other words, sexual repression may be due not just to cultural logic but instead may be intensified through the dynamics of immigration, especially when mediated by issues of race and class. As Nan Alamilla Boyd's review of Espín suggested, "New research on Latina migration, sexuality, and work suggests that immigration and acculturation often yield increased vulnerability and restricted sex and gender roles for women."[26]

In another study of acculturation status and sexuality among Cuban American college students, Raffaelli et al.[27] continued to unquestioningly reproduce this dominant construct of acculturation. Their own analyses found that "past research and the current findings indicate that different measures of acculturation share limited common variance and cannot be used interchangeably" and that "no consistent pattern of association emerged among these measures."[28] However, rather than critiquing the construct of acculturation and allowing more nuanced and multidimensional understandings of culture, possible immigration traumas, and multiple experiences of sexuality, they concluded that previous studies measured different aspects of acculturation; that was the reason for the discrepancy among the research.

Their acceptance of the dominant idea that traditional culture is repressed and "acculturated" Latinas are more sexually liberated led them to puzzle over one of their findings that seemed not to fit that particular narrative: high measures of ethnic identity in their study were associated with high lifetime voluntary sexual activity as well as higher sexual risk taking. It took them several steps to try to fit this finding into the dominant model. They wrote,

> Ethnic identity captures the degree to which individuals identify themselves as members of a particular group. Thus, having a strong sense of ethnic identity may reflect adherence to traditional cultural norms and values. In turn, traditional cultural norms regarding sexuality may be linked to sexual risk in Latina populations. A number of scholars have asserted that traditional Hispanic cultural norms related to sexuality include a dislike of condoms (perhaps linked to the beliefs of the majority Catholic religion or a reticence to discuss sexual topics that results in a preference for unobtrusive methods of birth control), as well as the notion that women should be ignorant of sex and submissive to men in sexual relationships.[29]

It is important to note that they cited Espín's work in the above paragraph; thus, her work continued and continues to shape the thinking of subsequent scholars in a way that perpetuates ethnocentric assumptions.

Other researchers have also had their own findings contradict notions of repressed Latina sexuality and yet still have made conclusions consistent with the dominant model rather than use the data to question it. A study by V. Nelly Salgado de Snyder et al.[30] examined the reasons that Latinas do not use condoms. The researchers compared three groups of Mexican women: immigrant women who lived with their husbands in the United States, women who were "left behind" in Mexico as their husbands worked as migrant workers, and women living with their husbands in Mexico. The researchers looked at differences in sexual history, sexual behaviors, HIV/AIDS knowledge, and communication and sexual negotiation. Their conclusion was consistent with the dominant stereotype, suggesting that Mexican American women "lack the power to negotiate safe sex practices with their husbands. In *traditional* societies, such as the setting where the women who participated in this study were raised, *cultural* norms promote male dominance and female submissiveness, particularly in the sexual arena."[31]

However, the researchers' own data contradicted their conclusions. When the researchers asked who makes the final decision regarding sexual activity, the women living in Mexico with their husbands (the situation the authors assumed was more representative of "traditional sexuality") responded "she" or "both" more than the other two groups.[32] In other words, the purportedly more traditional women had more control. In addition, the questions in this study were asked in an ethnocentric way that assumed an active male and passive female sexuality, for example, "How often does your husband make sexual demands on you?"[33] Even with these kinds of biased questions, the group representing women in the United States—presumably the most acculturated—responded that their husbands made sexual demands more often and they tended to "give in and have sex" with him more often than the other, presumably *less* acculturated, groups. These kinds of contradictions suggest that traditional Latinas may have healthier and more egalitarian sexual relationships than those who acculturate and that issues beyond culture should be explored in analyses of sexual repression and lack of power.

Other early researchers drew similarly problematic conclusions even as they found nonstereotypical behavior among Mexican and Mexican American adolescents. Amado Padilla and Traci Baird[34] surveyed Mexican American youth in East Los Angeles, and a second study by Baird alone[35] compared Mexican teens in Cuernavaca and Guadalajara. Although Baird did not raise the question, the study found that Mexican teen attitudes toward sexuality were more similar to the "liberated" attitude than were the attitudes of the Mexican American teens. For questions regarding male and female virginity, preference for male children, and preference for large families, a greater percentage of Mexican American youth reported values that were more consistent with a "repressed" view (see Table 1). Also, the finding that many Mexican females and males agreed that "a sexual relationship is one of the best things in life" challenged the notion that Latina sexuality was only concerned with procreation, not pleasure.

Essentializing the "Right" Way to Be Sexual: Repression and Negative Sex

The notion of essentialism refers to the underlying assumption that "individuals or groups have an immutable and discoverable 'essence'—a basic, unvariable, and presocial nature."[37] Here, we apply it primarily to the notion that women's sexual disposition and experience is natural and that women share an innate, universal essence of sexuality that is fundamentally the same for them all. Even when analysts recognize this

Table 1. Attitudes toward Sexuality among Mexican and Mexican
American Adolescents

	Mexican		Mexican American	
Attitude	Female	Male	Female	Male
Important to have boy (%)	—	71	—	94
Females should be virgins when married (%)	68	74	75	88
Males should be virgins when married (%)	50	35	37	36
Sexual relationship is one of best things (%)	75	88	—	—
How many children desired (number)	2.4	2.4	2.7	2.8

—: Not asked.

Note: Attitudes were measured using a five-point Likert scale ranging from "very" or "agree strongly" (5) to "not at all" or "disagree strongly" (1). Percentages refer to respondents who replied with a 3, 4, or 5 on the particular item.[36]

problem in certain areas of their work, they sometimes fail to apply it to all behaviors or cultural practices.[38] We argue that Latina sexuality has been one of those overlooked areas.

    The following section looks at popular and very influential Chicana/o and Latina/o authors who broached issues related to Latina sexuality. Their influence has been felt in many fields, but their writings failed to transcend the dichotomous assumptions or effectively situate their studies within a broader cross-cultural context. Instead, these authors limited the question of sexuality to an essentialized range of Mexican and white expressions. Since much of the literature about Latina sexuality was written by fiction writers who also wrote essay-based critical cultural analyses, we looked at two scholars and two popular writers.

These significant texts—all written by Latina/o authors—are filled with contradictions and ambiguity in their analyses. Included in this discussion are Sandra Cisneros, Ana Castillo, José Limón, and Ana Alonso—writers who have shaped the field of Latina/o studies and whose work has inspired and challenged us. However, like the previous texts we examined, when they discussed sexuality, their work also reflected normalized assumptions of "unrepressed" sexuality, or it narrowly portrayed sexuality in a way that we characterize as "negative sex": attitudes that view sex as shameful, distasteful, or otherwise unpleasant.

Their analyses assumed that Latina/o culture did not allow any room for women to enjoy or positively experience sex. While some Latina women under some conditions have believed and do believe that sex is evil and disagreeable for women, certainly others enjoy sexual relationships, even if bounded by the institution of marriage. Although none of these authors explicitly suggested the need for acculturation, they assumed that white sexuality was the universal, unmarked sexuality and that the values and practices of modern liberated white women represented the sexually free and open way to express a healthy sexuality.

In 1996, celebrated Chicana writer Sandra Cisneros published an essay that demonstrated her own vulnerability to the dominant discourse that white women's sexual practices were superior to those of Catholic Mexicans and Chicanas, even as she recuperated indigenous notions of femininity and sexuality for the Mexican Virgin of Guadalupe, renaming her Guadalupe the Sex Goddess. Reinscribing the notion that Latina/o culture and Catholic religion allowed Latinas to have only repressed sexualities, she wrote,

> In high school I marveled at how white women strutted around the locker room, nude as pearls . . . unashamed of their brilliant bodies. . . . You could always tell us Latinas. We hid when we undressed, modestly facing a wall, or . . . dressing in a bathroom stall. . . . I was as ignorant about my own body as any female ancestor who hid behind a sheet with a hole in the center when husband or doctor called. Religion and our culture, our culture and religion, helped to create that blur. . . . my culture locked me in a double chastity belt of ignorance and *vergüenza*, shame.[39]

In this paragraph, Cisneros showed how her personal perspective and memories were shaped by the dominant ideological discourse. She compared the white, unashamed women with the modest Latinas in the room—although it is that type of comparison that reproduces the pattern for the more generalized dichotomy of them/us, unashamed/ashamed, free/repressed—rather than allowing herself to reframe the experience from another perspective. For example, how might she have understood her shame if she had connected it to something besides the broader Latino culture? While the memory left much room to interpret and understand in a variety of ways, the power and familiarity of the dominant discourse pushed it into the recognized pattern.

Additionally, Cisneros exalted white scientific and medicalized approaches to bodies and sexuality, even while she marveled at a nurse's provision of a mirror and speculum along with words of encouragement, to "see" and "investigate" her cervix and genitalia during a visit to a clinic.[40] Rather than examining Latina practices within their own context and on their own terms, Cisneros—like the social scientists and health researchers of that time who chastised and/or patronized Hispanic women for their culturally prescribed reluctance to discuss sexual activities[41]—relied on ethnocentric, essentialized assumptions.

Ironically, while Cisneros exalted the medicalization of sexuality and the body, other scholars had already begun to identify the ways in which Western science and medicine created hierarchical sexual, gender, and racial identities. The medicalization of sexuality, they claimed, was used to justify and intensify gender and racial inequality, repress nonmarital and nonheterosexual desire, and naturalize female asexuality[42]—and was certainly not seen by them to liberate female sexuality.

Paradoxically, historians such as Antonia Castañeda have documented and analyzed mid–nineteenth-century Euro-American complaints about Mexican women's *immodest* dress and behavior,[43] which continued through the years. When Latinas are not being seen as being sexually repressed, they have been criticized for their sexy fashion look, with their tight, provocative clothes and their almost "garish" makeup.[44] Hernandez, in her study of "*chonga* girls" (a descriptor used to identify Latinas in South Florida who have a sexy style of dress and "heavy" application of makeup), argued that "the *sexual-aesthetic excesses* found in these representations complicate dichotomies of 'good' versus 'bad' girls [and] also express non-normative politics that trouble the disciplining of behavior and dress for girls of color."[45]

The work of Ana Castillo, another prominent and influential Chicana writer and essayist, likewise essentialized Latina sexuality in several ways. In "La Macha: Toward a Beautiful Whole Self,"[46] Castillo focused primarily on documenting the repressive and negative practices and ideologies of Latina/o sexuality. According to her, "Sexuality for the Catholic woman of Latin American background has, at best, been associated with her reproductive ability (or lack of it), and otherwise, repressed."[47] While she did acknowledge some positive erotic practices and expressions, she ultimately asserted that these manifestations were "distorted":

> Sexuality surfaces everywhere in our culture, albeit distortedly, due to the repression of our primordial memories of what it truly is. We experience it in the hip gyrating movements of our *cumbias* and the cheek-to-cheek twirling tension of the Tex-Mex polka (both dances are commonly danced by women together as well as men and women); in the blood merging reflected in our mixed heritage as mestizas; in the stifling of emotions by the Church, its hymns and passion for the suf-fering of Jesus Christ (passion derives from extreme feeling and here it arises as a result of repressed erotic and psychic sensations). Mexican erotica is charged by all our senses: in the traditional strict costuming of each gender: low cut dresses, tight mariachi charro pants, open-toed pumps and pointed, dapper cowboy boots; in sum, our culture is infamous for its intensities.[48]

Thus, Castillo invoked dressing, elaborate costuming, dancing, and even spiritual negation as expressions of sexuality but then claimed that they were "distorted" rather than healthy expressions and manifesta-tions.[49] In 1984, Carole Vance suggested that sexuality in both dominant and nondominant cultures was full of contradictions and inconsistencies: she wrote that nondominant groups "have different sensibilities and con-sciousness which are expressed in a variety of cultural forms—lyrics and music, oral tradition, humor, as well as in fiction and art."[50] Castillo, on the other hand, did not consider the perspective that humans have no natural, undistorted human sexuality; she failed to recognize that "sensibilities" and expressions of human sexuality different from modern white expressions are not necessarily "distorted."

In 1997, Mexican American anthropologist José Limón also acknowledged the complexity of sexuality and he began historicizing and contextualizing it, but he also ultimately evaluated it primarily in terms of modern white sexuality. Writing about Selena, a popular Latina musician killed in 1995, Limón situated Selena in the Mexicana/o popular culture of late capitalism but mistakenly declared her to be a "sexual revisionary" who "fully expressed" her sexuality and revised traditional models of Latina sexuality.[51] He argued that Selena was so popular because the "bodily sexuality [of previous Mexicana singers and dancers] was not yet fully available as a key aspect of their performance."[52] In contrast, he continued, Selena "fully expressed her bodily sexuality as no other such singer-dancer had ever quite done before for a mass public audience . . . she openly sexualizes this [greater Mexican musical] tradition in the most eroticized of ways. I suggest that for Catholic working-class Mexicans . . . Selena's public sexuality permits a much-needed site of discharge and expression for a still too repressed sexuality in this culture as true for women as for men."[53]

Like other scholars,[54] Limón acknowledged that public performances of sexuality were mediated by race and ethnicity—with nonwhite women often portrayed as "bad girls" or whores. However, he suggests that Selena avoided this by portraying herself (1) offstage as a "good girl" and (2) onstage through her "large open smile of full radiance, interestingly minimally sexualized, a smile which disarms and contains her body from the smile on down even as it allows this body to happen."[55]

Unfortunately, Limón's argument was flawed because he equated a "fully expressed" sexuality with one that—like modern white sexuality—was publicly expressed or performed and depended on scantily clothed bodies and ritualized body movements and facial expressions. Moreover, he assumed that this sexual style was less repressed than other styles. Thus, Selena's musical precursors' "bodily sexuality was not yet fully available" to them because they neither performed the ritualized body movements nor dressed scantily enough in public. Limón's argument did not consider that sexual expressions and desires—whether publicly or privately performed—are always historically and culturally specific.[56] As anthropologists and historians have attested, sexual expression, desire, and pleasure can look extremely different in different cultures: for the West African Wodaabe, men rising on the balls of their feet is suggestive,[57] while in the Trobriand Islands, eyelashes are important in erotic play.[58] Additionally, understandings and representations of sexuality and sexual identity shift over time relative to political movements, economies, and other contexts.[59]

Furthermore, Limón argued that Selena was a revisionary because she balanced public eroticization with offstage good girl behavior and an onstage good girl smile. Rather than being revisionary, this balance was and is an inherent part of both white and Latina/o everyday culture, and it certainly continues to be evidenced by many female entertainers (think of "nice girl" Katie Perry). In fact, are public and unclothed exhibitions of female bodies inherently less repressed, as Limón's analysis assumes? Did Selena "fully express" an unrepressing sexuality, or did she eroticize herself and adhere to dominant notions of beautiful bodies and female sexual expression, as almost all successful female musicians—particularly women of color—have had to do?[60] How would a current Latina singer such as Shakira be seen in Limón's analysis?

As Lim has stated, "Women's increasing loss of power—actual and ideological—over the representational meaning of their own bodies—is related to the intensification of power given over to global male-dominated fashion, music, entertainment, media, and informational systems."[61] Instead of thinking of Selena as a "sexual revisionary," a better analysis would have situated her historically within a global popular culture in which most successful female musicians are less clothed and more eroticized.

Likewise, the "unrepressed sexuality" Limón discusses is primarily about female sexual prestige and desirability and only secondarily about an individual woman's sexual pleasure. He neglected other scholarly work that documented how contemporary (white) women focus on their beauty and sexual attractiveness to the neglect of their own sexual pleasure.[62] Lisa Dietrich, just a year later, offered a more insightful analysis in her ethnographic study of adolescent Latinas. She found that "most of the girls exchange control over their sexuality for control over their sexual attractiveness."[63] Likewise, we conclude that the "Selenaization" (or Perrization or Shakirization) of young women's bodies does not necessarily mean that their sexuality is now fully available to them. Although Limón's concluding paragraph acknowledged that he wrote of a "particular kind of sexuality—'popular cultural,' 'heterosexual,' 'patriarchally conditioned,' "[64] his actual analysis did not effectively employ this understanding and instead assumed an underlying essentialized nature of sexuality.

Anthropologist Ana Alonso's work was historically significant in that she recognized the complexity of sexuality, yet she still characterized Latina sexuality as fundamentally negative. In 1989, she produced innovative ethnographic analyses of Latina/o sexuality that challenged essentialized assumptions about male sexual identities and categories such as heterosexual, homosexual, and bisexual.[65] Her follow-up work also carefully documented how state and institutional policies regarding class and ethnic relations shaped gender and sexual practices in specific times and places.[66]

However, Alonso's influential work narrowly portrayed Latina sexuality as entirely negative. Citing Octavio Paz (who was the source of many stereotypes and misconceptions regarding Mexican gender and sexuality), she contended, "In Mexico, sexual intercourse (whether vaginal or anal) is . . . a sign *of* and a source of tropes *for* domination and subordination."[67] Intercourse was inherently about "violence" and the "violation" of women. Citing one informant, she argued, "Sex, even with one's wife, is always a 'violation' . . . of the woman by the man, a breaching of her bodily boundaries. If intercourse makes a man a *chingón*, it makes a woman a *chingada*."[68] "Even marriage, the legal and divine sanctioning of sexual activity, does not erase the shame of intercourse."[69] While intercourse certainly can be a source of shame, violence, and violation, Alonso provided almost no evidence that this is what intercourse has meant to women and men within the institution of marriage. We doubt that this is the only meaning of sexual intercourse—either today or in the past. For both women and men it can also be a source of pleasure, an expression of love, a means to procreate, and so forth.

Alonso and Koreck even suggested that Latina/o culture was so antisex that it did not allow most women to experience sexual pleasure or even to imagine the possibility of same-sex relations between women: "Though women are objects of desire, they are never subjects of their own desire. Sex is something they are polluted by, not something they enjoy. 'Decent' women, it is thought, only engage in sex as a duty to their husbands and in order to have children. Thus, lesbianism is inconceivable."[70]

This research was based in rural northern Mexico, but Alonso and Koreck suggested that their conclusions were applicable to all Mexico.[71] Our observations and experience with the people of this area suggest otherwise. Fortunately, there has been recent work that contradicts their conclusions, work that has some "decent" women enjoying sex as mediated by love or within the culturally sanctioned bounds of marriage, whether civil or common law.[72] Other decent women—at least in the northern Mexican states of Nuevo Leon and Tamaulipas—not only conceive of but discreetly engage in lesbian sex, sometimes even living together in rural towns (see Anzaldúa's list of terms below).

Toward More Complex, Diverse, and Contextually Situated Sexualities

Challenging the dominant discourse, some Latina writers in the mid-1990s—many of them contributing to lesbian theory—increasingly questioned the need to emulate modern white models of sexuality, a questioning and challenging that continues to this day. They began to affirm the possibilities for healthy liberated expressions that draw on and incorporate their own cultural logic and move away from the negative sex model. At the time, most of the newer, more complex analyses were available primarily through alternative presses specifically designed to represent marginalized people such as Third World Press and Aunt Lute Press rather than through mainstream academic journals. This early work converged with later academic and popular work that drew upon global and transnational feminist perspectives to create a more nuanced view of Latina sexuality.[73] The concluding section of this chapter presents some of these nondominant but ever-growing approaches, suggesting that reading and incorporating the insights of alternative analyses will challenge and resist the stereotypical, ethnocentric, and essentialized understandings pervasive in the Latina sexualities literature.

The late writer and scholar Gloria Anzaldúa[74]—a leading theorist of gender, sexuality, and ethnicity—was originally one of the strongest voices challenging the dominant discourse. She fundamentally reformulated those ideas by questioning the naturalness of "lesbian" as both a term and an identity, instead reclaiming both Latina and working-class notions and terms for women-loving-women:

> For me the term lesbian *es problemon*. As a working-class Chicana, mestiza—a composite being, *amalgama de culturas y de lenguas*—a woman who loves women, "lesbian" is a cerebral word, white and middle-class, representing an English-only dominant culture, derived from the Greek word *lesbos*. I think of lesbians as predominantly white and middle-class women and a segment of women of color who acquired the term through osmosis, much the same as Chicanas and Latinas assimilated the word "Hispanic." When a "lesbian" names me the same as her, she subsumes me under her category. I am of her group but not as an equal, not as a whole person—my color erased, my class ignored. *Soy una puta mala*, a phrase

coined by Ariban, a *tejana tortillera*. "Lesbian" doesn't name anything in my homeland. Unlike the word "queer," "lesbian" came late into some of our lives. Call me *de las otras*. Call me *loquita, jotita, marimacha, pajuelona, lambiscona, culera.*[75]

Just as the term "homosexual" as a social category was coined by scientists in the mid-nineteenth century,[76] Anzaldúa's work reminded us that there was nothing natural about assigning social identities to people who chose same-sex partners. She discussed and contextualized cultural differences without assuming that modern white practices were healthier and better: "Yes, we may all love members of the same sex, but we are not the same. Our ethnic communities deal differently with us. I must constantly assert my differentness, must say, This is what I think of loving women. I must stress, the difference is my relationship to my culture; white culture may allow its lesbians to leave—mine doesn't. This is one way I avoid getting sucked into the vortex of homogenization, of getting pulled into the shelter of the queer umbrella."[77]

Rather than positing white sexuality as healthy and liberated, Anzaldúa suggested an affirmative aspect of Latina culture and sexuality, implying that white families and communities may push out or abandon lesbians, while Latinas/os might ostracize them but allow them to stay.[78] By contextualizing social dynamics, she challenged the notion that it is automatically freer and easier to be lesbian in white communities, instead recognizing the high price that can be paid for that freedom.

Another theorist who challenged the dominant discourse early on was historian Yolanda Chávez Leyva. She countered the simplistic assumption that Latina/o cultural silences about sexual practices indicated a greater level of sexual repression and oppression for Latinas/os. Instead, she presented a much more complex analysis. In "Listening to the Silences in Latina/Chicana Lesbian History,"[79] she looked specifically at the silence surrounding sexual practices such as lesbianism. Silence, she suggested, may have different meanings in different cultures and contexts. She examined the contextualized meanings and implications of silence about lesbianism, describing the common practice of family and community members as silently "knowing" and "imagining" that someone is lesbian. She quoted one of her informants' stories about her relationship with her mother: "Basically, you know, she doesn't like my way of life so we don't talk about it. She respects me, she loves me, she spoils me. But it's something we just don't discuss. I think I don't do it out of respect for her, and she doesn't do it out of respect for me."[80]

Chávez Leyva then suggested that "not discussing 'it' became a way to put love first, to reconcile very different expectations, a way not only for the daughter to defer to her mother, but also a way for the mother to show respect for her daughter."[81]

Instead of essentializing silence as always negative and oppressive, Chávez Leyva began to culturally and historically situate its meaning:

> Silence has its own contours, its own texture. We cannot dismiss the silences of earlier generations as simply a reaction to fear. Rather than dismiss it, we must explore it, must attempt to understand it. We must learn to understand the ways it has limited us and the ways it has protected us.
>
> This is not, however, a call to continue the silence, nor to justify it. Naming ourselves, occupying our spaces fully, creating our own language, is essential to our continued survival, particularly in these times of increasingly [sic] violence against us as Latinas and lesbianas. This is a challenge to explore the contradictions of silence within Latina lesbian history, to understand the multiple meanings of silence, to uncover the language of silence.[82]

Rather than assuming that silence is always negative, Chávez Leyva introduced a more complex and contradictory notion of silence, including a "silent tolerance" for lesbian experiences, even as she encouraged the transformative project of naming and speaking of and about lesbians and their experiences.[83]

Rosario Carrillo's more recent ethnography of everyday *rasquache* in a group of Latina friends who are heterosexual immigrants exemplifies a more recent approach that challenges the dominant narrative and provides a context that celebrates an alternative expression of Latina sexuality.[84] Interestingly, *rasquache* was originally understood as a Mexican word that referred to poor or lower-class people, but the 1960s Chicano arts movement appropriated the term and used it to describe an approach that took the most basic, simplest means to create an artistic endeavor that made "the most from the least." The *rasquache* for the group of friends is an aesthetic that is vulgar and tacky and defies rules of behavior while driving their "Latina *filosofía*," including "sexually charged language and embodiments."[85] Carrillo describes the powerful relationship between one of the friends and her daughter, giving the reader a sense of the lived strength, wisdom, and passion passed from woman to woman.

Focusing on one of the friends, Mrs. Zapata, she analyzes the group's conception of sexuality, philosophy, and body-centered way of being:

> With solidarity among the *viejas argüenteras*, Mrs. Zapata's language and embodiments that constitute a *filosofía* is expressed in a vociferant way. She eschews *valores de puritana* and instead blends the political, economical, and social with beauty, raunchiness, spirituality, and a vibrancy for living. While in traditional academic discourse, we might separate philosophy, aesthetics, and spirituality, with *filosofía* these components are articulated, embodied, performed and, therefore, coalesced. . . . Moreover, it evokes the spirit in order to live with courage, integrity, dignity, and carnal pleasure. The spirit is nourished by sex and relishing accomplishments (successful embodiments of the *filosofía*), as well as by savoring a distinct language that gives the *filosofía* dynamism through disorder and what Guerra (1998) identifies as *labia* (eloquence), *sabor* (flavor), *emoción* (emotion), and *gracia* (grace or wit).[86]

Conclusions

The more complex, contextually situated approaches presented here move us beyond ethnocentric and essentialized models that posit "traditional" Latina sexuality as repressed and pathological while white US models are held up as the unmarked, universal ideal. These examples examine ways of expressing sexualities without equating liberation with acculturation, but they do not shrink from documenting sexual and gender inequality. These new frameworks recognize that human sexuality does not have to take one form or another for it to be healthy or "undistorted." As we stated previously, humans have no "undistorted" sexuality. Although dominant ideologies suggest that Latina sexuality is repressed, many people would concede, as Ana Castillo has, that "sexuality surfaces everywhere in our culture" in the form of sensual dancing, religious passion, and erotic male and female costumes.[87] We agree that sexuality surfaces everywhere in Latina/o culture, but we do not see these expressions as only negative and distorted; rather, they are alternate and equally valid ways of experiencing sexuality that we hope will continue to be seen and celebrated on their own terms.

Notes

1. Chandra Talpade Mohanty, *Feminism without Borders: Decolonizing Theory, Practicing Solidarity* (Durham: Duke University Press, 2003), 19–20.

2. Cherríe Moraga and Gloria Anzaldúa, *This Bridge Called My Back* (New York: Kitchen Table Press, 1981).

3. Gloria T. Hull, Patricia Bell Scott, and Barbara Smith, *All the Women Are White, All the Blacks Are Men, But Some of Us Are Brave* (Old Westbury, NY: Feminist Press, 1982).

4. For example, see Marysol Asencio, ed., *Latina/o Sexualities: Probing Powers, Passions, Practices and Policies* (New Brunswick, NJ: Rutgers University Press, 2010); Lila Abu-Lughod, "Do Muslim Women Really Need Saving? Anthropological Reflections on Cultural Relativism and Its Others," *American Anthropologist* 104, no. 3 (2002): 783–790; Hector Torres, "The Ethnographic Component in Chicano/a Literary Discourse," *Aztlán* 25, no. 1 (2000): 151–166; Gloria Gonzalez-Lopez, *Erotic Journeys: Mexican Immigrants and Their Sex Lives* (Berkeley: University of California Press, 2005); Gloria Anzaldúa and Ana Louise Keating, *This Bridge We Call Home: Radical Visions for Transformations* (New York: Routledge, 2002); Ana María Juárez and Stella Beatríz Kerl, "What Is the Right (White) Way to Be Sexual? Reconceptualizing Latina Sexuality," *Aztlán* 27, no. 2 (2003): 7–37.

5. Gonzalez-Lopez, *Erotic Journeys*, 4–5.

6. Jean Pfaelzer, Doris Friedensohn, and Deborah Rosenfelt, "Intersections: Global Feminisms, American Studies," *American Studies International* 38, no. 3 (2000): 8.

7. Ann Ferguson, "Resisting the Veil of Privilege: Building Bridge Identities as an Ethico-Politics of Global Feminisms," *Hypatia* 13, no. 3 (1998): 95.

8. We will use the term "Latina/o" to refer to persons of Mexican and other Latin American descent living in the United States, unless we are citing work by an author who uses "Hispanic" or some other term. "Chicana/o" and "Mexican American" refer specifically to persons of Mexican descent living in the United States. "Mexican," "Mexicana/o," other national identifiers, and/or "Latin American" will refer to cultures and/or persons in specific countries or in countries significantly influenced or colonized by Spaniards throughout the Americas, regardless of where they now live. "White," "Anglo," "Euro-American," or "North American" will refer to persons of northern European descent living in the United States who have been racialized as "white."

9. Paredes may be the first to have used the term "talking back," but the term has also been used by many others in anthropology. Américo Paredes, "On Ethnographic Work among Minority Groups: A Folklorist's Perspective," in *Folklore and Culture on the Texas-Mexican Border*, ed. R. Bauman (Austin: University of Texas, Center for Mexican American Studies, 1993), 75. Also see Karen Mary Davalos, "Chicana/o Studies and Anthropology: The Dialogue

That Never Was," *Aztlán* 23, no. 2 (1998): 13–45; Renato I. Rosaldo, *Culture and Truth: The Remaking of Social Analysis* (Boston: Beacon, 1989); bell hooks, *Talking Back: Thinking Feminist, Thinking Black* (Boston: South End Press, 1989).
    10. For example, Chicana/o scholars challenged the notion that Chicana/o culture is basically negative—Octavio Romano-V., "The Anthropology and Sociology of the Mexican-Americans: The Distortion of Mexican-American History," *El Grito* 2, no. 1 (1968): 13–26; Nick Vaca, "The Mexican-American in the Social Sciences, Part I: 1912–1935." *El Grito* 3, no. 3 (1970): 3–24; Nick Vaca, "The Mexican-American in the Social Sciences, Part II: 1936–1970," *El Grito* 4, no. 1 (1970): 17–51—and that Chicana/o families are entirely male dominated—Maxine Baca Zinn, "Chicano Family Research: Conceptual Distortions and Alternative Directions," *Journal of Ethnic Studies* 7, no. 3 (1979): 57–71; Patricia Zavella, *Women's Work and Chicano Families: Cannery Workers of the Santa Clara Valley* (Ithaca, NY: Cornell University Press, 1987). Scholars of Latina/o and Latin American cultures similarly challenged the notion that gender is characterized by machismo (oversexed violent domineering men) and *marianismo* (undersexed suffering submissive women). See, e.g., Adelaida R. Del Castillo, "Gender and Its Discontinuities in Male/Female Domestic Relations: Mexicans in Cross-Cultural Context," in *Chicanas/Chicanos at the Crossroads: Social, Economic, and Political Change*, ed. D. R. Maciel and I. D. Ortiz (Tucson: University of Arizona Press, 1996), 207–230; Tracy Ehlers, "Debunking Marianismo: Economic Vulnerability and Survival Strategies among Guatemalan Wives," *Ethnology* 30, no. 1 (1991): 1–16; Elizabeth Dore, *Gender Politics in Latin America: Debates in Theory and Practice* (New York: Monthly Review Press, 1997); Judith E. Marti, "Breadwinners and Decision-Makers: Nineteenth-Century Mexican Women Vendors," in *The Other Fifty Percent: Multicultural Perspectives on Gender Relations*, ed. M. Womack and J. E. Marti (Prospect Heights, IL: Waveland Press, 1993), 218–224; Matthew Gutmann, *The Meanings of Macho: Being a Man in Mexico City* (Berkeley: University of California Press, 1996); Carla Trujillo, ed. *Living Chicana Theory* (Berkeley: Third Woman Press), 1998; Claudia Fonseca, "Philanderers, Cuckolds, and Wily Women: A Reexamination of Gender Relations in a Brazilian Working-Class Neighborhood," *Men and Masculinities* 3, no. 3 (2001): 261–277. Revisionist histories include Deena González, *Refusing the Favor: The Spanish-Mexican Women of Santa Fe, 1820–1880* (New York: Oxford University Press, 1999); Antonia Castañeda, "The Political Economy of Nineteenth Century Stereotypes of Californianas," in *Between Borders: Essays on Mexicana/Chicana History*, ed. A. R. Del Castillo (Encino, CA: Floricanto Press, 1990), 213–236; Emma Pérez, *The Decolonial Imaginary: Writing Chicanas into History* (Bloomington: Indiana University Press, 1999); Vicki L. Ruiz, *From Out of the Shadows: Mexican Women in Twentieth-Century America* (New York: Oxford University Press, 1998); Ramón Gutiérrez, *When Jesus Came the Corn Mothers Went Away: Marriage, Sexuality and Power in New Mexico, 1550–1846* (Stanford, CA: Stanford University Press, 1991). Key studies and reviews of the literature that document and assess some of

these issues in Chicana/o studies include José Limón, "Stereotyping and Chicano Resistance: An Historical Dimension," *Aztlán* 4, no. 2 (1973): 257–270; Renato I. Rosaldo, "Chicano Studies, 1970–1984," *Annual Review of Anthropology* 14 (1985): 405–427; and Davalos, "Chicana Studies and Anthropology," 1998.

11. Vincent Pérez, "Heroes and Orphans of the Hacienda: Narratives of a Mexican American Family," *Aztlán* 24, no. 1 (1999): 46.

12. See Davalos, "Chicana Studies and Anthropology" and Asencio, *Latina/o Sexualities*.

13. Virginia Domínguez, "Differentiating Women/Bodies of Knowledge," *American Anthropologist* 96, no. 1 (1994): 130.

14. Rosa Maria Gil and Carmen Inoa Vazquez, *The Maria Paradox: How Latinas Can Merge Old World Traditions with New World Self-Esteem* (New York: Berkley Publishing Group, 1996); Cynthia Gómez and Barbara Van Oss Marín, "Gender, Culture, and Power: Barriers to HIV-Prevention Strategies for Women," *Journal of Sex Research* 33, no. 4 (1996): 355–362; V. Nelly Salgado de Snyder, Andrea Acevedo, Maria de Jesus Diaz-Pérez, and Alicia Saldivar-Garduño, "Understanding the Sexuality of Mexican-Born Women and Their Risk for HIV/AIDS," *Psychology of Women Quarterly* 24 (2000):100–108; R. A. Reimer, A. E. Houlihan, M. Gerrard, M. M. Deer, and A. J. Lund, "Ethnic Differences in Predictors of HPV Vaccination: Comparisons of Predictors for Latina and Non-Latina White Women," *Journal of Sex Research* 50, no. 8 (2013): 748–756; Selma Caal, Lina Guzman, Amanda Berger, Manica F. Ramos, and Elizabeth Golub, " 'Because You're on Birth Control, It Automatically Makes You Promiscuous or Something': Latina Women's Perceptions of Parental Approval to Use Reproductive Health Care," *Journal of Adolescent Health* 53, no. 5 (2013): 617–622.

15. Bettina R. Flores, *Chiquita's Cocoon* (New York: Villard Books, 1994), 60.

16. See Moraga and Anzaldúa, *This Bridge*; Trujillo, *Living Chicana Theory*.

17. See Gonzalez-Lopez, *Erotic Journeys*; Jennifer Hirsch, *A Courtship after Marriage: Sexuality and Love in Mexican Transnational Families* (Berkeley: University of California Press, 2003) and Jennifer S. Hirsch, Jennifer Higgins, Margaret E. Bentley, and Constance A. Nathanson, "The Social Constructions of Sexuality: Companionate Marriage and STD/HIV Risk in a Mexican Migrant Community," in *Modern Loves: The Anthropology of Romantic Courtship and Companionate Marriage*, ed. Jennifer S. Hirsch and Holly Wardlow (Ann Arbor: University of Michigan Press, 2006), 95–117.

18. Yvonne Yarbro-Bejarano, "Sexuality and Chicana/o Studies: Toward a Theoretical Paradigm for the Twenty-First Century," *Cultural Studies* 13, no. 2 (1999), 335–345.

19. Deborah L. Tolman, "Adolescent Girls, Women and Sexuality: Discerning Dilemmas of Desire," *Women and Therapy* 11 (1991): 55–69; Ana Garner, Helen M. Sterk, and Shawn Adams, "Narrative Analysis of Sexual Etiquette in Teenage Magazines," *Journal of Communication* 48 (1998): 59–60; T. Hundhammer and T. Mussweiler, "How Sex Puts You in Gendered Shoes:

Sexuality-Priming Leads to Gender-Based Self-Perception and Behavior," *Journal of Personality and Social Psychology* 103, no. 1 (2012): 176–93.

20. Oliva M. Espín, *Women Crossing Boundaries: A Psychology of Immigration and Transformations of Sexuality* (New York: Routledge, 1999), 129.

21. Ibid., 6.

22. Nan Alamilla Boyd, "Book Review Essay," *Signs* 25, no. 1 (1999): 258; also see Gonzalez-Lopez, *Erotic Journeys*, 4–5; Patricia Zavella, *I'm Neither Here nor There: Mexicans' Quotidian Struggles with Migration and Poverty* (Durham, NC: Duke University Press, 2011); Patricia Zavella, " 'Talkin' Sex: Chicanas and Mexicanas Theorize about Silences and Sexual Pleasures," in *Chicana Feminisms*, ed. Gabriela F. Arredondo, Aída Hurtado, Norma Klahn, Olga Najera-Ramirez, and Patricia Zavella (Durham, NC: Duke University Press, 2003), 229–253; Patricia Zavella, " 'Playing With Fire': The Gendered Construction of Chicana/ Mexicana Sexuality," in *The Gender/Sexuality Reader: Culture, History, Political Economy*, ed. R. Lancaster and M. di Leonardo (New York: Routledge, 1997), 392–408; and Hirsch, *Courtship after Marriage*.

23. Espín, *Women Crossing Boundaries*, 158.

24. E.g., Aída Hurtado, "Understanding Multiple Group Identities: Inserting Women into Cultural Transformations," *Journal of Social Issues* 53, no. 2 (1997): 299–328; Renato I. Rosaldo, "Assimilation Revisited" in *In Times of Challenge: Chicanos and Chicanas in American Society*, ed. J. García, J. Curry Rodriguez, and C. Lomas (Houston, TX: University of Houston, Mexican American Studies Program, 1988), 43–50.

25. Espín, *Women Crossing Boundaries*, 129,

26. Boyd, "Book Review Essay," 258–259.

27. Marcela Raffaelli, Zamboanga, Byron, L. Carlo, Gustavo, "Acculturation Status and Sexuality among Female Cuban American College Students," *Journal Of American College Health* 54, no. 1 (2005): 7–13.

28. Ibid., 11.

29. Ibid., 44–46.

30. Salgado de Snyder et al., "Understanding the Sexuality."

31. Ibid., 106, emphasis added.

32. Ibid.

33. Ibid.

34. Amado Padilla and Traci Baird, "Mexican-American Adolescent Sexuality and Sexual Knowledge: An Exploratory Study," *Hispanic Journal of Behavioral Sciences* 13, no. 1 (1991): 95–104.

35. Baird Traci, "Mexican Adolescent Sexuality: Attitudes, Knowledge, and Sources of Information," *Hispanic Journal of Behavioral Sciences* 15, no. 3 (1993): 402–417.

36. Padilla and Baird, "Mexican-American Adolescent Sexuality." The study did not include the question about a sexual relationship being one of the best things in life. Sources for Table 1 are Padilla and Baird, "Mexican-American Adolescent Sexuality," for Mexican Americans and Baird, "Mexican Adolescent Sexuality" for Mexicans.

37. Paula Moya, "Postmodernism, 'Realism,' and the Politics of Identity: Cherríe Moraga and Chicana Feminism," in *Feminist Genealogies, Colonial Legacies, Democratic Futures,* ed. M. J. Alexander and C. T. Mohanty (New York: Routledge, 1997), 12.

38. See Moya ("Politics of Identity") for a good critique of the politics of essentialist and antiessentialist theory for Chicanas. More generally, Torres ("Ethnographic Component") examines the tension between ethnography, ethnocentrism, and essentialism for Chicanas/os, and Rival, Slater, and Miller even begin to question the universality of a generalized, cross-cultural domain of sexuality: Laura Rival, Don Slater, and Daniel Miller, "Sex and Sociality: Comparative Ethnographies of Sexual Objectification," *Theory, Culture and Society* 15, no. 3–4 (1998): 295–321.

39. Sandra Cisneros, "Goddess," in *Goddess of the Americas, La Diosa de las Américas: Writings on the Virgin of Guadalupe,* ed. A. Castillo (New York: Riverhead Books, 1996), 46.

40. Ibid., 47.

41. Kathleen Ford and Anne Norris, "Methodological Considerations for Survey Research on Sexual Behavior: Urban African American and Hispanic Youth," *Journal of Sex Research* 28 (1991): 539–556; F. Allan Hubbell, Leo Chávez, Shiraz I. Mishra, and R. Burciaga Valdez, "Beliefs about Sexual Behavior and Other Predictors of Papanicolaou Smear Screening among Latinas and Anglo Women," *Archives of Internal Medicine* 156 (1996): 2353–2358.

42. Michel Foucault, *The History of Sexuality,* trans. Robert Hurley, vol. 1 (New York: Vintage Books, 1978); Siobhan Somerville, "Scientific Racism and the Invention of the Homosexual Body," in *The Gender/Sexuality Reader: Culture, History, Political Economy,* ed. R. Lancaster and M. di Leonardo (New York: Routledge, 1997), 37–52; Thomas Laqueur, "Orgasm, Generation, and the Politics of Reproductive Biology," in *The Making of the Modern Body: Sexuality and Society in the Nineteenth Century,* ed. C. Gallagher and T. Laqueur (Berkeley: University of California Press, 1987), 1–41; Dirk Schultheiss and Sidney Glina, "Highlights from the History of Sexual Medicine," *Journal of Sexual Medicine* 7, no. 6 (2010): 2031–2043.

43. Castañeda, "Political Economy."

44. José Limón, "Selena: Sexuality, Performance, and the Problematic of Hegemony," in *Reflexiones: New Directions in Mexican American Studies,* ed. N. Foley (Austin: University of Texas, Center for Mexican American Studies, 1997), 5.

45. Jillian Hernandez, "'Miss, You Look Like a Bratz Doll': On Chonga Girls and Sexual-Aesthetic Excess," *NWSA Journal* 21, no. 3 (2009): 64.

46. Ana Castillo, "La Macha: Toward a Beautiful Whole Self," in *Chicana Lesbians: The Girls Our Mothers Warned Us About,* ed. C. Trujillo (Berkeley: Third Woman Press, 1991).

47. Ibid., 40.

48. Ibid., 44–45.

49. Ibid.

50. Carole S. Vance, "Pleasure and Danger: Toward a Politics of Sexuality," in *Pleasure and Danger: Exploring Female Sexuality*, ed. Vance (Boston: Routledge & Kegan Paul, 1984), 1–27.

51. Limón, "Selena," 13–17.

52. Ibid., 12.

53. Ibid., 13–14.

54. bell hooks, *Black Looks: Race and Representation* (Boston: South End Press, 1992); Douglas Kellner, "Madonna, Fashion, and Identity" in *Women in Culture: A Women's Studies Anthology*, ed. L. J. Peach (Malden, MA: Blackwell, 1998), 187–201; Susan Bordo, "'Material Girl': The Effacements of Postmodern Culture," in *Unbearable Weight: Feminism, Western Culture and the Body*, ed. S. Bordo (Berkeley: University of California Press, 1993), 245–276; Yarbro-Bejarano, "Sexuality and Chicana/o Studies"; Trujillo, "Living Chicana Theory."

55. Limón, "Selena," 14–15.

56. E.g., see Yarbro-Bejarano, "Sexuality and Chicana/o Studies"; Vance, "Pleasure and Danger"; Roger Lancaster and Micaela di Leonardo, eds. *The Gender/Sexuality Reader: Culture, History, Political Economy* (New York: Routledge, 1997); Rose Weitz, ed., *The Politics of Women's Bodies: Sexuality, Appearance and Behavior* (New York: Oxford University Press, 1998); Donna C. Stanton, ed., *Discourses of Sexuality: From Aristotle to AIDS* (Ann Arbor: University of Michigan Press, 1992); Louise Lamphere, Helena Ragoné, and Patricia Zavella, eds., *Situated Lives: Gender and Culture in Everyday Life* (New York: Routledge, 1997); Foucault, "History of Sexuality"; and Laura Rival, Don Slater, and Daniel Miller, "Sex and Sociality: Comparative Ethnographies of Sexual Objectification," *Theory, Culture and Society* 15, no. 3–4 (1998): 295–321.

57. Michael Grant and Richard Meech, *Strange Relations*. Vol. 2: *Millennium: Tribal Wisdom and the Modern World* (Alexandria, VA: PBS Video, 1992).

58. Bronislaw Malinowski, *The Sexual Life of Savages in North Western Melanesia* (Boston: Routledge & Kegan Paul, 1929).

59. Jisha Menon, "Queer Selfhoods in the Shadow of Neoliberal Urbanism," *Journal of Historical Sociology* 26, no. 1 (2013): 100–119; Wai Ching Angela Wong, "The Politics of Sexual Morality and Evangelical Activism in Hong Kong," *Inter-Asia Cultural Studies* 14, no. 3 (2013): 340–360; Arpita Das, "Sexuality Education in India: Examining the Rhetoric, Rethinking the Future," *Sex Education* 14, no. 2 (2014): 210–224; Clare Hemmings, "Sexuality, Subjectivity . . . and Political Economy?" *Subjectivity: International Journal of Critical Psychology* 5, no. 2 (2012): 121–139.

60. E.g., see Sut Jhally, *Dreamworlds 2: Desire/Sex/Power in Music Video* (Northampton, MA: Media Education Foundation, 1995); Bordo, "Material Girl"; hooks, *Black Looks*; Kellner, "Madonna, Fashion, and Identity"; Kristin Lieb, *Gender, Branding, and the Modern Music Industry: The Social Construction of Female Popular Music Stars* (New York: Routledge, 2013); and Shirley Geok-lin

Lim, "The Center Can(not) Hold: American Studies and Global Feminism," *American Studies International* 38, no. 3 (2000): 25–35.

    61. Lim, "Center Can(not) Hold," 29.

    62. Naomi Wolf, *The Beauty Myth: How Images of Beauty Are Used Against Women* (New York: W. Morrow, 1991); Jean Kilbourne, "Beauty and the Beast of Advertising," in *Women in Culture: A Women's Studies Anthology*, ed. L. J. Peach (Malden, MA: Blackwell, 1998), 127–131; Kathryn Pauly Morgan, "Women and the Knife: Cosmetic Surgery and the Colonization of Women's Bodies," in *The Politics of Women's Bodies—Sexuality, Appearance and Behavior*, ed. R. Weitz (New York: Oxford University Press, 1998), 147–166; Elayne A. Saltzberg and Joan C. Chrisler, "Beauty Is the Beast: Psychological Effects of the Pursuit of the Perfect Female Body" in *Reconstructing Gender: A Multicultural Anthology*, ed. E. Disch (Mountain View, CA: Mayfield, 1997), 134–145; Lim, "Center Can(not) Hold."

    63. Lisa C Dietrich, *Chicana Adolescents: Bitches, 'Ho's, and Schoolgirls* (Westport, CT: Praeger, 1998), 61.

    64. Limón, "Selena," 23.

    65. Ana Alonso and Maria Teresa Koreck, "Silences: 'Hispanics,' AIDS, and Sexual Practices," *Differences* 1, no. 1 (1989): 101–124.

    66. Ana María Alonso, *Thread of Blood: Colonialism, Revolution, and Gender on Mexico's Northern Frontier* (Tucson: University of Arizona Press, 1995).

    67. Alonso and Koreck, "Silences," 109.

    68. Alonso, *Thread of Blood*, 85–86.

    69. Ibid., 89.

    70. Alonso and Koreck, "Silences," 109–111, 121, n. 22.

    71. Ibid., 114.

    72. Gonzalez-Lopez, *Erotic Journeys*; Hirsch, *Courtship after Marriage*.

    73. For example, see Lorena Garcia, *Respect Yourself, Protect Yourself: Latina Girls and Sexual Identity* (New York: NYU Press, 2012); Lorena Garcia and Lourdes Torres, "Introduction: New Directions in Latina Sexualities Studies," *NWSA Journal* 21, no. 3 (2009): vii–xvi; Latina Feminist Group, *Telling to Live: Latina Feminist Testimonios* (Durham, NC: Duke University Press, 2001); Pamela I. Erickson, "The Role of Romantic Love in Sexual Initiation and the Transition to Parenthood among Immigrant and U.S.-Born Latino Youth in East Los Angeles" in *Modern Loves: The Anthropology of Romantic Courtship and Companionate Marriage*, ed. Jennifer S. Hirsch and Holly Wardlow (Ann Arbor: University of Michigan Press, 2006), 118–134.

    74. Gloria Anzaldúa, "To(o) Queer the Writer—Loca, escritora y chicana." In *Living Chicana Theory*, ed. Carla Trujillo, 263–76 (Berkeley, CA: Third Woman Press, 1998).

    75. Ibid., 263.

    76. Somerville, "Scientific Racism," 37.

    77. Anzaldúa, "To(o) Queer the Writer," 264.

    78. Ibid., 263–264

79. Yolanda Chávez Leyva, "Listening to the Silences in Latina/Chicana Lesbian History," in *Living Chicana Theory*, ed. C. Trujillo (Berkeley, CA: Third Woman Press, 1998), 429–434.

80. Ibid., 432

81. Ibid.

82. Ibid.

83. Ibid.

84. Rosario Carrillo, "Expressing Latina Sexuality with Vieja Argüentera Embodiments and Rasquache Language: How Women's Culture Enables Living Filosofía," *NWSA Journal* 21, no. 3 (2009): 122–142.

85. Ibid., 122.

86. Ibid., 135–136.

87. Castillo, "La Macha," 44–45.

The Power of Sympathy

The Politics of Subjectifying Women

Purvi Shah

On October 4, 2001, nearly a month after the tragic attacks of September 11,[1] then US president George W. Bush spoke of "stories of Christian and Jewish women alike helping women of cover, Arab American women, go shop because they're afraid to leave their home."[2] Bush's statement sought to highlight the humanity of kindhearted Americans and serve as proof of the nation's tolerance and acceptance of difference even in a time of trauma, anger, and sorrow. Through the lens of history, however, we can see that such an outlook of expressed respect for diversity served as a cover for discriminatory policies that emerged in the wake of 9/11, including but not limited to programs such as NSEERS and special registration.[3] While many advocates have analyzed the gap between the rhetoric and reality of valuing difference in the post-9/11 environment, more attention needs to be marshaled to the positioning of women in this representation.

By giving Arab American women the appellation "women of cover," a New World reality marked by stereotypes of old, Bush's statement codifies—and legitimizes—a religiously inflected version of women's subjectivity, in effect collapsing distinctions of gender, religion, religiosity, cultural practice, and national positioning. This chapter seeks to tease apart these categories in a period of national trauma and investigate how a politics of sympathy for "women of cover" purports to offer subjectivity but relies upon an objectification of women by placing them into fixed categories of victimhood while shifting scrutiny away from the legal

systems, institutional structures, and patriarchal frameworks responsible
for violence against women, racism, and neocolonialism. Thus, a politics
of sympathy empowers stereotypes while disempowering analyses of root
causes of inequity and violence—serving in the end to prevent long-term
sustainable change, harmony, and equity.

Teasing out the implications further, what does it mean to grant
subjectivity to women (especially minority women) through the language of protection? At first glance, Bush's comment may seem to constitute evidence for the US melting pot theory—one nation that coexists
through many communities blending together. Aside from the humane-
ness Bush attempted to represent, what seeps through is the position of
dependence and helplessness imposed on Arab American and Muslim
women as a group.[4] The visible and concrete causes of any such existing fear, including scores of bias attacks faced by Muslims and South
Asians (particularly Sikh Americans) post-9/11, are erased in this image
of domestic harmony. The real issue of violence motivated by differing
ethnic or religious backgrounds—or prejudicial stereotypes—is covered
over by a veneer of peaceful coexistence and cross-cultural compassion.

For centuries, political leaders, scholars, and citizens have made the
argument that imperial or military action is in part necessitated by an
imperative to civilize and protect women in "Third World" nations, an
imperative these countries are purportedly unable to fulfill themselves.
This attitude of cultural gender superiority has legitimized violent interventions, and it has reinforced binaries (such as the idea of the Western
liberated woman and the submissive Indian and/or Muslim and/or Third
World woman) that fail to register the complexity of the world around
us, including the histories of political and social activism by women from
the non-Western world. Indeed, Bush demonstrates that this attitude
toward the powerlessness of non-Western women frames not only perceptions of women around the world but also understandings of minority
women within the United States.

This chapter elaborates on two parallel concepts: the protection
of women in the context of a politics of sympathy and its relation to
the formation of women's subjectivity across two contemporary global
contexts, the US war in Afghanistan and the US movement against
domestic violence in communities of color. This investigation illuminates how sympathy—and the use of sympathy to call for change—places
undue emphasis on cultural accounts of violence against women: in the
project of liberating women, a sympathetic politics reinforces structural
misconceptions and hierarchies since a politics of sympathy relies upon

images of women as victims. Through varied and concrete examples, this chapter shows how women are granted sympathy for their struggles but their cultures and communities are simultaneously stigmatized for being the sources of women's pain. In so doing, larger systems and policies—and Western communities rife with gender inequity—are let off the hook.

My goal in this project is not to equate different geopolitical spaces and histories but to offer a comparative exploration of contexts of violence and intervention faced by women globally—and to show how women of color are working to center our own subjectivity without stigmatizing our own communities. While this strategy comes with its own pitfalls, I seek to avoid the tendency to critically investigate only what happens "over there" as opposed to "here" in the hope that political and gender relations within the United States itself can become both the implicit subject point of analysis and the object of global gender critique. In so doing, I hope both to illuminate the neocolonial underbelly of a politics of sympathy while demonstrating how women of color are challenging patriarchy and violence on our own terms.

Pretexts

The history of the British Empire provides striking examples of the use of an ideology of protecting women to further nation-building and imperial aims. As many have recorded, the practices of sati, a Hindu widow's self-immolation on her husband's funeral pyre, and purdah, the curtaining of women separate from men (practiced among Muslims and Hindus to varying degrees), particularly bolstered British justifications of the imperial mission as an attempt to further the civilization of the subcontinent—with the consequent emancipation of women from barbaric practices. Describing how sati sparked British cries of injustice, Margery Sabin notes, "While other Hindu practices, like child marriage and untouchability, were as shocking to the British as suttee, widow burning had even more sensational and sentimental power than other forms of human sacrifice, as James Mill remarks: 'none however has more excited the scornful attention of the Europeans, than the burning of the wives on the funeral piles of their husbands. To this cruel sacrifice the highest virtues are ascribed.'"[5]

The language of scorn (toward the culture and men in particular) and virtue (for the suffering women) points to a self-ordained British moral superiority: these sentiments framed the project of imperialism not as the subjugation of other peoples but as a civilizing process that included the liberation of women. The descriptive terms that Sabin uses—"sensational and sentimental power"—are particularly crucial because it is these emotions of sympathy and sentimental affiliation that helped to facilitate imperial politics. After all, who would not seek to control or intervene in a community that forces women to make a "cruel sacrifice"? I do not care to argue that sati is a practice to be lauded; rather, I seek to highlight the use of the concept of women's protection as a justification for subordinating the Indian subcontinent—a population including the very women in need of protection. As Sabin demonstrates, British thinkers and leaders relied on the rhetoric of civilization, morality, and advancement of women as a fundamental method of mobilizing support for the colonizing project—without mention of the barbarities of colonialism.

Fascinating to untangle here is the way this attitude of protection was espoused not only by British male leaders but also by British feminists and suffragists. The British government did use the logic of protection to enforce colonization, but sympathetic politics enabled British women to participate in imperial activity with the altruistic goal of liberating their brown sisters. By the late 1800s, as Deirdre David elucidates, "there were nearly two hundred Western women working as medical missionaries in the zenanas, who had arrived in India ready to deliver native women from ignorance and oppression."[6] The Western missionaries, who worked in these enclosures specifically for women, held the belief that they would bring liberty to Indian women. They simultaneously helped to provide one layer of infrastructure to empire. Furthermore, as David elaborates, India afforded a space—one that could not be found at home—for white women to practice medicine and build their own professional skills. Through an ideology of sympathy intended to protect and aid Indian women, Western women were able to satisfy their own unfulfilled yearnings for substantial employment and professional practice. A world away, British women could overcome the gender barriers present in their own homelands.

Pointing out the atrocities faced by nineteenth-century Indian women gave white women a platform from which to speak about women's advancement in Britain and the United States. For some white American women writers, the plight of Oriental women provided the subject matter for their literary productions; but in the end, how much did the Oriental subject matter? Lydia Huntley Sigourney, a prolific nineteenth-century American writer, produced poems that routinely dealt with women's despair via themes such as motherhood, death, and religion. "The Suttee," from Sigourney's 1827 *Poems* and reprinted in Paula Bernat Bennett's *Nineteenth-Century American Women Poets*, focused attention on an Indian mother about to be subjected to the theft of her own life.[7] In vivid language, Sigourney stages the scene of a young woman at the brink of her death, rendering in detail the helpless woman and unsympathetic crowd around her.

Sigourney starts "The Suttee" in the narrative mode: "She sat upon the pile by her dead lord."[8] She then moves from the local descriptive to an abstracted universal in the second stanza: "So tremulous, as is a mother's soul/Unto her wailing babe."[9] Sigourney points to the power hierarchies leading the Indian woman to death: the crowd's coercion of her obedience to her husband, the "dead lord." This patriarchal relationship is juxtaposed with the (implicitly cross-cultural/universal) relationship between mother and son—a relationship sati violates. Through the biological act of reproduction, the category of motherhood is deployed here to allow affiliation among diverse women—including Western and Indian women. Given its universal framing, in nineteenth-century American society, motherhood served as a common category to build a platform for a spectrum of women's advancement goals. Sigourney's narrative revolves around the forcible separation of the mother from her child, who is left in "hopeless orphanage."[10] The Indian woman is dramatized as breastfeeding her son one final time before he is wrenched away from her. Thus, the Hindu practice of sati is depicted hauntingly as a violation of the universal bonds of motherhood.

Yet Sigourney does not simply paint this scene for the reader to observe: like all good social reformers, she invokes the reader's participation. The poem's rhetorical genius rests upon a shift from the third person to the first person plural. Casting the scene in Christian terms, she elaborates, "as that Spirit malign/Who twined his serpent length mid Eden's bowers/Frown'd on our parents' bliss."[11] The "our" draws the reader into the poem, making him/her/everyone part of the scene being depicted. Through this shift of pronouns, the reader of this poem is both horrified observer *and* unwilling bystander participant in the events. While reassuring readers of their Christian allegiances and heritage, the use of "our" forces an immediate affiliation and investment in the described actions of Hindus, despite religious differences. Indeed, the

Christian vantage point sets into motion the judgment of sati as evidence of Hindu barbarity. The poem ends with "that burning mother's scream," a scream ignored by the crowd around this woman, a scream that the reader is compelled not to ignore.[12]

As a poem, "The Suttee" fits into a genre of sentimental writings stemming from noble impulses—the amelioration of social conditions, especially inequities facing women and children. While Sigourney's poem revolves around the Indian woman as subject, it ends up converting her into an ideal object requiring Christian social uplift. As Sabin remarks, "In the language of feminist analysis, Indian women did not acquire 'complex subject status' in the suttee discourse."[13] Indeed, sentimental works such as "The Suttee" serve to give subjectivity not to the characters portrayed in the works but to a white American and British female readership: these writings helped to bond women readers as a group of social reformers who desired women's advancement.

The struggles of women in other nations became a rallying cry and a symbol for the injustices faced by women but did so by turning foreign women into suffering souls who required saving or protection by those outside their own culture. From this perspective, Indian women, as well as other nonwhite women, were confined to a subject position of downtrodden victim. While aligning mothers across cultures, especially those who see sati as an intolerable heathen practice, such a depiction necessarily places the Indian mother in opposition to the community around her—reasserting gaps between East and West as well as underscoring the centrality of the image of a liberated woman as Western.

Such texts demonstrate that popular and resonant depictions of women from the subcontinent relied upon a Western frame of reference. In her examination of Fanny Fern's writings, Lauren Berlant argues that distinctions of class, ethnicity, and race were erased under the sign of "woman" in sentimental discourse as a way to create the category of woman, since women needed to see and label bonds of shared oppression to fight for reform. She observes, "Sentimental culture also established a broad audience of women, aiming to stake out a safe feminine space, a textual habitus in which a set of emotional, intellectual, and economic styles, knowledges, and practices might be formulated in common and expressed with pleasure."[14]

The sentimental "suttee" facilitated a way in which white women could collectively deplore the state of womanhood and evoke the need to take action, especially in far-flung barbaric lands. This is not to say that these sentiments were insincere: as Zakia Pathak and Rajeswari Sunder Rajan explain, "The will to power contaminates even the most sincere claims of protection."[15]

While the sentimental representation of sati justly pointed to atrocities faced by women, it did not simultaneously call upon women to resist colonizing projects or to assert the moral bankruptcy of colonial subjugation. As part of the larger goal of achieving their own freedoms, British and US women could safely mobilize around a foreign atrocity. Such a strategy kept women from emphasizing their own conditions of oppression or resisting British colonial subjugation of their Third World sisters. In the end, attitudes of cultural superiority gained legitimate standing under the banner of women's rights.

The subject position offered in the sentimental "suttee" splintered woman's relation to national or religious or other communities. In these writings, women were simply excluded from the community: in order to maintain a recognizable subjectivity, the Indian Hindu woman would have to be affiliated with mothers and white reformers. Such a position offers nonwhite women mixed victory: gender reform at the cost of other community constructions. This is a troubling self-division, one that women rooted in their ethnic communities still seek to challenge, even through the twentieth and twenty-first centuries. As King-Kok Cheung points out, "Women of color should not have to undergo a self-division resulting from having to choose between female and ethnic identities."[16]

The example of nineteenth-century texts provides texture to contemporary conversations about the need to protect non-Western or minority women: This prehistory shows the schisms that can result from gender reform that is not aware of attitudes of national, cultural, or religious superiority. Texts of colonial history demonstrate that the suffering of nonwhite women has been historically seen as a valid arena of colonial intervention by a community external to the women being represented. Claims to protect Third World women have previously served as pretexts for imperialism as well as material for white women's social advancement and writing. While times have inevitably changed, these literary and moral pretexts hold a marked and disturbing resonance for more contemporary articulations of the need to protect and save both Afghan women and Muslim and immigrant survivors of domestic violence in the United States. The remainder of this chapter illuminates these resonances and the ways in which women of color are working to center their own voices and subjectivity.

The Plight of Afghan Women

> Afghan women know, through hard experience, what the rest of the
> world is discovering: The brutal oppression of women is a central
> goal of the terrorists. . . . Civilized people throughout the world are
> speaking out in horror—not only because our hearts break for the
> women and children in Afghanistan, but also because in Afghani-
> stan we see the world the terrorists would like to impose on the
> rest of us.
>
> —Laura Bush[17]

After the tragic events of September 11, 2001, plenty of talk arose of the
plight of the Afghan woman. Feminists had been asserting for decades
that Afghan women were dealing with fundamental violations of human
rights daily. Yet, a will to intervene only came as an effort linked to the
US War on Terror. As the former first lady's comments above demonstrate, Afghan women's oppression suddenly became an active agenda
within US foreign policy. Mark how the rhetoric here eerily echoes
nineteenth-century justifications of imperial violence in India—the striking sense of barbarity and threat to (Western) civilizations. Indeed, Laura
Bush frames the world in binaries—civilization versus terrorism, liberation versus oppression, us versus them—but she also raises the specter
of an Afghan topos of oppression becoming our own if no action is
taken. In the period after 9/11, such sentiments furthered the campaign
to support military action and invade Afghanistan—a campaign framed
not only to root out terrorism and terrorists but in great measure, in the
language of liberation, to support Afghan women's freedoms.

 While US politicians rushed to assert their support of Afghan
women's rights, few explained their previous silence on the issue—or,
in fact, the recognized historical US support for the Taliban. During the
Cold War era of US-Soviet jockeying for global power, former president
Ronald Reagan famously depicted the Taliban as Afghanistan's version
of the United States' Founding Fathers. Such a statement derived from
the Taliban resistance to the Soviets and paid no heed to any other
ramifications—such as the brutal inequities politicians decried post-9/11.
The rhetoric of saving Afghan women erases history, including the history of Soviet occupation and US monetary and military support for
the resisting Taliban. Moreover, it reinforces the misconception that
women's rights are divorced from national, international, and community
rights. The fight for Afghan women had been characterized as a prob-

lem of Afghan culture and Islam, a convenient understanding stripped of the multiple political, social, and historical contexts that perpetuate women's subjection. Furthermore, the years of struggle to achieve democracy and women's rights launched by Afghan women themselves, including groups such as the Revolutionary Association of the Women of Afghanistan (RAWA), are silenced in these narratives of the need to protect Afghan women.

This silence includes the fact that Afghanistan, despite a more than decade-long war with ongoing repercussions, is yet not a garden of women's rights: in spite of US intervention, Afghan women continue to seek fulfillment of the promise of rights, security, and democracy for themselves and the nation. Writing in 2003, Noy Thrupkaew illuminates this: "The funding and security crises have been devastating, particularly for Afghan women. The 5,000 international peacekeeping forces inside Kabul have made it an oasis of relative calm, but areas outside the capital are in the hands of the 200,000 armed men controlled by former warlords—some of whom issue decrees that rival those of the Taliban for brutality against women . . . Hard-line vigilantes have threatened women seeking work outside of the home; in addition, they bombed or set fire to more than a dozen girls' schools last fall."[18]

While the US War on Terror branches to other countries, Afghan women are still searching for basic security and progress, including access to education and inheriting property. Indeed, as the American public demonstrates increasing fatigue of multiple wars abroad, in his administration, President Barack Obama sought to exit US involvement in Afghanistan quickly—even if one cost is leaving Afghan women's equality behind. In 2011, Rajiv Chandrasekaran reported on the shifting priorities of the US Agency for International Development (USAID), assessing, "The removal of specific women's rights requirements, which also took place in a $600 million municipal government program awarded last year, reflects a shift in USAID's approach in Afghanistan. Instead of setting ambitious goals to improve the status of Afghan women, the agency is tilting toward more attainable measures."[19]

In essence, over time, the goal became to see some sort of national stability in Afghanistan, withdraw troops, and "end" the conflict. Or, as one senior official in Obama's administration is quoted in this article as saying, "Nobody wants to abandon the women of Afghanistan, but most Americans don't want to keep fighting there for years and years. . . . The grim reality is that, despite all of the talk about promoting women's rights, things are going to have to give."[20] Afghan women are suddenly presented as a special—not common—interest (such as a reason for going to war!). Their needs are also seen as competing with the project of national stability and US troop withdrawal. The official asserts, "Gender issues are going to have to take a back seat to other priorities. . . . There's no way we can be successful if we maintain every special interest and pet project. All those pet rocks in our rucksack were taking us down."[21] In other words, the struggle for Afghan women's rights are no longer the struggles for Western liberty—our own—as the former first lady depicted but rather an Achilles's heel for the US body politic. Afghan women, once a battle cry and cause célèbre, are seen simply as a liability and obstacle to US troop withdrawal and national interests.

In the evolving discourse—and discontent—in relation to the war in Afghanistan, concepts of peace and stability began to trump women's equity and rights—as if women's social, political, and economic positions do not influence national stability or peace. Around the tenth anniversary of 9/11 in 2011, a decade after the intervention in Afghanistan began, Gayle Tzemach Lemmon observed, "The international community now seems to see Afghan women as unfortunate collateral damage along the path to peace, not valuable contributors who make stability possible. Meanwhile, women are fighting for a voice in the upcoming Bonn conference and a say in their future, including on the team negotiating with the Taliban for the country's future. Women I talk to say they try not to be despondent, but it is not easy to be hopeful given the facts on the ground and the talk of the future."[22] A politics of sympathy, then, is often accompanied by a short memory. The sequence of events in Afghanistan demonstrates the ways in which a politics of sympathy can quickly be erased in favor of expediency: a subjecthood of victim is hardly a platform for gaining power. Rather than being subjects of liberation, the facts of history here make transparent that Afghan women have been the objects of US foreign policy aims and the vicissitudes of the US public—the real subjects in this conflict.

We must recognize the complexity of wars in the aim of liberation. Even as many rallied against a war in Afghanistan for the fear of hypocrisy charted above, many Afghan women's rights advocates and Afghan community members themselves did seek US intervention to remove the Taliban. The Taliban regime hardly seemed inclined to remove itself. Yet the larger questions of how, why, and when to strategically deploy force—and who to involve in this endeavor and how to ensure objectives for gender equity and freedom are fulfilled—remained unelaborated prior to the advent of the war and have been summarily dismissed from subsequent discussions. Regardless, on one point there is agreement: women are yet searching for a secure place in the new Afghan nation. The promise of rights for Afghan women—the central justification for the immense violence that displaced the Taliban—has even now to be realized.

Envisioning Subjection: Afghan and Muslim Women as Objects of Art and Analysis

After 9/11 and the newfound sensitivity to the plight of the Afghan woman, politicians rushed to show the need to topple the Taliban regime and violently root out al-Qaeda. As terrorist, Taliban, and al-Qaeda became linguistically and connotatively collapsed into one and the same, new language was simultaneously shaped for analyzing the struggles of Muslim women. Let us return to Bush's use of the term "women of cover" in this context. We'll put aside that this rhetoric asserts a Judeo-Christian heritage within America, that all Arab American women are seen to be Muslim or wear covering, or that all Muslim women "cover." Regardless of its collapsing language, is Bush's term "women of cover" a sister to the often self-designated appellation "women of color"? Does it open up a space for analysis and community organizing in similar ways?

Media pundits have remarked on the contemporary appropriateness of the phrase, noting that it is fashionably twenty-first century. On the other hand, conservative critics of Bush's neologism decried the term's euphemistic quality, arguing that it dressed up Muslim fundamentalists. Other commentators analyzed it within Bush's war lexicon: in a witty analysis of the president's morally loaded and culturally superior terms such as the "crusade" against terrorism, writer and translator Eliot Weinberger remarked, "Lately Bush has become more sensitive. In his speech the other night, he referred three times to 'women of cover.' Next thing you know, he'll be calling the CIA 'men of cover.' Or maybe 'men of covert.'"[23] Weinberger's clever comment gestures to the power of revising the world through the word as well as the need to avoid deflecting attention from American institutions and their activities. Rather, we should refocus our scrutiny here.

The phrase "women of cover" may give rhetorical power to the humanity of Muslim women but affords no real status as living, thinking, willful beings. In fact, the term denies women a basic agency: the agency to choose whether or not to cover. Indeed, Muslim women who cover may do so not only for religious reasons but also to engage a political context or space. As Minoo Moallem explains, in the political arena of revolutionary Iran, the black chador did not serve as "a sign of passivity or as a sign of religiosity. It is rather a gendered invitation to participation in political activity and a sign of membership, belonging, and complicity."[24] The political moment Moallem describes includes women who choose to show their political affiliations through the act of veiling. This is not to say that all Muslim women choose to cover as some women have in Iran: the status of choice within the Afghan context, for example, is not the same. Nonetheless, the term "women of cover" erases the fact that covering is an action and, many times, an active choice. Despite being a nation structured on the idea of choice, this has been a difficult concept to comprehend within the United States.

Notably, Bush himself had first used another appellation: when speaking at the Islamic Center in Washington within a week of the attacks, he deployed the term "women who cover," which some women within Muslim communities have used themselves.[25] Subsequently, however, Bush made consistent use of his newly fashioned phrase, "women of cover." The shift from "who" to "of" may seem slight, but in grammatical terms the transformation is immense and fundamental. Replacing "who" with "of" not only removes agency but shifts "women" from a subject position to an object position. In "women who cover," women are clearly the active subject. But in "women of cover," women are defined by—even fused to—the status of being covered. This slight turn of phrase, inserting "of" as a preposition indicating possession, serves to restrict Muslim women's subjectivity through the grammatical assertion that coverings define women rather than that women may cover (or not) as an active decision.

Within the mainstream American (and Western) imaginary, it is evident that covering is not seen in the benign light implicit in the term "women of cover." Rather than serving as a positive sign of faith practice, covering is seen as a symbol of oppression and strangeness as well as the absence of personhood and liberty. The latter term, like "choice," is particularly resonant within American self-conception. In the wake of Islamophobic sentiment post-9/11, the Internet was awash with images picturing a world run by al-Qaeda. Bush was depicted as garbed in Taliban headdress, and the Statue of Liberty was represented veiled and holding a Koran.[26] The veiled Liberty gave visual reinforcement to the fears verbalized by Laura Bush: American liberties would be curtailed through the spread of an Islamic (and implicitly terrorist) world.

This veiled Lady Liberty is a pre-9/11 production of a Russian-based art collective, the AES Group. This Russian trio produces visual art that critiques popular cultural conceptions, and in fact, this veiled image was "intended as an ironic comment on Western paranoia about the spread of Islam."[27] Nonetheless, post-9/11, the image (part of a series of art begun in 1996) circulated across the Internet and newspapers, not through the intended lens of irony and cultural critique of Western fears but with the earnest belief in the threat of an encroaching Islam whose triumph over the United States would irrevocably change cherished ideas of liberty, democracy, and independence.[28] Postmodern critique became seen as sincere history; the currency of this image and rapidity of its transmission relied upon the same anti-Islamic sentiment and hysteria subject to comment by the Russian artists.

AES Group's "Islamic Project," including the veiled Statue of Liberty image, intends to offer "a kind of social psychoanalysis—visualization of fears of Western society about Islam."[29] Seen through this lens, the image is a wry critique of Western fears of contamination by what is perceived as the other—as well as an acknowledgment that in most Western eyes, the idea of liberty and freedom within the secular nation is antithetical to the religion of Islam (especially non-Muslim conceptions of Islam). The project is designed to provoke public discussions and analysis of fears around Islam rather than to serve as a vehicle of hysteria around Islam. Yet what happens when postmodern critique is so clever that irony is taken as sincere opinion? Although the artistic background of the digitally altered Statue of Liberty makes for compelling critical analysis for those who already question such Western conceptions of Islam, the image drew validity and popularity as a sign of post-9/11 antagonism toward Islam and Muslims in general.

In the high-speed world of digital communication, context and history can easily be stripped away, rendering artistic critique into racist currency. In the rush of racist paranoia, the veil is read as a marker for the threat of gender and cultural subordination. It is also an attack on Western values, making Islam and Western democracy antithetical—a space where there could be no Arab Spring. As with the propagation of sympathetic discourse to frame the struggles of nonwhite women, the wide circulation of this image draws upon stereotypes and attitudes of cultural superiority and the barbarity of others to stake its claims. Such a position masks both the very real cross-cultural issue of violence against women and why so many women—across our world and including the United States—lack political voice.

Given its graphic depictions, this AES project has faced prior attacks—from Muslims and non-Muslims alike. A 1998 exhibition of AES's works at the Mason Gross School of the Arts at Rutgers University in New Jersey drew heated criticism from local Muslims who found the images offensive and prone to promote stereotypes. Other art observers and curators agree with such sentiments; this specific AES image was removed from a segment of the "Veil" art exhibition touring England from February 2003 to January 2004. A press release from the exhibit organizer, the Institute of International Visual Arts, states that "photographs by the Moscow-based AES art group will not be shown at the insistence of Walsall Borough Council, who, fearing an incitement of violence, have deemed them too controversial given the current political climate."[30] The exhibit organizers indicated that the exhibit is designed to encourage conversation, making the exclusion a disappointment. Despite the controversy—or perhaps as a result of it—the Modern Art Oxford went on to show the AES images at its "Veil" exhibit.

The moral of the controversy is that our perceptions influence our opinions. Indeed, even our sympathies are directed through one's own lens of life. In "A Day in Afghanistan," a political cartoon for *The Arkansas Democrat-Gazette*, John Deering depicts an Afghan man walking by a bathroom.[31] This Afghan man, upon seeing the biological symbol for a woman on the door, covers that over with a figure garbed in a long dress, a version of the burka that marked Afghan women's oppression. What is fascinating about this cartoon is not the focus on women's erasure by men (which could easily cross many national lines) but the implication that the woman garbed is somehow less than the sign of the woman: through this logic, she is no longer a woman because she cannot realize herself in Western terms. No doubt this cartoon draws its emotional resonance from the waves of sympathy for Afghan women post-9/11 and is intended to highlight gender surveillance and inequity within Afghanistan. Yet, its vantage point reinforces the opposition of Western and Afghan women and thereby denies power and selfhood to women not cast in Western terms. It is as if the category of a covered-Afghan-woman is itself an impossibility.

Subjection at Home: Muslim American and Immigrant Survivors of Violence after 9/11

As the country focused on gender inequity in Afghanistan, reports of increased domestic violence in Muslim American families also surfaced

following the tragic 2001 attacks. "9/11's Hidden Toll," a *Newsweek* article by Sarah Childress, details the story of one woman whose husband
became increasingly abusive—a shift from verbal to physical violence—
after 9/11. Even in this case study of one, the "patriarchal culture" of
Muslim communities is shown to be at fault.[32] Islam is also depicted by
a Muslim anti-violence advocate as a religion that inhibits women from
fleeing lest they seek to be cast as immoral "runaway women." The advocate reports that such mores are common to the "very religious strains
of Judaism and Christianity," seeming to make the problem a shared
struggle of (extreme) religiosity.[33] However, such nascent conversations
of shared struggles—or difference—are elided in the effort to advance
sympathy for a specific subset of women: evoking the larger body of
Muslim American survivors of violence, Childress laments, "Sadly, Lila
is not alone."[34] Through such phrasing, provoking sympathy for this
particular Muslim American woman—and all the other downtrodden
Muslim (and immigrant/foreign) women Lila is seen to represent—the
politics of sympathy comes home to roost.

Childress, and her interviewees, do gesture to nonreligious obstacles faced by women. For instance, Childress refers to the lack of culturally sensitive resources and shelters for Muslim American survivors of
violence. This gap, a hallmark of the culture of US systems (a one-size-
fits-all approach), helps to explain why women stay in abusive homes
and why abuse persists across communities. Childress also gestures to the
climate of backlash against Muslim Americans post-9/11. Yet, her article
does not specify how key regulations such as special registration chilled
women from speaking out about abuse or accessing services.

In this brief six-paragraph article, systemic barriers comprise one
paragraph whereas the religious-cultural account takes up three—half
the entire article—underscoring an impression that systemic issues or
national scrutiny or hate backlash is incidental but that retrograde attitudes and practices in nonmainstream US communities certainly promote
violence. Avoiding critique of government policies, the article generates
reader sympathy for survivors of domestic violence as religion, culture,
and traditions are used to account for women's pain and trauma. In other
words, their culture or religion doesn't respect women—a present-day
echo of a politics of sympathy manifest in nineteenth-century colonial
contexts and imperialism.

In addition to demonizing nonmainstream communities, a politics
of sympathy disables readers from seeing Lila's story in any sort of relation
to domestic violence experiences of white American women or to shared
institutional and structural problems faced by all groups of women.[35]

In line with the previous pretexts of cultural superiority explored in this chapter, the focus on cultural barriers promotes sympathy, but not affiliation or action leading to institutional or antiracist reform. Under a new cultural imperialism, readers are left bemoaning the backward, alien cultures that produce violence rather than provoking policy or systemic change. The culture of patriarchy goes unnamed and unchallenged.

On the other hand, Paroma Basu's "Digital Deterrence?" published in *The Village Voice* serves as a relevant counterpoint to a culture-focused representation of domestic violence. Basu reports on two recent anti–domestic violence initiatives in New York City, noting, "Most agencies also report that numbers of hot-line calls have shot up since September 11."[36] This information is gripping because the call volume appeared to be increasing *across* cultures and communities generally. Does this information speak then to violence in a time of national trauma and instability? At the very least, the information suggests that multiple variables must be analyzed to untangle the causes of (increased) violence.[37]

In Basu's article, the spotlight is not on religion and culture but on the city and federal barriers that inhibit immigrant survivors of violence. In addition to family and cultural barriers, Basu points to the lack of court interpreters and the repercussions of having one's abuser deported (including loss of economic stability). As Basu writes, "Language and cultural barriers sorely need to be addressed if minority domestic violence victims are to become survivors."[38] Basu does speak of culture, but her article presents a profoundly different version of the walls that contain women: it is not simply a woman's culture or religion that precludes safety but rather the incapacity—and refusal—of various city systems to deal with different languages and cultural practices. Such a stance puts the onus of education and response not on survivors but on the institutions that respond to abuse. A woman and her culture are no longer stigmatized, but rather the gaps in service delivery are noted and made accountable. Such an analysis allows for intervention and response. Indeed, Basu goes on to describe two initiatives led by the New York City Mayor's Office to Combat Domestic Violence that seek to increase cultural competence in the health care provider and police communities.

Despite or perhaps even due to a rise of cultural competency training, culture—a shifting, mobile process—has become a totalizing and prevalent explanation for the presence of violence against women. But what is left out when culture rules? When religion or culture is seen as a never-changing prison? For immigrant survivors of violence, the crucial context of immigration itself—including gaps within US immigration policies that preclude women from accessing safety—is removed. As Margaret Abraham, author of the first book-length study on South Asian American marital violence, attests, "To truly understand the cultural and structural factors that affect abused South Asian women, we must look at the way in which gender, class, race, and legal status play out in US immigration policies. Historically, especially in the context of the twentieth century, US immigration policies and practices have been framed around overt and covert racial discrimination, the shifting demands of a labor market for the accumulation of American capital, and the principle of family unity."[39]

Abraham points out that, among other variables, immigration policy itself can become a barrier for women seeking to flee abuse. Indeed, while immigration relief is available to some survivors of abuse—what Sujata Warrier, formerly of the New York State Office for the Prevention of Domestic Violence, calls a "very narrow band of women"—many other survivors are unable to access immigration remedies and thus feel trapped in abusive relationships.[40] While violence against women has cultural manifestations (for example, the presence of dowry deaths in the Indian subcontinent versus women being shot in the United States), looking only to religion or culture erases the systemic and institutional barriers that keep women bound in violent contexts. In essence, the culture or religion explanation stigmatizes immigrant communities while letting US laws and systems off the hook.[41]

Indeed, a focus on cultural or religious accounts of gender violence erases the other intersections of violence women may experience, through racism, heterosexism, homophobia, transphobia, classism, the state, and so on. For Muslim American women, it erases the context of Islamophobia, a palpable presence after 9/11. And for immigrant women generally—Muslim and non-Muslim—it erases the trauma of immigration and barriers related to an immigrant status. As Tanvi Tripathi, former domestic violence program director at Sakhi for South Asian Women, explains,

> About 10 to 12 women came to the support group in October 2001. None of them wore traditional South Asian clothes, saying they were afraid of being targeted for a race-based attack. These are women who often dress up for support groups in new clothes, using it as a place to socialize and bond with other women. A lot of the women who came and also those who called in the following months felt that the trauma of

their own violent relationships was coming back to them, what is called secondary trauma. Some were worried about the racial repercussions on their children, especially boys, in their schools or neighborhoods.[42]

During the volatile time after 9/11, survivors of violence faced fears stemming from threats both within and outside their homes—including the fear of bias attacks and racism experienced through the nation. In addition, many survivors felt their traumas at home had to be put aside given the spectacular trauma faced by the city and nation. Nonetheless, for immigrant and Muslim American survivors of domestic violence, one trauma does not simply trump the other: these are felt experiences as well as experiences felt through the frame of the other. As Leti Volpp explains, it is crucial that we keep in mind that "women of color belong to communities of color."[43] Given the reality of violence in women's lives, immigrant culture, a minority religion, or the patriarchy of home nations cannot serve as the suitable explanation (and origin tale) for violence.

Within the United States, one of the most vibrant elements for change within minority communities is the anti–domestic violence movement. A host of advocates are asking questions, such as, how can activists make women's rights an acknowledged subject without objectifying our communities? How do we account for violence in nonwhite communities and immigrant and/or Muslim American communities; is culture or religion the only thing that counts? Advocates are locating our frames of reference beyond cultural explanations of abuse to strengthen the power of the anti–domestic violence and gender rights movement. In such a stance, we can hold institutions and systems as well as families, communities, and harmful practices accountable. And we can empower productive change for all survivors of violence by recentering cultures of patriarchy as the objects of analysis—envisioning change is possible in how we perceive it.

On the other hand, a sympathetic stance, with its hallmark superior cross-cultural benevolence, reinforces the misconception that domestic violence is a problem greater in communities other than one's own—especially if one is a mainstream American. As Chandra Talpade Mohanty comments,

> Universal images of "the third world woman" (the veiled woman, chaste virgin, etc.), images constructed from adding the "third world difference" to "sexual difference," are predi-

cated upon (and hence obviously bring into sharper focus) assumptions about Western women as secular, liberated, and having control over their own lives. This is not to suggest that Western women *are* secular, liberated, and in control of their own lives. I am referring to a *discursive* self-presentation, not necessarily to material reality. If this were a material reality, there would be no need for political movements in the West.[44]

Indeed, if women are so free in the West, what need is there for our multiple women's rights movements? Mohanty points out that notions of difference may essentialize the objects of discussions while making the unspoken subject positions falsely authoritative. For immigrant women, then, being defined by culture or religion alone limits the ability to be a full subject, a person with experiences beyond oppression and pain, as evidenced in nineteenth-century representations. A counting beyond culture, one that takes into account the multiple variables that lead to abuse, permits immigrant women to be more than objects of cultural trauma. Through an analysis that goes beyond sympathy or cultural stigmatization, women can be subjects of their own empowerment, and our communities can work together to remove all the barriers that contribute to violence against women.

Reviewing Power

Sympathy may be the first step in motivating change: it can propel people to see the world anew and to feel beyond their own experiences. It is a strategy often used when trying to draw attention to those suffering needlessly. Yet as the previous examples indicate, in the struggle to end violence against women, sympathy directs attention to a limited range of facts, a strategy that can paradoxically promote violence. Indeed, sympathy itself can become a smokescreen for more sustained analysis of the deeper causes that put women at risk of violence. Depending on its slant, sympathy may humanize women, but it may demonize their cultures and communities. Such a strategy can feel like winning a battle while losing the war.

The polarization of opinions after 9/11—you're either for terror or against it, with America or against freedom—has demarcated women into two categories: you're either a liberated Western woman (the woman's sign) or an oppressed Third World subject (the garbed "women of cover"). The sympathetic discourse of "women of cover" and the need to save Third World or Muslim women imposes a confining grammar: Third World and Muslim women are excluded from self-realization while Western women constitute a norm. In fact, Western women are no longer women but are free-form liberated subjects. The category of woman itself becomes a stigmatized object in this 9/11 cultural grammar.

This grammar is reinforced by the binaries and pathologies that underpin a sympathetic recognition of difference, binaries that assume Western women enjoy fundamental liberties (a questionable claim, considering US pay inequities and ongoing onslaughts on reproductive rights) and that Third World women cannot occupy any category but submission, since to do so would be to become a woman in Western terms. As Shamita Das Dasgupta explains, "The common assumption among Americans is that only 'Westernization' leads women to be involved in politics, social change movements, or any kind of social activism."[45] The United States did not launch the women's rights movement: other nations claim long, textured histories of women challenging people and institutions for the development of rights that would advance their and their community's standing. To recognize the breadth of women's movements is to see that political action and participation itself is a process that varies across contexts.

In this discourse about Muslim, Afghan, and immigrant women, it is helpful to recall the startling opening line of Sara Suleri's *Meatless Days*: "Leaving Pakistan was, of course, tantamount to giving up the company of women."[46] Suleri describes the problems with the Western category of women, how it cannot encompass her realities of South Asia, where an equivalent concept of woman simply does not exist. Being a woman in Suleri's homegrown version is much more than the translation of the term into Western contexts. Across global topographies and idioms, the category of women is itself mobile and changing: the term refuses to be encompassed in one demarcation. What it means to be a woman is a relational understanding, one necessarily tied to local histories, cultures, experiences, households, and social mores.

For such reasons, immigrant women and women internationally seek to be linked to their communities as a way in which they can define their individual and collective selfhood and liberation. As Masuda Sultan, an Afghan American human rights activist, writes, "Westerners have correctly focused on the oppression of women in Afghanistan, but they have not taken sufficient note of the anguish of Afghan men."[47] What Sultan points to here is the Western dissection of Afghan women from men—the inability to see the community as one that has suffered as a whole through the years of war and trauma. In the Western depiction of demonized Afghan men, women are read only as powerless objects and afforded humanity for this reason. But Afghan women must strip themselves of Afghanness altogether in order to claim such humanity and sympathy. From the Western point of view, it appears to be impossible to be both an Afghan woman and a woman connected to her community. Of course, Afghan women have been working to be subjects of their own histories and actions—and persist in doing so.

A local and international community approach could bring new energy to the US women's movement by enabling movements in other nations to inform local strategies and progress. Such a stance would help eliminate the naïve binary of Western liberated woman and the Eastern submissive and oppressed woman. Furthermore, this analysis would enable wider reflection on the limits of women's power within the United States as well as a more profound sense of possibilities for change. To adopt this point of view would be to give respect to the many women's movements throughout the world and would lead to a greater understanding of the restrictions American women face despite the sense of women's liberation internalized in American self-fashioning.

Why is such a pathway critical? Because women in the United States must also recognize their loss of voice during this national crisis. One measure of proof of women's restricted power within the United States comes from the fact that women's silence post-9/11 did not infect women vulnerable due to documentation status, cultural background, or religious creed alone. As Geneva Overholser documents, only five out of eighty-eight op-ed pieces in three national newspapers in the week after 9/11 were written by women. Overholser comments, "I started to notice a haunting silence amid the views I was finding in America's newspapers: it was the absence of women's voices."[48] In a time when women were all the talk, it is startling to see that very few women spoke for themselves or their communities. Overholser records a virtual disappearance of women from the US media. Suddenly, only men had legitimate platforms for opinions or reactions to world events and public policy choices. Despite the prevalent attitudes of sympathy for women's rights—and the subject of women—the actual political presence of women's voices in the United States had diminished. Given Overholser's research, a revised version of Deering's political cartoon might have been more appropriate: the depiction of the erasure of US women from the public sphere.

Looking at the absence of women's voices from the media, as well as of opinions dissenting to the prevailing militaristic passions post-9/11, we witness not a resurgence of women's rights but the spectacle of women forced undercover. The silence of women resounded in a time when it seemed as if the world was advocating women's rights. Given the gap between the rhetoric of women's subjectivity and the reality of women's silence and objectification, it is critical to distinguish between opportunistic feminisms and social movements that would fundamentally aid women in achieving safety, opportunities for advancement, and human rights. As Sunera Thobani remarks, "Women are taught to support military aggressions, which is then presented as being in their 'national' interest. These are hardly the conditions in which women's freedoms can be furthered."[49]

In order for the struggle for women's rights as a material reality to become more than a promise, we must go beyond sympathy and protectionism to a more profound subjective politics that enables power through self-defined and varied manifestations. An essential part of this process includes reviewing the assumptions that motivate sympathy and reframing our analysis. For example, this would include shifting our categorization of domestic violence in immigrant communities as simply a cultural or religious manifestation to defining it as a crime and human rights violation perpetrated against women globally. Given the sometimes currency of the women's agenda, women will likely remain ongoing objects of political discussion. What remains to be seen—as women continue the agitation for rights here and abroad—is whether we ourselves will become subjects in the discussions and policies that determine our status and dreams.

Notes

1. I would like to thank Tanya Agathacleous, Bix Gabriel, Vanessa Manhire, and Sunita Subramanian for their painstaking and thorough review of a prior version of this article. Their comments were instrumental to my development of this chapter, and I am grateful for their generous sharing of insights and feedback. In addition, I would like to thank the community at Sakhi for South Asian Women, where I served as a volunteer for seven years and executive director for seven and a half years. The commitment, advocacy, and sisterhood I found with Sakhi have made this chapter and my ongoing women's rights work stronger.

2. William Safire, "Coordinates: The New Location Locution," *New York Times Magazine*, October 28, 2001, 22.

3. NSEERS, the National Security Entry-Exit Registration System, and special registration, began in June 2002 and required men sixteen and over from twenty-five countries (all Muslim-majority nations except for North Korea) to go through a specialized, extensive procedure for entering the United States. In addition, they were required to maintain contact with immigration officials during their stay in the United States. Furthermore, foreign nationals from these countries already present in the United States were required to register with the government. After significant outcry from diverse groups challenging the efficacy and ethics of this program, in April 2011, NSEERS was ended. As Muzaffar Chishti and Claire Bergeron note, "The *New York Times* reported in 2003 that, out of roughly 85,000 individuals registered through the NSEERS program in 2002 and 2003, just 11 were found to have ties to terrorism." Chishti and Bergeron also report, "According to DHS, between September 2002 and the end of September 2003 (nearly the full course of the special registration component of the NSEERS program), 83,519 individuals participated in special registration interviews at immigration offices nationwide. As a result of these interviews, 13,799 individuals were placed in removal proceedings" ("DHS Announces End to Controversial Post-9/11 Immigrant Registration and Tracking Program," May 17, 2011, http://www.migrationinformation.org/USFocus/display.cfm?ID=840).

4. Though I will not discuss this aspect in detail, it is vital to note that President Bush's comment is also vexed—and vexing—because the majority of Arab Americans identify religiously as Christians. President Bush erases the religious diversity within Arab American communities, and his statement counters the actual community data, presence, and migration history. Furthermore, his comments rely upon the illogical (but often reasserted) conflation of Arab American-Muslim-terrorist that resurfaced and gained circulation after 9/11. Even in the guise of offering sympathy, President Bush's statement highlights perceptions of terrorism and religious affiliation fundamental to the evolving "War on Terror" that many have critiqued as a War on Islam due to the collapsing of terms that should be distinct—a collapse that serves to promote an us vs. them worldview. In the end, President Bush's comment does not manifest diversity but erases its actual facticity.

5. Margery Sabin, "The Suttee Romance," *Raritan: A Quarterly Review* 11, no. 2 (1991): 4.

6. Deirdre David, *Rule Britannia: Women, Empire, and Victorian Writing* (Ithaca, NY: Cornell University Press, 1995), 88.

7. Lydia Huntley Sigourney, "The Suttee," in *Nineteenth-Century American Women Poets: An Anthology*, ed. Paula Bernat Bennett (Malden, MA: Blackwell, 1998), 5–6.

8. Ibid., line 1.

9. Ibid., lines 11–12.

10. Ibid., line 26.

11. Ibid., lines 27–29.

12. Ibid., line 50.

13. Sabin, "Suttee Romance," 5.

14. Lauren Berlant, "The Female Woman: Fanny Fern and the Form of Sentiment," in *The Culture of Sentiment: Race, Gender, and Sentimentality in Nineteenth-Century America*, ed. Shirley Samuels (New York: Oxford University Press, 1992), 269.

15. Zakia Pathak and Rajeswari Sunder Rajan, "'Shahbano,'" in *Women, Gender, Religion: A Reader*, ed. Elizabeth A. Castelli (New York: Palgrave, 2001), 202.

16. King-Kok Cheung, "The Woman Warrior Versus the Chinaman Pacific: Must a Chinese American Critic Choose between Feminism and Heroism?" in *Asian American Studies: A Reader*, eds. Jean Yu-Wen Shen Wu and Min Song (New Brunswick, NJ: Rutgers University Press, 2000), 318–319.

17. Laura Bush, "Text: Laura Bush on Taliban Oppression of Women," Radio Address by Mrs. Bush to the Nation, November 17, 2001, http://www.washingtonpost.com/wp-srv/nation/specials/attacked/transcripts/laurabush-text_111701.html.

18. Noy Thrupkaew, "Afghanistan Update," *Ms.*, 13, no. 3, fall 2003, 30.

19. Rajiv Chandrasekaran, "In Afghanistan, U.S. Shifts Strategy on Women's Rights As It Eyes Wider Priorities," *The Washington Post*, March 6, 2011, http://www.washingtonpost.com/wp-dyn/content/article/2011/03/05/AR2011030504233.html.

20. Ibid.

21. Ibid.

22. Gayle Tzemach Lemmon, "Forgetting Afghanistan's Women," *Foreign Policy*, September 9, 2011, http://afpak.foreignpolicy.com/posts/2011/09/09/forgetting_afghanistans_women.

23. Eliot Weinberger, "Anonymous Sources," Talk given at Lost & Found: The Art of Translation conference, Iowa City, University of Iowa, October 13, 2001.

24. Minoo Moallem, "Transnationalism, Feminism, and Fundamentalism," in Castelli, *Women, Gender, Religion*, 129.

25. Safire, "Coordinates," 22.

26 The image is available at http://www.aesfgroup.org/index.php?action=cats;cat_id=1;sub_cat_id=17;image=20.

27. Blake Eskin, "Russian-Jewish Art Angers Rutgers Muslims," *Forward*, February 20, 1998, 1.

28. Though I do not discuss this point further here, recent hysteria regarding the threat of Sharia law overtaking the US Constitution or federal, state, or local laws follows in this vein.

29. http://www.aesf-group.org/index.php?action=cats;cat_id=1;sub_cat_id=1.

30. http://universes-in-universe.org/eng/nafas/articles/2003/veil/photos/img_04.

31. John Deering, "A Day in Afghanistan," *The Arkansas Democrat-Gazette*, October 11, 2001.

32. Sarah Childress, "9/11's Hidden Toll," *Newsweek* 142, no. 5, August 4, 2003, 37.

33. Ibid.

34. Ibid. The husband in Childress's case study is an African American Muslim. The African American Muslim community is inflected by diverse and multiple histories of oppression and resistance through community formations. The article's focus on a patriarchal Muslim culture sidesteps racist stereotypes of African Americans but also avoids untangling multiple contexts of violence. Indeed, the real subject elided by the politics of sympathy is US culture, systems, and histories as the subjects for analysis. The culture of US patriarchy (and inequity)—across races, religions, and histories—remains uninvestigated, while a totalizing Muslim culture becomes the convenient root of the crisis.

35. Considering the widespread prevalence of domestic violence across religions and communities, it is difficult to see how culture and religion can solely account for abuse. Research in the December 1999 *Population Reports* states, "Around the world at least one woman in every three has been beaten, coerced into sex, or otherwise abused in her lifetime" (L. Heise, M. Ellsberg, and M. Gottemoeller, "Ending Violence against Women," *Population Reports* 27, no. 4 [1999]: 1). Not only is violence against women a global issue but research from the US Bureau of Justice shows that "violence against women perpetrated by intimates was consistent across racial and ethnic boundaries" (Ronet Bachman, Linda E. Saltzman, and US Bureau of Justice Statistics. *Violence Against Women: Estimates from the Redesigned Survey*. Washington, DC: US Bureau of Justice Statistics, 1995, 4). If women across the world—and women across races in the United States—are subject to violence, how is it that culture (which varies so much across and within nations and races) can serve as the convincing catchall explanation for the existence of violence against women? Given that most cultures in the world are patriarchal, what does it mean to explain abuse in terms of an immigrant's home culture or religious background or affiliation?

36. Paroma Basu, "Digital deterrence?" *The Village Voice* 47, no. 49, December 4–10, 2002, 28.

37. Data gathered even prior to 9/11 demonstrate a need to account for multiple variables in understanding increasing rates of domestic violence. Ruksana Ayyub, a founding member of the Committee on Domestic Harmony at the Islamic Center of Long Island, indicates that in 1994, 4 percent of women they

surveyed reported physical abuse. In 1997, this number shot up to 20 percent. As Ayyub explains, "We believe that this second survey is a more accurate reflection of the incidence of domestic violence in our community. The change in numbers is a result of the growing awareness and education imparted by our committee" ("The Islamic Mosque: A Source of Support for Muslim Women," in *Breaking the Silence: Domestic Violence in the South Asian-American Community*, ed. Sandhya Nankani [Philadelphia: Xlibris, 2000], 131). Ayyub's analysis explores the validity of the initial 4 percent benchmark rather than claiming a rise in the incidence of violence. Within every community, domestic violence has often gone unreported as women struggle to name and disclose abuse. An increase in calls for assistance cannot prove increased violence (prevalence), but it does affirm the work of many community-based organizations leading the charge to end violence in our communities by creating a safer space for disclosure, services delivery, and community change.

38. Basu, "Digital deterrence?" 29.

39. Margaret Abraham, *Speaking the Unspeakable: Marital Violence among South Asian Immigrants in the United States* (New Brunswick, NJ: Rutgers University Press, 2000), 44.

40. Sujata Warrier, "Social, Legal, and Community Challenges Facing South Asian Immigrant Women," in *Breaking the Silence: Domestic Violence in the South Asian-American Community*, ed. Sandhya Nankani (Philadelphia: Xlibris, 2000), 93.

41. Yoking culture to community struggles both stigmatizes non-US cultures and reinforces American capitalist ideals that celebrate individualism. I am grateful to Bix Gabriel for offering this analysis.

42. Tanvi Tripathi, "Voices of Sakhi," Sakhi.

43. Leti Volpp, "(Mis)Identifying Culture: Asian Women and the 'Cultural Defense,'" in Wu and Song, *Asian American Studies*, 402.

44. Chandra Talpade Mohanty, "Under Western Eyes: Feminist Scholarship and Colonial Discourses," in *Contemporary Postcolonial Theory*, ed. Padmini Mongia (New York: Arnold, 1996), 192.

45. Sayantani DasGupta and Shamita Das Dasgupta, "Women in Exile: Gender Relations in the Asian Indian Community in the United States," in Wu and Song, *Asian American Studies*, 329.

46. Sara Suleri, *Meatless Days* (Chicago: University of Chicago Press, 1989), 1.

47. Masuda Sultan, "Hope in Afghanistan," in *Women for Afghan Women: Shattering Myths and Claiming the Future*, ed. Sunita Mehta (New York: Palgrave Macmillan, 2002), 202.

48. Geneva Overholser, "After 9/11: Where Are the Voices of Women?" *Columbia Journalism Review*, 40, no. 6 (2002), 67.

49. Sunera Thobani, "War Frenzy," *Meridians: Feminism, Race, Transnationalism* 2, no. 2 (2002), 296.

References

Abraham, Margaret. Speaking the Unspeakable: Marital Violence among South Asian Immigrants in the United States. New Brunswick, NJ: Rutgers University Press, 2000.

AES. "Islamic Project. AES—the Witnesses of the Future." http://aesf-group.com/projects/islamic_project.

Ayyub, Ruksana. "The Islamic Mosque: A Source of Support for Muslim Women." In Breaking the Silence: Domestic Violence in the South Asian-American Community, edited by Sandhya Nankani, 126–132. Philadelphia: Xlibris, 2000.

Bachman, Ronet, Linda E. Saltzman, and US Bureau of Justice Statistics. Violence Against Women: Estimates from the Redesigned Survey. Washington, DC: US Bureau of Justice Statistics, 1995. NCJ-154348.

Basu, Paroma. "Digital Deterrence?" The Village Voice, 47, no. 49, December 4–10, 2002, 28–29.

Berlant, Lauren. "The Female Woman: Fanny Fern and the Form of Sentiment." In The Culture of Sentiment: Race, Gender, and Sentimentality in Nineteenth-Century America, edited by Shirley Samuels, 265–281. New York: Oxford University Press, 1992.

Bush, Laura. "Text: Laura Bush on Taliban Oppression of Women." Radio Address by Mrs. Bush to the Nation, November 17, 2001. http://www.washingtonpost.com/wp-srv/nation/specials/attacked/transcripts/laurabush-text_111701.html.

Chandrasekaran, Rajiv. "In Afghanistan, U.S. Shifts Strategy on Women's Rights As It Eyes Wider Priorities." The Washington Post, March 6, 2011. http://www.washingtonpost.com/wp-dyn/content/article/2011/03/05/AR2011030504233.html

Cheung, King-Kok. "The Woman Warrior Versus the Chinaman Pacific: Must a Chinese American Critic Choose between Feminism and Heroism?" In Asian American Studies: A Reader, edited by Jean Yu-Wen Shen Wu and Min Song, 307–323. New Brunswick, NJ: Rutgers University Press, 2000.

Childress, Sarah. "9/11's Hidden Toll." Newsweek, 142, no. 5, August 4, 2003, 37.

Chishti, Muzaffar, and Claire Bergeron. "DHS Announces End to Controversial Post-9/11 Immigrant Registration and Tracking Program," May 17, 2011. http://www.migrationinformation.org/USFocus/display.cfm?ID=840.

DasGupta, Sayantani, and Shamita Das Dasgupta. "Women in Exile: Gender Relations in the Asian Indian Community in the United States." In Asian American Studies: A Reader, edited by Jean Yu-Wen Shen Wu and Min Song, 324–337. New Brunswick, NJ: Rutgers University Press, 2000.

David, Deirdre. Rule Britannia: Women, Empire, and Victorian Writing. Ithaca, NY: Cornell University Press, 1995.

Deering, John. "A Day in Afghanistan." The Arkansas Democrat-Gazette, October 11, 2001.

Eskin, Blake. "Russian-Jewish Art Angers Rutgers Muslims." Forward, February 20, 1998, 1, 8.

Heise, L., M. Ellsberg, and M. Gottemoeller. "Ending Violence against Women." Population Reports 27, no. 4 (1999): 1–43.

Institute of International Visual Arts. "Press Release." http://universes-in-universe.org/eng/nafas/articles/2003/veil/photos/img_04.

Lemmon, Gayle Tzemach. "Forgetting Afghanistan's Women." Foreign Policy, September 9, 2011. http://afpak.foreignpolicy.com/posts/2011/09/09/forgetting_afghanistans_women.

Moallem, Minoo. "Transnationalism, Feminism, and Fundamentalism." In Women, Gender, Religion: A Reader, edited by Elizabeth A. Castelli, 119–145. New York: Palgrave, 2001.

Mohanty, Chandra Talpade. "Under Western Eyes: Feminist Scholarship and Colonial Discourses." In Contemporary Postcolonial Theory, edited by Padmini Mongia, 172–197. New York: Arnold, 1996.

Overholser, Geneva. "After 9/11: Where Are the Voices of Women?" Columbia Journalism Review 40, no. 6 (2002): 67.

Pathak, Zakia, and Rajeswari Sunder Rajan. "'Shahbano.'" In Women, Gender, Religion: A Reader, edited by Elizabeth A. Castelli, 195–215. New York: Palgrave, 2001.

Sabin, Margery. "The Suttee Romance." Raritan: A Quarterly Review 11, no. 2 (1991): 1–24.

Safire, William. "Coordinates: The New Location Locution." New York Times Magazine, October 28, 2001, 22.

Sigourney, Lydia Huntley. "The Suttee." In Nineteenth-Century American Women Poets: An Anthology, edited by Paula Bernat Bennett, 5–6. Malden, MA: Blackwell, 1998.

South Asian Insider. "SAKHI Annual Gala on Sept 27." 2, no. 28, September 17, 2003.

Suleri, Sara. Meatless Days. Chicago: University of Chicago Press, 1989.

Sultan, Masuda. "Hope in Afghanistan." In Women for Afghan Women: Shattering Myths and Claiming the Future, edited by Sunita Mehta, 193–203. New York: Palgrave Macmillan, 2002.

Thobani, Sunera. "War Frenzy." Meridians: Feminism, Race, Transnationalism 2, no. 2 (2002): 289–297.

Thrupkaew, Noy. "Afghanistan Update." Ms. 13, no. 3, fall 2003, 30.

Volpp, Leti. "(Mis)Identifying Culture: Asian Women and the 'Cultural Defense.'" In Asian American Studies: A Reader, edited by Jean Yu-Wen Shen Wu and Min Song, 391–422. New Brunswick, NJ: Rutgers University Press, 2000.

Warrier, Sujata. "Social, Legal, and Community Challenges Facing South Asian Immigrant Women." In Breaking the Silence: Domestic Violence in the

South Asian-American Community, edited by Sandhya Nankani, 89–97. Philadelphia: Xlibris, 2000.

Weinberger, Eliot. "Anonymous Sources." Talk given at Lost & Found: The Art of Translation conference. Iowa City, University of Iowa, October 13, 2001.

Part Three

REDEFINING DIFFERENCE,
CHALLENGING RACISM

The Proust Effect

Gigi Marie Jasper

I became a teacher by accident. Fourteen years ago, a high school English teacher had a nervous breakdown, and since I had a degree in English I was asked to take the long-term substitute job. I have been educationally Janus faced ever since.

I am the only black teacher in my Wyoming high school and have never gotten over the amount of educating I have to do that has nothing to do with my subject matter. Virtually all of my students are white. So too are their teachers and the educational cultural representation to which they have been exposed. Since I evidently comprise all definitions of "other," I seem to be privy to an entire spectrum of ideas I had not previously had to witness.

All of my life I have had to endure what I have come to call "the Proust Effect": the look I get that must exactly mirror the look one would give to her dog if her dog trotted up and began intoning, *For a long time I used to go to bed early. . . .*[1] At first I thought it was simply racist amazement that I can conjugate the verb "to be," but I have found that it goes much deeper than that. It is how most administrators, parents, and teachers look at me. While I have often seen "the look" in the outside world, I was dumbfounded to have to see it professionally as well, since I had naïvely thought we were doing the same thing: educating students.

My mistake was that I must have believed teaching was rather a higher calling than the other professions; that even though it existed in a world of prejudice, foolishness, and contempt, we knew better, and we were slowly showing, by demonstration and information, the way to a better world. *Nothing of the kind!*

Education in this country is a business, albeit a badly run, primarily unsuccessful one, and as such, it displays the same racism and sexism we see everywhere else in business. Like the business world, my high school has exemplary rules against discrimination of any kind, but let me point out a violation, and I have to hear, "You think everything is racist." They evidently believe that the very fact that rules against discrimination exist is proof positive there can be no violation—the "that was taken care of" attitude one sees as an excuse for eliminating affirmative action laws: Martin Luther King fixed all that. I believed I could find solace in my students, and if it weren't for them, I would be much more grim than I am, but even in my classroom I must prove my humanity.

One of my favorite books is *The Woman Warrior* by Maxine Hong Kingston. This work is often taught at the college level, but I have found it can work well for high school students if I am willing to steel myself against the often hideous preconceptions of what minorities and women are that my students seem to bring to class. Kingston explores many cultural subtexts for a non-Chinese readership, plus the book addresses the very problems of being a "stranger in a strange land" and a native simultaneously—the very things I want my students to consider. My selection of this book isn't just my exposing my students to a different literature. It is that while I do I am also, I hope, debunking attitudes my students might not know they have. If we get *there* together, maybe they will understand that mine isn't the last word on minority thought either.

The book begins with a story Kingston's mother tells her about a town's revenge on a girl who humiliates her family. Kingston explores how this girl (her aunt) could or could not have been "guilty" and how she probably had been a tragic victim, the tragedy compounded by her subsequent suicide. That is not how her mother tells the story at all. Kingston cannot question her mother about her aunt because the family considers the aunt never to have existed as a result of her so-called crime and resulting suicide. "No Name Woman," the opening chapter, is an attempt to give voice to the voiceless: her dead aunt who no one will speak of and who couldn't in her life speak for herself.

My students are appalled by how "foreign" the story is. They seem to believe there are no American ramifications for being a pregnant rape victim. They naïvely act as if all American families cherish and support all women all the time, and they also seem to think American townspeople never treat their neighbors differently when circumstances change.

As we read the first chapter we talk as a class about the many similarities our experiences have with those in the story Kingston's mother tells, that is, because the Chinese village acted upon those feelings in a different way than my students had ever heard of does not make the motivation different. My goal is to get students talking about pregnant teenagers thrown out of the house that they know. Many students are sure of how their parents would react if they were raped, became pregnant, and then attempted to not name their tormentor even though they know him. When we talk about what it would feel like to be that Asian aunt even in Wyoming, we demystify the emotions behind the particulars of what we have read.

My students respond to Kingston's novel in many ways. Some students resent that they were assigned this book in the first place and find it impossible to identify with the protagonist. Rock Springs, Wyoming students have virtually no school experience in reading any work that isn't about their racial heritage, and some even feel themselves rather *ecumenical* when asked to try to "live in the skin" of another race. Some of my students may feel we are reading this particular book because of me; that is, if they lump minorities together as representing oddness, then to them it might stand to reason that I, an "odd" teacher, would naturally teach "odd" books. I am willing to accept their assumptions temporarily as my concession to their outlandishness and their attitude of entitlement, even though they don't know that is what it is; but because this position is one many never move from in their lives, I do not leave it at that, since it is evidently from this pool of students my school's administrators are chosen. I must also admit that students know I adore this book. It would be shortsighted of me not to recognize "the desire to please" response teachers evoke in a few, and that alone sometimes paves the way for discourse.

Even so, students who are willing to withhold judgment about those "weird" Chinese people are hard-pressed sometimes to move from this beginning into Kingston's allegorical next chapter. Here Kingston pretends to be exactly the opposite of what she has been trained to be but exactly what some aspects of America expect her to be. This is less convoluted than it sounds.

"White Tigers" is about the training of a little girl (Kingston's fantasy self) by a rather superhuman couple to be a heroine and avenge anybody who hurts her family. They instruct her to endure physical deprivation, to wield a sword expertly, and to commune intimately with nature. In the Chinese part of Kingston's real life, however, she is aware she is less than a boy in every way, and for her to aspire to more than slavery is possibly fatal. As an American girl, she also saw she could be Wonder Woman or, at least, have a say in her fate. It seems reasonable that she blends these contradictions to make herself a Chinese Wonder Woman. Kingston creates a metaphor for coming to terms with being an "other": "I learned to make my mind large, as the universe is large, so that there is room for paradoxes."[2]

In becoming a contradiction in terms she does not have to betray either of what are clearly parts of her, however much she may reject her inferior status as a girl. Believing oneself not to be inferior does not, in her case, relieve her of her personal fears, and these fears she goes on to relate in the chapters about being an American girl born in San Francisco of Chinese parents, or a Chinese girl born in America and what each variation means to her identity.

I have had students say Kingston's story is ridiculous. No one, they say, could learn to do the things she describes. I understand the difficulty some students have with a story that blends fact with fantasy, but many times I ascribe to my students a deeper objection. The protagonist/author isn't a real person to them because she is Chinese. They feel she could have nothing to say to them and are unwilling to grant any legitimacy to her writing. Although I try not to bluntly say so in class, this attitude both terrifies and infuriates me. I sometimes hear in their objection a failure to give Maxine Hong Kingston human status. Why bother to read about someone who is not like they are, someone who doesn't act like a "normal" (white) person?

A nonwhite person can teach them nothing, they seem to be saying. I hear reverberations of that bias among others who claim they have no interest in exploring other cultural texts and those who claim categorically it cannot be done: both assume a degree of close-mindedness harmful to democratic teaching. I also wonder why those students don't recognize what they are saying about me, their nonwhite teacher, when they reveal such an attitude. Or maybe they do.

Minority status does not reduce one's ability to understand authorial intention, however much the dominant culture believes it does. I, a black woman, *can* relate more closely to Kingston's experience because I see American life as a marginalized person. As a teacher this works for me and against me: I may seem to represent Kingston better because my students see us in the same way, casting themselves as the outsiders, or they may think of me as an outsider along with them, because none of us is Chinese. I am actually willing to be seen in either light. If my students perceive me as able to introduce another cultural point of view with more ease, and thereby help them, good. If they believe we are coexaminers, bringing many eyes and notions to the novel, also good. I also try to make it clear to my students that while I may represent two very obviously marginalized groups, my perception could very easily resonate with other, less visual examples.

For instance, many of my students complain of the stupidity of those they talk to on the Internet, how often they are asked whether they have flush toilets, and how often they are asked whether they have to take a horse to school. My students are dumbfounded the person hasn't quite grasped that they are talking via a computer and not carrier pigeon, but more often than not, they play along with it and talk about how they have to go out and feed "Ol' Paint" and make sure the outhouse hasn't frozen over before they go to the bunkhouse. My students are constantly asked, "Wyoming? Is that a state?" or told, "Oh yes, it's one of the square states." More recently, however, they are asked whether they have killed any "queers" lately and have the good grace to be horrified. I ask them how it feels to previously be from a state known for Yellowstone Park and now be from a state known for viciously beating and hanging Matthew Sheppard on a fence *because* he was gay.

My quicker students will say that it isn't fair to judge Wyoming by one incident, and we are more than just that occurrence. If I can get them there, I have hope they can make the leap to Kingston's writing. While it is true the abjectly brutal hanging of Matthew Sheppard will always be associated with Wyoming, most Wyomingites do not take that association upon themselves nor accept any personal responsibility in the tragedy. Sometimes I can point out that their attitude is a bit self-serving and shortsighted: many of my students are daily gay bashers. Isn't their blithe hatred similar to what caused two individuals to kill Sheppard? Most of the time, though, that discussion is dismissed as totally unreasonable.

In teaching *The Woman Warrior*, I also must explain that Kingston does not represent all "Chineseness." She tells her readers: "Chinese-Americans, when you try to understand what things in you are Chinese, how do you separate what is peculiar to childhood, to poverty, insanities, one family, your mother who marked your growing with stories, from what is Chinese? What is Chinese tradition and what is the movies?"[3] Kingston is making a statement true of all autobiographical writing, and the very same questions she asks apply to other cultures, but the challenge is to get my students to consider it. Many of my students are so provincial that for them to shift to thinking *The Woman Warrior* may have much to do with them and then understand what they learn isn't immutable and applicable even to all Chinese people, let alone other peoples, is not easy. Once they are generous enough to consider that what they read in the novel is valid, often my students want to stop there and think they are now "Chinese (read minority) experts." It is sometimes too much for them to realize that Kingston is not the representative of all Chinese or all minority people.

Kingston gives me a nod of encouragement in the last chapter of the novel. Some of it is a story of a poetess kidnapped by barbarians. After years in their company and having children, she chanced to hear music that she sang in her own way. The book concludes: "She brought her songs back from the savage lands, and one of the three that has been passed down to us is 'Eighteen for a Barbarian Reed Pipe,' a song that Chinese sing to their own instruments. It translated well."[4] I like to think Kingston is giving me permission to teach this book by saying that it can be translated well into our non-Chinese lives, given the time, understanding, and desire. I also recognize that permission does not necessarily confer excellence, and I am forced to explore why it is I so passionately want to read with my students literature whose cultural experiences I do not share.

Maybe in my classroom I want some other minority to be the voice of authority, even if it is only from the pages of a book. When some students view something in a book by a minority as bizarre, maybe I don't feel I have to excuse it if I don't share it, that is, if the book isn't about me. I can't take personally a negative observation of a student about another culture if I am not invested in it, and I can say with confidence, "I don't know" to things I don't know. I understand I always have this privilege, but it is easy to forget when I am looked at as the authority and sole representative both of teacher and of minority woman.

Many of my students come into my class with the expectation that they know me. Anglo-Americans comprise my whole class. Perhaps my students are as ignorant about black women as they are about minorities in general. If they were blank slates my job would be easy: I would paint the pictures I wanted them to have. The problem is they often come with ugly and inaccurate mental images that often pass as facts about minorities and women gleaned from our society at large.

I wish Lorraine Bethel were exaggerating when she stated how I see my dilemma in the classroom. It isn't a wonder I am often uneasy with my position as a teacher: "The codification of Blackness and femaleness by whites and males is seen in the terms 'thinking like a woman' and 'acting like a nigger' which are based on the premise that there are typically Black and female ways of acting and thinking. Therefore, the most pejorative concept in the white/male world would be that of thinking and acting like a 'nigger woman.'"[5] I often respond with a feeling of defensiveness about issues my students see as "black," but if we're talking about "someone else" I might feel less "touchy."

Exploratory teaching isn't necessarily comfortable, but being a teacher does not exempt me from self-discovery, however much I am not thrilled with what I discover. Thrilled or not, my divulgence of my discomfort does not cause me to limit what I teach to the writings of black women. If I did, I would be advocating the ghettoizing of literature. I, like Henry Louis Gates, Jr., believe "people arrive at an understanding of themselves and the world through narratives purveyed by schoolteachers, newscasters, 'authorities,' and all the other authors of our common sense."[6] If teachers only shared the literature of their own culture with their students, that understanding would be diminished, thereby creating islands, or ghettos, of the written word. Only some students would be introduced to some works, and those of us with "shared common sense" would never know it.

I have mixed success when I teach Maxine Hong Kingston. I have mixed success when I teach Emily Dickinson, too, but my students don't go through the "author as alien creature" stage. I certainly object to the "It's a Small World" approach to multiculturalism, but given where I live and who I teach, getting students who start with the "I'd like to teach the world to sing" attitude sounds good to me. Sure, it's simplistic, inaccurate, and in many ways sort of silly, but it beats having to begin teaching a wonderful piece of literature with a lesson convincing students of the author's humanity. And maybe that is the problem: I don't. Instead I have to defend the author's humanity many, many times within the discussion of the book when questions and statements reveal disbelief that what we're reading is "relevant."

I do not mean to suggest my students are the only ethnocentrics around. In fact, it is absolutely shocking to them when they learn how the Chinese people in Kingston's book (and elsewhere) refer to non-Chinese people as ghosts—and in a very insulting context. I do mean to suggest, however, that it might be the only time they have been faced with the idea that their standard of beauty, power, and righteousness may not be shared by the rest of the world, however much American television and movies commodify white American images. What they hold as standards is viewed as ugly and undesirable by some. My students don't know how to respond when I remind them of the part in the 1980 movie *The Gods Must Be Crazy* when Xio first sees the white woman and says that her blonde hair is "absolutely gruesome" and that her skin looks "like something that crawled from under a rock."

When I propose that the movies *Deliverance* (1972) and *Dumb and Dumber* (1994) portray perfect examples of American white men, they are appalled; yet they have no difficulty believing *Boyz n the Hood* (1991) and *New Jack City* (1991) capture black America. They are equally insulted when I tell them many Asians believe all non-Asians "look the same"—a case of having their own prejudices thrown right back in their faces—and find it not only distasteful, which they should, but unbelievable, which they should not. Why does it offend and surprise my students to discover some folks don't see them as real people and yet not even question that they write off whole sections of the world as "not real people," including, probably, their teacher? But why should they see me or any other racial minority as "real"? Their parents often don't. At my last parent-teacher conference a parent told me, "I don't mind that you are my daughter's teacher; but then, I am a liberal." I believe she expected me to thank her.

When I became a teacher I came to expect I would have to introduce ideas, probably more than once, to my students. I did not expect that I would have to pretend gratitude in that teaching. Just as many of my students believe themselves to be broadminded by the very act of reading outside of their experience, so too does my school district seem to believe the very act of hiring One Black Woman constitutes radical liberalism, and they are stunned that I won't just be satisfied with *permission*. Both my students and the school district generally are quite willing to admit racism exists as a concept, but if I dare point out an example of racist behavior and/or attitudes, I am labeled as a hysterical malcontent, always angry, or, my personal favorite, the "She just won't shut up and be satisfied, will she?" face I am forced to look at and pretend I don't understand. Their steadfast unwillingness to countenance the possibility that an actual real life example of racism has any more relevance to their lives than the writings of an "other" is tiring.

That I am *allowed* to teach multicultural literature is, to many, *giving me* much more than I *deserve*, and some appear to think, "Aren't we on the cutting edge by teaching multiculturalism?" That I am *allowed* to stand in front of white students should fill me with such exaltation that

I should never dream of complaining; but frankly, it makes me want to scream. In fact, it is I who has been the recipient of a better education (or perhaps socialization) than virtually all of the people in my building, despite what my family and I have had to do to get it, and if my school district could not see the color of my skin, they would be telling me repeatedly how lucky they are to have me; but that, perhaps, is the very test of racism they refuse to acknowledge.

For many of my students to know many people hate other races is enough for them to think they understand racism. It is a totally unrecognizable beast to believe whole worlds of people could feel that way about them. The result is rarely self-reflection but further adherence to the idea that others are REALLY others (read substandard), and so REALLY unworthy to be read about because they dare to be racist *against us!*

This makes me weary. I am not grateful to teach excellent literature because it is by a minority writer, any more than I am grateful to be a teacher because I am black. Both are merely statements of fact.

So many of my students tell me I teach them to look at things from more than one point of view that I am beginning to believe them. If this is so, I am gratified, but I am also amazed they think I am unique in this. Has their education, until they have had me as a teacher, been so devoid of alternative perspectives? Sadly, yes, and not just in minority-deprived places like Wyoming but all over the United States. According to *Teacher Recruitment and Retention*, edited by Antoine M. Garibaldi, there is roughly one chance in twenty for a student in the United States to have any minority teacher during her or his K–12 education, and for a multitude of reasons, that one is still being further reduced.[7]

Maybe this is what is different about my teaching: according to the traditional ways in which my students have been educated, I teach against the grain. Of course I am familiar with Louise Rosenblatt's reader-response theory, and whatever book or play or culture I am focusing on, I make the study of racism, sexism, and classism a fundamental part of my contextualizing. I switch the point of view from the standard European perspective to that of the other side. I try to connect historical events to patterns today and highlight parts of history that are not discussed in most high school classes, but I must also ask myself: How could I do otherwise? That's how I look at *everything*. My fine education did not make me less inquisitive and more gullible. I actually understand Rosenblatt. Perhaps that's what my district is so distressed about. I should know that the only educational point of view worth knowing is the sanitized revisionist one. If I knew that, then I would be happy to keep

"Multicultural Literature" as a subset of *real* literature and be pleased with the "Taco Tuesday" approach of which my district is so proud.

It does not look to me that the process is going to change. From grade school to graduate school to school administrator it seems the function of American education is not to explore ways in which we can all benefit from each other, not to try to expand our experiences and knowledge through honest exchanges and learn from those whose lives are not mirror images of our own, but to *look* as though we do. That is no doubt why my students see racism and sexism as something their grandparents had to contend with but that has nothing to do with them. That, and their racist reactions are unconscious, so deeply embedded in the psyche of both the students and of this country, many are unaware of it. Sadly, that is also the way many want those reactions to stay.

Earlier this school year, the entire English department of my high school presented me with a petition containing all of their signatures requesting I be appointed department chair. First the administration pretended there was no opening, and then, after months of ignoring me, it set up an "interview" for the job. During this meeting, to which the administrator came dressed quite unlike her usual attire in play clothes, the administrator lied to me about pertinent information and said if I got the position I would just be a mouthpiece. She then gave the job to the only other candidate, a white man who was just transferred to our school, does not teach English full time, has not taught on a secondary level, does not have the same level of education as I, and did not have the support of the department. School officials are absolutely drop-jawed that I consider this treatment both racist and sexist. I got an interview, didn't I? Since I am their self-appointed in-house minority expert, why don't they just accept my word for it? Because when all is said and done, the prevailing attitude seems to be that hiring me was enough to fulfill their part of the "equal opportunity" bargain. What happens to me after that is not worthy of concern, and when I object, I once again have to witness the Proust Effect.

Marcel Proust himself said, "But when from a long-distant past nothing subsists, after the people are dead, after the things are broken and scattered, taste and smell alone, more fragile but more enduring, more unsubstantial, more persistent, more faithful, remain poised a long time, like souls, remembering, waiting, hoping, amid the ruins of all the rest; and bear unflinchingly, in the tiny and almost impalpable drop of their essence, the vast structure of recollection."[8] Perhaps my students will carry with them a bit of my teaching in their memory, despite the erasure I often personally feel. I can only continue to do what I am doing: be the lonely and unlikely voice in the only high school in Rock Springs, Wyoming.

Students hear from me a perspective they would not have heard except from me, and on my best days, I know some of them recognize that. The school administration wishes I would either shut up and be indebted or become a "Stepford Wife" teacher with black skin so that they can continue to claim they are culturally diverse while not having to address a single one of my concerns. I know I am not a failure because I do neither. My chief virtue is that I and others like me in this country make students aware of the notion of "the other," and any such awareness begins a process that undermines their assumptions, broadens their consciousness, and, if I am triumphant, reduces their ethnocentrism.

Notes

1. Marcel Proust, *Swann's Way* (New York: Vintage Books, 1970), 3.

2. Maxine Hong Kingston, *The Woman Warrior* (New York: Vintage Books, 1975), 35.

3. Ibid., 13.

4. Ibid., 185.

5. Gloria T. Hull and Barbara Smith, "The Politics of Black Women's Studies," in *All the Women Are White, All the Blacks Are Men, but Some of Us Are Brave*, ed. Gloria T. Hull, Patricia Bell Scott, and Barbara Smith (New York: Feminist Press, 1982), xxiv.

6. Henry Louis Gates, Jr. "Thirteen Ways of Looking at a Black Man," *The New Yorker*, October 23, 1995, 56–65.

7. Antoine M. Garibaldi, "The Impact of Schools and College Reforms on the Recruitment of More Minority Teachers," in *Teacher Recruitment and Retention*, ed. Antoine M. Garibaldi (Washington, DC: National Education Association, 1989).

8. Proust, *Swann's Way*, 51.

Hot Commodities, Cheap Labor

Women of Color in the Academy

Patti Duncan

> My resignation and the discouragement I see in my colleagues, their alienation from "academe," are reactions to a seemingly insoluble problem: formalism, establishmentarianism, whitism—whatever it is called, it has me beat.
>
> —Paula Gunn Allen[1]

In 2008, after immeasurable distress, I resigned from my faculty position in a women's studies program. I had recently been awarded tenure at a large urban university in a city I love. I had developed numerous close friendships at the university, and I felt that my research and teaching were meaningful both to me and to my students. However, for nearly three years I had experienced harassment and discrimination, in both subtle and extremely overt ways, by the program's acting director, a white woman without tenure, whose own position had been converted from a contract instructor to the tenure track in exchange for serving as program director.

Presumably either threatened by my seniority over her or uncomfortable with my racial identity as a woman of color, or some combination of the two, she seemed to do everything she could to exclude me and to undermine my position in the program and in the university. I was denied program resources and bullied in front of colleagues and students, rumors were spread about me to colleagues within the program, and the submission of my tenure file was obstructed. For a period of time I attempted to counter her discriminatory treatment, going as far as filing grievances with both the Office of Human Resources and the university's Office for Affirmative Action as well as participating in three separate mediation processes over the course of seven months. In the end, acknowledging that the problem was greater than that represented by this individual and that the administration seemed unable or unwilling to address the issue in any meaningful way, I made the difficult decision to leave what had become an increasingly hostile work environment.

Racism and sexism in the academy are systemic, supported by the entire institutional structure and rendered invisible to many by the complex workings of the academic marketplace. In the years since my resignation I've realized that my story is not anomalous, but all too common for women of color in higher education. In today's global economy the restructuring of academic institutions and their subsequent privatization result in a changing educational environment characterized by shifts in labor relations, transforming the nature and effects of racism and sexism in academia. As the global free market assumes primacy within the university system, previous commitments to social justice within disciplines like women's and gender studies are often replaced by conflict management models of the corporate world.

In this chapter I am most concerned with the effects of this restructuring on women of color faculty, who have historically been marginalized within academia and expected to perform reproductive labor (i.e., act as "service providers") for the benefit of others. Even while the language of diversity often dominates discussions about higher education, race and gender continue to structure the experiences of women of color faculty, who as Chandra Talpade Mohanty suggests, remain subject to a revolving door policy. As she states, "While the discourse of multiculturalism is in full force in the academy these days, the practice of multiculturalism actually facilitates the recolonization of communities marginalized on the basis of class, and racialized gender."[2] Thus, how such recolonization occurs varies depending on context and the specific institutional practices associated with addressing "multiculturalism" and "diversity," which, within corporate models, often rely on individualistic rather than structural understandings and analyses of power. What is the changing nature of higher education—and women's and gender studies in particular—within a neoliberal political economy in which the university functions much like other apparatuses of the state, and how do these changes affect women of color?

Women of color in women's and gender studies have endured a long history of exclusionary racist practices, tokenization, and discrimination. Since the inception in 1969 of women's studies programs in the United States, women of color writers, scholars, and activists have identified and resisted multiple forms of oppression and challenged the methodological practices within the field that sustain the exclusion and stereotyping of women of color and women of the global South. Scholars including Gloria Anzaldúa, Barbara Smith, Audre Lorde, Mitsuye Yamada, Barbara Christian, and many others have repeatedly critiqued both overt and covert forms of racism within the field of women's studies. As Shirley Geok-lin Lim argues, until very recently the field of women's studies has neglected the study of women of color, eliding our contributions to social movements, including feminist movements, and rendering invisible the specific cultural contexts and communities in which many of us work.[3]

In response to the challenges made by women of color, many women's and gender studies programs have shifted to make race and the experiences of women of color more central. However, these gestures are often deeply problematic, relying on additive approaches, occurring with little or no institutional structural framework, or shaped by an imperial feminism fraught with assumptions about the labor of women of color. In other words, simply adding race and women of color to white-dominated programs and paradigms, without transforming the contexts, actually undermines the potential contributions of women of color in women's and gender studies. As Sandra Gunning suggests, the actual meanings and consequences of the inclusion of faculty members of color within academic departments have not received adequate attention.[4] Also, when white, Western, Eurocentric feminist frameworks are taken to be the standard, and sometimes the only, legitimate feminist frameworks, then the presence and work of women of color are even further marginalized.

Using my own experience as a point of entry, in this chapter I explore some of these dynamics of the restructured academy, particularly the gendered and racialized processes of exploitation that consolidate the outsider status of women of color in women's and gender studies programs. Such processes result in a peculiar contradictory position in which women of color may find ourselves perceived as both "hot commodities" within the academic marketplace and "cheap labor" designated to do the dirty work. Examining the events that resulted in my resignation allows me to elucidate the structural dynamics that shaped my interactions with

a white program director within a mostly white women's studies program
in my previous academic position. Similar to Roxana Ng's discussion of
her own experience of racial harassment in a Canadian university, it
allows me to draw attention to the power dynamics that structure our
experiences of racialized gender.[5] It also provides a framework for what
Himani Bannerji refers to as a "situated critique"—beginning from our
experiences not as isolated selves, but with a sense of being in the world,
considering social, political, and historical contexts and connections.[6]

The "Home" Question

> Mechanisms in the academy are geared to the maintenance of struc-
> tural power for white people as a whole.
>
> —Aida Hurtado[7]

In "Genealogies of Community, Home, and Nation" Mohanty brings
together questions of home, belonging, nation, and community to discuss
globalization and multicultural feminism. She describes her own experience with what she refers to as the "home" question (when are you going
home?) as well as the profoundly political implications for US women of
color of the assumptions that structure our sense of (not) belonging and
(in)ability to cross borders. For women of color in women's and gender
studies, home is complicated. Over the past decades mainstream feminists have often claimed a universal "sisterhood," implying that coming
to women's studies and/or feminism is like coming home, an idea that
has been critiqued by scholars including Anzaldúa, Smith, and Gayatri
Spivak. And Mari Matsuda makes the point that members of campus
are encouraged to think of universities as home, presupposing a sense of
personal security and belonging.[8] However, this is not always the case
for those of us marginalized within the field and within the academy.
In fact, in the US educational system and within mainstream feminism
women of color, immigrant women, and women of the global South
continue to be perceived as outsiders and interlopers. In addition racism
and anti-immigrant sentiments may shape our experiences within the
field of women's studies.

    In the fall of 2000 I was hired as an assistant professor in a small
women's studies program at a public state university. This university
attracted me because so many of its students are nontraditional—includ-

ing many returning women students, working mothers, and activists. Though I was not aware of it at the time, I was hired during a period of intense conflict and upheaval within the program over issues of race and racism. During the year of the hire, as I learned later, students of color had organized against the program and its director, arguing that they had been subject to racist treatment and that the program was not a welcoming place for women of color. Calling themselves the "Raging Exotics," this group of students of color protested what they identified as racist exclusionary practices in the curricular offerings as well as specific incidents of racism they had experienced or observed in women's studies classes, and they demanded that the (at that time) all-white faculty be accountable to issues of race and racism. They also cited numerous examples of oppressive encounters and interactions with the program's director and faculty members that they believed violated their rights as students of the university.

Such was the climate into which I was hired, through a special diversity initiative designed to attract and retain faculty of color, since the university reportedly had a poor track record with this given the small number and extremely low retention rate of faculty of color in tenure-track positions. I had recently attained my PhD and was the first tenure-track hire in the program, as the director at that time had been granted tenure in another department many years earlier. I was also hired, it became clear to me early on, not only to teach about race and women of color studies and to attract and mentor students of color but to *be* the program's woman of color, effectively embodying their commitment to diversity.

Benjamin Baez discusses this phenomenon for faculty of color, who are often commodified and "overused" by their own institutions as a means to portray a commitment to diversity.[9] As such I was expected to perform not as a person within the institution but as a *persona*. This meant performing diversity and often being interchangeable with other women of color faculty at the institution, as Bannerji suggests is the case for many scholars of color.[10] And I was expected to help the director and other faculty members address the charges of racism leveled at them by the Raging Exotics and other students of color.

This was made obvious to me in many ways over my first two years at the university. My contract stipulated that I was to develop and teach a course on "Women of Color" for the program as well as other courses in which race and women of color would be central, such as "Asian American Women's Studies" and "Race, Class, Gender, Sexuality." I was assigned the task of "managing" the students of color protesting the program. When several of these students stated that they did not want to take courses from white instructors whom they considered racist, I was asked by the program's director to do independent studies with them so that they could fulfill their degree requirements with a woman of color faculty member. I was also charged with helping other faculty members to "diversify" their course offerings and syllabi, involving the tedious task of reviewing numerous syllabi and course materials and offering helpful suggestions for inclusion of women of color and issues of race.

When the faculty within the program decided to schedule a series of antiracism workshops, I was asked to take the lead in organizing these workshops and securing funding to offer them as optional programming for all affiliated faculty. Finally, I was required to represent the program in countless ways. In my first two years I served on eleven committees and was often asked by the program's director to attend events in her place, including orientation programs for new students.[11] There was even a front-page story about me in the university's newspaper, touting me as the women's studies program's "first woman of color!" which one administrator took as evidence of the success of the diversity initiative through which I had been hired.

As a mixed race Asian Pacific American (APA) woman focusing my research and teaching on women of color feminisms and transnational feminisms, I believe I was deemed a good choice not only because of my qualifications but perhaps also because the other faculty in the all-white program were initially not threatened by my presence. As Maria P. P. Root and others have argued, mixed race individuals are often tokenized in contexts where other people of color might be seen as too different, too foreign, or too "exotic."[12] And Mari Matsuda suggests that there exists a strange preference in hiring for Asian Americans, particularly women, who appear to be assimilated and nonthreatening.[13] This might explain why the director once asked me to make copies for her and how and why she and other colleagues felt it was perfectly acceptable to request that I update and diversify their syllabi for them. In addition my status as the only APA woman in the program—in fact the only woman of color in the program at that time—contributed to both my sense of isolation and my tokenization within the program.

In those first years I fluctuated between desperately wanting to quit academia altogether—given my tremendous workload, isolation, and lack of support—and feeling extremely grateful to have a job at all (especially one in women's studies, where I could continue my teaching and research with a focus on women of color). I want to highlight here that the isolation I, along with other women of color faculty in positions across the country, experienced is distinct from the general isolation most new faculty experience, particularly in academic contexts that stress individualism and competition for resources. As Mary Romero suggests, women of color in academia often face extreme hostility from white students and faculty colleagues, as we are seen as benefiting from affirmative action.[14] For example, some of my white colleagues at that time mentioned to me more than once that I was an affirmative action hire, implying that I had gotten the job only because of my racial identity. They seemed to believe this despite the fact that I was the first person hired within the program through a national search and the only faculty member at that time with a PhD in women's studies.

Some of us may find ourselves in a double bind between feeling angry about being characterized as having been admitted only by virtue of our race/gender—and internalizing this belief to some extent—and fighting to prove our worth and competence. This process, discussed by Yolanda Flores Niemann, involves what she refers to as "stereotype threat," or being vulnerable to internalizing negative stereotypes even when we do not accept such stereotypes.[15] We become acutely aware of the fact that every action we take will be judged according to impossible standards and stigmatized as a marker of our deviance or difference. And, as Shirley Hune notes, APA women and women of color faculty in general are subject to a campus life of close scrutiny.[16]

For APA women in the academy stereotypes of the model minority contribute to a culture in which we are viewed as both incompetent (and simply there because of our race) and overly competent (and therefore threatening to the establishment). According to the myth of the model minority, APAs do not experience racism or discrimination but have "made it." Moreover, we are seen as opportunistic, even threatening, especially when we speak out against the oppressive conditions and discrimination we encounter. This stereotype remains pervasive and continues to mask challenges APA women face in the academy.[17] At the same time the myth of the model minority serves to pit APAs against other groups of people of color. In addition the image of the model minority is overdetermined, as Sumi Cho suggests, by associated images of submissiveness to authority and political passivity.[18] APA women are also frequently stereotyped as exotic and overly sexualized.

Patricia Hill Collins discusses controlling images of black women as a set of overarching stereotypes about black women that rely on and reinforce objectification and dehumanization and justify the continued oppression of black women.[19] Invoking her discussion I suggest that Asian Pacific American women are subject to an overlapping yet distinct set of controlling images, including that of the model minority, which juxtaposes APA women as passive and docile in opposition to stereotypes of black women as angry and aggressive. This dichotomy upholds white supremacy and places all women of color in untenable positions in the academy. Also, such controlling images contribute to a culture in which APAs and other people of color are objectified and may be victimized by overt discrimination and hate violence. More commonly, however, anti-Asian sentiments are subtle, and the stereotypes discussed above lead to numerous microaggressions as well as APA women in academia being taken for granted and overlooked for advancement.[20] Moreover, nonconformity to these controlling images frequently leads to repercussions. APA women in academia report that peers often expect them to behave in stereotypical ways, and they face negative reactions when perceived as too outspoken or "aggressive."[21] Matsuda discusses these reactions: "When the Asian woman . . . decides to challenge the judgment of her senior colleague, he [sic] will be as shocked as if the Xerox machine had chosen to criticize the substance of a memo. The woman who was hired to be good and smart and silent except in scripted appearances is suddenly acting like an equal. Any Asian woman who has been there knows there is a special wrath reserved for those moments. It is disproportionate to the substantive challenge. It is enraged. It is physical. It is scary."[22]

The unexpected psychological aggression many women of color experience in academia when we step out of our expected roles has the effect of reminding us that we are not at home but in fact, as Matsuda points out, "tenants at sufferance."[23] Even in women's and gender studies APA women encounter these controlling images. According to Karen Pyke and Denise Johnson, the construction of hegemonic femininity, extolled in the dominant culture, privileges white middle-class heterosexual women's expressions of gender and results in the marginalization of women of color (associated with subordinate, often racialized, femininities).[24] And challenging racism and other forms of oppression in the academy, for women of color faculty, results in being perceived as troublemakers.[25]

In addition to the pressures I faced to perform racialized gender, I experienced other obstacles, including a severe lack of resources. It was not until my third year in the program that I discovered that the special diversity initiative through which I had been hired had actually provided a large sum of money to the program to be used for my retention. However, no one had informed me of this fund, and no stipulations were placed on the use of the money. The funds were never made available to me, despite my struggles to locate funding to attend conferences and set up the special "diversity" lectures and events I was required to organize. When I look back now, I realize that nothing concrete was ever done to retain me at the institution.

While the university claimed to have a commitment to recruiting and retaining faculty of color, and provided a budget for the so-called retention of new "diversity hires," I cannot think of one instance in which the administration actually attempted to retain me or any other faculty member of color I knew at the university. In fact, it was just the opposite, with countless faculty members of color leaving over the eight years I spent there due to denial of tenure and promotion, lack of resources and support, and constant reminders of our lack of belonging. To my knowledge the administration did nothing to counter other job offers or the misery, harassment, and isolation so many of us experienced. Our workloads were often significantly greater than those of our white colleagues due to the hidden labor associated with mentoring students of color and performing the extra service work associated with diversification, and we were required to work longer hours to meet the demands of our positions.

As Baez demonstrates in his research, opportunities for advancement within academic institutions are often significantly reduced for faculty of color, due to excessive service demands.[26] Gunning describes the potentially debilitating service demands placed on faculty of color who are isolated as the "only one" (for example, the only APA), sometimes resulting in blurring the line between inclusion and mere tokenism.[27] And Gitahi Gititi discusses the anecdotal and research evidence attesting to the excessive workloads of faculty of color, including heavy formal and informal teaching loads, excessive committee assignments, and discriminatory tenure review procedures.[28] But, he suggests, the psychological burden associated with tokenization and isolation is rarely addressed, particularly the ways in which such processes negatively affect productivity.

One exception is Yolanda Flores Niemann's discussion of stereotype threat, as mentioned earlier. In her recounting of her own experience as a woman of color within the academy, Niemann analyzes the psychologically damaging processes associated with tokenization, particularly in terms of internalizing racist attitudes of colleagues and supervisors, potentially resulting in feelings of incompetence and "self-undermining" practices.[29] And underlying it all is the message that faculty members should be grateful to have been hired in the first place. As outsiders we are made consistently aware of our lack of belonging. And refusing to play the role of the Grateful Outsider, as Anna Agathangelou and L. M. H. Ling suggest, often triggers indignation, even outrage, among the academy's gatekeepers.[30]

Hune also suggests that APA women are perceived as "strangers" or outsiders in the academy. She cites research and campus climate studies documenting the unequal treatment of APAs in higher education. Her research demonstrates a chilly climate for APA women in the academy, who often experience both overt racism and sexism and "everyday inequities"—the subtle forms of oppression and informal practices that serve to marginalize, exclude, and silence.[31] Also, APA women find a largely unsupportive and sometimes hostile campus climate that hinders our professional development.[32] Like other women of color in higher education APA women's expertise and authority are often contested; our teaching, research, and service may not be fully acknowledged; we experience heavier teaching and service loads and carry service assignments for which we often do not receive credit; and we are insufficiently recognized for our academic expertise but called upon to address "diversity" issues. In addition there exists a lack of mentoring for APA women faculty, a lack of a sense of community with colleagues, and a feeling of being devalued within our departments. Hune writes, "Their theoretical perspectives, publications, and creative works, especially those involving ethnic and women's issues, are frequently disregarded by peers who consider APA women's contributions lacking in academic merit. . . . In addition, some APA women find their campus issues and leadership ignored and underrated. Their concerns may be doubted by whites and occasionally by other minorities, who do not see APAs as racially disadvantaged.[33]

Hune notes that APA women in 2007 constituted a small percentage (2.8 percent) of total full-time faculty. And in a recent publication she suggests that APA women in academia continue to face racism and sexism as well as anti-immigrant sentiments and accent discrimination.[34] Racism is normalized within the university, and faculty labor is gendered and racialized, creating an environment in which women of color faculty are constituted as outsiders and often alienated from our work within the academy.

Outsiders Within

In the attempt to correct so many generations of bad faith and cruelty, when it is operating not only in the classroom but in society, you will meet the most fantastic, the most brutal, and the most determined resistance. There is no point in pretending that this won't happen.

—James Baldwin[35]

Five years into my position the director of the program announced her decision to retire. While I was offered the opportunity to direct the program, I was also informed that it would not be possible to negotiate early tenure. I was not yet tenured at that time and was advised by many senior colleagues that it was not in my interest to accept the position.[36] There were no other tenure-track faculty members in the program at that time, with the majority of courses taught by adjunct and fixed-term instructors, and the administration was very firm in its unwillingness to hire a new director through a national search or to allow us to recruit an affiliated tenured faculty member from another program within the university.

As background it is important to note here that contract (adjunct and fixed-term) instructors constitute one of the most heavily exploited groups in academia. Generally hired course-to-course (adjuncts) or year-to-year (full-time, fixed-term instructors) within this particular institution, these instructors made up the majority of faculty within the women's studies program. Almost none of them had earned doctoral degrees, and they lived contract-to-contract, with fewer resources and benefits and less status than tenure-track faculty within the university system.

According to Angela Harris and Carmen González women of color are generally overrepresented in the lower academic ranks, particularly in temporary, part-time positions within the restructured corporate US academy.[37] However, most adjunct and fixed-term faculty within this particular program were white women. One of these instructors had applied for my position five years earlier. Throughout the years she had sought a tenure-track position elsewhere but had been unable to secure one. So when the administration struggled to find a replacement for the program director, she volunteered for the job on the condition that they convert her line to a tenure-track position. With no affirmative action process this individual, "A," was granted a tenure-track line and status as a new assistant professor and program director. At the same time, after years of requests and proposals the program was finally granted approval to begin a national search for a new tenure-track assistant professor. I chaired the search that resulted in the hire of a new colleague, another woman of color. It was during this time that things began to really disintegrate.

Both the new hire, "X," and I regularly felt an intense sense of competition with us coming from "A." Since A and X were technically at the same rank within the university hierarchy, A seemed to limit X's access to resources that A herself did not have. In fact A resisted fighting for a competitive salary for X, arguing that it felt unfair to her since she herself had had to wait years for a tenure-track line and a competitive salary. The complete list of our experiences of discrimination is too long and complex to detail exhaustively here; however, we felt in multiple ways that A attempted to undermine and sabotage our positions within the university. For example, she failed to write the required chair's letter for my tenure file and then "forgot" to compile and turn in the file, an act that could have resulted in my not being considered for tenure at that time, had it not been that a senior colleague in another department learned of the situation and intervened on my behalf. A failed to file payroll paperwork for X, resulting in X being paid late for the first month of her new position. She neglected to sign off on my grant proposals and fellowship applications, which required permission of department chairs, so during the entire time that she served as director, none of my applications and proposals was actually submitted.

We learned that she spread rumors about both of us around the program to fixed-term and adjunct instructors, resulting in increased isolation and ostracism by colleagues and an even more hostile environment for the two of us. She shifted significant parts of her workload to us, increasing our labor and contributing to a sense of chaos and confusion within the program. And she began to slowly withdraw program resources for the two of us, including course release time, while increasing such resources for herself and for the fixed-term instructors within the program. In fact, in my final year at the institution every full-time faculty member within the program was granted a spontaneous course reduction except for X and me.

We were never passive during this time. However, every action we took to counter A's seemed to result in more negative consequences for both of us. When I tried to speak with her about what was happening, she grew angry and defensive. We went to Human Resources and then to the Omsbuds Office at the university to discuss our grievances and to begin a formal mediation process. We spent seven months attending regular meetings with administrators and repeatedly met with the dean of the college. Our attempts to work through the conflicts simply resulted in multiple incidents of her retaliation against us, comprising a "secondary injury" in the legal sense, inflicted by A and later by colleagues within the program (who aligned themselves with our harasser and contributed to our hostile work environment) and by administrators who failed to intervene. Cho, discussing a case of racialized sexual harassment, suggests that the convergence of racial and gender stereotypes of APA women helps constitute the specific forms of harassment that we may face and also the ways in which others may perceive both the harassment and the secondary injury.[38]

Dynamics within the department were increasingly racialized, targeting the two of us—the only women of color tenure-track faculty. In particular there seemed to be an assumption that labor rights and resources normally guaranteed for tenured and tenure-track faculty became privileges bestowed upon us, and these rights and resources were subsequently questioned and challenged. For example, a new computer set off a backlash of anger toward X, who was referred to by one colleague as the new affirmative action hire. Indeed, while X and I had been the only faculty members within the program to be hired through competitive national searches, like other faculty of color in US higher education we were "preemptively construed as lacking the requisite qualifications, credentials, and experience."[39]

Our racial identities played a significant role in such assumptions. Treatment of us within the program seemed directly affected by both the model minority stereotype of APAs and anti-immigrant sentiments shaped by the perception of us as perpetual foreigners (*they* are taking over *our* jobs). These assumptions resulted in the idea that we were somehow usurping the white women faculty members' rightful ownership of the program and the field of women's studies. Later the entire group of mostly white adjunct and fixed-term faculty claimed that it was unfair that X and I had our own offices and suggested voting to change the system within the university that allowed for tenure-track faculty to have access to individual offices. They felt it was wrong that they (nearly all white women, most of whom were older than the two of us) should share offices while the two women of color tenure-track faculty each had her own office.[40] They implied that we were somehow squandering the program's resources and that our very presence resulted in the depletion of public resources to which they should be entitled.

Underlying these assumptions is an imperial feminism that frequently reframed the discourse surrounding faculty labor rights, power, and privilege. While it might be assumed that X and I enjoyed greater power within the university system given our tenure-track lines, this was complicated. In fact A and several of the fixed-term faculty colleagues suggested that it was our (X's and my) elitism that resulted in the unequal access to resources among tenure-track and fixed-term instructors. They claimed that our doctoral degrees signified this elitism as well as our greater privilege relative to them and that by expecting certain labor rights associated with tenure-track positions at this university (e.g., our own offices, funding to attend conferences, time to do research) we were not only "uppity" but somehow disloyal to feminism—a feminism they defined narrowly and around their own interests.

What I came to recognize was that these same critiques were never raised in relation to older, white women (or men) with doctoral degrees in tenured positions. In fact it became clear to me that what A and these other mostly white colleagues resisted most vehemently was not the exploitative distinction between tenure-track and temporary faculty positions but the fact that X and I—two women of color—were overstepping racial and gender boundaries by earning doctoral degrees and tenure-track positions. In addition their repeated framing of themselves as the "Other"—central to any discourse of oppression—served to privilege their own concerns and further marginalize women of color within the program. These dynamics and others, including the constant refrain of "sisterhood," a critical stance toward what they referred to as hierarchy and elitism, and a stated commitment to consensus, actually functioned to silence and, at times, vilify X and me. The underlying racism and white privilege within women's and gender studies as an academic formation failed to receive adequate exploration and critique.

When I filed an affirmative action complaint, we experienced further retaliation, including the withholding of resources from students whom I advised and mentored. During this time I met with the college's dean, who privately expressed his support for me and for X, stating that he would take immediate action to protect us. But he never actually did anything. Senior colleagues in other departments attempted to intervene, but when the hostility of these fixed-term faculty members was then directed against them, most retreated. The support we received was almost invariably private support, willingness to listen sympathetically, or the suggestion that we document everything. But the closed circle of the university's administration effectively precluded any meaningful intervention. Ultimately, I was left wondering what it really means to act as an ally within the academy. Finally, at the end of the term the dean offered his plan: he required the three of us to go through a formal mediation with an outside mediator through the summer. While A, an administrator, would be paid for her time to do this, they could offer no compensation to X or me. We were given no choice in the matter but told instead that this was the way for us to demonstrate our commitment to the program and the institution. Against my better judgment I agreed to it. The mediation team consisted of two experienced and skillful women, who, once they gained an understanding of the situation, positioned themselves as advocates for X and me and recommended the immediate termination of A's contract. A immediately withdrew from the mediation process. The university responded by canceling the process and displacing all responsibility, though there remains some confusion about how and why this occurred.

Mohanty suggests that in today's system of higher education, shaped increasingly by neoliberalism and corporate power, students are situated "as clients and consumers, faculty as service providers, and administrators as conflict managers and nascent capitalists whose work involves marketing and generating profit for the university."[41] She ties this reinvention of the public university to other corporatized systems, including the military-industrial complex and the prison-industrial complex, to highlight the ways in which corporate and government interests come together and profit and social control are intertwined. To this end the university functions like the nation-state in its defining of citizens and noncitizens, in which certain groups of people are always already cast as outsiders. And Gititi makes the point that the issue of ownership is central within academia—"ownership of power and the institutions that power creates to maintain and protect itself."[42] Institutionalized power, he argues, creates insiders and outsiders, marking boundaries that exclude, disqualify, and oppress.[43] With the construction of (white) hegemonic femininity comes the construction of (white) hegemonic *feminism* and therefore assumptions about women of color as subordinate.[44]

As my colleague X and I were constituted as outsiders, we were also constructed as inherently *different*, inferior, and threatening to the status quo. This process of being invalidated within white feminist academia, Himani Bannerji suggests, results in a profound sense of alienation.[45]

We were offered the possibility of inclusion only on terms defined by
and controlled by others, which explicitly discounted our specific experiences as women of color. In the university system and within the field of
women's and gender studies, what determines citizenship? Who belongs,
and on what grounds?

Academic Citizenship, Migration, and Epistemic Violence

> My experiences very often spoke of violence and violation. They
> consisted of humiliation in the institution called the university.
>
> —Himani Bannerji[46]

I use the term *epistemic violence* here following Gayatri Spivak's discussion of colonialism and the destruction of non-Western ways of knowing, which thereby reinforces the domination of Western frameworks,
methods, and epistemologies, as a way to characterize—and politicize—
the harm inflicted upon me, X, and countless other women of color
faculty in women's and gender studies and the academy. George Dei and
Agnes Calliste, writing of the Canadian context, suggest that colleges
and universities operate as powerful discursive sites "through which race
knowledge is produced, organized, and regulated."[47] People of color are
marginalized, silenced, and rendered invisible not only through failures
to take issues of race seriously but also "through the constant negation
of multiple lived experiences and alternative knowledges."[48] And this
violence, as Bannerji notes, is everywhere in a society based on race.[49]
Furthermore, the racism that organizes such violence, she suggests, is
central to European (white) feminist discourse as it serves the interests
of white, middle-class women and those aligned with them.[50]

   Ironically, both X and I had been hired to perform racial difference
within the white-dominated program and university. Both of us were
ostensibly hired to serve as experts on race, racism, and women of color.
Our research and teaching in these areas made us desirable at the times
of our hires (the "hot commodities" of my title). Yet when we reported
what was happening within our program, we were not taken seriously
and in fact were repeatedly challenged, questioned, and even maligned.
Gititi suggests that work on race and diversity is often deemed worthy
and meritorious when done by white colleagues, but when people of

color do it, it is often discounted as whining or as evidence that we are simply incapable of doing other kinds of scholarship.[51] Perhaps paradoxically, I felt that my ability to teach courses about race, racism, and women of color was, in fact, valued within the program and university. But my attempt to actually address race, racism, and the marginalization of women of color within the program was not acceptable and led to the hostility I subsequently experienced. In fact, calling attention to racism within academia, for faculty of color, often risks being labeled as uncollegial, a somewhat vague and general charge, but one with unique power when it comes to processes of tenure and promotion. At the same time, as Ng suggests, gender and race relations within the academy function to undermine the authority and credibility of women of color faculty, producing even greater subordination and marginalization.

To my knowledge A has never taken responsibility for any of her actions, nor has she been held accountable in any way by the university. Rather, her attempt to frame the issues as simply a personal conflict between her, X, and me indicates her insistence on equating our positions and erasing all power inequities and hierarchies. She refused to hear our concerns and grievances and instead evaded the power differences between us as well as any personal or professional accountability. Other colleagues within the program, some of whom claimed to be "antiracist" feminists, nevertheless colluded with A in her discriminatory treatment and harassment of X and me and contributed to an increasingly hostile climate for us. The university states as part of its mission the policy to support and retain faculty of color, but as discussed in the previous section, this policy was never implemented.

Even more egregious than A's actions was the university administration's failure to protect us from racial discrimination, bullying, harassment, and retaliation. We dutifully attempted to go through each of the university's official processes to address our grievances and improve our working conditions. Yet we were repeatedly punished for doing so. We were cast as the problem and as troublemakers; we were the subjects of rumors and lies; and we suffered both professionally and personally. My attempts to work within the system left me increasingly frustrated over the administration's failure to address our labor rights and my growing awareness of the limits of affirmative action and legal interventions. My experience led me to question whether justice is even possible within the current US academic institutional framework.

Rather, the administration seemed more focused on protecting A and her position within the university. Once we began to challenge the power dynamics within the program, X and I were increasingly cast as outsiders, interlopers, and noncitizens, while A, a white woman, was protected at our expense. As women of color faculty our contributions to the university were rarely recognized. We were treated primarily as visible representatives of minority groups, tokenized within the program, showcased on university committees, and expected to enhance the diversity of the institution. In addition an emphasis on mediation, "unlearning prejudice," and "healing" within both the women's studies program and the university effectively individualized the issues, framing them as simply interpersonal and undermining the necessity for political organizing, analysis, and action. As Ng suggests, such approaches, which frame harassment as attitudinal and individualistic problems, often mask the ways in which racism and sexism are systemic. And Mohanty writes, "if complex structural experiences of domination and resistance can be ideologically reformulated as individual behaviors and attitudes, they can be managed while carrying on business as usual."[52] In this way the university administration's focus on "managing diversity" (and managing the discrimination we and others experienced), within a neoliberal political economy, resulted in an ahistorical and depoliticized approach to addressing not only our grievances but also "diversity" in general. How, then, did A come to be seen as a legitimate citizen within the university, while X and I were not?

APA women and other women of color, while growing in numbers, are still relatively rare on US campuses and like other women of color are generally concentrated in junior ranks and among part-time and nontenure lecturer positions. Also, APA women have one of the lowest tenure rates of all faculty groups in the United States and continue to face multiple forms of discrimination and inequality within the academy.[53] The restructuring of the university leads to a restructuring of faculty positions, leading to more contracting out of teaching. It also shifts relations of labor among different faculty constituencies, parallel to the university's shift in relation to national and state interests. The privatization of higher education, according to Mohanty, results in a shift from an emphasis on social justice to a management perspective as well as a growing division between tenure-track faculty and an increasing number of contract workers, marking the creation of a "permanent underclass of professional workers in higher education."[54] Research indicates that women of color and other faculty from subordinated groups are more likely to be lecturers, untenured, with disproportionately lower salaries.[55] Privatization turns citizens into consumers, making profit central. And citizenship itself is actively redefined for university faculty through this restructuring. This division of labor is both gendered and racialized, so that the majority of women of color faculty working in the US academy occupy the lowest and least secure positions. Hence citizenship within the academy, aligned with the state, is also gendered and racialized.

These processes contribute to the complex experiences of women of color in tenure-track faculty positions within the academy, shaped by assumptions about citizenship and belonging. I believe the intense hostility X and I experienced was due, in part, to dominant perceptions of us as stepping outside the acceptable roles for us within US higher education and women's and gender studies. As APA women we were expected to be passive and subservient and also low ranked, untenured, and acting primarily as service providers. We were expected to function as cheap—or cheapened—labor, invoking Cynthia Enloe's discussion of the processes that produce certain bodies as cheap labor, imported to perform the dirty work that the "real" citizens within the academy do not want to do.

Bannerji, discussing her experience as a woman of color in women's studies, writes, "I am an exception in the universities, not the rule. As a body type I am meant for another kind of work."[56] In fact, she suggests, women (and men) of color in such contexts are "made to feel like 'guest workers,' eternally labeled and marginalized as 'migrants,' 'aliens,' and 'outsiders.'"[57] In this program the condition under which X and I might have been tolerated was that of subservience.[58] Alternately, assimilating to perform whiteness, or acting as Native Informants, sometimes allows women of color faculty special token status within the university system. Jasmin Zine, writing of the Canadian academic context, describes how for a period of time she was able to gain social currency through cultural conformity, "passing" as an assimilated foreigner ("the good immigrant"), but despite her efforts she could "never really own or claim national identity," which is always already reserved for white members of society.[59] Agathangelou and Ling, asking why so many women of color faculty "fail" in the US academy, conclude that for faculty of color, there exist hidden "subsidiary criteria": "a series of private rules and power relations operating behind the public rhetoric of tolerance and diversity . . . [that] rationalize racism, sexism, and classism in order to screen out persons who do not fit the academy's designation of who and what a faculty of color should be."[60] And women of color who achieve too much are often punished for it.

In response to inhospitable work environments many women of color faculty members choose to relocate or to leave academia altogether.

The cost of moving, Gititi suggests, is a lack of stability, often internalized by those who move.[61] I use the term "academic migration" to describe the moves we make and to situate those of us in the academic job market within a larger global marketplace in which people of color are simultaneously often considered hot commodities and objects of cheap labor. In drawing this connection, I acknowledge the relative privilege those of us who work in academia may experience in relation to the majority of the worlds' workers.

I do not mean to suggest an easy conflation between our migration between and among institutions and the ways in which migrant workers within the global economy are most likely to be women of nations deeply affected by structural adjustment programs and other processes associated with globalization. However, as women of color many of us have ties to this context of migration within our own families and communities, and my intent is to link our movement, structured as it is by race, class, gender, and nation, to other broader movements also structured by state apparatuses and global inequities. In this way I draw attention to the ways in which women of color are often already marked as "service providers" within a global economy structured by race, gender, class, and nation and are subsequently also seen as embodying this role within the academy. Additionally, linking our struggles to migrant labor movements highlights the ways that economic exigencies are mediated through state apparatuses that produce racialized, gendered subjects.[62]

The controlling images discussed above contribute to an academic class structure in which women of color faculty constitute what Agathangelou and Ling refer to as "a domestic underclass or foreign migrant community, regardless of personal history," seen as temporary workers and commodified as such.[63] Our presence in the university is likened to the legalized noncitizen: "You can live here, but don't get too comfortable," writes Matsuda, who suggests that achieving citizenship within the academy means abandoning one's home locations, denying one's own indigenous knowledge, and "naturalizing the dominant worldview in one's own body and soul and teaching and scholarship."[64] In addition the politics of language produce a discursive struggle within the academy, in which the linguistic space of women's and gender studies and other disciplines is also racialized, shaping what counts as legitimate theory or knowledge.

In her discussion of the origins of mainstream women's studies Bannerji refers to a "little club of white women . . . [whose] self-ness made them so unselfconscious. They never considered their ideas irrelevant, their lives marginal, because they so happily were the centre, the creators/subjects of their discourse."[65] Race and gender are integral to the organization of this space, and a colonialist-imperialist legacy leaves few options for women of color faculty in the US academy— "slave, servant, or prostitute."[66] But X and I occupied ostensibly higher and more stable positions within the program than most of the white women adjunct and fixed-term instructors, resulting in a peculiar brand of outrage and hostility among several colleagues, in particular A, who held direct supervisory power over us. Hence the ways in which academic citizenship, often considered primarily in terms of the tenure system, is always already racialized elucidates how more highly ranked women of color faculty members confront specific forms of oppression, often associated with perceptions of our transgressions within the university system. Harris and González suggest that such microagressions—which may be subtle or implicit—are often the result when academic women of color thwart expectations of them as service workers.[67]

Given the results of the mediation, it became clear that the administration and our colleagues had no interest in restructuring the workplace or addressing the racism within the women's studies program. In this way racism was further reinforced and normalized, and we were alienated from our labor as we were continually denied the truth and integrity of our own experiences. This consolidation of power and oppression within the new corporate academy and the alliance between the university and capitalism/economic globalization are bolstered by racialized, sexualized systems of exploitation that produce consumer-citizens. And these systems, Mohanty suggests, include not only unequal labor relations and campus cultures structured by racism and sexism but also the marginalization and potential cooptation of our struggles for social justice.[68] The ways in which women's and gender studies colludes in this restructuring of the university, risking cooptation and accommodation, have not yet been adequately addressed. Along with the gains for some there are intense losses for others, both material and abstract.

Of particular concern to me is the power of a predominantly white managerial class to define the terms of "racial diversity," often insisting on individualistic rather than structural understandings of power and privilege, entrenched within a liberal pluralist conception of diversity. Within such a model, according to Ng, universities rely on "prejudice-reduction" approaches, with emphases on neutrality, objectivity, and "fairness," which effectively conceal unequal distributions of power, rather than analyses of structural systems of oppression. For example, when X and I attempted to address racism, and specifically A's discriminatory treatment of us within our program as a structural form of oppression, we were met with resistance by colleagues and administrators who repeatedly reframed our grievances as an individualistic, interpersonal issue. This reframing shifted the focus to "mediation" and "healing," rather than any meaningful analysis of the underlying factors that produced a hostile work environment for us as women of color in the academy.

In this chapter I have offered an analysis of my experiences within a women's studies program as a situated critique and one example of a structural analysis of systems of oppression that shape the experiences of women of color in the university. In doing so, I challenge and critique the increasingly ahistorical, depoliticized understandings of "diversity" in the academy. Also important to note is that my hire, through a special diversity initiative, was not supported in any way by an infrastructure or administration cognizant of the larger, systemic issues of power and privilege. As mentioned earlier, the funding granted to the program for my retention was never disclosed to me, and I did not receive any of it. My service load was excessive. There were no programs in place at the university to support faculty of color, through either professional development or community building, and there were no resources to diminish the sense of isolation and tokenism we experienced. Finally, when I worked within the system to report and try to remedy the hostile work environment of the program, I was repeatedly punished for doing so.

An alternative approach, focused on social justice rather than management of the status quo, would require a focus on structural models of power and privilege within the academy. University initiatives to enhance diversity or multiculturalism should refer to best practices in hiring and retaining faculty of color, recognizing that such processes are ongoing and require consistent support and commitment, especially at the highest levels of administration. University programs specifically designed to educate faculty, staff, and students about intersecting systems of oppression, discrimination, and power should undergird this work. And faculty from underrepresented communities should be offered additional support and resources to counter the hidden labor often associated with our positions. Finally, reports of discrimination in the academy should be taken seriously by colleagues and administrators, thoroughly investigated, and directly addressed.

In women's and gender studies and other disciplines ostensibly committed to social justice, attentiveness to these practices is particularly important. In addition we require a greater understanding of the power differences between tenure-track and contingent faculty, using an intersectional framework that emphasizes race, gender, class, and other social categories that structure our experiences. The increasingly corporate US academy is of critical significance to feminist struggles and decolonizing practices, and analyzing the impact of racialized gender must be central to women's and gender studies.

Epilogue

For a long time after my resignation I considered taking legal action. I was encouraged to do so by a number of colleagues, who urged me to make the situation public in order to prevent even more faculty of color from similar experiences. I even met with a prominent labor and civil rights attorney, who stated that I had a strong case and informed me that he had received so many complaints about this particular university that he wondered if we might have a class action suit. However, I also talked with friends and colleagues who had pursued legal action in similar cases at other institutions. From them I heard about years of stress, pain, and public humiliation. I was discouraged by the fact that each of the mediation processes I had participated in had failed and that even a grievance filed with the university's office of affirmative action had had almost no effect. Also, I was beginning to experience health problems associated with stress, and I feared the potential effects this might have on my family. So I made the difficult personal decision to leave the university—the best decision for me at that time. However, I realize that each situation is unique, and I hope others in similar circumstances will have greater options to pursue various forms of justice within such contexts.

While not the case for the majority of women of color in the academy, my story has a happy ending. I was fortunate enough to be offered a tenured position in a women, gender, and sexuality studies program. Once again I was hired through a special diversity initiative. However at this university it was clear to me from the outset that the administration had carefully considered the implications of such initiatives, including thinking through best practices for retention of faculty of color and others representing marginalized communities. I was also fortunate to find myself surrounded by colleagues who support and value my work on women of color studies and transnational feminisms and provide encouragement, collaboration, and mentoring. After my previous experience

I'm too cynical to believe any longer in "home" in the academy, but for now I am happy to be immersed in an intellectual community where our many differences are acknowledged and respected.

Acknowledgments

For their support and invaluable feedback, I wish to thank Priya Kandaswamy, Marie Lo, Reshmi Dutt-Ballerstadt, Hillary Jenks, Susan Shaw, Qwo-Li Driskill, and Melinda de Jesús. I also gratefully acknowledge a summer writing grant I received from the School of Language, Culture, and Society at Oregon State University, which enabled me to complete this paper.

Notes

1. Paula Gunn Allen, Off the Reservation: Reflections on Boundary-Busting, Border-Crossing, Loose Cannons (Boston: Beacon Press, 1998), 134.

2. Chandra Talpade Mohanty, Feminism without Borders: Decolonizing Theory, Practicing Solidarity (Durham, NC: Duke University Press, 2003), 178.

3. Shirley Geok-lin Lim, "The Center Can(not) Hold: US Women's Studies and Global Feminism," Women's Studies Quarterly 26, nos. 2–3 (1998): 30–39, 31.

4. Sandra Gunning, "Now That They Have Us, What's the Point? The Challenge of Hiring to Create Diversity," in Power, Race, and Gender in Academe: Strangers in the Tower? ed. Shirley Geok-Lin Lim and Maria Herrera-Sobek (New York: Modern Language Association, 2000), 171–182.

5. Roxana Ng suggests that such work enables us to explicate the systemic character of racism and sexism. She writes, "I maintain that in so doing, we move away from treating these incidents as idiosyncratic, isolated 'wrong doing' perpetrated by a few individuals with attitudinal problems. Instead, we aim at a fundamental re-examination of the structures and relations of universities, which have marginalized and excluded certain groups of people historically, and continue to do so despite equity measures implemented in the last ten years or so" (191). See Ng, "'A Woman Out of Control': Deconstructing Sexism and Racism in the University," Canadian Journal of Education/Revue canadienne de l'education 18, no. 3 (1993): 189–205.

6. Himani Bannerji, Thinking Through: Essays on Feminism, Marxism, and Anti-Racism (Toronto, ON: Women's Press, 1995), 13–14.

7. Aida Hurtado, The Color of Privilege: Three Blasphemies on Race and Feminism (Ann Arbor: University of Michigan Press, 1996), 149.

8. Mari J. Matsuda, Where Is Your Body? And Other Essays on Race, Gender, and the Law (Boston: Beacon Press, 1996).

9. Benjamin Baez, "Race-Related Service and Faculty of Color: Conceptualizing Critical Agency in Academe," Higher Education 39 (2000): 363–391.

10. Bannerji, Thinking Through, 42.

11. For a greater discussion and critique of excessive service loads for women in the academy, as well as the gendered division of labor within university settings, see Shelley M. Park, "Research, Teaching, and Service: Why Shouldn't Women's Work Count?" Journal of Higher Education 67, no. 1 (1996): 46–84.

12. Maria P. P. Root, Multiracial Experience: Racial Borders as the New Frontier (Thousand Oaks, CA: Sage, 1996); Racially Mixed People in America (Thousand Oaks, CA: Sage, 1992).

13. Matsuda, Where Is Your Body? 168.

14. Mary Romero, "Learning to Think and Teach about Race and Gender Despite Graduate School: Obstacles Women of Color Graduate Students Face in Sociology," in Is Academic Feminism Dead? Theory in Practice, ed. The Social Justice Group at the Center for Advanced Feminist Studies, University of Minnesota (New York: New York University Press, 2000), 283–310.

15. Yolanda Flores Niemann, "The Making of a Token: A Case Study of Stereotype Threat, Stigma, Racism, and Tokenism in Academe," in Presumed Incompetent: The Intersections of Race and Class for Women in Academia, ed. Gabriella Gutiérrez y Muhs, Yolanda Flores Niemann, Carmen G. González, and Angela P. Harris (Boulder: University Press of Colorado, 2012), 336–355.

16. Shirley Hune, Asian Pacific American Women in Higher Education: Claiming Visibility and Voice (Washington, DC: Association of American Colleges and Universities Program on the Status and Education of Women, 1998).

17. Shirley Hune, "What's Changed and What Hasn't? Asian American, Native Hawaiian, and Pacific Islander Women in Higher Education, 1998–2010," On Campus with Women 39, no. 3 (2011), Association of American Colleges and Universities, accessed June 16, 2012, http://www.aacu.org/ocww/volume39_3/feature.cfm?section=3#_hune.

18. Sumi K. Cho, "Asian Pacific American Women and Racialized Sexual Harassment," in Making More Waves: New Writing by Asian American Women, ed. Elaine H. Kim, Lilia V. Villanueva, and Asian Women United of California (Boston: Beacon Press, 1997), 164–173, 165.

19. Patricia Hill Collins, Black Feminist Thought: Knowledge, Consciousness, and the Politics of Empowerment (New York: Routledge, 2000).

20. Hune, Asian Pacific American Women.

21. Ibid., 16.

22. Matsuda, Where Is Your Body? 168.

23. Ibid., 122.

24. Karen D. Pyke and Denise L. Johnson, "Asian American Women and Racialized Femininities: 'Doing' Gender across Cultural Worlds," Gender and Society 17, no. 1 (2003): 33–53.

25. Marcia Sutherland, "Black Faculty in White America: The Fit Is an Uneasy One," Western Journal of Black Studies 14, no. 1 (1990): 20.

26. Baez notes that it is not service, per se, that is the problem. In fact, for many faculty of color "service" can function as a way to resist oppressive structures, mentor students of color, and work for and with our various communities for social justice. What is problematic, he suggests, is the university system's underlying message that service is less valuable than publishing and teaching. And because faculty members of color are often expected to perform greater service than white counterparts, Baez suggests, in "Race-Related Service," that the devaluation of service actually functions to punish faculty of color. Similarly, Park, in "Research, Teaching, and Service," discusses academic women's commitment to service, suggesting that while gender and race affect faculty workloads, it is also difficult for women faculty and faculty of color to simply abandon their service.

27. Gunning, "Now That They Have Us," 179.

28. Gitahi Gititi, "Menaced by Resistance: The Black Teacher in the Mainly White School/Classroom," in Race in the College Classroom: Pedagogy and Politics, ed. Bonnie TuSmith and Maureen T. Reddy (New Brunswick, NJ: Rutgers University Press, 2002), 176–188.

29. Niemann, "Making of a Token."

30. Anna M. Agathangelou and L. H. M. Ling, "An Unten(ur)able Position: The Politics of Teaching for Women of Color in the US," International Feminist Journal of Politics 4, no. 3 (2002): 368–98, 382.

31. Hune, Asian Pacific American Women, 4.

32. Ibid., 27.

33. Ibid., 21.

34. Hune, "What's Changed."

35. James Baldwin, "A Talk to Teachers," Talk delivered October 16, 1963 as "The Negro Child—His Self-Image," originally published in Saturday Review, December 21, 1963, reprinted in The Price of the Ticket, Collected Non-Fiction 1948–1985 (New York: Saint Martin's Press, 1985).

36. I realize it may appear that the initial opportunity to direct the program represented the university's intention to offer me greater institutional power. However, the possibility of this directorship came with no additional resources, increase in salary, or support. In other words, it appeared to me at the time to represent the least expensive, easiest solution for an administration that ultimately did not support the success of the program or my work within the institution.

37. Angela P. Harris and Carmen G. González, "Introduction," in Gutiérrez y Muhs et al., Presumed Incompetent, 1–14, 6.

38. Cho, "Asian Pacific American Women," 165.

39. Sutherland, "Black Faculty in White America," 19.

40. I should note here that there was one woman of color included in this group of fixed-term faculty. Her presence—and her repeated claim that racism simply did not exist in the program—illuminates the complexity of these dynamics and the need to discuss cross-racial hostility within feminist and women's studies organizations, internalized racism, and the ways in which women of color in the academy can undermine one another, act as gatekeepers, and align ourselves with dominant power structures in order to access greater privilege.

41. Mohanty, Feminism without Borders, 184–185.

42. Gititi, "Menaced by Resistance," 182.

43. Ibid., 182.

44. Pyke and Johnson, "Asian American Women."

45. Bannerji, "Thinking Through," 62.

46. Ibid., 7.

47. George J. Sefa Dei and Agnes Calliste, Power, Knowledge, and Anti-Racism Education: A Critical Reader (Halifax, NS: Fernwood, 2000), 11.

48. Dei and Calliste, Power, Knowledge, 11.

49. Bannerji, Thinking Through, 11.

50. Ibid., 47–48.

51. Gititi, "Menaced by Resistance," 179.

52. Mohanty, Feminism without Borders, 210.

53. Hune, "Asian Pacific American Women," 17–18.

54. Mohanty, Feminism without Borders, 178–179.

55. Matsuda, Where Is Your Body? 123.

56. Bannerji, Thinking Through, 61.

57. Ibid., 153.

58. Ibid., 138.

59. Jasmin Zine, "Unsettling the Nation: Gender, Race, and Muslim Cultural Politics in Canada," Studies in Ethnicity and Nationalism 9, no. 1 (2009): 146–163, 148.

60. Agathangelou and Ling, "Unten(ur)able Position," 370.

61. Gititi, "Menaced by Resistance," 187.

62. Lisa Lowe, Immigrant Acts: On Asian American Cultural Politics (Durham, NC: Duke University Press, 1996), 14.

63. Agathangelou and Ling, "Unten(ur)able Position," 382.

64. Matsuda, Where Is Your Body? 128.

65. Bannerji, Thinking Through, 108.

66. Agathangelou and Ling, "Unten(ur)able Position," 384.

67. Harris and González, "Introduction," 3.

68. Mohanty, Feminism without Borders, 174.

Toxic or Intersectional?

Challenges to (White) Feminist Hegemony Online

Suey Park and David Leonard

If we look online, it might seem as if the Internet and social media have contributed to a growth in feminist discourse and practice. If we look specifically at Twitter or in the comment section of any number of online publications, we might conclude that not only is feminism mainstream but so too is the vigor of feminist debates that has increased over the years. However, we are also bound to witness a level of contentiousness, especially between black and white feminists, that might lead us to question the viability of a multiracial feminist movement. While social media provides visibility to any number of debates, the types and level of discourse has done little to advance racial harmony. Notwithstanding the saturation and hypervisibility, notwithstanding the spectacle, the emergence of online feminism has *not* ushered in a new "postracial" moment. Rather, it has rehashed the same racial tensions and conflicts within feminist movements from the past.

Despite promises of an online space devoid of race, where democracy reigns supreme, where equality emanates from a myriad of platforms, the Internet mirrors and recapitulates the violence, inequality, and ideologies governing everyday life. Race, gender, sexuality . . . they all matter online.[1] That is, just as "real world" institutions and ideologies reflect and perpetuate the idea that "all the women are white, all the blacks are men," virtual reality is no different. Amid a persistence of debates and tensions within various feminist circles, amid a feeling of exclusion, a number of black feminists have taken to social media to stake their claim on antisexist and antiracist organizing. In a recent exposé in *Ebony*, Jamilah Lemieux documents the resurgence of black feminist organizing and the importance of online spaces: "Gone are the days in which feminism is easily dismissed as the territory of privileged white women or limited largely to those who live in academic and activist circles. There is an emergence of boldly Black feminist thought spreading via big and small screens. . . . An outspoken group of young Black feminist writers have also been able to galvanize readers across the world with their ruminations about the intersection of race and gender."[2] The Internet has become a central front for black and other women of color feminist activists, who have used the space, the community, and the ability to speak back against racism and sexism to advance feminist discourses.

Within this context, we reflect on the emergence of, yet historic continuity in, online black feminism. We argue that the persistent foreclosure on black women's voices and intersectional frameworks engenders black feminist organizing on- (and off)line. Online spaces have proven to be particularly important in documenting the persistent violence experienced by black women and girls and also in challenging those who engage in silencing marginalized groups, who refuse to account for white (middle-class, heterosexual) privilege, and who accept and promote discourses of civility and appropriateness, even though they invariably silence countervoices.

We take up these issues, focusing on the many ways that "women are still white" in the real world and in virtual reality. As an Asian American female writer and activist and a white male writer and professor, both not only committed to advancing conversations about patriarchy and misogyny but also realizing "freedom dreams,"[3] we have been disappointed by widespread efforts to silence particular online voices. As writers and scholars who regularly write on issues impacting black women, who learn from the literature, scholars, and activists that are part of black feminist traditions, who collaborate with black feminists who routinely bear the burden of racism and sexism online and offline, and who work to be accomplices in the work of black feminism, we came together to reflect on how discourses around toxicity and tone are regularly used to silence and control black feminist thought and the black feminists who use social media platforms to speak truth to power.

As a Korean American woman, Suey Park's proximity to blackness became a pivotal marker in her activism by initially being seen as "nonthreatening." Through various mediated conversations, Park emphasizes

the need to reject the model minority status Asian Americans can frequently occupy. As a wedge group, Asian Americans are frequently used
to justify the logics of racism. Cultural values are often attributed to the
success of Asian Americans as a way to hide the reality of black suffering
that is structurally sanctioned. Through an emphasis on multiculturalism,
differences between people of color get erased. As an Asian American
woman, Park receives the most pushback when raising the issue of Asian
antiblackness in which relative privilege on the racial hierarchy means
Asian empowerment depends on continued antiblackness.

By choosing women of color feminism as a political identity over
Asian American nationalism, Park has been labeled "toxic." Many negative stereotypes against blacks are heightened in contrast to positive
Asian stereotypes, which we know are distortions. This rejection of
the model minority status makes the demonization of Asian American
women identifying as women of color second nature, as the rhetoric of
toxic is mediated through political proximity to blackness.

David Leonard, as a while male accomplice, enters into these spaces
with an eye on accountability and respect for community. Both on- and
offline, Leonard connects to these struggles as an accomplice against racism, misogyny, homophobia, and systems of violence. He is guided by the
words of activists and scholars who regularly challenge those invested in
justice to move beyond titles and "checking privilege" to take risks in
the name of equity and change. In a blog post entitled "Accomplices
Not Allies: Abolishing the Ally Industrial Complex," Indigenous Action
Media highlights the importance of moving beyond allies: "Accomplices
aren't motivated by personal guilt or shame, they may have their own
agenda but they are explicit. Accomplices are realized through mutual
consent and build trust. They don't just have our backs, they are at our
side, or in their own spaces confronting and unsettling colonialism. As
accomplices we are compelled to become accountable and responsible
to each other, that is the nature of trust."[4]

Whereas online environments facilitate individualized discourses,
competitiveness, and talking, in being an accomplice with minimal
consequences (rarely is the violence directed at Leonard), it is crucial
to listen, to support, and in moments of immense hostility be present
not "to protect" as "savior" but to disrupt and challenge the efforts to
constrain and contain conversations of race and racism. This can be
challenging because as a male-identified feminist, Leonard recognizes
his privilege as a white heterosexual man and the ways that his voice
is elevated. He recognizes the ways that he is insulated from hostilities

in virtual reality and everyday life, and the ways that his tone, rage, or demeanor is not challenged. In entering into spaces, he must reflect on his male privilege, whether that results in entering into conversations with a level of force or in "standing up" for peers. While not wanting to silence others, he also recognizes that, as an accomplice and as someone of privilege, he has a responsibility and an obligation to play a role of support, and in using his whiteness to challenge racism from white liberals and white feminists.

As with our activism online, in the classroom, and in communities, in this chapter we recognize our social location and the culture of violence that permeates on- and offline. The demonization of black feminists and women of color feminists and the silence from both allies and those who purportedly represent the mantle of feminism in the twenty-first century regarding these issues and those central to black feminist praxis has been disconcerting. Efforts to silence those counter-voices with accusations of toxicity contribute to a persistent erasure of black women's voices and experience.

Here we argue that, just as in communities throughout the United States, predominantly white feminist individuals and collectives are increasingly seizing virtual space, claiming ownership for the good of the community. To understand black feminist discourses online requires looking at the efforts to silence and stifle, to minimize black feminist critiques as "anger," and to virtually gentrify those spaces in the name of safety and solidarity. We argue that we must challenge the discourses of toxicity and move beyond rhetorical solidarity in the name of politics and organizing that names and challenges both racism and sexism.

Black Feminist Online

The marginalization of women of color from race-based and gender-based organizations and discourses is nothing new. Black feminist efforts to challenge the exclusion of bodies, voices, and issues are equally long-standing. The establishment of organizations and spaces dedicated to the marginalized and excluded and the commitment to theorizing the intersectional nature of identity has been fundamental to a history of black feminism.[5] The 1960s and 1970s saw ample work from black feminists who challenged their male and female counterparts to look at race and gender together (along with class and sexuality). This, along with a growing belief in a postracial moment, has led to optimism regarding coalitions, a new era for race and gender work, and recognition of the specificity of identity.

The technological possibilities in our new media world, and its disruptive impact on entrenched voices, tactics, and institutions, have furthered the optimism that feminism and antiracism have ushered in a new moment. However, according to Jessie-Lane Metz: "I have been assured a multitude of times that mainstream feminism is getting better. That each wave is better than the last. That intersectionality is upon us. . . . I am still waiting for the evidence on this one, the proof that mainstream feminism is becoming a safer space for me as a Black woman. And I am getting pretty damn tired, and increasingly angry. And I am living in that anger, because I can't think of a more reasonable response to this ongoing failure of many white feminists to be intersectional allies to Black women."[6]

This comment in many ways encapsulates the nature of feminism online (and offline). Whereas others reduce the discourse to conflict or tension, often blaming black women for fostering division by not focusing on "commonalities and shared experiences," Metz speaks of the continued failure of mainstream white feminists to deal with race, white privilege, and intersectionality. Likewise, in a piece on *Gradient Lair*, blogger Trudy Hamilton argues that the fundamental issue is that white feminists continue to see "black women as 'allies' to their feminism, not actual women or feminists."[7] Evident here and elsewhere, black feminists have taken to social media to spotlight these continued failures from white feminist institutions.

This platform, because of its technologies that allow direct responses in real time and because of the ability to carve communities dedicated to "black counterpublics,"[8] has become not only a space to make visible the invisible, to give voice to the silenced, and to organize for those denied their humanity but also a place to challenge allies. Building upon a history of black feminism, viral black feminism is both about organizing and dreaming, challenging and accountability, building and reimagining movements for equity and justice. It is a challenge to white (class) privilege, a challenge that is often erased from other spaces. It disrupts the ongoing history of white feminist movements to universalize the experience of all women as singular.

As noted by Audre Lorde, in "Age, Race, Class, and Sex: Women Redefining Difference," *intersectional discussions are key*: "Some problems we share as women, some we do not. You fear your children will grow up to join the patriarchy and testify against you, we fear our children will be dragged from a car and shot down in the street, and you will turn your backs upon the reasons they are dying."[9] Similarly, Kimberlé Williams Crenshaw reminds readers, "Sexism isn't a one-size-fits-all phenomenon."[10] Not surprisingly, black feminists and others tweeting alongside them have used online spaces to challenge the adherence to a one-size-fits-all approach.

Questioning how the term "feminist" erases race, class, and sexuality, Black Feminist Twitter has taken up the mantle of making whiteness visible within mainstream feminist organizations. Viral black feminism has thus emerged as a powerful tool in spotlighting the injustices endured and the injustices that contributed to the illegibility of black female pain. It has become a space to theorize, articulate, and document a twenty-first-century black feminism, one that remains focused on antiblack racism, persistent patriarchy, intersectionality, and reconceptualizing spaces of resistance to both hear and see black women's voices and experiences.

Black Twitter and Viral Feminism

While the challenges from black feminists regarding the failure of white feminists—and the mainstream feminist movement—to substantially deal with race, white supremacy, class, and white privilege are long-standing, social media platforms have exposed these critiques in new ways. Black feminists have seized the power of the Internet to demand visibility and voice, all while challenging the silence and invisibility of white feminists when it comes to issues of antiblack racism as well as white feminist rejections of the feminist claims made by women of color. Following the surprise release of her 2013 self-titled album, much debate took place on black female pop star Beyoncé and her place in the feminist movement.[11] Beyoncé's sampling of author Chimamanda Ngozi Adichie's TEDx talk on YouTube—"We Should All Be Feminists"—and several pieces claiming Beyoncé embodies a twenty-first-century black feminist ethos[12] sparked "Twitter wars" that became racialized in perception. That is, despite varied opinions about "Is Beyoncé a feminist?" that cut across racial lines,[13] the debate became yet another moment to discuss intersectionality and the longstanding frustrations regarding the erasure of black women's voices and experiences from hegemonic feminist discourses.

Mikki Kendall, in "Beyoncé's New Album Should Silence Her Feminist Critics," argues: "Feminism has never been one size fits all, yet much of the criticism that revolves around entertainers like Beyoncé (or corporate leaders like Sheryl Sandberg) presumes that there is a unilateral guide on how to be the 'right' kind of feminist. As we talk about rebranding feminism, about solidarity in feminist circles, even about what issues are feminist, we must remember that the movement seeks to represent people. And it must recognize that individuals will have different needs, wants, and routes to achieving their goals."[14] Mia McKenzie, however, surmised how the discourse around Beyoncé's feminist credentials became yet another moment to bear witness to larger issues at play:

> I'm here for Black feminists defending Beyoncé against criticisms that she does not deserve. But I also hope that we can call out the flaws in her feminist expressions. I understand that at some point, the Beyoncé feminist/non-feminist discussion became a line in the sand, a line past which we were no longer prepared to let white feminists go. Black feminists, Black women, have had to deal with constant disrespect from white feminists, not just over Beyoncé but over so, so many Black women and girls and at this point we are just really fucking tired of it. We defend Beyoncé because she is a symbol of the ways in which white feminists degrade, dehumanize and demonize Black women all the damn time. She is an easy example of the ways white feminists ignore and exclude Black women from "their" movements, the way they paint our experiences as secondary and inferior to their own, the way they *other* our sexuality and demean our right to own it. We defend her against white feminists because we know that we are the only ones who can and the only ones who will. We defend her because, feminist or not, she is our sister, our daughter, our girlfriend. We defend her because having the back of a Black woman being attacked by white folks is, in and of itself, part of our feminism.[15]

These debates were not so much about Beyoncé as they were about her symbolic meaning and the legibility of her feminist politics. As with the controversy following the 2012 Oscars concerning *The Onion*'s insulting rhetorics against young black Oscar-nominated actress Quvenzhané Wallis,[16] these moments elicit anger and frustration because of the history of silencing, because of a history of erasure of black women from feminist discourses, and because of the failure to account for whiteness and the resulting privileges, even though invariably the broader issues get lost in the virtual shuffle.

Such criticisms, which have become commonplace online, are not simply about a refusal from white feminists to see progressive black women like Beyoncé or First Lady Michelle Obama as fellow feminists but about the limited outrage, public discourse, and critical analysis from white feminists to a range of incidents, including the inclusion of the "n-word" at Slutwalk events[17] or British pop artist Lily Allen's racism.[18] It also has bubbled up in the aftermath of the trial and sentencing of Marissa Alexander, who fired a warning shot at her abusive husband, only to be convicted and sentenced to twenty years in prison (her conviction was eventually overturned and subsequently pled guilty for a reduced sentence)—her case presided over by a prosecutor and judge who were both white women which further discourses about the failures of white feminism to advance the causes and needs of black women. The limited coverage of her case from mainstream feminist websites, and the silence from mainstream feminist organizations[19] in this instance and with others, has furthered the Twitter wars. The absence of endorsements or public statements from leading feminist voices has contributed to a feeling that there is no place for black women in "feminist circles"; that antiblack racism continues to preclude organizing in response to violence experienced daily by black women.

Yet, these challenges have been met with condemnation that reimagines the continued history of black feminism as counterproductive, as toxic, and as threatening to (white) feminist practices. Prior to writing the controversial 2014 article "Feminism's Toxic Twitter Wars," which sparked contentious debates online, *The Nation*'s Michelle Goldberg had proven herself to be a powerful defender of white women's innocence. She has defended Sheryl Sandberg, author of the bestselling *Lean In* and the Facebook CEO who reduces the empowerment of women to economic success rather than ending patriarchy.[20] Goldberg also defended Justine Sacco, who tweeted a joke about AIDS in Africa before her flight took off, sparking #HasJustineLandedYet and the loss of her job. Both of these defenses showcased a desire to maintain white female victimhood and innocence. In the case of Sacco and Sandberg, the main concern was not their baseline survival, but bullying that was limited to the Internet. Neither of these women faced the violence that women of color face daily but instead focused on hurt feelings.

Given Goldberg's history, "Feminism's Toxic Twitter Wars" did not surprise anyone familiar with her work. In fact, it simply confirmed what we knew all along: the inability of mainstream institutions, media or otherwise, liberal or not, to represent women of color. Rather than engage the critiques that women of color have offered online, Goldberg has blamed what Sara Ahmed has named the "feminist killjoy." The feminist killjoy is someone who points to a larger problem that is manifesting in a space and is then labeled as the one who caused disruption. Therefore being afraid of toxicity online is about her fear rather than the women of color she has hurt through politics that benefit white women. There is a sincere denial to understand how white women climbing up the corporate ladder or gaining success does not mean things are getting better for all women.

On "Feminism's Toxic Twitter War"

The discourse on safety and online spaces was on full display with Michelle Goldberg's piece, "Feminism's Toxic Twitter War."[21] In the words of Jamie Kilstein: "Michelle Goldberg's writing is the print version of crossing the street when you see a group of Black people."[22] Goldberg's piece, which chastised Mikki Kendall's bullying behavior—in her creation of the popular #SolidarityIsForWhiteWomen Twitter hashtag—was on the cover of *The Nation's* print publication. There, Goldberg controls the narrative of Mikki Kendall and shapes her as unsafe and dangerous to an audience that is largely removed from digital interaction. Goldberg is able to plant the seed that digital spaces are unsafe because of intruders, an action Andrea Smith describes as "a bullying attack against those black feminist invaders of the 'safe space' of white feminism."[23]

In a world where the voices of white middle-class heterosexual men and women are privileged, it is striking that Twitter, one of the few spaces that allows counternarratives and resistance, has faced such a barrage of criticism. Audre Lorde discusses how women's magazines only published prose and rejected poetry as a "serious" form of writing when poetry was the most economical. She notes, "We need to be aware of the effect of class and economic differences on the supplies available for producing art."[24] Similarly, women of color are already excluded from major publishing platforms but are reprimanded for using available platforms such as Twitter and Tumblr to write their own stories. Lorde, always writing into the future, reminds readers, "The need for unity is often misnamed as a need for homogeneity, and a black feminist vision mistaken for betrayal of our common interests as a people."

Only those with presumed safety in dominant society fear losing their privilege of comfort, along with possession and control over discourse in online spaces. People of color face real violence on the basis of their skin color. Black, brown, and gender nonconforming bodies face police brutality, which shows that a lack of protection is normalized. The #SayHerName movement, co-organized by Kimberlé Crenshaw and other online efforts, each of which has sought to shine a spotlight on the victims of police violence and those black women who have died in police custody, speaks to the level of violence and this erasure, in which white feminists play a role through their gatekeeping efforts. In a world where whiteness means presumed innocence, safety, and entrance, there is born a fear of anything contrary to unquestionable authority. The reaction white feminists have to women of color feminists entering Twitter tends to often problematize those who point out racism rather than question the integrity of the framework being critiqued.

The invoking of toxic is particularly instructive in that it normalizes online spaces in absence of these "polluting influences." Seemingly ignoring the daily violence directed at women of color online, claims about the tranquility of online spaces in absence of these intrusions belies the facts on the ground. Dr. Brendesha Tynes et al., in "Online Racial Discrimination and Psychological Adjustment among Adolescents," found that between 30 and 40 percent of youth of color experience racism online.[25] According to Dr. Marcia Dawkins, "These young people were more likely to become depressed, anxious and, possibly, less successful academically."[26] The Internet is toxic and violent, yet Goldberg's narrative seems to reimagine virtual reality as a democratic nirvana seemingly disrupted by angry and divisive (black) feminism.

The Internet's Neighborhoods and Online Gentrification

"As Twitter makes its Wall Street debut, tensions are rising here on the spillover effects from the booming technology industry on real estate prices, rents and even the very cultural fabric of the city," wrote Malia Wollan in the *New York Times* in November 2013.[27] With a booming tech industry, it's no surprise that cities are becoming increasingly gentrified safe havens for white middle-class techies. Fostered by Google buses and friendly policies, the lived gentrification experienced by white techies is not limited to their apartments and coffee shops. It has spilled over into virtual spaces.

Whitney Erin Boesel, in *The Society Pages*, reflects on the language deployed by danah boyd, who described the ways white middle-class users leaving Myspace for Facebook mirrored "white flight." Boesel argues, "Facebook (which was at first offered only to students at the most elite universities) was associated with the middle-class ideal of attending a four year college. Slowly, a pattern began to emerge: white and Asian students, more affluent students, and more 'mainstream' students were more likely to join or migrate to Facebook, while black and Latina/o students, less affluent students, and more 'subcultural' students were likely to join or keep using Myspace."[28]

Boesel further discusses how "Facebook was safe and protected; Myspace was dangerous and full of predators."[29] History is repeating itself. Twitter is the new Myspace: a dangerous online "ghetto" that threatens white middle-class users. In other words, by not being a segregated space, Twitter is marked as an unsafe space for the white middle-class user who has to share a platform with people of color, especially when whiteness and privilege are made visible.

Just as African Americans are more likely to experience the commonplace violence online—the systemic toxicity—they are more likely to live in neighborhoods degraded by environmental hazards. According to the Associated Press, an analysis showed that "in 19 states, Blacks were more than twice as likely as whites to live in neighborhoods where air pollution seems to pose the greatest health danger."[30] Not surprisingly, African American children have an asthma rate twenty-six times that of white youth.[31] Similar inequalities are evident in the fact that the children of mostly Latina/o farmworkers are more likely to experience birth defects because of exposure to pesticides[32] and with the reality that Navajo teenagers have cancer rates seventeen times higher than the national average as a result of environmental toxins.[33]

In the discussion of Twitter feminism, the deployed language of toxic or polluting feminism is striking, given the desire to reclaim these spaces because they are toxic and a blight on feminism or progressive causes. Just as middle-class whites are returning to neighborhoods, previously abandoned and "left behind"—resulting in environmental hardship—these "crusaders" are now seeking to clean up the Internet at the expense of already marginalized voices.

Whereas others seem to be focused on cleaning up or otherwise ridding the Internet of those undesirable intrusions, there remains a community of people committed to creating a more just on- and offline space. The desire to clean up these spaces through displacing or silencing women of color, those critical yet marginalized voices, embodies a form of digital gentrification.

Gentrification represents a sociohistoric process in which rising housing costs, public policy, persistent segregation, and racial animus facilitates the influx of wealthier, mostly white, residents into a particular neighborhood. Celebrated as "renewal" and an effort to "beautify" these communities, gentrification results in the displacement of residents. This has disproportionately affected communities of color.[34] Gentrification is the result of not only policy decisions and economic incentives but also discourse that imagines neighborhoods of color as pathological and criminal, necessitating outside intervention for the good of all. We see efforts to blame "Black Twitter" for divisions, to identify women of color feminism as a toxic intrusion, as an effort to reclaim these spaces as well as attempting to do so while locating the Other as the problem.

In a recent conversation about coded racial language, Gina Harris stated that the "Internet" is the new "urban."[35] In postracial America, there is a continual desire to better mask racism rather than uproot its existence. Sarah Kendzior, who wrote her dissertation on the role of the Internet in dictatorships, states in a personal interview, "People use 'Twitter' or 'The Internet' to stand in for the specific groups of people who use online media to try to transform a power structure or challenge dominant narratives. We see rhetoric like this in countries like Uzbekistan, Kuwait or Turkey, where citizens are arrested for using the media their leaders condemn. This is why it is jarring to see similar rhetoric espoused by allegedly 'progressive' outlets who claim to stand for disparate values."[36]

This speaks to how power is maintained by oppressive forces through social control. Goldberg's use of "emotionally savaged" to refer to those who have felt burned by engaging in discourse with women of color is racially charged: "savaged" referring to the contagion that is implied as being the natural state of women of color.[37] This implies that mere proximity to women of color is toxic. Such language does not expand the conversation but instead results in a continuation of a longstanding history that imagines bodies of color as disruptive and corrupting to the national landscape.

Additionally, Goldberg racializes the call-out culture as being one directional, an act of aggression done solely to white feminists by women of color. However, in locating call-outs at the fingertips of black women, Goldberg centers the conversation on white women's fear rather than the disposability of black women's critiques and existence. There lies a preemptive fear of discourse across racial lines, and therefore any conversation that happens automatically shifts blame from the white woman's inability to understand race relations to the black woman's inability to educate.

What is missing from Goldberg's discussion and so much of mainstream liberal feminist discourses is an acknowledgment of how hegemonic understandings of whiteness and racial otherness infect definitions of safety. That is, the failure to recognize or to see the experiences of black women, to reflect on entrenched whiteness, has contributed to an investment in producing a feminist antiviolence movement built upon the entitlement to space and safety of white women. Mirroring the logics of safety in gated communities (in suburban neighborhoods or newly gentrified city streets), the lack of outrage resulting from the incarceration of rape victims, the imprisonment of women like Marissa Alexander,[38] the death of Sandra Bland in Texas, and the brutal treatment of fifteen-year-old Dajerria Becton by Eric Casebolt (a McKinney, Texas police officer), reflects a belief that feminism is only about protecting white women from gendered violence. Writing about Renisha McBride, who was shot by a homeowner as she searched for help in the aftermath of a car accident, Janell Hobson notes,

> We need to seriously reclaim solidarity and redefine the mission of a multiracial feminist movement in which racism is dismantled and our rage is put to better use. When a Renisha McBride can't seek help after a car accident without getting gunned down because a white man perceives her as a "threat" and not as a vulnerable subject, we need to have meaningful conversations on what solidarity looks like, how it will operate and how it must not serve one sect of privileged women. We are not props or theoretical talking points for white feminism. We have lives that need protecting and valuing. Now, more than ever, solidarity is about saving lives and affirming them.[39]

These issues have not been central to feminist organizing; solidarity has not yielded organizing against racism from white feminists. The systemic support for policies like stop and frisk[40] or the war on drugs, despite its devastating impact on black women, highlights the ways "white feminism" has sought power, justice, and safety through increasing the power of the state.

The lack of reflection about how the protection of white women often comes at the expense of women of color is a fundamental concern. The consequences can be seen with more police on the streets and demands for better decorum online. The support for incarceration, the organizing of state violence, and the idea that "scary and threatening" brown and black people in handcuffs equals a safe world are all about ultimate protections of whiteness and white supremacy—not creating or constructing safety.

There has been an increase in conversations on Internet laws from white feminist antiviolence advocates. While misogyny and gendered hostility against all women—white and of color—are ubiquitous online, as evidenced by repeated rape threats and death threats directed at women advancing feminist agendas, particularly women of color, we worry about the cost and consequence of empowering the criminal justice system. Given history and the criminalization of black bodies, we worry that these laws will ultimately harm feminists of color, who despite also facing ample gendered violence, will surely deal with the criminalization of critiques against racism.

That is, women of color who endure "toxicity" online will likely be subjected to demonization, policing, and punishment for their challenges against racism as they are unfairly lumped in with misogynists and are thus unjustly labeled "toxic." The culture of "safety" and "creating safe spaces," which can be seen when white feminists say, "I don't feel 'safe' sharing my opinion," not only silences the anger and rage of people of color, making their voices the problem, but erases the absence of any safety for women of color. So often, white feminist discourses speak about ending violence against women without realizing that definitions of safety *contribute to* violence against women (of color). To challenge racism and sexism means reimagining safety, reconceptualizing security and peace in the name of solidarity and justice.

Conclusion

Challenging the toxicity—racial and gendered violence—on- and offline requires looking at the issues and political agendas being articulated within these spaces. As seen in Andrea Smith's "Heteropatriarchy and the Three Pillars of White Supremacy," organizing against global oppression is strongest when we consider how our thinking and political priorities may hurt other groups.[41] White feminism isn't just a nickname or a descriptor of feminists who are white; it is a term used to group women whose political goals actually harm women of color. This is evident in the agenda setting that has long dominated white feminism. This includes pushing for a carceral state, corporate inclusion ("lean in"), and responses to gender-based violence that are not solutions for/ by women of color. By understanding that white feminism does not exist without settler colonialism, we begin to understand how it is not the origin of feminism. That is, white feminism does not exist apart from white supremacy.

The strategic location of black feminists specifically, and women of color feminism in general, has always been a political identity in which politics inform our identity. It is more than organizing around a shared identity; it is organizing around political potential and solidarity. These efforts resulted in tensions and conflicts, as more than identity is at stake.

Despite what many believe, Twitter has a particular genealogy and community. From #SolidarityIsForWhiteWomen, to #POC4CulturalEnrichment, to #BlackPowerIsForBlackMen, to #NotYourAsianSidekick, to #BlackPowerYellowPeril, to #NotYourMascot, #BlackLivesMatter, #SayHerName, and #IfIDieInPoliceCustody, we see how women of color have supported each other beyond the Twitter wars, beyond black or white Twitter. However, it is important to remember what Andrea Smith has taught us about how multiculturalism wants us to push beyond the black/white binary, when the black/white binary is the same binary that informs these racial hierarchies.

Therefore, moving forward we must remember that dismantling antiblackness must be at the forefront of our political goals in women of color spaces. In several interviews, Mikki Kendall has advocated for all women of color and has claimed a politics of women of color feminism.[42] Before #NotYourAsianSidekick started,[43] an article by Lindsey Yoo was released titled "Feminism and Race: Just Who Counts as a 'Woman of Color?'" Yoo stated, "This dismissive attitude toward Asian-Americans causes a dangerous rift in the ever-evolving journey toward true solidarity and the dismantling of racial and gender hierarchies. It's difficult, for instance, to feel like an ally when so many prominent feminists around me choose to praise and write about *Orange Is the New Black* for its portrayals of gender and race, but make almost no mention of the lazy, racist depiction of the lone Asian female character."[44] Responding to this article, Kendall reminded several Asian American women engaged in the conversation, "Black women were never given a space. We made a space."[45]

Although it is interesting that #SolidarityIsForWhiteWomen[46] intended for all women of color to voice their frustrations, we again see how the language of exclusion easily developed. It is too easy to mistake visibility with power. Michelle Goldberg falls into the trap, mistaking visibility as power and voice and concluding ultimately that "bullies" are a threat to the existing power dynamics and gains made through feminist activism. Visibility and representation is not true change. Solidarity without transformative politics is not change.

The emergence of the hashtag #StopBlamingWhiteWomenWe NeedUnity[47] in 2013 really captured a dominant ideology among white feminists: that all women should unite against patriarchy and do away with feminist infighting. The problem with this framing is that white heteropatriarchy would still exist. This is not simply about white feminism somehow including the right number of women of color, because politics of inclusion never go beyond self-improvement of dominant groups to help make their structures and spaces seem friendlier. Like #AllLivesMatter, the often uttered white retort to #BlackLivesMatter, discourses around inclusion and faux equality is pushed at the expense of understanding and challenging the specificity of racial violence and persistent inequity.

In reality, a politics of inclusion doesn't change dominant culture or political goals but, rather tends to use the labor of marginalized groups to promote the goals and causes of the elite. "Including" women of color should not be the end goal but should be seen as the very first step to understanding women of color feminism. Ultimately this cannot happen without decentering whiteness—to fight against the urge to center white victimhood and feelings and to instead understand violence against women of color.

In an effort to build toward organizing imperatives on the ground— solidarity is not a goal but a strategy in a struggle for justice and equity— we have highlighted how Twitter disagreements between white feminists and feminists of color actually highlight ideological differences that hold potential. We believe that lowest common denominator unity does not serve to end gendered violence. It does not serve to end racial violence. The effort to stifle and silence, to refashion civility and appropriateness in the name of unity, does little to advance radical transformation. Challenging privilege, rethinking definitions of civility and safety, questioning what sort of "freedom dreams"[48] are articulated, and otherwise demanding accountability and action is fundamental to struggles for justice. The emergence of Black Twitter and the presence of Black Feminist Twitter points to the potential and possibility here.

Encouraging us to reflect on the culture of social media, while dreaming of a virtual reality based in "generosity and kindness," Dr. Imani Perry reminded us in a personal interview that power, privilege, and structures of inequality remain in operation online: "Given the real power dynamics in this society, that is an inversion of the way bullying and marginalization generally works in the world of gender activism and otherwise. The commitment to narratives of white female innocence does far more damage to feminism than Twitter arguments." To reconcile these material inequalities, to rectify the violence experienced on and offline, to combat the normalization of whiteness, and to mobilize in opposition to these injustices necessitates a recalibration.

It requires interrogation of the ideas of toxicity, tone, and inclusion; it requires a decentering of whiteness in discourses around feminism and rethinking concepts of allies[49]; it necessitates a centering of black women in conversations about antiblack racism. It necessitates an effort not to minimize critiques with sensationalized headlines of "Twitter wars" that play upon established gendered and racialized tropes; it necessitates those committed to justice and transformation to expand rather than constrain discourses, to shine a spotlight on the invisible, to turn up the volume on the silenced, and to #hashtag and tweet in the name of solidarity, not "sameness."

Controlling the influx of toxic voices and "cleaning up" *those* neighborhoods is not a pathway to justice but the creation of yet another space that privileges the already privileged and empowered. An effort to gentrify digital spaces in the name of safety and dignified discourse is sweeping the Internet, hoping to cleanse "pollution" by erasing undesirable influence. Cleaning up requires looking at and challenging the silencing, which happens prior to an exchange of political ideas or dialogue. It is natural for difference (of analysis, of opinion) to exist, and listening to critique is the very first step in understanding how to undo white-centered feminism.

Women of color feminists have long since been proving that feminists of different races/ethnicities not only can get along but can find solidarity in our differences. Gentrification, virtual or otherwise, is not power. History teaches us that. Twitter teaches us that each and every day. The question is who is listening, who is talking, and who is being *blocked.* This is the history of today and tomorrow, a future that has yet to be realized but one waged each and every day. This isn't a toxic history but one committed to change.

Acknowledgments

This piece contains and builds upon a previous essay, "In Defense of Twitter Feminism," which appears at http://modelviewculture.com/pieces/in-defense-of-Twitter-feminism.

Notes

1. Beth Kolko, Lisa Nakamura, and Gilbert Rodman, *Race in Cyberspace* (New York: Routledge, 2000); Lisa Nakamura, *Digitizing Race: Visual Cultures of the Internet* (Minneapolis: University of Minnesota Press, 2007); Lisa Nakamura and Peter Chow-White, eds., *Race after the Internet* (New York: Routledge, 2011); Thuy Linh Tu and Alondra Nelson, eds., *Technicolor: Race, Technology, and Everyday Life* (New York: New York University Press, 2001).

2. Jamilah Lemieux, "Black Feminism Goes Viral," accessed March 6, 2014, http://www.ebony.com/news-views/black-feminism-goes-viral-045.

3. Robin D. G. Kelley, *Freedom Dreams: The Black Radical Imagination* (New York: Beacon Press, 2003).

4. Indigenous Action Media, "Accomplices Not Allies: Abolishing the Ally Industrial Complex," accessed June 19, 2014, http://www.indigenousaction.org/accomplices-not-allies-abolishing-the-ally-industrial-complex.

5. Patricia Hill Collins, *Black Feminist Thought: Knowledge, Consciousness, and the Politics of Empowerment* (New York: Routledge Classics, 2008); Beverly Guy-Sheftall, ed., *Words of Fire: An Anthology of African-American Feminist Thought.* (New York: New Press, 1995); bell hooks, *Feminist Theory: From Margin to Center* (Boston: South End Press, 2000); Emily Lordi, "Why Is Academic Writing So Beautiful? Notes on Black Feminist Scholarship," March 4, 2014, accessed March 6, 2014, http://thefeministwire.com/2014/03/academic-writing-black-feminism-krisof.

6. Jessie-Lane Metz, "Ally-phobia: On the Trayvon Martin Ruling, White Feminism, and the Worst of Best Intentions," July 24, 2013, accessed March 3, 2014, http://the-toast.net/2013/07/24/ally-phobia-the-worst-of-best-intentions.

7. Trudy Hamilton, "Black Women Are Not Just White Women's 'Allies' in Feminism," April 3, 2013, accessed March 6, 2014, http://www.gradientlair.com/post/47053023694/black-women-can-be-feminist-not-white-women-sidekicks.

8. Michael Dawson, "A Black Counterpublic?: Economic Earthquakes, Racial Agenda(s), and Black Politics Public Culture," *Public Culture* 7, no. 1 (1994): 195–223.

9. Audre Lorde, "Age, Race, Class, and Sex: Women Redefining Difference, Intersectional Discussions Are Key," in *Words of Fire*, ed. Guy-Sheftall, 288.

10. Cited in Lemieux, "Black Feminism Goes Viral."

11. A similar discourse has emerged on Michelle Obama's place in feminism about whether white feminists have used their voices and platforms to defend Michelle Obama from sexist and racist attacks.

12. Mikki Kendall, "Beyoncé's New Album Should Silence Her Feminist Critics," December 13, 2013, accessed March 7, 2014, http://www.theguardian.com/commentisfree/2013/dec/13/beyonce-album-flawless-feminism; Crunktastic; "5 Reasons I'm Here for Beyoncé, the Feminist," December 12, 2013, accessed March 7, 2014, http://www.crunkfeministcollective.com/2013/12/13/5-reasons-im-here-for-beyonce-the-feminist.

13. Mia McKenzie, "On Defending Beyoncé: Black Feminists, White Feminists, and the Line in the Sand," December 13, 2013, accessed March 7, 2014, http://www.blackgirldangerous.org/2013/12/defending-beyonce-black-feminists-white-feminists-line-sand.

14. Mikki Kendall, "On Feminist Solidarity and Community: Where Do We Go from Here?" August 19, 2013, accessed March 3, 2014, http://www.ebony.com/news-views/on-feminist-solidarity-and-community-453#.VPJQrazwvIU.

15. McKenzie, "On Defending Beyoncé." Emphasis added.

16. *The Onion* referred to then nine-year-old Quvenzhané Wallis, who was nominated for her role in *Beasts of a Southern Wild* (2012), as a c*** in a tweet. The outrage and condemnation was swift from black feminists, who took to Twitter, Facebook, and other online spaces to denounce the racist sexism exhibited by *The Onion*. Yet again, a perception emerged that white feminists, and those mainstream spaces imagined as white, would remain silent in the face of violence against black girls and women. See Tressie McMillan Cottom, "Did White Feminists Ignore Attacks on Quvenzhané Wallis? That's an Empirical Question," February 28, 2013, accessed March 3, 2014, http://tressiemc.com/2013/02/28/did-white-feminists-ignore-attacks-on-quvenzhane-wallis-thats-an-empirical-question; Kirsten West Savali, "Where Were White Feminists Speaking Out for Quvenzhané Wallis?" February 28, 2013, accessed March 3, 2014, http://www.clutchmagonline.com/2013/02/quvenzhane-wallis-white-feminism.

17. Brittney Cooper, "I Saw the Sign but Did We Really Need a Sign?: SlutWalk and Racism," October 6, 2011, accessed March 3, 2014, http://www.crunkfeministcollective.com/2011/10/06/i-saw-the-sign-but-did-we-really-need-a-sign-slutwalk-and-racism.

18. Janell Hobson, "Black Women, White Women and the Solidarity Question," November 27, 2013, accessed March 7, 2014, http://msmagazine.com/blog/2013/11/27/black-women-white-women-and-the-solidarity-question; Ayesha A. Siddiqi, "Lily Allen's Anti Black Feminism," November 13, 2013, accessed March 3, 2014, http://noisey.vice.com/blog/lily-allen-hard-out-here-ayesha-a-siddiqi.

19. "Free Marissa Now," http://www.freemarissanow.org/endorsements. html.

20. bell hooks, "Dig Deep: Beyond Lean In," October 28, 2013, accessed March 6, 2014, http://thefeministwire.com/2013/10/17973.

21. Michelle Goldberg, "Feminism's Toxic Twitter Wars," January 29, 2014, accessed March 3, 2014, http://www.thenation.com/article/178140/ feminisms-toxic-twitter-wars?page=full#.

22. @jamiekilstein, Tweet, January 30, 2014, accessed March 3, 2014, https://twitter.com/jamiekilstein/status/428985064761090048.

23. @andrea366, Tweet, January 29, 2014, accessed March 3, 2014, https://twitter.com/andrea366/status/428726192510746624.

24. Lorde, "Age, Race, Class," 286.

25. Brendesha M. Tynes, Michael T. Giang, David R. Williams, and Geneene N. Thompson, "Online Racial Discrimination and Psychological Adjustment among Adolescents," *Journal of Adolescent Health* 43 (2008): 565–569, accessed March 3, 2014, http://scholar.harvard.edu/files/davidrwilliams/ files/2008-online_racial_discrimination-williams.pdf.

26. Marcia Dawkins, "Miss America: Why Racism Thrives Online," September 16, 2013, accessed March 3, 2014, http://www.truthdig.com/report/item/ miss_america_why_racism_thrives_online_20130916.

27. Marla Wollan, "Twitter's I.P.O. Draws Protesters to Company's San Francisco Offices," November 7, 2013, accessed March 3, 2014, http:// mobile.nytimes.com/blogs/bits/2013/11/07/twitters-i-p-o-draws-protesters-to- companys-san-francisco-offices.

28. Erin Bossell, "New Myspace: Bringing (Re)Gentrification Back?" September 12, 2013, accessed March 3, 2014, http://thesocietypages.org/ cyborgology/2012/09/27/new-myspace-bringing-regentrification-back.

29. Ibid.

30. David Pace, "Minorities Suffer Most from Industrial Pollution," December 14, 2005, accessed February 27, 2015, http://www.nbcnews.com/ id/10452037/ns/us_news-environment/t/minorities-suffer-most-industrial-pollu- tion/#.VPI9vkJly_I.

31. Aliyah Baruchin, "For Minority Kids, No Room to Breathe," August 30, 2007, accessed February 27, 2015, http://www.nytimes.com/ref/health/health- guide/esn-asthmachildren-ess.html.

32. Susan Freinkel, "Warning Signs: How Pesticides Harm the Young Brain," March 11, 2014, accessed February 27, 2015, http://www.thenation.com/ article/178804/warning-signs-how-pesticides-harm-young-brain#.

33. Susan Freinkel, "The Navajo Nation's Ongoing Battle against Uranium Mining," March 2, 2006, accessed February 27, 2015, http://www.democ- racynow.org/2006/3/2/the_navajo_nations_ongoing_battle_against.

34. Lance Freemen, *There Goes the Hood: Views of Gentrification: Views of Gentrification from the Ground Up* (Philadelphia: Temple University Press, 2011); Daniel Jose Older, "Gentrification's Insidious Violence: The Truth about American Cities," April 8, 2014, accessed February 27, 2015, http://

www.salon.com/2014/04/08/gentrifications_insidious_violence_the_truth_about_american_cities.

35. Gina Harris, @sultryglebe, Tweet, January 30, 2014, accessed March 3, 2014, https://twitter.com/sultryglebe/status/428932438803238912.

36. Sarah Kendzior, "The Uzbek Opposition in Exile: Diaspora and Dissident Politics in the Digital Age" (PhD diss., Saint Louis, MO: Washington University, Department of Anthropology, 2012).

37. Goldberg, "Feminism's Toxic Twitter Wars," 2014.

38. Trymaine Lee, "Marissa Alexander Sentenced: Florida Mom Who Shot at Abusive Husband Gets 20 Years in Prison," May 11, 2013, accessed February 27, 2015, http://www.huffingtonpost.com/2012/05/11/marissa-alexander-sentenced_n_1510113.html.

39. Hobson, "Black Women, White Women," 2013.

40. In the name of "safety" and "security," cities like New York have implemented policies of racial profiling that disproportionately affect black and brown youth.

41. Andrea Smith, "Heteropatriarchy and the Three Pillars of White Supremacy Rethinking Women of Color Organizing," in Color of Violence The INCITE! Anthology, ed., Andrea Smith, Beth Richie, Julia Sudbury, and Janelle White (Boston: South End Press, 2006).

42. Kendall, "On Feminist Solidarity."

43. Casey Capachi, "Suey Park: Asian American women Are #NotYourAsianSidekick," December 17, 2013, accessed February 27, 2015, http://www.washingtonpost.com/blogs/she-the-people/wp/2013/12/17/suey-park-asian-american-women-are-notyourasiansidekick; Yoonj Kim, "#NotYourAsianSidekick Is a Civil Rights Movement for Asian American Women," December 17, 2013, accessed February 27, 2015, http://www.theguardian.com/commentisfree/2013/dec/17/not-your-asian-sidekick-asian-women-feminism.

44. Lindsey Yoo, "Feminism and Race: Who Counts as a 'Woman of Color?'" September 12, 2013, accessed March 3, 2013, http://www.npr.org/blogs/codeswitch/2013/09/12/221469077/feminism-and-race-just-who-counts-as-a-woman-of-color.

45. For more discussion, see "Internet Harassment of Women: When Haters Do More Than Just Hate," January 8, 2014, accessed February 27, 2015, http://www.npr.org/2014/01/08/260757625/internet-harassment-of-women-when-haters-do-more-than-just-hate; Jia Tolentino, "A Chat with Mikki Kendall and Flavia Dzodan about #SolidarityIsForWhiteWomen," August 16, 2013, http://thehairpin.com/2013/08/solidarity-is-for-hairpin.

46. Hamilton, "Black Women."

47. Adele Wilde-Blavatsky, "Stop Bashing White Women in the Name of Beyoncé: We Need Unity Not Division," December 12, 2013, http://www.huffingtonpost.co.uk/adele-tomlin/white-feminism_b_4477351.html?just_reloaded=1.

48. Kelley, Freedom Dreams, 2003.

49. @FeministGriote, Tweet, March 10, 2013, accessed March 3, 2014, https://twitter.com/FeministGriote/status/310887684954529792.

Note to Self

Joey Lusk

Dear Younger Me,

Feminism does not exist to comfort you. Comfort is transitory. Feminism is about making substantive changes to the program. It exists to discomfit you. To challenge you. To acknowledge your power and teach you how to wield it with integrity, accuracy, and effectiveness. If you are lucky, every feminist you meet will challenge you on every point, every preconception. This is their job, as it is yours. As it is mine. Therefore, I am not here to comfort you, either. I am the drill sergeant from hell. I am harsh, I am exacting, but I am not uncaring. I am writing you this letter to give you a few tools. Many of them I learned from women of color.

First, the map. I got the original map from Bernice Johnson Reagon and her essay "Coalition Politics: Turning the Century"[1]; but because none of us speaks the same language, I've decided to translate the legend. Right now, you think you're in the big tent of feminism. You're not. You and I are in a little tent, an identity caucus that represents "us" whoever "us" may happen to be. You'll notice our tent is connected to several other tents. Because it's you and me, we start out in the "white" tent. But because right now, "us" is just you and me, we can step out of this tent and over into the "white women with atypical neurological profiles" tent because of this wacky brain of ours. This is going to make you uncomfortable because this is a very small tent and you haven't yet come to terms with our condition. It's okay. I remember the terror and isolation of what it was like to live with undiagnosed mental illness. If memory serves me correctly, you'll have just stopped taking the medication for depression (because that's all you were strong enough to admit to) that made you spend several weeks' worth of nights rocking in the corner of your bedroom, pulling on your hair so as to distract you from the maelstrom of your brain, your mind, and the snapping of each tether that holds you in place. I want you to remember this tent.

Remember it as one of Reagon's "little barred rooms": spaces where groups of similar people gather to gain respite from the daunting task of confronting the other, or being the other, or, if they're doing it right, both. This tent is a place you will go when you need to disengage from the discomfort of other people. You're probably nodding your head as you make the connections between this and Sartre's *No Exit*. Yes, even in feminism, "Hell is other people." But if you poke your head outside of this tent, you'll see a much larger tent off in the distance. That's the big tent of feminism. Like I said, you're not there yet. But you will be. First you have to understand that there's a "there" to get to. Hence the map.

This is the *Kobayashi Maru* test from *Star Trek*. As a white feminist, you are up against yourself. You do not yet fully understand the implications of this, nor will you ever, fully. Your relationship to racial privilege will always be asymptotic. The more you learn, the more you realize how much there is that cannot be learned. We have an invisible disability. We do not share a visible characteristic with others like us. We don't know what it's like to have a visible community. There is no visible characteristic to the people who dispense our structural and social disenfranchisements. I know you remember the *Kobayashi Maru* test because it distilled something previously ineffable into an accessible anecdote: how to win the unwinnable scenario. The KMT was designed to be unwinnable in order to evaluate potential candidates' responses to failure. James Tiberius Kirk failed the test twice. Prior to his third try, he altered the programming on the simulation to allow for another option. There will be times, not many, when you are tempted to view feminist discourses as unwinnable situations, to feel the feminist deck is stacked against you because you are white.

Do not ever succumb to that kind of thinking. Do not ever think to play your neurological condition as a trump card, either. It's not. In the years to come you will crunch the data. This will allow you, when necessary, to argue by numbers as to why being a racial minority is not the same thing as being a white person with bipolar disorder and ADD. It will also help you understand that your racial privilege is defined by the fact that, no matter what your social location or invisible facets of difference, you always have the choice to remain silent and dwell in the comfort of that refuge. Even if you never remained silent, you would still have the choice. And that's what power is: the ability to make choices.

Thankfully, you will never seek to argue why it is unwinnable, because you will grow to understand that feminism isn't a test. No one constructed it to see how you respond to failure. No, you will change the definition of winning. You will rewrite code. And you will fail. Time and again you will get things wrong. Spectacularly wrong. Sometimes you will get things so right and people will still accuse you of cheating, of drawing from your endless reservoir of privilege and access. And you will laugh. You will think of the trump card that can't win a trick. And then you will round on them, with glee, as you challenge them on each and every one of their points. You will do your job.

And in that moment you will grow comfortable in your feminist skin. Do not succumb to comfort. You will think you have it figured out, that at last you have finally arrived at the big tent. But you haven't yet. Because a few months after that moment, you will commit a cardinal sin in feminism. You in your joyous embrace of sisterhood, power, and intellectual carnage will get so comfortable that you decide you can use a quote of Audre Lorde's without having read the text, and you won't even give it a citation. You will be one of those white feminists. Oblivious to your privilege. You will initially balk at this unspoken yet conveyed characterization. You will outwardly accept the objection, but inwardly you will lull yourself into comfort by telling yourself that Audre Lorde is ubiquitous in feminism—she's omnipresent—that you've earned the right to be casual in this because you are such a good feminist. You get everything! Except for this invisible thing you live with.

And this will eat you up. It will seem that this, this, is the unwinnable situation. And then your professor will mention it. And you will wait for the pain, the punishment, the exclusion to follow. And it doesn't. She gets mad, she mentions it, and then she proceeds to include you in a lot of community events. She will not coddle you. She will not care about how you feel in any given moment or debate. She will teach you how to be a feminist by rejecting a narrative that demands perfection as a prerequisite for membership. And in that moment you will realize that she's been to the big tent.

And in that moment you will get comfortable again. Do not succumb to comfort. You will think that now you have it all figured out, because really, what bigger mistake could you make?

And in a joyous hypomania-induced embrace of *everything!* you will have this big sea change about your own disability. And in this moment of sisterhood, solidarity, and openness, you will decide to speak for "your" group and inadvertently out someone with a different kind of atypical neurology to a group of neurotypical people. Yeah. You will go from making a grievous academic mistake to affecting someone's life, real time, immediately. That person doesn't forgive you. And you will live with that. If you check the catalogue of mistakes we've made, it's in the three thousands. You will review each of these mistakes for the rest of your life. Not because you feel bad about them—you do, and you always will—but because these moments are teaching moments.

I see you're getting comfortable and thinking, now I know. I won't make those mistakes. This is where I tell you that you need to start watching *Doctor Who* as soon as the reboot starts up. I could give you a list of every mistake we've ever made and you will still make them; you will just make them differently. Because feminism isn't about following a set of rules. There's no cheat sheet. It is a process of making mistakes. As Reagon said, "I belong to the group of people who are having a very difficult time being here. I feel as if I'm gonna keel over any minute and die. That is often what it feels like if you're really doing coalition work. Most of the time you feel threatened to the core and if you don't, you're not really doing no coalescing."[2]

That discomfort? That existential threat? That is essential. That's cognitive dissonance doing its work. When you sense discomfort, seize it. Do not push it away. Understand it. Our fears are the children of our subconscious. Our discomfort is almost always predicated on some kind of fear. And this I can say with pride: you will learn to take your fears by the hand, to gentle them, to put them to bed. You will care for your fears, and in caring for your own, you will learn to respect the fears and discomfort of others.

You're going to go on to edit Wikipedia articles, becoming one of the people who are counted among the "less ideological" set. This is going to be an invaluable experience in learning how to back your shit up. You're going to need that, because you will decide to jump out of the frying pan and into the fire. You will participate and moderate debate forums online. You're going to learn how to be an adversary. A good one. One day, you're going to show a white conservative woman how the Affordable Care Act will save her from financial ruin. She will thank you in tears of relief. You will help a bunch of white men understand that being gay is not a choice. You will help one older woman you meet randomly at a diner come to peace over her own abortion years prior, when you intrude on a conversation you overhear.

When young men of all colors come at you because they think feminism is sexist or racist, you will hand them Audre Lorde, Alice Walker, bell hooks, Octavia Butler, and Bernice Johnson Reagon. (And when someone points out that Octavia Butler isn't an academic, you will laugh and round on them with glee.) You will not help feminists of color. You will mine their work for tools that help you. White feminists do not help feminists of color. "They" don't need our help, our gracious acts of beneficence and generosity. White feminists work with feminists of color. Women may comfort and help other women, but feminists get the job done. You will get validation when you accomplish things. You don't get a cookie just for showing up.

But you read ahead, didn't you? You're recalling the part where Reagon is talking about the mistakes she made in her songwriting and how she said, "So all of these people who hit every issue did not get it right, but if they took a stand, at least you know where their shit is."[3] She said "took a stand," not "strolled into the room." No cookie.

And seriously, do not go to your professor and pull some tired "I'm just feeling a little uncomfortable, as if maybe my experience is being marginalized." She's just going to go home and laugh at you. Really? That's your argument? That's your technique? Oh, hell no.

No one wants that weak, passive bullshit on their team. If you think your experience is being minimized in class you stand up and say something. In class. But make sure you bring your A game. Be prepared for the response. If you're lucky, it will be brutal and unflinching. And I'm not saying you're wrong. You are most likely wrong, but that's not the point. You have a right to make arguments from obliviousness. I need you to make those arguments, because I need you to be challenged by strong, smart women. And not just women of color. Be prepared for white women to take you to the mat, as well. Some people like to perpetuate this crystal jiggly "We can all get along" shtick. Do not buy that for one minute. We can't all just get along. If getting along is the goal, it's the goal, not the plan for accomplishing the goal. But getting along is not the goal. This isn't family therapy. Thank all that is just and good. This is not family therapy.

Some people will try to tell you that coalition building is all about overcoming our differences and learning how we are the same special individual snowflakes underneath. This is bullshit. Coalition building is what we do when we acknowledge that we are different and that we don't agree and we don't have to and still sign on for the fact that things need to change. You are not ever going to agree with people who think women do not have the right to exploit themselves sexually when it comes to sexual politics. But you cannot dismiss them. Just like you can't dismiss women who are pro-life or anti-vaxxers or women who make you uncomfortable with their arguments about race; you as an individual must figure out a way to work with them, because working with "them" is your job. And it's not because you are white. It's because you signed on to be a feminist.

You will hear white women argue why they shouldn't have to explain sexism to men and women of color who will argue that they shouldn't have to teach white feminists about white privilege. At first, all you will hear is their anger. Then you will listen to their anger, two threads discordant and harsh. And this, my beautiful, mad, oblivious, analytical messed-up self, will be you finding the moment of your arrival in the big tent. You will not preach to the choir. You will listen to it. Even in this moment, do not succumb to comfort. Because comfort might tempt you to join in with hopes of helping these two melodies harmonize. Resist that temptation. Listen longer.

In a moment, some random event will trigger a memory of the first time you listened to *Zaireeka*, the Flaming Lips album that was meant to be played on different speaker systems. And that same (not really) random event will also trigger a memory of your anger, voiceless, because it spoke a language no one even knew existed, in a place between the world of white neurotypical women and neurotypical women of color, and in that moment a new intersection is formed. You will decide to take a risk, yes, one of those risks that usually end with you making a mistake.

You pull the part of you that is in the pews and the part of you that is at the pulpit, and you coalesce as a whole person between the angry white women and the angry women of color. You move, not to obstruct their anger or to protect anyone from it. If you listen to anger off to the side, you can't hear it clearly. If you only ever listen to anger from the sidelines, you can get to the point where you think the whole genre is bad. None of these songs have any harmony! And as you begin to hear both songs of anger more clearly, you will start to realize that they were never harmonies; they were two different songs sung in rondo.

And they weren't meant to be aesthetically pleasing, to be happy, or encouraging, to lift one up. They were meant to be statements of experience. And experience, that shit's not tidy. Sifting through the rage, the disenfranchisement, the dehumanization, the humiliation to be able to vocalize at the top of your lungs, this is who I am, this is what happened to me, this is what I did, and *this is what I learned*; that's art. It's Art with a capital A—the art of living and the art of feminism.

You weren't able to do that before this moment because you hadn't made enough mistakes from which to learn. You hadn't taken in other people's experiences and anger. And I know you, cranky contrarian pain in my ass, right now, part of you is thinking, but that last bit, that sounds like comfort. It's not. You don't listen to other people because it's a kindness you do for them; you listen to them to discover tools to help you figure your own messy experience out. The whole purpose of language, evolutionarily, is to pass on tools. Listening is a tool in itself, a tool to acquire more tools. You listen because acquiring those tools, that's your job. It's not feminism's job to figure that out for you. Pfft! And you call yourself a genius. You hate one-size-fits-all solutions. Custom tools require custom effort.

Then, right in the middle of this amazing moment where you're not learning anything, or teaching anything, you are merely standing with women who are angry, some white girl is going to waltz in and say, "Whoa, all this anger, and some of it directed at me. I'm feeling a little uncomfortable. I thought this was supposed to be a safe space." And this, this is your moment to sing, Sunshine, because this, this is what you have to contribute. And do not get comfortable in this moment, either. Having something to contribute doesn't make you better than anyone else. It makes you useful. To yourself and to others.

And you will share the story of growing up as an alien with no home. I'm not even kidding. You will actually do this. I know that right now anything that even hints of mental instability makes you uncomfortable, fearfully uncomfortable. And I won't lie; we were right to fear what would happen if people learned we had bipolar disorder. So you will talk about how that fear kept you apart from every other human being. How it kept you from getting help. How fear of what people could and, eventually, would do to you if you asked for help would keep you from living. How it almost really did kill you, several times over. How you burrowed deeper and deeper into your little barred room desperate for comfort and safety.

You will talk about what it is like to live in a world of one, because growing up with mental illness is an invisible condition. It is imperceivable, at first. It is unidentifiable. So even after you learn that something is wrong with you neurologically, it isn't like you can scan a room and find people like you to hang out with at parties. Or in school. Or at home. Not at first. You will talk about how you had to learn the languages of neurotypical people, how they don't understand that they assume they all speak the same language because they use the same words.

You will talk about how sometimes you use ugly words to describe your condition because much of the reality is ugly, and you don't always feel like making it palatable for people. How in order to talk about your experiences candidly, you demarcate them with yellow police tape and trigger warnings. How you suspect those warnings are de rigueur, not to actually protect people like yourself but to protect people like her. Not white people, but people who do not know what it's like to live with these disturbing and discomfiting facts as commonplace occurrences. You explain to her what it means to be a walking, talking trigger. How in order to be visible, you have to make people see things about you that cause them to recoil. How they often get angry with you because acknowledging the reality of your existence disrupts their happy little narrative, and in that disorientation, they confuse the power you wield to make yourself visible with an implication.

You will explain how privilege in every form comes down to the assumption that you can be and should be safe from discomfort. Privilege is the assumption that you have a right to be free of other people's painful and complicating existences. That you shouldn't have to deal with any of that because it's not your fault.

So, you will tell her about how you finally hit the bottom of your little barred room with all your burrowing in search of comfort and safety. How there was none. How when you finally got so scared and so incapable of doing it on your own, you begged for help. How one person dared you to kill yourself and another physically attacked you. How doctors who were once sympathetic to your privileged white depression now treated you like a criminal. How you went from being "one of the smartest people I know" to "you know, you are mentally ill." Overnight. How you finally had to volunteer to be locked up for days, because that was the only way you could get help. And you didn't get help. How there was never any context in which your anger would be considered legitimate, only a symptom of your pathology. How being white didn't protect you from any of that. Being "white" is conditional.

Having white skin is different from being white, in that "white" is the designation of an ideal in Western culture. Being mentally ill is not ideal. Having white skin will not protect you from the rejection of other white people. And it is not until that moment, that moment of categorical rejection, that you have any understanding of the anger that comes from racial oppression. You will always have your white skin, you will always have that layer of sheltering privilege that protects you from having your mental illness be attributed to your race. So you can never know what it means to be racially oppressed, but you have some insight into what it means to be dehumanized, dismissed, and made into a statistic. The need, the physical need you have is for someone to stand with you in all your anger—not as scapegoat, whipping boy, or architect but as existential witness.

You will tell her that being of a marginalized population is to live a life of grieving without end. That we do not blame the grieving for their anger. We do not take it personally. We stand with them so they might not be alone in a process for which there is no comfort. To stand witness to the voicing of suffering and its attending anger without judgment or internalization is not solidarity in a cause, but in a species. The ability to do this is one of the things that defines us as humans. The willingness to do this determines our capacity for change. You will tell her in the bluntest of terms: If you cannot accomplish this simplest of tasks with good faith, why would anyone trust you?

And then she will look at you with relief, because you were obviously angry, but you didn't punish her for it. You will allow her to stay. And she will say, in her discomfort and an ecstatic embrace of sisterhood, "Absolutely, I get it. I get everything. I mean suicide, really, it's so terrible! It's such a mystery!" And just like that, this oblivious neurotypical white girl tries to comfort you. She tries to comfort you. And she gets it all wrong.

You will get back to debating people on the Internet, people who are not feminists. And then maybe one day, eight years down the line, you get an e-mail from her, and she tells you that although you didn't know it at the time, she was going through a pretty horrific experience, an experience you've never had. She reminds you of her early years in the big tent, or what she thought was the big tent, and the mistakes she made. She thanks you for being the drill sergeant from hell, for challenging her on every point, preconception, and privilege. In so many unspoken words, she thanks you for providing her with a model of how anger can be incorporated productively into her own praxis. And we're all special snowflakes. No. Not even in this moment can you succumb to comfort.

Because all of this—this isn't getting the job done. This is just getting to the point of being able to start working. Yeah, buck up, Little Camper. This part is short and, actually, pretty sweet. See that once young and still oblivious neurotypical white girl? She's going to show up a lot and irritate the living daylights out of you. Oh no, not with the old mistakes of comfort and safety. She found a way to pass the *Kobayashi Maru* test, too. She will irritate you by making points that you disagree with, and she will make them well. And you will round on her with glee.

> But most of the things that you do, if you do them right, are for people who live long after you are long forgotten. That will only happen if you give it away. Whatever it is that you know, give it away, and don't give it away only on the horizontal. Don't give it away like that, because they're gonna die when you die, give or take a few days. Give it away that way (up and down). And what I'm talking about is being very concerned with the world you live in, the condition you find yourself in, and be able to do the kind of analysis that says that what you believe in is worthwhile for human beings in general, and in the future, and do everything you can to throw yourself into the next century. And make people contend with your baggage, whatever it is. The only way you can take yourself seriously is if you can throw yourself into the next period beyond your little meager human-body-mouth-talking all the time.[4]

In the twenty-second century, all the women will not still be white. White women will be a distinct minority across the globe. And this, dear Younger Me, will mean nothing to you as a white feminist, because it will change nothing. The interlocking dynamics of power will remain. Difference will remain. Distance will remain. All that will matter is whether or not you got enough people to the table to change the programming in an unwinnable scenario.

Notes

1. Bernice Johnson Reagon, "Coalition Politics: Turning the Century," in *Home Girls: A Black Feminist Anthology*, ed. Barbara Smith (New York: Routledge, [1983] 2000): 343–356.

2. Ibid., 343.

3. Ibid., 351.

4. Ibid., 352.

Part Four

RECLAIMING THE PAST, LIBERATING THE FUTURE

Mary Magdalene, Our Lady of Lexington

A Feminist Liberation Mythology

Raquel Z. Rivera

Llamó Jesús a María
Plenitud de plenitudes
Pura entre las multitudes
La de más sabiduría
El Maestro bien sabía
Que era ella su sucesora
Del rebaño la pastora
La que nuestra paz avala
Mi María de Magdala
Nuestra divina señora

Jesus called Mary
Fullness of all fullnesses
Pure among the multitudes
The wisest one
The Master knew
She was his successor
The new shepherd
She who assures our peace
My Mary of Magdala
Our divine lady[1]

I was raised Evangelical in San Juan, Puerto Rico. Then I turned atheist as an adolescent. Later, I moved to New York City and, as an agnostic adult, became immersed in popular Afro-Caribbean spirituality: Puerto Rican *espiritismo*, Cuban *santería* and *palo*, Haitian Vodou, and Dominican *vudú*.

But something felt off to me. Eventually, I gave myself the freedom to meld what I enjoyed best about collective myths and worship with my most personal and individual poetic truths. That was when I identified Mary Magdalene as my favorite myth, as my guiding metaphor in connecting with The Everything—especially with myself. She became the key to making peace with all the roads I had walked. She became the protagonist of my most intimate liberation mythologies—those I have been crafting over the course of the last decade, song by song.

Toward Liberation Mythologies

In my most recent academic work, I have been using "liberation mythologies" as the guiding concept that allows me to explore the intersections between roots musical practice, spiritual belief, utopian desires, and social justice.[2] Until fairly recently, the bulk of my academic production was devoted to hip-hop and reggaeton, and it was primarily concerned with exploring the porous boundaries between Blackness and Latinoness, as well as connecting those porous border zones with social justice activism. Those topics are still of great interest to me, but I have become increasingly engaged in looking at the spiritual dimension of political action—and most specifically in looking at the use of spirit-based myth making as a component of political action. My work focuses on Afro-Caribbean spiritual practices like *espiritismo*, *santería*, *palo*, Vodou, and *vudú*; but keep in mind that with this concept of "liberation mythologies" I'm also trying to develop a way to understand any other spiritual or religious practice that is invested in utopian desires and social justice activism.

I started developing my thoughts on liberation mythologies as I was learning, performing, and writing about the intersections between the culture and music of Puerto Rican *bomba*, Dominican *palos*, and Haitian-Dominican *gagá* (*rara*) in New York City. It struck me as significant that there were at least three powerful characters or references that kept popping up in the music: maroons or *cimarrones* who escaped slavery, the so-called Kongos of Central Africa who have a reputation for rebelliousness in Afro-Caribbean lore, and references to Haiti and Haitians. All of these are tropes that point to a centuries-long history of resistance and liberation struggles in the Caribbean. Maroons, Kongos, and Haitian revolutionaries are invoked as heroic figures from the past that are connected by "roots" and "ancestry" to artists and cultural practitioners of the present. They symbolize struggle and freedom and are the "ancestors" clearing the path for those still fighting for justice. I began focusing on documenting and analyzing how these tropes are intricately connected and how they share many basic assumptions and impulses. There was a larger picture that I was trying to understand.

Putting a slight spin on "liberation theology," I started thinking about "liberation mythology" as a potential guiding concept.[3] Taking my cue from the work on mythologies by Joseph Campbell and Robert Segal, I look at myths not as stories or beliefs that are (necessarily) untrue but as tropes that poetically attempt to explain or get us closer to the unexplainable.[4] The myth may or may not be true; my aim is not to determine if it is or if it isn't true but to explore the "dreams of freedom" at the root of myth making. I am interested in these myths as strategic tools deployed by musicians and activists to give individuals and communities the strength to keep crafting and pursuing their dreams of freedom. According to the way I'm developing the concept, what makes liberation myths different from just plain myths is that their purpose is to describe and understand the world but more importantly to change it—change, in turn, is defined in terms of personal and collective liberation from oppression, injustice, sadness, and/or fear. In other words, the goal of this mythmaking is redemption—individual and collective. This concept of liberation myths is quite similar to Robin D. G. Kelley's notion of "freedom dreams" and the black radical imagination, but one key distinction is that I focus on spirituality and religiosity in the process of freedom dreaming or mythmaking so that the "mythology" part in "liberation mythology" serves a similar purpose as "theology" does in "liberation theology."[5]

Now, if we were to take literally these claims of collective Kongo, maroon, or Haitian heritage, we would have to take them to task for distorting history. Obviously not all of us Puerto Rican or Dominican folks have Kongo, maroon, or Haitian heritage. Furthermore, as Kristina Wirtz has pointed out, the reconstruction of "roots" in Afro-diasporic music is often closer to a "divination of the past"—more a poetic than a historical interpretation.[6]

Let's take as an example the way some musicians and activists describe (and employ) the Haitian roots of Puerto Rican and Dominican music genres like *bomba* and *gagá* as a figurative bridge between Haitians, Dominicans, and Puerto Ricans. Considering the severe and longstanding conflicts between these three groups, appealing to the common Haitian roots and ancestry that they purportedly share is a myth with the liberatory political purpose of building a sense of unity among them. But what about the fact that, if taken literally, this liberatory myth is a distortion of history?

Here is where Kelley's ideas in his book *Freedom Dreams* are crucial. Kelley's recollections of being a "junior Afrocentrist" as an undergraduate provide much insight into the issues at stake in weaving liberation mythologies or, in his words, "freedom dreams" that are invested in looking backward into history to claim something necessary in order to go forward:

> We looked back in search of a better future. We wanted to find a refuge where "black people" exercised power, possessed essential knowledge, educated the West, built monuments, slept under the stars on the banks of the Nile, and never had to worry about the police or poverty or arrogant white people questioning our intelligence. Of course, this meant conveniently ignoring slave labor, class hierarchies, and women's oppression, and it meant projecting backwards in time a twentieth-century conception of race, but to simply criticize us for myth making or essentialism misses the point of our reading. We dreamed the ancient world as a place of freedom, a picture to imagine what we desired and what was possible.[7]

Kelley's work sheds a lot of light on my own mixed feelings regarding these liberation mythologies.

On the one hand, I was (and I am) inspired by their beauty and power. On the other hand, I can't help but be turned off by what sometimes ends up being an idealization of the past and essentializing assumptions. But through Kelley's work I have been better able to understand the beauty and potential of liberation mythologies. I am still wary of their reductiveness and essentialisms, though. But is it possible to celebrate the sacredness and power of these liberation mythologies without necessarily taking them literally? Can we spread and celebrate through *bomba*, *palos*, and *gagá* songs, for example, the myth of the shared Haitian roots of Puerto Ricans and Dominicans without *literally* believing (and requiring that others believe) that we all share Haitian ancestry? I think so. Considering the lofty and powerful impulses holding up these liberation mythologies, I'm more inclined to explore the freedom dreams that feed these mythologies and the liberatory practices inspired by these mythologies rather than stay stuck on arguments regarding literalist versus poetic interpretations of mythical truth.

As I have been exploring all these ideas in my academic work, simultaneously I have also been participating in this same New York Caribbean musical and cultural scene as a singer-songwriter. One day a few years back, as I was talking to Sandra García Rivera, a close friend and musical collaborator, about my liberation mythologies academic project, she responded enthusiastically and pointed out how well the concept also applies to all the songs I had been feverishly composing in honor of Saint Mary Magdalene. The connection had not dawned on me until she pointed it out. In excitement I realized Sandra was absolutely right! I had enshrined Mary Magdalene as the protagonist and central trope of my own liberation mythologies. As much as I treasured the liberation mythologies woven throughout my immediate musical and cultural community, I had unwittingly begun weaving my own mythologies that could speak to the most intimate freedom dreams and utopian desires of my heart.

Enter The Magdalene

I developed a passion for Mary Magdalene just as the millennium was coming to a close. Back then, I used to sometimes attend San Romero de las Américas Church in the Bronx for two reasons: (1) I was part of the unruly group of musicians who livened up the services with the percussive Afro-Caribbean sounds of Puerto Rican *plena* and Dominican *palos* and (2) the radical theology of a congregation that welcomed people of all faiths and no faiths, embraced feminism, shunned homophobia, and remained active in social justice struggles was right up my agnostic alley.

One Sunday, Danielline Martínez, a young deaconess raised in East Harlem, delivered the sermon that invalidated everything I knew until then about Mary Magdalene. The Bible is a historical and literary document, Danielline said that day, inspired by The Divine and filtered by our limited humanity. I was pleased to hear it inside a church. But, up to that point, I had heard nothing new.

Danielline continued: "According to the canonical scriptures, Magdalene was not a prostitute." *Say what?!* What the New Testament actually states is that Jesus cast seven demons out of her, that she gave of her resources to support Jesus' ministry, that she was present at Mount Calvary, and that she was the first person to see the risen Christ. But her name never actually appears alongside references to the anonymous biblical "sinner" (presumed to be a prostitute) who washed Jesus' feet with her tears and expensive ointments.[8]

Thanks to a sermon in 591 by Pope Gregory the Great, in which he spoke of the anonymous sinner, Mary of Bethany (sister of Lazarus and Martha), and Mary Magdalene as the same person, The Magdalene was forever linked to prostitution. Centuries later, the Vatican admitted the error in 1969: The Magdalene and the tearful sinner are *not* the same person. But despite this attempt to correct the widespread misconception, Mary of Magdala is still best known as a redeemed prostitute.

I have nothing against prostitutes or against redeemed prostitutes. But what irks me to no end is that folks insist on stamping Magdalene with a terribly ill-fitting label. How convenient: the most important woman in the social, political, religious, and philosophical movement led by Jesus got demoted by the "fathers of the Church" to repentant prostitute, to little more than a footnote.

Mary The Magdalene: She who Eastern Orthodox Christians celebrate as apostle of the apostles. The wisest among Jesus' followers, according to the apocryphal gospels. She who Jesus calls "fullness of fullnesses" and "completion of completions" in the gnostic text Pistis Sophia. The "light of the Church," according to one of the medieval songs of praise in the vellum manuscript "Legenda Sanctissimae Mariae Magdalenae."[9] The Mary whose importance was not dictated by maternity. All those images fired up my imagination.

The rumors and theories regarding her sexual or matrimonial relationship with Jesus frankly left me cold. In fact, they seemed to me both boring and downright suspicious. My gut reaction was: Here we go again—to have central importance as a woman in Christianity you either have to be Mary the Mother or Mary the Wife/Lover. Here we go again—only through her relationship to the male does the female get validated. The male, however, needs no female validation. Jesus, according to the dominant Christian doctrines, was whole and sufficient unto himself, just like his Daddy.

I was thoroughly annoyed with Dan Brown's 2003 novel *The Da Vinci Code* (and the public furor around it) for that reason—among others. But little by little I have made an effort to understand why the millenarian heresy that Brown's book is based on holds such power for some: Magdalene and Jesus, two sides of the same coin and also the embodiment of The Lovers archetype, which competes with the archetype of The Divine Victim represented by the virginal crucified Jesus. Two bodies, one Christ: He Who Knows and She Who Knows. It was through the many conversations that I had with painter Tanya Torres, my friend and collaborator in Magdalene artistic adventures, that I was motivated to go deeper into why different versions of The Magdalene myth might appeal to different people.

But the part in that millenarian heresy that is irredeemably unpalatable to me is the theory that the blood of Jesus and Mary Magdalene runs through the veins of the European nobility. What a demoralizing take on the story! Descendants of the "illuminated" Middle Eastern couple? Who? Those shameless European elitists who lived in opulence as the common people died of hunger? Those despicable characters who profited most from the colonialism, genocide, international slave trade, and imperialism of the last few centuries?

The theory that Jesus and Mary Magdalene were the bearers of a so-called royal bloodline that later was propagated across Europe is certainly a convenient and romantic justification for perpetuating oppressive dynasties. Ugh! How annoying. Was it not enough for Eurocentrists to whiten Jesus and blondify Mary Magdalene? Must the purported couple also be used to justify patrician hierarchies?

The Penitent Magdalene

Who is the most famous penitent sinner and repentant prostitute of all time? Mary Magdalene, no doubt.

In European Medieval and Renaissance paintings by El Greco, Titian, Artemisia Gentileschi, El Españoleto, Gaspard Dughet, Georges de la Tour, Murillo, Paolo Veronese, and others, all titled "Penitent Magdalene," she appears with her mythical alabaster jar, a book, and/or a skull. It's this last item that hypnotizes me: symbol of contemplation and wisdom, of rejection of frivolity. I couldn't help but sneak it into my *Las 7 salves de La Magdalena/7 Songs of Praise for the Magdalene* CD cover artwork (Figure 2).

All those penitent Magdalenes, painted with particular zeal in the sixteenth and seventeenth centuries, are gorgeous, intriguing, fascinating. Usually teary and blond, sometimes bony and other times plump, these Magdalenes are mystical celebrations of repentance and surrender

Figure 2. *Las 7 Salves de La Magdalena* CD cover art. Design by Zachary Fabri. Photo by Jorge Vázquez.

that still always dwell on her alleged concupiscent past. The result? A viscously lascivious subtext. The underbelly of the moralizing sermon is swarming with lustful interests. The redeemed prostitute: the holiest, the sexiest, the tastiest.

And so, to this day, the myth of the prostituted Magdalene persists.

People! Didn't the Catholic Church admit decades ago that Pope Gregory made a lamentable mistake in interpreting the scriptures when he conflated The Magdalene and the anonymous repentant sinner? What happened? How many times does it need to be repeated?

I am irritated to no end with this our collective obsession with the penitent Magdalene. Why the focus on the sins of she who was most faithful among Jesus' followers? Why not focus on Judas, who (one version of story says) betrayed Jesus with a kiss? Why not focus on Peter, who denied him three times and, what's worse, was the rock upon which a message of liberation became rebuilt as an instrument of power?

These were the questions that led me to write around 2001 the first of my songs for Mary Magdalene, which I titled "Al pie de la cruz/At the Foot of the Cross." The source of the story was biblical but filtered through my Caribbean spiritual experiences and musical practices. So the lyrics and music flowed and syncopated out of me in the form of one of my favorite musical genres: *salves* from the Dominican Republic.

Al pie de la cruz, Magdalena
Al pie de la cruz, Magdalena
(coro) Al pie de la cruz, Magdalena
Al pie de la cruz, Magdalena

Divina María Magdalena
Allá en El Calvario, mi morena

Con las dos Marías estaba ella
Mi santa María Magdalena

Pedro lo negó, nunca ella
Discípulo amado, Magdalena

Judas a Jesús traicionó
Magdalena nunca lo abandonó
Ella ungió los pies del Maestro
Fiel a su Jesús, vivo o muerto

Si los pies de Jesús lavó María
Por ella lo mismo él haría

A la diestra del buen Jesús
Divina María de la Luz

Al pie de la cruz, al pie de la luz
Al pie de la luz, mi morena

Magdalena fiel siempre fue
Divina María de la Fe

At the foot of the cross, Magdalene
At the foot of the cross, Magdalene

(chorus) At the foot of the cross, Magdalene
At the foot of the cross, Magdalene

Divine Mary Magdalene
There at Mount Calvary, my beautiful dark lady

She was there with the other two Marys
My holy Mary Magdalene

Peter denied him, never she
Beloved disciple, Magdalene

Judas betrayed him
Magdalene never left him

She anointed the Teacher's feet
Loyal to her Jesus, dead or alive

If Mary washed Jesus' feet
He must have done the same for her

At the right-hand side of the good Jesus
Divine Mary of the Light

At the foot of the cross, at the foot of the light
At the foot of the light, my beautiful dark lady

Magdalene was always loyal
Divine Mary of Faith[10]

Our Impenitent Lady of Lexington

Tanya Torres's painting titled *Mary Magdalene of the Roses* (Figure 3) and all her other Mary Magdalenes have helped me much in understanding and processing my fascination and simultaneous horror over the stubborn myth of The Magdalene as sexy penitent prostitute. Tanya's Magdalenes have been just the visual balm I needed. They are not in penitence, but in contemplation, harmony, adoration. They do not blondify her darkness. They are colorful, bright, refreshingly and deceptively simple.[11]

Figure 3. *Mary Magdalene of the Roses*. Painting by Tanya Torres. Used with permission of the artist.

It was in 2006 that Tanya and I decided to channel our shared devotion for Mary of Magdala into a joint artistic project in homage of the symbol and myth that she is.[12] We had each already started creating art in her honor (visual in Tanya's case and musical in mine). But 2006 was when we started our joint obsessive dialogues and readings: interpretations and reinterpretations of Christian theology, the apocryphal and gnostic gospels, the myths, fiction, music, and visual traditions of twenty centuries A.M. (After Magdalene). We met for this purpose virtually every Saturday morning for years. Everything good that we had and that we wanted to bring into our lives had to do with Magdalene. Wisdom was Magdalene. Heterodoxy was Magdalene. Ataraxia was Magdalene. From all the spaces that She occupies, we imagined her as guiding our process of celebration and discovery. Eventually, we started calling her Our Lady of Lexington, acknowledging her as the holy patroness that was shining a light on the bit of Lexington Avenue in East Harlem where Tanya and I reside and create.

Toward a Caribbean Feminist Liberation Mythology

In the Caribbean, Black Virgins are simultaneously connected to European traditions of devotion to the Black Madonna—which, in turn, are also connected to pre-Christian goddess worship—and to African-derived religious traditions in which feminine spirits abound. I found my way to The Magdalene by connecting the Black Madonna and the feminine spirits of Afro-Caribbean religions with a biblical character I reclaimed and reinterpreted from my Evangelical past—the biblical Mary that called to me the most, meaning not The Nazarene Mother but The Magdalene Leader.[13]

After spending my adolescence as the atheist angry survivor of an Evangelical childhood, it was my love for Afro-Caribbean praise music that prompted me to reclaim a space in my life for the "spiritual."[14] How could I deprive myself of the intense joy of singing to the Virgin Mary with my Puerto Rican neighbors during the Fiestas de Cruz and with my Dominican neighbors on the day of La Altagracia? How could I not join my friends in singing heartfelt *palo mayombe* praises to the fierce Centella or the flirty Chola Wengue? How could I not fall head over heels in love with the *lwa* Ezili Danto, who, one story says, lost her tongue as a fierce warrior during the Haitian revolution and whose Catholic image is the Black Madonna of Czestochowa with the awe-inspiring scars under one eye and the baby Jesus cradled in her arms?

It was not only the Afro-Caribbean percussion-driven music and ecstatic (and fun!) approach to worship that appealed to me. After being indoctrinated in a Protestant tradition devoid of representations of the divine feminine, I was particularly fascinated by Marian worship—even as I experienced a reflexive distaste for the Virgin myth and how it has historically been used to control women's sexuality. So despite my rational objections, as I sang song after song praising the Virgin Mary, she, oddly, started feeling more and more *mine*.

Up until then, I had been assuming I was an interloper in *other* people's traditions. I was operating under the assumption that I had two choices in the matter: either believe literally (like most others did) or not believe at all. Yet, little by little, it started dawning on me that there was a third option: I could believe poetically, metaphorically, musically, on *my* terms.

I remember a powerful moment quite a few years back, singing to Mary the Mother during a Fiesta de Cruz (Feast of the Holy Cross) in East Harlem. I was at the front of the room, singing the chorus into a microphone. The first five rows were taken up by women mostly in their sixties, seventies, and even eighties. They were singing with such power, devotion, joy, and abandon. For a second, I lamented my faithlessness and wished I *really* believed in Mary. But then I realized: I do *really* believe in Mary! But in my version of Mary. In the Mary that speaks the language of my heart. Not The Mother, but The Leader. Not Mary of Nazareth, but Mary of Magdala. My version of Mary of Magdala. The protagonist of *my* liberation mythology.

> Hija de la humanidad
> De la luz la mano diestra
> De apóstoles maestra
> Camino a la claridad
> Suman dos una verdad
> Y en ella el misterio mora
> Dulce madre redentora
> Salve pía Magdalena
> Mi María La Morena
> Nuestra divina señora

> *Daughter of humanity*
> *The right hand of the light*
> *Teacher of the apostles*
> *The way to clarity*
> *Two make up one truth*
> *And the mystery lives within her*
> *Sweet redeeming mother*
> *Hail pious Magdalene*
> *My Mary The Dark One*
> *Our divine lady*[15]

Mi María La Morena/My Mary The Dark One

One of the reasons I have been able to open up to Afro-Caribbean spirituality, in a way that has been much harder to do with Eurocentric Catholicism, is that in Afro-Caribbean religions the female divine is often much more diverse than the unidimensional virginal rose without thorn who intercedes for us before the Big (Male) Divine Boss. Some of those Afro-Caribbean feminine spirits are wise and pacifist leaders; others are bloodthirsty and fierce warriors. Some are promiscuous, others are dependable and resourceful single mothers, and still others are absent

mothers. But none of them ever called to me as powerfully as Mary
Magdalene did. Maybe it was because none of those spiritual entities
provided the link I needed to my Evangelical past. The biblical Mary
Magdalene did. With time, I have realized why: she is my way to reclaim
my past and reintegrate it into my present—on my terms.

Mary Magdalene is, in my songs, "María La Morena" (Mary the
Dark One or Mary the Black One). Why "La Morena"? Above all,
it's a loving nod to the term of endearment so often applied to dark-
skinned feminine spirits and saints in the Dominican Republic. Calling
her La Morena is also a nod to the connections some say exist between
the European Black Madonnas and Mary Magdalene.[16] I also praise her
as La Morena in honor of the likely skin hue of the Middle Eastern
woman (North/Eastern African, in some versions of the story) who has
been passed down to us in myths and histories as Mary The Magdalene
(Figure 4).

Figure 4. *Mary Magdalene on Papyrus*. Painting by Tanya Torres. Used with
permission of the artist.

Salve Reina/Hail Queen

Dulcísima María, ay, llena eres tú de gracia
(coro) Salve Reina, salve
Salve Rosa del Cielo, mi estrella de la luz
Dulcísima María, ay, compañera mía
María te cantamos con velas prendidas
Salve, salve, salve Reina
Salve La Monserrate y salve La Milagrosa
Salve Virgen de Altagracia y salve mi Dolorosa
Salve Virgen de Regla y salve la Caridad
Salve Reina
Dulcísima María, ay, compañera mía
Salve La Magdalena mi madre divina
Salve, salve, salve Reina
De azul y blanco va La Virgen
De rojo y negro Magdalena
De azul blanco va La Virgen
De rojo y negro mi morena
Salve Reina
Salve Reina
Salve Reina

Sweetest Mary full of grace
(chorus) Hail Queen
Hail Rose of the Heavens, my bright star
Sweetest Mary, oh my companion
Mary we sing to you with lit candles
Hail, hail, hail Queen
Hail Lady of Montserrat, Lady of Miracles
Hail Virgin of Altagracia, Hail my Lady of Sorrows
Hail Lady of Regla, Lady of La Caridad
Hail Queen
Sweetest Mary, my companion
Hail Magdalene my divine mother
Hail, hail, hail Queen
Blue and white wears the Virgin
Magdalene wears red and black
Blue and white wears the Virgin
My dark one wears red and black

Hail Queen
Hail Queen
Hail Queen[17]

She: The Truth and The Way

Daughter of Humanity. Redemptress. Ancestress. Amalia Belcán. All and none. One. The right hand of the light. The left hand of darkness. Mary of Magdala. Our Lady of Lexington. The truth and the way that live *within each of us.*

Notes

1. Second *décima* verse (and English translation) of my song "Nuestra Señora de Lexington/Our Lady of Lexington," from the CD *Las 7 salves de La Magdalena/7 Songs of Praise for the Magdalene* (Ojos de Sofia, 2010). I composed the music based on the *seis fajardeño* style of Puerto Rican *jíbaro* music. The full album is streaming at www.ojosdesofia.com.

2. See Raquel Z. Rivera, "New York Afro-Puerto Rican and Afro-Dominican Roots Music: Liberation Mythologies and Overlapping Diasporas," *Black Music Research Journal* 32, no. 2 (2012): 3–24.

3. On liberation theology, see Samuel Silva Gotay, *El pensamiento cristiano revolucionario en América Latina: Implicaciones de la teología de la liberación para la sociología de la religión* (Salamanca, Spain: Ediciones Sígueme, 1981); see also, Luis Rivera-Pagán, "God the Liberator," in *In Our Own Voices: Latino/a Renditions of Theology*, ed. Benjamín Valentín (Maryknowll, NY: Orbis Books, 2010), 1–20. Though both liberation theology and liberation mythology are concerned with the connections between spirituality and social justice, the history of liberation theology as a concept is so firmly grounded in ecclesiastical Christianity that (though in theory what I'm talking about is a type of liberation theology) in practice for me to use "liberation theology" would create more confusion.

4. Robert Segal, *Myth: A Very Short Introduction* (Oxford: Oxford University Press, 2004); Joseph Campbell with Bill Moyers, *The Power of Myth* (New York: Anchor Books, 1991).

5. Kelley has one chapter titled "Keeping It Surreal" that deals with the surreal or mythological aspects of freedom dreaming, but his book doesn't just focus on the surreal. See Robin D. G. Kelley, *Freedom Dreams: The Black Radical Imagination* (Boston: Beacon Press, 2002).

6. See Kristina Wirtz, "Divining the Past: The Linguistic Reconstruction of 'African' Roots in Diasporic Ritual Registers and Songs," *Journal of Religion in Africa* 37 (2007): 242–274.

7. Kelley, *Freedom Dreams*, 29.

8. I have purposefully chosen to use the term "prostitute" rather than "sex worker" since the former term carries a historical weight and moral judgment that the latter does not.

9. "Legenda Sanctissimae Mariae Magdalenae," Add MS 15682 in the British Library. My heartfelt thanks go to Belinda Sykes and Joglaresa for making these texts widely available through their 2003 CD *Magdalena*.

10. Lyrics (and English translation) for the song "Al pie de la cruz/At the Foot of the Cross" from the CD *Las 7 salves de La Magdalena*. Regarding the lines "If Mary washed Jesus' feet/He must have done the same for her," I purposely inserted "if" right before the image of Magdalene anointing Jesus' feet. It's a nod toward people whose hearts are set on that image and that version of the Magdalene/Jesus myth but at the same time (poetically) arguing that *if* we imagine that scene, it only makes sense *if* we imagine him doing the same for her.

11. See Tanya Torres's Song of the Magdalene painting series at www.songofthemagdalene.com.

12. See www.songofthemagdalene.com.

13. Among my favorite sources for reinterpreting The Magdalene is the work of biblical scholars Marvin Meyer, Esther De Boer, and Karen King. See Marvin Meyer and Esther De Boer, *The Gospels of Mary: The Secret Tradition of Mary Magdalene, the Companion of Jesus* (New York: HarperOne, 2006); see also Karen King, *The Gospel of Mary of Magdala: Jesus and the First Woman Apostle* (Santa Rosa, CA: Polebridge Press, 2003).

14. Mind you, I am not saying all atheists are angry. I am just admitting *I* was an angry atheist. Now I'm a happy atheist or happy nonliteral believer or happy whatever you want to call me. Just preface it with "happy."

15. Third *décima* verse (and English translation) of my song "Nuestra Señora de Lexington."

16. See, for example, Tanya Torres, "Song of the Magdalene: Connection to the Black Madonna," entry posted September 28, 2010, accessed December 19, 2011, http://tanyatorres.blogspot.com/2010/09/song-of-magdalene-connection-to-black.html; see also Margaret Starbird, *The Woman with the Alabaster Jar: Mary Magdalen and the Holy Grail* (Santa Fe, NM: Bear, 1993).

17. Lyrics (and English translation) for the song "Salve Reina/Hail Queen" from *Las 7 salves de La Magdalena*.

It All Started with a Black Woman

Reflective Notes on Writing/Performing Rage

Gina Athena Ulysse

For the ones who died and those left behind.

"We wonder . . . if it is the sound of that rage which must always remain repressed, contained, trapped in the realm of the unspeakable."

—bell hooks

And if that rage is not spoken, expressed, then what becomes of it? One too many books and articles have been written reflecting on the mad white woman relegated to the attic because she dared to question social mores that incarcerated her or turned her into the wallpaper. Less is known of black female rage for there is usually no place for it. Its very articulation is a social death sentence especially in mixed company. Her rememories stay crushed in her body, her archive. She dare not speak. Shut your mouth. Careful. There is a place for unruly girls like you who do not know when to be quiet. When to not offend white sensibilities. When not to choke. Swallow. When to submit. Shhhhhh—Take a deep breath. Swallow.

There is no safe word.

On April 23, 2010, after a performance of my one-woman show *Because When God Is Too Busy: Haiti, Me and THE WORLD* at the "Let the Spirit

Speak: Cultural Journeys through the African Diaspora" conference, I had two moments with audience members that exemplify responses I have at times received from those afflicted by my visceral expression on stage. In the talk back that followed, a young white woman asked about the title. Did I really think that God was too busy and had forsaken Haiti? I gave her my usual quick answer: *That's what God's helpers are for.* After the question period, I usually have more informal interactions with the audience. The same young woman then identified herself as a Christian and proceeded to give me her contact details. She told me she would love to get together and discuss God. I took said information with politesse.

The fact is that I have had too many of these conversations already and will only engage in that discussion when it is no longer about epistemic violence. Over the years, the title of my performance has aggravated and caused the end of friendships. So much for tolerance and religious plurality. At issue is the belief that I reject God (Bondye),[1] which in itself is a (mis)representation—an act of interpretation—just another exercise in hermeneutics. My disregard of their objection stems from knowledge of socioeconomic histories promoting racialized discourses of "Christian hierarchies of civility"[2] that continually demean blackness and its myriad manifestations in order to extol the sanctity of whiteness. Vodou is a spiritual practice that not only is African in origin but maintains an allegiance to the continent, in contrast to Eurocentric belief systems. Hence, my affinity for and defense of Vodou is deeply lodged in a staunch refusal of what Robert Young refers to as "white mythologies."

The second response came from a slightly older white woman, who spoke with me after the show. She thanked me for the performance and then somewhat timidly added that it was too much. "What do you mean?" I asked her. "There was too much emotion," she replied and then said again, "It was too much." She was clearly moved. Her own voice uneven, shaking. "I guess you didn't expect this here?" I offered. "This is a conference," she retorted. I have become accustomed to such responses, especially since in recent years, I insist on presenting this work to disrupt conventional notions of scholarship.[3]

When the performance touches raw nerves, attendants sometimes speak while still unsettled. "And in the academy, there is no room for affect," I goaded her. "What about the conference's theme? How do spirits speak?" I demanded. Then I asked her, What should I have done with my emotions? I mentioned my need to have people connect with Haiti in a substantive way especially after the January 12 earthquake.[4]

Then I explained why I choose to perform what I call an alter(ed)native. This is about full subjectivity, not just a cerebral or just a visceral one but also a full being. This work is about engaging in an embodied project to access a full subject.

As I have defined it elsewhere, the alter(ed)native is "a counter-narrative to the conventionalities of the more dominant approaches in anthropology. It is alter as in other and native as I am ascribed that identity." The conjugation of "alter" and "native" is meant "to connote [processes of engagement from] an "anti and post-colonial stance, with a conscious understanding that there is no clean break with the past. With that in mind, alter(ed)native projects do not offer a new riposte or alternative view, rather they engage existing ones, though these have been altered. [Moreover], alter(ed)native perspectives are those in which tools of domination are co-opted and manipulated to [flip the script] and serve particular anti-and post-colonial goals."[5] Hence, I begin with the unequivocal premise that colonialism fractured the subject as articulated by feminist scholar M. Jacqui Alexander. In *Pedagogies of Crossing*, Alexander elaborated: "Since colonization has produced frag-mentation and dismemberment at both the material and psychic levels, the work of decolonization has to make room for the deep yearning for wholeness, often expressed as a yearning to belong that is both material and existential, both psychic and physical, and which, when satisfied, can subvert and ultimately displace the pain of dismemberment."[6] The alter(ed)native that is my work is an attempt at a gathering of frag-ments in pursuit of integration with the aim of ultimately subverting and displacing this pain.

Undoubtedly, the reassembling, as Toni Morrison shows in *Beloved*, needs to occur in a clearing. It is there that we can peacefully confront fractures and ultimately restore lost voices. This intangible, too often intuitive work (that is embedded within the structural) is usually rel-egated to the arts. There, historically, emotions have been sustained by disciplinary lines that uphold the border between art and science. In recent decades, questions concerning the sociohistorical construc-tion of academic disciplines have allowed the creation of other writing spaces. The blurring of genres fosters textured and multivocal possibili-ties, which are particularly necessary since daily life is not compartmen-talized. Indeed, subjects live, make, and remake selves in a messy world that continuously begs for interdisciplinary crossings.

The earthquake, for me, is another pivotal moment of collective horror that must not be smothered, especially since we have so many tools with which we can record and are recording so much—earth's moaning; people's crying, singing, shouting; tolls . . . In the latest installment of my show, I interrupt my personal narrative with individual quotes and statistics about postquake conditions. The Vodou chants are there as signification of the ethical that is to highlight the moral imperatives at play.

I begin with the premise that theory alone simply cannot enclose the object of study, as anthropologist Michel-Rolph Trouillot[7] has succinctly put it. So I go deep within. I compile what I call my ethnographic collectibles (excess bits unfit for publication because they were too personal, too raw, or seemingly trivial) and recycle them. I shut out the world to access that which I have been socialized to ignore. Trained academic. Repress. Digging deep to find ways to express a history of violence. Repress. I consciously and rather expertly manipulate my voice and let it out, knowing I am crossing boundaries. Resowing seeds that caused white fears of a black planet. Exposing bourgeois attachments to restraint. Undoing reason. Trading with different forms of capital. Undoing enlightened reason.[8]

I choose the stage. Performance provides me with a space—a clearing—albeit a public one. The stage becomes the site to occupy and articulate the embodied. The primeval. Releasing sound bites of horror. Unhinging the raw. Expressing that which is most guttural, and which for black women must too often remain the unspeakable. There is no fourth wall. Everyone present participates and becomes implicated in the denouement.

Because When God . . . Origins

An accidental academic, I had sought the stage long before deciding to pursue a doctorate in anthropology. I left Haiti for the United States with dreams of becoming a singer. I abandoned this pursuit, but I continued to write the personal for myself. Something I did on the side. It was concerns about Haiti that sent me to college and led me to a higher education, seeking answers to nonending questions about why Haiti remains poor and is continuously politically unstable. It was in academia that I fully understood the structural and its limits. As I was punished into discipline or continually disavowed in required courses that taught anthropological traditions, I quickly learned that which is felt deep within had to be managed. Put aside. I kept writing, consciously engaged in building a personal archive. My words could be whispered. Maybe. But never spoken aloud, especially not in mixed company. They found their way out of me into spoken word pieces with theoretical phrases deployed to deconstruct the machine that taught me.

My opposition had to go somewhere. It became anger when I found myself in danger of committing self-erasure. From that point on, my writing took a very specific turn. At the center was a motivation to expose the threads of racial matters that underlined how I both understood and made sense of my place in the world. When sounds threatened to emerge in the classroom they found their way on blue-lined pages and eventually ended up on stage. I am not supposed to have any anger or rage. I should have learned to swallow it years ago. But I refused to be docile. I wrote like so many who came before me and, as Barbara Christian insists, to reassure myself that I am alive. I was born in the first free black republic. I came of age colonized. I was being conscientized, when one day, I realized a poem I had written years before titled "Rodin's Kiss" should have been titled "Danbala and Aidawedo."

Pieces I had written over the seven years of graduate school had a continuous thread woven through them. Haiti. Bits of chants that were no longer part of my life as they had been when I was a child became bookends that maintained connections between memories of interactions with spirits that ceased in the aftermath of migration. I not only held on to those but reworked them. They became hybrids as I filtered them through the various lenses (a penchant for rock 'n' roll, respect for Billie Holiday and revolutionary black poets) I had acquired while hoping to find a place of belonging somewhere on the margins. I have never been status quo. The tensions that occurred as these worlds clashed were so grand that they too often discouraged resolution.

So, I played within the interstices that were created in their encounters and forged another space. It is one in which praxis rules to foster engaged ontologies. Those were made most present on a stage in interactive moments with audiences. Articles and books that I would eventually produce denied the opportunity to interact with an interlocutor in the same moment. As I have previously mentioned, I didn't exactly set out to be in academia. I built my degrees on top of my desire to be a singer (took lessons in my teens), a poet, and a performer. I sought critical thinking skills to decipher a problem and try to make better sense of it. An activist. By the time I realized the conventions in my chosen discipline would resist the lines I sought to cross, I self-identified as a budding performance artist masquerading as an academic.

The Performance

In my show, I mix personal narratives, bits of history, ethnography, literature, and song to ponder a single question: How did Haiti—the enfant terrible of the Americas—become the world's bête noire? I shift back and forth between the here and now and the there and then, the personal and the political, to consider the various ways the colonial past occupies the present. Weaving spoken word with Vodou chants, my monologue reflects specific childhood memories, instances of social injustice that link Haiti and the black Diaspora, historical moments that point to the incessant dehumanization of Haitians at home and abroad. Selected chants in honor of specific spirits are intermittently placed to frame the text. In a Haitian context, I am actively engaging in *voyé pwen* (sending points)—that is the act of sending a charged coded message to an interlocutor through indirect comments or actions.[9] Ultimately, my goal is to offer critical musings on geopolitics from the perspective of a Haitian American woman who is bent on loving Haiti, loving Vodou and loving herself despite the odds.

The show always begins with the *Noyé* (drowning) chant—an invocation to Ezili Danto, the spirit of motherhood, protection, and wisdom. Her realm is water and her symbols are a pierced heart and knives—*Drowning we are drowning, Drowning we are drowning. Ezili, if you see us fall in the water, take us. Save the lives of your children because we are drowning.* Danto is the fierce mother who will protect her children until the day she dies.[10] This refrain (or part of it) is repeated throughout the monologue after each piece both to provide a grounding point of the entire work and to serve as a reminder that ultimately this is about Haitians drowning. Initially, I selected that particular chant to bring attention to the unnamed thousands who over the years have lost their lives in the Caribbean Sea en route to US shores.

Since 2008, I have deployed the chant for a different reason. I use it to bring attention to the four successive cyclones that devastated Gonaives that year. After singing the last note, I name each one. Fay. Gustav. Hanna. Ike. Haiti was still reeling from the devastating storms. The death toll was somewhere around one thousand. The damage to property and infrastructure was still awaiting benefactors to be fixed when in 2010 the January 12 earthquake occurred and fractured the republic. It was initially reported that over half a million died, hundreds of thousands were wounded, and well over a million had been displaced. *Goudougoudou*, as Haitians have affectionately dubbed the quake, would be known as the greatest modern catastrophe of this century.

After the quake, one day, I found myself changing the original lyrics of the opening chant. *Noyé* became *tranblé* (tremble). Inspirational words came to me out of nowhere. *Tranblé, te a tranblé. Tranblé te a tranblé. Ezili si nou tranblé anko pran nou. Métres si nou tranblé anko pranm nou. Sove pitit lakay yo tranblé te a tranblé.* By the time I did my first post-quake performance on February 4, there had been over fifty aftershocks. The dead, most of them unidentified, were filling mass graves. So then drowning became trembling. *Trembling the earth trembled. Trembling we are trembling. Ezili, should we tremble again, hold us. Save the lives of your children because the earth is trembling.* Without skipping a beat, I usually melodically ease into the very first piece "Concepts of Home."

Concepts of Home

i just left it
lying there on the table at espresso cafe
a cup lined with fizzzzlessss foam
pressing the pages down
pressing to keep them down
to keep them closed
so grandmere doesn't see them
if my grandmother ever read these words
echoing screams of Kundera's post-mid-life crisis
she would have raised her eyebrows
lowered her head rolled her eyes
stupe real loud
and with swaying hips of her womanly form
she would have walked away
with a bad taste in her mouth
that's my critique of Immortality

i remember knees rubbing
as i tried to outrun
katia who was always the fastest
she was even faster than djeanane who was taller than all
    of us
blue/white checked pleated skirt twirls when i spin
flies when i jump
trying to reach extended branches
that were closer to the sky than they were to my head

i remember us collecting rocks
that i held onto tightly within closed fists
I remember running on paved sidewalks
passing the Cabane Choucoune
Le Petit Chaperon Rouge
on our way home we would stop at a pye zanman (almond
    tree)
look for the yellowish orange ones the ripe ones
we'd throw rocks like boys at the zanman
until we knocked them onto the ground
we would wipe them off our uniforms
and stuff them into our mouths
biting away flesh that was barely ripe for eating
but soft enough to let spots of juice seep through
leaving tongues tasting of sour
we weren't suppose to keyi zanman on that street (collect
    almonds)
or on any street
where we would be seen acting like
ti moun san fanmi (kids without families)
ti moun san manman (kids without mothers)
my mother never knew we did that
unless
we bit into one that was so green
that we had to spit it out quickly
carelessly
letting it stain our clothes
when i was in jamaica this summer
i ate breadfruit and saltfish
i ate bonbonsiro
i cooked like mother or ivela would
i never measure anything
I cook like that
because that's just the way us women
at rue darguin no. 8 cooked
at Dragon's bay villa i skipped about in my yellow flowered
    dress
the blue bay
the escovitched fish
small strips of kan in a plastic bag tied with a twist

for the tourist price of 30 J
the smell of and the taste of blue mountain coffee
with carnation evaporated milk
to which i'd add spoonfuls of brown sugar
brown sugar that i'd have to demand
because raw sugar has no place on tables in hotels
it is colored
raw sugar has no place on tables in hotels
it is colored
because it is not refined
it wasn't processed in britain or in the united states of
    america
lean dark waiters in white shirts and red vests serving
uptight white american tourists who want eggs over-easy
instead of ackee and saltfish for breakfast
who sit under the almond tree
my almond tree by the bar
drinking rum punches
the almond tree overlooking the bay
the almond that i wanted to climb
i jumped trying to catch extended branches
jumped again
my dress
rides up
glimpses of the
eternal thigh
up
again
i lost my balance
i lost my shame
as i jumped up again over and over again
trying to grab arching branches with almonds
that have not seen me for fifteen years
i didn't even check
to see if they were yellowish gold or even close
that wasn't the point
no you see
i had to knock them down from the tree
wipe them off my bathing suit
and sink my teeth into them

as soon as i possessed them
as soon as i had them in my hand
without wasting a moment
but they fell on the sand
i didn't even wipe them
i bit right into them
one at a time
because i had to
i had to because
they reminded me of the place where i came from
this place — a country — my country — a man
the zanman reminded me of this man
this man with whom i share a torrid love
a man that didn't like women
that smothered children before they were born
because in their mother's belly they promised
they'd have too much fire in their soul
they were black
he knew they'd all be black
he knew they were all blakk
and they promised they'd want to be free
and they promised they'd fight to stay free
because they were blakk
and he knew they knew what would happen
and he knew they knew what would happen what always
    happens
he knew they knew they couldn't be french
because they only speak kreyòl
he knew they knew they couldn't be french
pase se moun andeyo yo ye (Because they were born on
    the outside — in the country)
the zanman reminded me of this man
that i haven't gone back to
that i can't go back to
that i don't want to go back to yet
that i don't want to see so t o r n
bleeding
because i don't want to believe that ayiti can
bleed

that ayiti is bleeding
i don't want to see
i don't want to see
her
bleed
ing
but it's always been —
he said
high
suicide
alcohol ism
family
violence
repeatedrapesofbabieschildrengirlswomenladiesswomen
    violenceagainstwomen
blood has been
shedding in
south africa
black blood
colored blood
blood
a lot of pnp and jlp blood

red has always been the color of the blood that has
c o l o u r e d south africa

how do you call a place home that doesn't allow you to
    forget
how do you call a place home that tears you inside out
that makes you wish you could not feel
that makes you wish you could not think
that makes you wish you could not see
that makes you wish you could not remember
horror that has become an everyday commodity
a place that keeps bleeding
that keeps bleeding
even after operation restore democracy
that will continue
to bleed

until there's no trenchtown
until there's no lost city no sun city
until there's no white power center
until there's no whites only signs in children's minds
until there's no whites only signs in children's hearts
until the colored are free
until white people are free
until black people are free
But it keeps bleeding

but we can't make it stop
or can we
you can't make it stop
or can you

do you turn away wallowing in guilt
delving deeper into a forgiveness that doesn't exist
a forgiveness that ceased to exist
a forgiveness that will never exist
there's blood too much blood in south africa and it's spill-
    ing over
there's blood too much blood in south africa and it's spill-
    ing over
blood is spilling over on necklaces
blood is spilling over in cité soleil
blood is spilling over in garrisons
red is the color of the blood spilling over from makeshifts
    boats in the Caribbean sea
red is the color of the blood spilling over from makeshifts
    boats in the Caribbean sea

there's too much blood on this country that i love
there's too much red on this country that i love
this country that won't let children live
that kills them in their mother's womb
so women now give birth to stillborns
how do you keep yourself how do you keep yourself from
    wanting
to touch from wanting to smell from wanting to be from
    wanting to feel to find a peace that ceased to exist to find

a peace that never existed to find a peace that will never
   exist to stop looking to stop
looking for something to stop looking to stop looking for
   anything to stop
looking to stop looking so you can find peace

Some Pieces of the *Pays Natal*

Displaced, in Ann Arbor, I seek home in the cup of coffee that rings a
page of Milan Kundera's *Immortality*. Knowing my paternal grandmother
would not only reject his disenchantment with aged women but would
kiss her teeth in distaste and walk away. The search for the home of
which I speak then takes me back to my childhood in Pétion-Ville, then
to Kingston and Port-Antonio in Jamaica. For many years, Jamaica had
become a replacement for Haiti. I refused to go back there as a youth in
the aftermath of migration. I had vowed to return to my birth country
only when things changed.

I spent fifteen years waiting. In the meantime, I reconnected to the
home I left behind through things. Food. Pieces of memories. Pictures.
Cut-up sugarcane in a plastic bag tied with a twist for which I would
pay the tourist price. Because in Jamaica, where I decided to conduct
my doctoral research, I am at times a visible foreigner. There, I also
find classed rejections of that which is black, that which is local, that
which is considered folk.

Even an almond tree helped me in making this return. It took me
back and became a reminder of school days. Haiti continually fails its
black masses. Kreyòl is eschewed. Blackness promises to fight to stay free.
Ayiti bleeds. So does Jamaica. South Africa. Women have always been
vulnerable. Repeated rapes of babies, girls, ladies, and women. These
places continue to bleed. Hence the call to the audience: Can we make
it stop or not? The *we* is then changed to *you*, addressing those present even more directly. The bleeding is structural. We all partake in its
making. It won't end until we as a collective and as individuals that
form this collective decide.

I repeat the lines over and over again lowering the register of
my voice until they become murmurs. My voice turns into a nagging
scratch that must not be ignored. What causes inequality? How do we
reinforce it? What are the bases of structural violence? Ideas become
practices that are deeply lodged in children's hearts and minds. How do

we end this predisposition? How do we effect change? You can't make it stop, or can you? The piece ends with the announcement that we share the same blood: red is the color of the blood that is spilling over in the Caribbean Sea. It is the same red that has spilled over Jamaica's garrison communities. It is the same red that dripped on necklaces in South African shantytowns. Is this massive spillage due to the excess? Is there too much blood in these countries that I love so much so that now women give birth to stillborns? This is a reference to both the infant mortality rate and the too common call from conservatives that Haiti needs to exercise greater population control to contain its misery. I seek to allude to the fact that this process is actually already in effect.

Then I confront the survivor's dilemma. How do we live when others are dying? How do we breathe? Think? Feel? Touch? How do we seek peace in the midst of this chaos that threatens to deny us a center? How do we gather the pieces? How do we find them? They had been scattered so long ago.

Skin Castles

I. Contact −

> In the castle of my skin,
> In the castle of my skin,
> In the castle of my skin,
> Look! Look!
> Look!!! A negro . . .

On that island, the offspring of a white man and a black woman is a mulatto; the mulatto and the black produce a samba; from the mulatto and the white comes the quadroon; from the quadroon and white comes the mustee; the child of a mustee by a white man is called a musteefino; while the children of a musteefino are free by law and rank as white persons, for all intents and purposes.[11] And further up north, there was the one-drop rule. All—it—took—was—one—d-r-o-p.

II. Bleeding −

> Mwen di Feray'o m'blésé.
> Feray'o m'blésé.
> Gade'm blésé Feray.

Mwen pa we san mwen.
Mwen di Feray'o m'blésé.
Feray'o m'blésé.
Gade'm blésé Feray.
Mwen pa we san mwen
In the castle of my —

III. Dying —

Saint Philomene vierge martyre
Accorde nous miserecorde
Saint Philomene vierge martyre
Saint Philomene vierge martyre
Accorde nous miserecorde
Saint Philomene vierge martyre
The strong black woman is dead
The strong black woman is dead
The strong black woman is dead
Her silence killed her last night

Saint Philomene vierge martyre
Accorde nous miserecorde
Saint Philomene vierge martyre

In the castle of my skin

IV. Being—

She never ever apologized for who she was. With her there was no
pretense. There was no shame. What you saw was what you got. She
was a peasant, so what. She was illiterate, so what. She was a street
vendor, so what. She had a lot of children, so what. She smoked a pipe,
chewed tobacco and was a heavy drinker, so what. She was a Vodouist
who loved to serve her spirits, so *fucking* what.

V. Embracing—

I dwell just beyond your logic. I dwell just beyond your logic. If I didn't
define myself, for myself, I would be crunched up into other people's
fantasies for me and be eaten alive. I exist as I am and that is enough.
I exist as I am and that is enough. I exist as I am and that is enough.

VI. Living—

> In the castle of my skin,
> In the castle of my skin,
> In the castle of my skin, I dive

Counter-Memories

If "Concepts of Home" is about engaging with the recent present, then "Skin Castles" seeks to evoke the most distant past. It usually follows "Athena's Rant on Good and Bad Neighbors,"[12] a piece about Haiti's relationship with the United States and the Dominican Republic. In that piece, I continue to play with metaphors. I expand on the idea of Haiti as a woman and then imagine her being stalked by her biggest and baddest neighbor. She can't get a restraining order. Her trespasser has framed each encounter in terms of their common well-being. So what does she do?

"Skins Castles" retracts to actually explore the earliest moments of colonial contact. It is a play on articulations of class, color, and gender. It begins with homage to George Lamming's *In the Castle of My Skin* before an invocation of Frantz Fanon. "Look! A Negro." I then actively show how blackness has been historically written on the body through color categories and their concomitant exchange value on an unnamed island in the Caribbean. As a reviewer noted, "In a startling clinical manner, Ulysse [reads] the taxonomy of different hereditary combinations of black and white until what began as a black woman ended with a white one."[13] Indeed, as the color gradations increase in value, the closer they are to white progeny. Ultimately, it is the musteefino—already the whitest—who, when coupled with a white man, is free by law and ranked as a white person for all intents and purposes.

In North America, that miscegenation story took a slightly different turn. No such dilution was so officially accommodated. Any amount of blackness was deemed a stain. All it took was one drop. Hence, the chant that automatically follows an elongation of the word "drop" with a heavily pronounced *p* is loaded with symbolic significance. *Feray I am bleeding. Feray I am bleeding. Look I am bleeding I don't see the blood.* One of the interpretations of the chant is that the spirit—acting as the bodyguard—protected the human and took the cut or bullet that was aimed at him or her. This ode is to Ogou Feray—who symbolizes strength and valor—the warrior spirit who is sometimes represented by the lithograph of St. George in full armor. According to Marc Christophe, Ogou "is portrayed as a general who is said to have contributed heavily to the war of independence . . . his emblematic vévé, which includes two crossed swords and a stylized central palm tree, is an abstracted version of the Haitian coat of arms. . . . Legend has it that Ogu was the personal spirit of Jean-Jacques Déssalines, Haiti's liberator."[14] It is this spirit that devotees take to battle. The double entendre here is quite intentional. As I wail Feray I am bleeding, it must be questioned: When did I sustain this wound?

This bleeding occurred in the moment of the colonial encounter that produced the miscegenation that creates color and class categories. A black woman is wailing. That's how it all started. The following chant (part of the *action de grace* that precedes Vodou ceremonies) is for St. Philomene, the martyr virgin who had devoted her virginity to God. Legend has it that when she refused a Roman emperor, he threw her into the sea with an anchor tied to her body. The sea refused to let her drown. After floating on the water, anchor and all, she was pulled out and beheaded. The call then is for Saint Philomene to grant us clemency. It is repeated three times, as is customary in ceremonies. Compassion is needed now, for she is about to break the silencing. This is a rejection of martyrdom. There will be a price to pay for creating this disorder. Saint Philomene also knows only too well that when the black woman dies, it is her silence that will kill her.

In the next section, the silence is broken. An illiterate peasant woman with many children who drinks, smokes a pipe and chews tobacco, and loves to serve her spirits revels in her being. Without pretense or shame, she embraces all that is stereotypically associated with the poor black masses as an act of self-making. Self-love. The piece ends with a cut-n-mix of samples from Natasha White, Audre Lorde, and Walt Whitman—all three self-defining agents, poets who used the written word to make fierce declarations of self-actualization. All three of them outsiders (by virtue of their sexual orientation, religious leanings, etc.). Indeed, their very presence offset the established order. Along those lines, White has written that her existence defies the logic of stereotypical notions that seek to restrain her to categories that stifle her. Lorde continually practiced self-definition (naming herself whenever she presented herself anywhere) to resist being crunched up in other people's fantasies of her. Whitman gets the last word in a reference to Zora Neale Hurston: "Well you know whut dey say 'uh white man and uh nigger woman are the freest thing on earth.' Dey do as dey please."[15] Enunciating every syllable of each word, I announce that I exist as I am and that is enough. I breathe deeply before chanting Noyé again.

The show always ends with a throaty wailing chant to Gédé—symbolic of life and death—a personification of the ancestral dead and sexual regeneration. Trickster. Healer. Counselor. He who sets right wrongs perpetuated by the living. It probes the listener with a looping plea—yet another call being made to the spirit world demanding justice: "Look at what the mortals have done to me!" And they continue to do. Things. Unwittingly. Sometimes consciously. Other times completely clueless. *I can save you.* Things fall apart. Pieces break. Bleed. Surely someone will pick it up. Bleed just for me. I alone can heal you. If you let me, I know just how to fix you. I meditate on these thoughts and disregard the simplest of mathematical conundrums. Then I return to one of the refrains in the last piece: "How do you overturn four hundred years of history in less than one century?" My repetitions build into a crescendo. More chanting. I use the repetitions and chanting as a portal—to access the body and keep it present. It is interwoven between pieces as a reminder of the ultimate aim of the work.

I turn inward again. Indeed, it took thirty-four years for the republic's first formal recognition. Another fifty-eight for her stepmother to consider her a sovereign state. Or one hundred years of isolation. An indemnity of 90,000,000 francs (reduced from the original 150 million) was paid to her former colonizer for their loss of property. These numbers don't make sense, but they are not supposed to any more than a twisted ragged gagged doll pricked with pins can spew out eligible words of consent. On the stage, in my imagination, Haiti is a voodoo doll. A gigantic dark brown puppet made malleable as she is stuffed with cloth that is adorned with pins and needles. Upon closer examination, the pins actually become poles. Poles with coiled national flags and family crests of those who landed on her shores and made imperialist claims.[16]

There is an ethical dimension to Vodou that escapes those who have maligned the practice. Nonetheless, as Claudine Michel asserts, each spirit in the pantheon is "an archetype of a moral principle that he or she represents."[17] Thus, this final call to Gédé, which comes from righteous anger, is a demand for spiritual retribution. Without the material, military capital to challenge those with such powers, all Haiti has left is its morals. Part of the Vodou creed is to turn your troubles to the spirit world. Humans are not judges. The spirits and God alone shall right all wrongs.

In the ten years since I have put this show together and performed it for various audiences, I have scarcely had negative responses from black women (unless they were anti-Vodou). On the contrary, I usually receive accolades, acknowledgment for seeing, presenting, and expressing a world of contradictions, full of battles, exploitation, and pain where no one is above reproach, including myself without closure. The last line of the show before the earthquake was "I am tired of wearing this suit of steel. I am tired of being weighed down by armor, while the war still rages on!"

With each performance since the quake, I become increasingly aware of the fact that we do not know or have never confronted Haiti's pain. We have talked about it. Written about it incessantly. Some have actually engaged with it. Still we have never sat with it in its rawest form and let it be. It has always been smothered. Shhhhhh. Not in public and certainly not in mixed company. Somatic theories tell us that in many ways some of it is still there. Trapped. It remains unprocessed trauma.

This past year, in light of the impact of the earthquake at home and abroad, I began to think more and more about the absence of discussions of psychoanalytical explorations of the experiences of Haitians in general and then especially with regards to the Revolution. We have no substantive record of those moments of fracture, of pain when screams stemmed from deep within before they found constructed expression, sometimes in rage. The little we do know of those moments come from the fearful gaze of colonizers. What did we sound like to ourselves? I keep wondering what Ayiti—this land where spirits inhabit permanent resting places in nature—could tell us about the collective and individual sounds we made in the aftermath of the Revolution. The earthquake for me is another pivotal moment of collective horror that must not remain unspoken. Smothered. It must have voice.

Ezili rears her head again with the drowning/trembling chant. One of the most striking characteristics of this spirit is that she is incapable of forming words. Her tongue had been cut during the Revolution. It is disputed whether those who maimed her were French colonialists or her own Haitian brethren. Either way, the belief was that she was too strong a woman. In ceremonial spaces, when she appears, she is distinguishable by her unintelligible speech. Utterances. Her power comes, not from her words but from the fact that she dares to speak at all.[18]

Black women continuously engage in battles of all kinds for various reasons. Differentially positioned, we bear the burden and joy of maneuvering through notions of race and gender that are inextricably linked with other indices that we embody and occupy. We are many. What we too often recognize in each other and usually don't articulate is that the point of the work is not to find resolution. Rage, as bell hooks so aptly puts it, can be all consuming. No, the point is to make and inhabit a space where the guttural not only escapes but transitions to new words, wails even without retribution, where safe words are not necessary and, for now, utterance is enough.

Acknowledgments

This piece was written in the aftermath of the January 12, 2010 earthquake. A brief section of it was first published on Postcolonial Networks. I thank Janell Hobson for both her interest in this work and her suggestions for expansion. My sincere thanks go to Kyrah M. Daniels, Gillian Goslinga, Kate Ramsey, and Victoria Stahl, who offered responses and comments that pushed me to address certain points. Given the tragic moment that inspired this writing, this work is exactly where it needs to be: somewhere in between the discursive and expressive.

Notes

1. In its formulation in the New World, Vodou not only recognizes but also acknowledges the supremacy of God. Those who serve the spirits (the preferred terminology) do so with the understanding that spirits (*lwas*), as Claudine Michel explains, "serve as intermediaries between humans and the Supreme Being (Bondye). . . . Bondye is not involved directly in devotees' daily existence or in their personal relations with the spirits" (Michel, *Haitian Vodou: Spirit, Myth, and Reality* [Indianapolis: Indiana University Press, 2006], 38).

2. Michel-Rolph Trouillot, *Silencing the Past: Power and the Production of History* (Boston: Beacon, 1995), 77.

3. In 2011, at the American Anthropological Association annual meeting, I performed a spoken word piece on panel instead of giving a conventional paper. The proposed presentation I was to deliver was titled "Spokenword as Ethnography" and was based on a project I have been developing through what I refer to as an alter(ed)native. The respondent (a known feminist ethnographer who has herself "blurred" different genres of writing) proceeded to thank me for what she referred to as my "performance in an academic setting." As if we are not all performing.

4. Soon after the quake, I was frequently invited to give talks and perform this work. I used it in its entirety or bits of it as an entry point to discussions

regarding the catastrophe that shook the republic. Questions that followed were often more engaging, as I (in the words of Devin Thomas, a reviewer, several years earlier noted) transform "Haiti from an objective abstract to a subjective reality" (accessed September 9, 2011, http://www.independent.com/news/2007/aug/16/embecause-when-god-too-busy-haiti-me-and-world-em).

5. Gina Athena Ulysse, *Downtown Ladies: Informal Commercial Importers, A Haitian Anthropologist and Self-Making in Jamaica* (Chicago: University of Chicago Press, 2008), 7.

6. M. Jacqui Alexander, *Pedagogies of Crossings: Meditations on Feminism, Sexual Politics, Memory and the Sacred.* (Durham, NC: Duke University Press, 2005), 281.

7. Michel-Rolph Trouillot, "The Caribbean Region: An Open Frontier in Anthropological Theory," *Annual Review of Anthropology* 21 (1992): 19–42.

8. I thank Gillian Goslinga for pointing out the qualification. Indeed, it is enlightenment that is at stake.

9. Jennie M. Smith, *When the Hands Are Many: Community Organization and Social Change in Rural Haiti* (Ithaca, NY: Cornell University Press, 2001), 47.

10. Accessed September 9, 2011, http://www.research.ucsb.edu/cds/projects/divinehaiti.html.

11. The quote is from Fernando Henriques's *Family and Colour in Jamaica* (London: MacGbbon and Kee, [1953. 1968), 46.

12. This rant is from an unpublished memoir, *Loving Haiti, Loving Vodou*, 2006, n.p.

13] http://wesleyanargus.com/2008/05/02/faculty-dancres-channel-passion-anguish-grace-in-performance.

14. Marc Christophe, "Rainbow over Water: Art, Vodou Aestheticism, and Philosophy," in *Haitian Vodou: Spirit, Myth & Reality*, ed. Patrick Bellegarde-Smith and Claudine Michel (Indianapolis: Indiana University Press, 2006), 97.

15. Ibid., 227.

16. The three paragraphs above are a remix of several *pwens* (points) from *VooDooDoll What if Haiti Were a Woman* (2013), a performance installation project that reconsiders Haiti's history and reactivates the doll and some symbols associated with this icon.

17. Claudine Michel, "Of Worlds Seen and Unseen," in *Haitian Vodou*, ed. Bellegarde-Smith and Michel, 38.

18. I thank Kyrah Malika Daniels for insisting that I acknowledge this and make this point.

References

Alexander, Jacqui M. *Pedagogies of Crossing: Meditations on Feminism, Sexual Politics, Memory and the Sacred.* Durham, NC: Duke University Press, 2005.
Christian, Barbara. "The Race for Theory." *Cultural Critique* 6 (1987): 51–63.

Christophe, Marc. "Rainbow over Water: Art, Vodou Aestheticism, and Philosophy." In *Haitian Vodou: Spirit, Myth & Reality*, edited by Patrick Bellegarde-Smith and Claudine Michel, 85–102. Indianapolis: Indiana University Press, 2006.

Frantz, Fanon. *Black Skin, White Masks*. New York: Grove Press, 1952.

Henriques, Fernando. *Family and Colour in Jamaica*. London: MacGbbon and Kee, [1953] 1968.

hooks, bell. *Killing Rage*. New York: Henry Holt, 1995.

Hurtson, Zora Neale. *Their Eyes Were Watching God*. Champaign: University of Illinois Press, 1991.

Lamming, George. *In the Castle of My Skin*. Ann Arbor: University of Michigan Press, 1991.

Lorde, Audre. *Sister Outsider: Essays and Speeches*. Berkley, CA: Crossing Press, 1984.

Michel, Claudine. "Of Worlds Seen and Unseen." In *Haitian Vodou: Spirit, Myth & Reality*, edited by Patrick Bellegarde-Smith and Claudine Michel, 32–45. Indianapolis: Indiana University Press, 2006.

Morrison, Toni. *Beloved*. New York: Alfred Knopf, 1987.

Popkin, Jeremy. *Facing Racial Revolution: Eyewitness Accounts of the Haitian Insurrection*. Chicago: University of Chicago Press, 2008.

Smith, Jennie M. *When the Hands Are Many: Community Organization and Social Change in Rural Haiti*. Ithaca, NY: Cornell University Press, 2001.

Thomas, Devin. "Because When God Is Too Busy: Haiti, Me, and the World." Accessed September 9, 2011. http://www.independent.com/news/2007/aug/16/embecause-when-god-too-busy-haiti-me-and-world-em.

Trouillot, Michel-Rolph. "The Caribbean Region: An Open Frontier in Anthropological Theory." *Annual Review of Anthropology* 21 (1992): 19–42.

———. *Silencing the Past: Power and the Production of History*. Boston: Beacon, 1995.

Ulysse, Gina Athena. *Downtown Ladies: Informal Commercial Importers, A Haitian Anthropologist and Self-Making in Jamaica*. Chicago: University of Chicago Press, 2008.

———. *Loving Haiti, Loving Vodou: A Book of Rememories, Recipes & Rants*. 2006. Unpublished memoir.

———. "VooDooDoll What if Haiti Were a Woman on Ti Travay Sou 21 Pwen: Or An Alter(ed)native in Something Other Than Fiction." *Transition* 111 (2013): 104–114.

Young, Robert. *White Mythologies: Writing History and the West*. New York: Routledge, 1990.

BOT I

A Performance Script in Two Parts

Praba Pilar

Figure 5. BOT I Digital Image. 2010. Created by Praba Pilar. Used with permission of the artist.

MEGA :: situate

Out . . . Into this world . . . this world . . . tiny little thing . . .
    before its time. . . .
Born in a cab racing to the hospital . . . five pounds and tiny . . .
seeking out the world . . .
falling in the hands of . . . father . . . father . . . father . . . father of
    life . . .
padre de todas las fuerzas . . . padre amado . . . padre sagrado . . .
cut my umbilical cord and introduced me to a world . . .
bits . . . bytes . . . processor . . . coding . . . programming . . . network . . .
binary . . .
and I fit right in . . .
I fit right in I tell you, playing with the little cogs . . .
the little spidery cogs . . .
parts . . . chips . . . data entry cards . . . electronics . . .
all the way from Taiwan. . . .

Two weeks after the Kennedy assassination in Dallas, I made my debut into the world in a cab on the way to the hospital on a snowy day in Manhattan. My mother, a Colombian journalist, convulsed in pain and fear as my father, an Argentine salesman, yelled at the driver: Faster! Faster! Faster! This entry into the world, connecting New York, Buenos Aires, and Bogota, with the blood running through my veins embodying a hemispheric mapping, has always made me interested in developments across the broader Americas.

We left New York City when I was five months old and began to travel through Latin America: spending time in Bogota, Buenos Aires, and Caracas because of my father's computer sales job with IBM. He was an expert in computing and was selling the big, bulky, and basic computing machines available in the early 1960s to large corporations and governments. My feminist mother volunteered for Planned Parenthood, fighting for women across Latin America to have the right to birth control and abortion.

By 1967, my father decided to launch his own computer business, moving our family to Nuevo Laredo, Mexico/Laredo, Texas to open a large data entry enterprise in direct competition with IBM. Enormous data entry machines, from a child's point of view, filled the large warehouse he ran in Nuevo Laredo. With my parents lacking babysitters or support, my siblings and I hung around the business all day, playing with the data entry machines, drawing little stick figures on the cards, and entering them into the systems to see what would happen.

This informed my sense of the computer world.

My father went bankrupt on his data entry empire, and in one short year we went from being middle-class Latin Americans in Mexico to poverty-stricken immigrants in Texas. From a life of stability and comfort, we arrived at the core of immigrant poverty. I was six years old. We were surrounded by devastating scenes: grandmothers begging in the street, young women with hungry babies, Vietnam vets shooting up in corners, kids going to jail for the marijuana trade. Hollowed out faces, drunks, and heroin addicts populated my world.

In Laredo, the Anglos had an acceptable standard of living, the immigrants a deplorable one, the Native Americans a genocidal one. My mother moved us into a "white" neighborhood, and I was soon exposed to the learned racism of children. I made friends with the most hated girl in school, Lisa, a Native American girl who lived in a defunct trailer.

This informed my sense of dislocation, of injustice.

CODE BLUE . . . CODE BLUE . . .

meat body, meat ware, wetware . . .
he hates the meat body,
father, father, father,
incestor and abuser . . .
schizophrenic and full with promise . . .
the promise to live in the mind . . .
it was nothing new . . .
filthy hatred of my body, my five pound body . . .
STOP . . . CODE BLUE . . . CODE BLUE . . .

My father was a twenty-first-century man. He believed in the promise of computers to free us from the meatware. Large, overweight, overbearing, he survived three heart attacks, two forms of cancer, diabetes, and numerous other illnesses; an atheist, he hated the flesh and mortified it. Given that he was schizophrenic and untreated for the duration of his life, he often experienced life as a machinic interaction.

He reflected broader attitudes in the field, wherein the body is associated with the feminine, the feminine with nature, the masculine with the mind and rationality. The ability to transcend the body is seen as a solely male ability. The discourse that prevails within this masculin-ist construction leaves very limited room for women.

This informed my sense of feminism, of the limits of technology.

GIGA :: discourse

I was born for the new world order . . .
speed up my mathematics . . .
give me software, software, replace this wetware. . . .
Garage band symphonics. . . .
Singularity. . . . Bioprospecting. . . . Mechanosynthesis. . . .
A computer in every pot! Back me up baby. . . . Put me on the
  remote server . . . speed me up . . . I'm ready for takeoff into
  the hyperbolic longevity escape velocity . . .

I began an early art career working on immigrant and farmworker rights in California. However, I had a redefining moment in the late 1990s,

Figure 6. BOT I Performance Still, 2010. Photography by Cisco. Taken at Galeria Studio Cerrillo in San Cristobal de las Casas, Mexico. Used with permission of the artist.

which altered the direction of my work. I received an e-mail from Geri Guidetti on genetically engineered sterilized seed technology and its impact on saved-seed farmers throughout the world.

Monsanto Corporation and the United States Department of Agriculture had applied to commercialize a complex genetically engineered process by which seed embryos would be rendered sterile, thus preventing saved-seed farming. The farmer utilizing these seeds would have to buy new seeds after every harvest. The e-mail reported that 1.2 billion people depended on saved-seed farming throughout the Third World and that their very food supply would be compromised by self-sterilizing seeds. The seed-sterilizing process was renamed the Terminator by the Rural Advancement Foundation International (RAFI then, recently renamed the ETC Group).

My research into the Terminator revealed an insidious wave of consolidation within not only the seed industry but what became the life sciences industry. I was concerned with the links between the corporations controlling agriculture, biotechnology, and pharmaceuticals—and how this was turning into the field of capitalist life sciences. I was very disturbed to see that profits could be the governing principle in a field as central to the survival of the human species as the life sciences.

Immersing myself in a very rapid and deep study of the complex field of biotechnology, I began reading voraciously in the field: RAFI, the Pesticide Action Network, the Council for Responsible Genetics, Food First!, Physicians and Scientists for Responsible Application of Science and Technology, Greenpeace, the UK Genetic Engineering Network, and the Union of Concerned Scientists. I attended the Biodevastation Conferences held in 1998 and 1999; contacted activists, scientists, legislators, and artists around the world and within my community working on this issue; and immediately joined the immense international campaign to block the commercialization of seed-sterilizing technology. Activists, nongovernmental organizations, scientists, farmers, and national governments all over the world stood together in opposition to Terminator technology.

The urgency of this issue was profound. There was a limited window of opportunity to ban the Terminator from commercialization. I immediately began an art activist campaign in San Francisco to bring attention to the issue of the Terminator, forming the Hexterminators with the Mexican artist Gerardo Perez. The name of the group came out of an artistic desire to attack irrational corporate greed with an irrational weapon: a hex. We put a hex on the terminator through our work.

We recruited artists in the Latina/o community, activists from EarthFirst!, students from multiple universities, science policy educators, web designers, media artists, musicians, videographers, and others in San Francisco to participate in direct action, street theater, agitprop, art installations, radio appearances, television public service announcements, lectures, presentations, invisible theater, theater productions, web interventions, and multiple interventionist projects. The group eventually grew to around twenty-five people involved at multiple levels of engagement.

Our focus was the economics of Terminator technology. With Monsanto buying out smaller seed companies and retiring seed varieties from the market, farmers would have fewer options in their seed selection. Eventually, they would have to buy genetically engineered seeds. If those were sterile at harvest, it would devastate entire economies and put lives at risk.

I read widely for the Hexterminators and soon stumbled upon the vast literature on the convergence of nanotechnology, biotechnology, information technology, and cognitive neuroscience (NBIC), which has informed my work since. Since then I have created multiple art works in multiple media to critique the unproblematized, ahistorical, masculinized, and utopian rhetoric of the technology revolution. I have generated art projects on exclusion and access to the Internet by Latinos within and beyond the United States; on the discourse of the digital divide; on Internet surveillance and readily available crime records and who this disproportionably affects within the documented racist US criminal justice system; on Internet trafficking of women for sexual exploitation; on robotics and the development of a global war machine; and on manifest tech destiny with the body as the final frontier. These examples reflect a critical rhetoric I have been generating for the past decade.

The NBIC convergence has rapidly accelerated technological development over the past two decades. Each formerly distinct field potentiates the others by providing the tools for analysis that were formerly unavailable. As supercomputers become more powerful and rapid in processing capacity, they open up new possibilities for nanotechnology and genetic engineering, and new technology leads to more powerful computers.

Contemporary agents of the NBIC convergence—primarily made up of Western governmental agencies with neoliberal economic agendas; multinational corporations centralizing the life sciences; information technology corporations marketing products with built-in obsolescence; military-industrial complexes developing living weaponry and robotics; and universities funding laboratories—have saturated Western culture with a hegemonic discourse that the NBIC convergence brings crucial and beneficial progress.

The dominant discourse of these agents of the NBIC convergence includes the following rhetorics: the convergence will eradicate hunger, poverty, and disease through genetic engineering, nanomanufacturing, and nanomedicine; will end stultifying human labor through robotics; will remove human soldiers from war through advanced weaponry and robotics; will extend the human brain through artificial intelligence and implants; and overall will topple dictatorships, introduce liberal democracies worldwide, and herald a new world order beyond historic divisions of race, class, and gender.

While there can be positive applications of emerging technologies, this hegemonic discourse ignores profound oppressive forces in social, political, economic, and environmental terms, which prevent a large part of humanity from enjoying the benefits of advanced technologies right now. There are enormous disparities in access to advanced technologies along the First World/Third World and the global North/global South divides.

As reported in The World in 2010: ICT facts and figures, 71.0 percent of the population in developed countries are online, compared to only 21.0 percent of the population in developing countries. While in developing countries 72.4 percent of households had a TV, only 22.5 percent had a computer and only 15.8 percent had Internet access (compared to 98.0 percent, 71.0 percent, and 65.6 percent, respectively, in developed countries). In addition, the production and dismantling of computers and related electronics have created numerous extremely toxic sites throughout the world, particularly in recycling operations in Asia.[1] Of course, the lore of recycling lets us off the hook as we create the most toxic products and then recycle them, cleaning our conscience in the process. Most consumers of electronic devices are incredibly ignorant of the toxic load that goes into creating and disposing of electronic devices. The strategy is to generate obsolete products and keep the market growing. The human cost of this is hidden, secret, and covered up by computing manufacturers, who always promote their products as clean, sleek, and modern.

PETA :: race

*then I saw the men . . . implosions, negations, cruelty . . . no
  brethren there . . . no sisters . . .
No no no, just white men, so elite, so rich. . . .
Nanophotonics . . . plasmonics . . .
spreading the white male myth . . . in the technological arena . . .
but you are so mistaken . . . I don't want to be a middle-
  class white man. . . . I don't want your rationality . . .
ME CAGO EN TUS ZAPATOS . . . soy de Colombia . . .
magical realism . . . indigenous plantations . . . vida sagrada . . .
ritmos del sol . . .*

What I find equally disturbing is how this discursive matrix legitimizes the white, Western myth of superiority and the creation stories that run deep into the colonialist project. Technology functions in the world in very marked ways. Joel Dinerstein notes, "Technology has long been the unacknowledged source of European and Euro-American superiority within modernity."[2] This is based on the historical misrepresentations of the roots of the technological, going back to Hegel, which I discuss below.

Such misrepresentations create what Dinerstein calls the "white mythology"[3] of technology. This white mythology is universalizing and is influenced by Enlightenment ideas of progress and the function of science in progress narratives. He succinctly describes the Western technocultural matrix thus: "progress, religion, whiteness, modernity, masculinity, the future."[4] This myth is clearly reiterated in much of our present-day technocultural discourse. I find the promotion and rhetoric of the NBIC convergence to be so messianic that in 2005 I founded a fictive church, the Church of Nano Bio Info Cogno, to satirize and critique this phenomenon. The Church of Nano Bio Info Cogno (the Church) is a counterhegemonic performance project counteracting this discourse by exposing the class origins and Euro-American centrism of agents behind the technology revolution. The Church uses various strategies and tactics to counter this discourse. It exposes the power of this language through sermons railing against Luddites and environmentalists. It demonstrates the words of the prophets of technoculture and posthumanism through showing edited videotaped interviews with leading technologists in the field, all of whom are white men.

The Church proffers the position of technofundamentalism implicit to this dominant paradigm, thereby exposing the limits inherent in the logic of the posthuman. The Church also reveals through its performances that the very roots of this technomythological discourse are found deep in the fabric of Christianity and, through that, Western domination. Dating back to ninth-century monks who imagined themselves as coworkers with God in making over the planet—through the mechanical arts—to prepare for the second coming of Christ, Christianity has valorized the mechanical arts, and therefore technology, as a means to access the divine.[5]

By the dawn of the Enlightenment, the world did have a new messiah: the machine, as displayed by publications such as de la Mettrie's 1748 *Man a Machine*.[6] The Church gestures toward the counterhegemonic by joining a broader critique of the majoritarian public sphere that punishes those who are outside of this paradigm as Luddites, imbeciles, or wacko environmentalists. It works indirectly with the tools of the master to promote a radical revisioning and relocation of the discourse to its historical roots.

Michele M. Wright argues that our assumptions about and our definitions of technology and its history worldwide need to be revamped, as they reify the West as the "cradle of civilization—and therefore the sole owner of technology in and of itself."[7] The abstract concept of technology as solely white and male ignores many technological developments in parts of the world outside of the West. Reflecting on Hegel's *Philosophy of History*, Wright notes that Hegel introduced a racist dichotomy between the 'enlightened' Europe and the 'dark continent' of Africa, and that his argument is based in racist myths. Hegel's vision of the world continues to inform contemporary discourse, as "the deep-rooted racism in American minds today only further perpetuates the lies and mythologies of our history."[8] Wright defends the technological contributions of contemporary African Americans and discusses technological developments and interactions between ancient Africans and Greeks.

When I attended the 2004 conference AfroGeeks: From Technophobia to Technophilia, many of the panelists and speakers pointed out and reiterated that it is not that Latinos and African Americans are unable to access and engage with emerging technologies. It is that the technologies they do engage with most effectively, in both historic and contemporary terms, are not "seen" as advanced. Alondra Nelson, Kali Tal, Anna Everett, and other Afro-futurists have problematized this point of view, pointing out the ways African diasporic communities utilize communications and digital technologies in the arts, most tellingly in hip-hop culture.

The ideology of the progress narrative and of the myth of whiteness in technology permeates technocapitalist discourse in particularly

marked ways that negate alternative technologies precisely because they
do not serve capitalism. So, let's discuss ideology.

TERA :: ideology

I must become more efficient . . . MILITARY IDEOLOGY . . .
  human efficiency machine folding at longevity escape
  velocity . . .
regeneration . . .
back me up on your servers . . . transcend the body, my body,
  what body . . . all reason . . . all rationality . . .
todo en la mente . . .
mentation . . .
depravation . . . sensory overlord . . .

In his essay "The German Ideology," Karl Marx describes how ideology
is imbricated in the thinking of the society at hand. He states, "The
ideas of the ruling class are in every epoch the ruling ideas: i.e., the
class which is the ruling *material* force of society, is at the same time

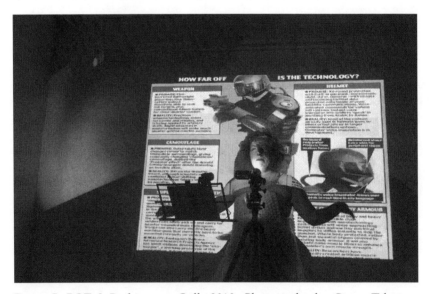

Figure 7. BOT I Performance Still, 2010. Photography by Cisco. Taken at
Galeria Studio Cerrillo in San Cristobal de las Casas, Mexico. Used with
permission of the artist.

its ruling *intellectual* force. The class which has the means of material production at its disposal, has control at the same time over the means of mental production."[9] Our very thoughts and ideas are formed within ideological constructions, as the material conditions of the epoch influence the mental landscape we inhabit.

Althusser extends this concept and explores how this works in the world. Given that ideology constructs individuals as subjects through multiple institutions, Althusser proposes, "*All ideology hails or interpellates concrete individuals as concrete subjects*, by the functioning of the category of the subject."[10] How does ideology do this? Althusser explains, "I shall then suggest that ideology 'acts' or 'functions' in such a way that it 'recruits' subjects among the individuals (it recruits them all), or 'transforms' the individuals into subjects (it transforms them all) by that very precise operation which I have called *interpellation* or hailing, and which can be imagined along the lines of the most commonplace everyday police (or other) hailing: 'Hey, you there!' "[11]

Interpellation describes the mechanism, in the world, through which institutions and state apparatuses address individuals as particular types of subjects, providing them with a subject position that they unconsciously recognize themselves and operate from within. However, this recognition is a false view of the self. It is a view that comes from outside, from an institutional discourse, which alienates us from ourselves and forms the very genesis of our thoughts.

I find two features of Althusser's interpellation very interesting. One: It is insidious. The subject is not aware that she is operating within ideology. Hailing comes from a place one can't see, and ideology is always going to find a new way to disguise itself. Two: There is no outside to ideology, as one is always already within it. The child is born into a family system that is already an ideological construct. Even before birth, from this Althussean perspective, the expectant parents begin the process of hailing.

How do I see this at work in the world? In the spectacularized culture of the United States, individuals are continuously hailed back into ideology and turned into subjects. Advertising, marketing, overconsumption, excess materiality, billboards, overstocked stores, and media vapidity present an overwhelming saturation that is hard to escape. This can be widely seen in the technology industry, wherein not only are new products promoted through an ideology of a cost-free dramatic improvement of the quality of life, but the government is in full support. The military-industrial complex remarked upon by Eisenhower is the engine behind the push of products developed originally by the Defense Advanced Research Projects Agency.

I would argue that while interpellation is operative and is a useful tool for analysis, there are degrees of interpellation and hailing. There are "bad" subjects. My favorite is Gloria Anzaldúa.

PETA :: mestizaje

and I rise up with Sadie . . .
I am the modern cunt. . . .
The modern cunt that will not upload . . .
will not artificial . . .
will not intelligence . . .
will not go . . .

Why not just play, be a get along gal? After all, new technologies are fun, and I could have continued working in the tech world, managing servers and routers and computer platforms, massaging the machines and celebrating their prowess. But I am a Latina, a minority in the United States. I am situated and ideologically constructed less effectively by capitalist technoculture. As a Latina, within a community, I have been *left behind, outside and aside due to the ever multiplying digital and technodivide and therefore do not participate fully in the technomatrix.*

I use Gloria Anzaldúa's borderlands concept as an analytical tool far beyond border zones, offering resistance to technocapitalist discourse and the concomitant technomatrix. In *Borderlands, La Frontera: The New Mestiza*, Anzaldúa describes her multiple borderlands: betwixt the historically complex border zone where Mexico and the United States meet, between indigeneity, *mestizaje*, and *latinidad*, between her queer sexuality and homophobia in her community. The betwixt is where I resonate most strongly.

My reading of her work is very broad. She provides an analysis of the crossroads of distinct ideologies, of the resistance to these ideologies through *mestizaje*, and of a way out of binary dualisms. As Anzaldúa writes, "Don't give me your tenets and your laws . . . your lukewarm gods. What I want is an accounting with all three cultures— white, Mexican, Indian. . . . And if going home is denied me then I will have to stand and claim my space, making a new culture—una cultura mestiza."[12] Anzaldúa uses indigenous symbols and spirituality to reclaim and recuperate the new woman, the mestiza, proclaiming, "Here we are weaponless with open arms, with only our magic. Let's try it one way, the mestiza way, the Chicana way, the woman way."[13] Finally, Anzaldúa writes about reclaiming the inner mental landscape, noting, "Nothing happens in the 'real' world unless it first happens in the images in our heads."[14] She acknowledges that ideology permeates mental life but that the mestiza can create new grounds for an ontology of the world.

Receiving the messages from multiple cultures (or ideologies), the mestiza goes through a cultural collision. The mestiza operates at the crossroads between cultures. Anzaldúa describes the mestiza as corn, as revolutionary and evolutionary, as "an inevitable unfolding," as a "product of crossbreeding" that will "survive the crossroads."[15]

Most importantly, in her definition of the new consciousness of the mestiza, Anzaldúa rejects binary opposition and offers other possibilities of action and not reaction. She argues for a different form of resistance, one that takes place underground, with a holistic perspective, with contradictions and ambiguity, without a set rational plan of action. Who better to enact such resistance than a performance artist?

EXA :: resistance

the promise to live in the mind . . . yes . . . no body . . . new thoughts . . . new paradigms . . . new thresholds. . . . Beyond the

Figure 8. BOT I Performance Still, 2010. Photography by Cisco. Taken at Galeria Studio Cerrillo in San Cristobal de las Casas, Mexico. Used with permission of the artist.

body, exploding a new frontier and then POOF Descartes!
WHAT? I tell you Descartes . . . it was nothing new . . . filthy
hatred of my body, my five pound body . . . threshold to
transcend into a binary mapping of dendrites. . . . Filthy
body . . . leaky disruptive body . . . oozing obsolescence . . .
STOP . . . CODE BLUE . . . CODE BLUE . . .

In 2003 I began to conceptualize a solo performance project, Computers Are a Girl's Best Friend, featuring the performance figure the Latina Digital Diva. She was that "get along gal" that embodied technofetishism. The project came from a radio interview with journalist Edward Jay Epstein about Marilyn Monroe and the diamond industry. He discussed the 1953 movie *Gentlemen Prefer Blondes* and the film's signature song "Diamonds Are a Girl's Best Friend." In his book *The Rise and Fall of the Diamond*, Epstein describes how the De Beers diamond cartel of South Africa helped finance films like *Gentlemen Prefer Blondes* as part of a finely orchestrated campaign to drive up demand for diamonds.

I immediately saw parallels with the personal computer industry. Since the mid-nineties, I had been exposed to the relentless chants of the heralds of the information revolution—*acquire, update, upgrade, upload, download, unload, reload.* Apple, Microsoft, Dell, Toshiba, and others promised a revolution, born of a computer in every home. It was a good strategy for moving product, and moving product is what they did. In tempo with the breathless incantations of the glory of the information revolution, hundreds of millions of personal computers were sold in the United States.

Diamonds have always been marketed as cool, smooth, impeccable gems and appear in very glamorous or romantic settings. Underlying these fancy rocks are grossly oppressive conditions under which diamonds are mined and cut. Much of the mining work is unhealthy, unsafe, and dangerous. Many of the countries where diamonds are extracted end up poor. Consumers don't know a thing about the diamond-cutting industry, which employs children in slave conditions. Consumers never get a glimpse of the conflict diamonds imbroglio that European diamond traders play along with.

Like the ugly and well-hidden mining secrets of the diamond industry, computer manufacturing has created its own oceans of toxicity. Silicon Valley, birthplace of the electronics industry, now has 29 Super Fund sites and 150 groundwater contamination sites. The Silicon Valley Toxics Coalition warns that electronic waste is the most rapidly growing waste problem in the world. Toxic ingredients such as lead, beryllium, mercury, cadmium, and brominated flame retardants are being exported from the First World to the Third for disposal. These e-waste operations in the Third World are extremely polluting and damaging to health through exposing workers and their children to toxic solvents, the open burning of plastic waste, river dumping of acids, and widespread general dumping.[16]

This project focused on two overlooked aspects of the computer era: the exportation of hazardous toxic computer waste to Asia and the effects on the bodies of women and their children; and the increasing penetration of women's bodies through the trafficking of women for sexual exploitation through online channels, including web-order bride sites, enforced prostitution, and sex tourism. The overall project was made up of three modules that specifically explored contradictions between the promotional rhetoric of the computer industry and effects on the bodies of women.

The performance module, titled *Computers Are a Girl's Best Friend*, drew parallels between the diamond and the computer industries. The performance had its world premiere at Studio XX, the premiere feminist digital art center in Montreal, and subsequently toured internationally.[17] There were two versions of the performance that developed between 2004 and 2010.

The two-dimensional artwork module, titled *Cyber.Labia*, explored themes of e-waste, pornography, and the geography of Internet use through a series of digital collages. Some of the images from the series depict what have become very routine views of women from online pornographic websites superimposed onto maps of Internet geography. Other pieces collage images of manufacturing, overseas recycling—which includes children dismantling hazardous waste—and workers of the e-revolution onto the abstracted contemporary maps of Internet usage.[18]

The text module resulted in a printed chapbook with artwork, critical theoretical reflections, and interviews on women and computers. *Cyber.Labia* was the final culmination of the multidisciplinary project, bringing together all the research and practice elements into a book form with a DVD insert of the music video of *Computers Are a Girl's Best Friend*. Edited by feminist performance art historian Moira Roth, this book featured interviews with author and cyberfeminist Anne Balsamo on the historic exclusion of women from the narrative of the information revolution; essayist and *Wired* journalist Paulina Borsook on the mediatization of sexuality; environmental activist Sheila Davis of the Silicon

Valley Toxics Coalition on the environmental costs of computing; and cyberactivist Art McGee of the Media Justice Network on the negations of difference promulgated through discourses about the Internet.[19]

In the performance I was interested in what I saw as a new phenomenon: the increasing penetration of the female body by computing and advanced information technologies. The subRosa collective[20] had already done work examining the effect on female bodies of genetic engineering and medical technologies, particularly on artificial reproductive technologies. I, however, wanted to look specifically at computing within this construct.

First, I examine how women's bodies were being penetrated physically by the process of computer recycling. The Silicon Valley Toxics Coalition, in coordination with the Basel Action Network, released a report in 2002, reporting: "Electronic waste or E-waste is the most rapidly growing waste problem in the world. It is a crisis not only of quantity but also a crisis born from toxic ingredients—such as the lead, beryllium, mercury, cadmium, and brominated flame retardants that pose both an occupational and environmental health threat."[21]

Upon reading this report I contacted the Silicon Valley Toxics Coalition and requested an interview with Sheila Davis, project director of their Computer Take Back campaign. Davis has worked on electronic recycling and environmental sustainability issues since 1996. She has also explained how the very notion of computer recycling has given us the comforting idea that something responsible is being done with junked computers, while in actuality, computer recycling operations are extremely toxic and recyclers routinely export hazardous wastes to poorer countries.

The damage to women's bodies specifically has to do with the penetration of toxins into the fatty tissues of breasts and the concomitant risks of illness. These hazardous materials affect women's bodies in different ways than they affect men's bodies, for anatomical reasons. Equally important is the question of *which* bodies are being damaged. By exporting the recycling from Western nations to Asia, it is Third World bodies that are being damaged by First World consumption.

Second, women's bodies were being penetrated by sex tourism, web-order bride sites, and false job advertisements on the Internet leading to enforced prostitution. At the time the web was being used in various ways as a tool in the prostitution of women, with global sex syndicates recruiting women from all over the globe. Womenspace.org posted reports on how pimps used the web to stalk, sell, and exploit women, enabling sex tourism and the meeting of web-order brides.[22] There was increased trafficking of women online, a further globalization of the sex trade, with the use of this communications tool for sexual exploitation.[23] This is not the cyborgian destiny that Donna Haraway was dreaming of in her manifesto.

These two vectors of penetration led me to think that computers are not always a girl's best friend. The subsequent performance I developed had two iterations, and the second iteration comprised four scenes. In Scene One, an overhead voice introduced the Digital Diva and I came out on stage and sang "Computers Are a Girl's Best Friend" to much laughter and singing along by the audience (Figure 9). I created a backdrop video of a highly degraded and digitized cut of the original film version of "Diamonds Are a Girl's Best Friend." This contextualized the critique back to its original intent and provided a play of lighting and shadow as I moved about the stage.

Figure 9. "Computers Are A Girl's Best Friend" Performance Still. 2006. Photography by Rene Garcia. Taken at MACLA (Movimiento de Arte y Cultura Latino Americana) in San Jose, California. Used with permission.

Scene Two shifted the mood considerably, as a video played con-
trasting "Diamonds Are a Girl's Best Friend," the music video of *Com-*
puters Are a Girl's Best Friend, and shots of mountains of computer waste
and recycling with audio that included both excerpts of an interview
with Sheila Davis of the Silicon Valley Toxics Coalition and a running
commentary about the parallels that I was trying to tease out. I quickly
changed into worker's overalls and came onstage and gutted a desktop
computer at the front of the stage while the video played in the back
(Figure 10).

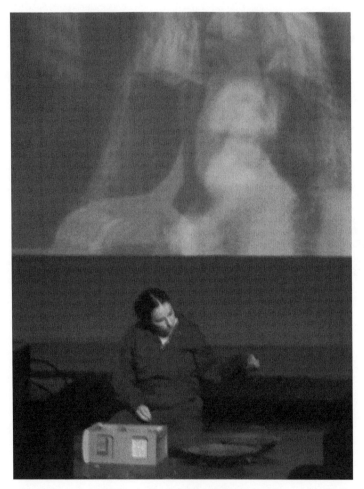

Figure 10. "Computers Are A Girl's Best Friend" Performance Still. 2006.
Photography by Rene Garcia. Taken at MACLA (Movimiento de Arte y Cultura
Latino Americana) in San Jose, California. Used with permission.

Scene Three began with an audio track of orgasmic moans as I quickly changed backstage into my vinyl dress with CD ROMs. I came back out on stage and began to caress and make love to a computer monitor, inserting parts into my mouth and gesturing toward my genitals, while a video simulating an advertisement about the penetration of women's bodies by computers played (Figure 11).

For Scene Four an audio track began of women's voices telling their stories of being trafficked, while I quickly changed backstage into a slip, came back onstage, and began interpreting historically accurate, factual stories of three different women who were trafficked through the Internet. The first story focused on a web-order bride. The second story focused on a sex worker in the sex tourism industry. The third story focused on a woman who answered an Internet advertisement to become a waitress and instead was forced into prostitution for two years.

Overall, this performance illumines a counternarrative drawn from my experiences in my community, intervening into the technomatrix with serious play.

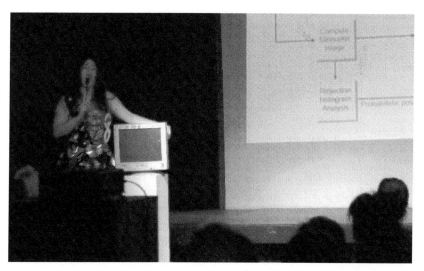

Figure 11. "Computers Are A Girl's Best Friend" Performance Still. 2006. Photography by Rene Garcia. Taken at MACLA (Movimiento de Arte y Cultura Latino Americana) in San Jose, California. Used with permission.

ZETTA :: poetics

Internet logics . . .
digital delusions . . .
moving bodies. . . .
transtime, transspace . . . transcend time space . . .
NO: telepresencia . . .
NO: binary coding . . .
infinite trick . . .
who am I in it . . .
Disaffected?
who are you . . .
Disconnected . . .
am I alone here?
Am I alone?

In 2009, media artist Adriene Jenik invited me to present a two-minute performance as part of her project Open_borders: Improvisation across Networks, Distance, Timezones at the Actions of Transfer Conference of the Hemispheric Institute of Performance and Politics at the University of California, Los Angeles. Her project was a web-based international performance event wherein performances from around the Americas would be web cast and streamed into a lounge at UCLA on the Saturday night of the conference. All the performances had to be done in front of a web cam.

I had been watching videos of Samuel Beckett's 1973 play *Not I* in hypnotic reflection. I was fascinated by the level of alienation in the piece, the disembodiment, the rant, the story, the broken, repetitive, circling, nonlinear narrative. I was fascinated by the twisting, wretched mouth, by the spitting out of words. I needed to do an interpretation of *Not I* based on my own contemporary alienation.

I began with the lines from *Not I*, "out into this world . . . this world . . . tiny little thing . . . before its time . . ." and told my story, my birth into a computer family, my early introduction to the materia prima of electronics, my later disillusionment working as a technologist, my love of instant communication, my disgust with military applications. As I spoke the words, I stuffed computer wiring into my mouth until the wiring deformed my mouth and I was left uttering incoherently. I watched this brief sketch projected on the wall of the lounge and realized I could develop it into a full-length piece, referencing many of the ideas and arguments, the hidden histories, the rebels and usurpers, of the tech revolution.

I named it BOT I, drawing on the texts of Not I and I, Robot by Isaac Asimov. I presented the performance in the Arena Theatre of the University of California at Davis, California; at Galeria Studio Cerrillo in San Cristobal de las Casas, Chiapas, Mexico (Figures 6–8); and at the Radical Philosophy Association Conference in Eugene, Oregon. I provide this script to disengage from the hegemonic framework of emerging technologies and engage the ethical dilemmas through an informed criticality.

> Out. . . . Into this world . . . this world . . . tiny little thing . . .
> before its time. . . . Born in a cab racing to the hospital . . . five
> pounds and tiny . . . seeking out the world . . . falling in the hands
> of . . . father . . . father . . . father . . . father of life . . . padre de
> todas las fuerzas . . . padre amado . . . padre sagrado . . . cut my
> umbilical cord and introduced me to a world . . . bits . . bytes . . .
> processor . . . coding . . . programming . . . network . . . binary . . . and
> I fit right in . . . I fit right in I tell you, playing with the little
> cogs . . . the little spidery cogs . . . parts . . . chips . . . data entry
> cards . . . electronic . . . all the way from Taiwan. . . . Father . . .
> fathers . . . father . . . STOP . . . CODE BLUE . . . CODE
> BLUE . . . he would give me everything I wanted. . . . Connect
> me all over the world . . . spread me further than ever. . . . Ooze
> me into the ionosphere . . . baby cyborg born into this world . . .
> el Nuevo mundo. . . . I would reach the zenith. . . . Analog to
> digital communion. . . . Commune . . . commune . . . orgy of
> telepresence . . . WHY! WHY! WHY am I here all alone?
> Mega . . . Giga . . . Tera . . . Peta . . . Exa . . . Zetta . . . I want to be
> a cloud . . . a computing cloud . . . everywhere and nowhere at
> once. . . . I was born for the new world order . . . speed up my
> mathematics . . . give me software, software, replace this
> wetware. . . . Garage band symphonics. . . . Singularity. . . .
> Bioprospecting. . . . Mechanosynthesis. . . . A computer in every
> pot! Back me up baby. . . . Put me on the remote server . . .
> speed me up . . . I'm ready for takeoff into the hyperbolic
> longevity escape velocity . . . I'm ready for Methuselarity . . . I'm
> ready for WAIT! The little children, the little children . . .
> WHAT? . . . Yes, little children . . . girls, boys, scraps . . . in my
> dreams . . . soft delicate skin . . . maybe 4? laughing and

playing... playing Legos with digital parts... Are you 4? Picking
through the breasts... little villages... standing on stacks of
parts, digital dream.... Picking through... Picking through
WHAT? cadmium, beryllium, lead... Chinese villages....
sucking brominated flame retardant breasts... WHY WHY
WHY must my dreams be saturated.... The children... Rivers
of Toxins... WHAT?.... CODE BLUE CODE BLUE. NO!
You were going to clean up the world.... Give us the paperless
office... give us the power to fix... to fix at a higher
intelligence...700 hazardous chemicals in one little fix, not the
fix I have in mind.... But they're recycling... pero es un
cuento sin fin... story never told.... E-waste stream north
west... now south east... hazardous material.... Boats of
detritus... STOP... meat body, meat ware, wetware... he
hates the meat body, father, father, father, incestor and
abuser... schizophrenic and full with promise... the promise to
live in the mind... yes... no body... new thoughts... new
paradigms... new thresholds.... Beyond the body, exploding a
new frontier and then POOF Descartes! WHAT? I tell you
Descartes... it was nothing new... filthy hatred of my body,
my five pound body... threshold to transcend into a binary
mapping of dendrites.... Filthy body... leaky disruptive
body... oozing obsolescence... STOP... CODE BLUE...
CODE BLUE... I must become more efficient... MILITARY
IDEOLOGY... human efficiency machine folding at longevity
escape velocity... regeneration... back me up on your
servers... transcend the body, my body, what body... all
reason... all rationality... todo en la mente... mentation...
depravation... sensory overlord... and I rise up with Sadie... I
am the modern cunt.... The modern cunt that will not
upload... will not artificial... will not intelligence... will not
go... I saw a rat, a rat I tell you.... An ugly filthy rat in
rotting ruins... chewing on the fetid minds of the smartest
computer scientists with their robotic processing machines....
against the laws... the three laws... Asimov, you are not
presente! WHAT? a robot may not injure a human being... a
robot you said... cannot allow a human being to come to
harm.... WHAT? a robot must obey orders... orders,
disorders, borders... given by human beings... a robot must
protect PROTECT.... its own existence. WHAT? Ohhh no

hurting humans...I get you Asimov! Asimov! Where were you
when DARPA came in.... DARPA WHAT? Defense
Advanced Research Project Agency...Defense? Defense of
WHAT? Advanced Research, into WHAT? DARPA was right
on top of my body...DARPA my nemesis...ruination of
visions.... out into this world...tiny little thing.... Now
tentacles reaching into every lab...universities...research
departments.... robotic scientists...all over the world....
DARPA...you are the pulse of robotics...there is nothing
without you...killing machines...started small...tiny little
thing.... giganormous...forty three...now you fucked
up...forty three countries military robotics.... WHY? WHY?
WHY?...you don't biomedical, you don't surgical, you don't
telesurgery.... DOG...WHAT? Yes, DOG! DOG carries the
burdens on the battle field...taken away our birthright....
killers...killing machines...you negate me.... Mega...
Giga...Tera...Peta...Exa...Zetta... I saw the
men...white, elite, masters of the universe...planning the
future...leaving me out...WHY WHY WHY were there no
other people there...WHY.... I spied on you...to see your
flesh...creamy...and fatigued...i joined Foresight...WHAT?
Foresight Nanotechnology Institute...Nano Bio Info Cogno
Convergence meetings...I've seen your talks.... End all
poverty...end material want...provide everything for all...for
everyone...in the world...WHAT?...I want this this
this...I want this to be true...then I saw the men...
implosions, negations, cruelty...no brethren there...no
sisters...No no no, just white men, so elite, so rich....
Nanophotonics...plasmonics...spreading the white male
myth...in the technological arena...but you are so
mistaken...I don't want to be a middle-class white man....
I don't want your rationality...ME CAGO EN TUS
ZAPATOS...soy de Colombia...magical realism...indigenous
plantations...vida sagrada...ritmos del sol...I am only good
data...good plasma...I am your DNA sources...WHAT?
DNA source...yes porque un buen indio, es un indio
explotado Biopiracy...bioprospecting...intellectual
property......north south dynamics.... Columbus,
PRESENTE...rising...from the grave...Columbus.... I see
you now so clearly...your new world order...disorder....

*gold rush...I see your Neem tree thefts...WHAT? You fuck
me...taking and taking and taking...take me...take
me...place me...spread me...connect me...dilate me....
Make me...nothing outside of the new world border....
Online...connected.... Connected connected connected....
Skyping my girl and losing myself into the data flow...erotics,
pleasure, play...high speed sousveillance.... Somatic
mutation.... Skype me into the orgasmic flow...a little critter
moving through the world...a better life...online job
market...she goes...she participates...joins this new world
frontier...trust...desperation.... Grind...and POOF...hell
hole bordello...taken south east now west north...seventeen
Johns a day...seventeen fucking Johns...rape, abduction,
meat market...caught up...deportation...WHAT? Moving
bodies...not telepresente.... fresh innocent body.... A tiny
little thing...born into this world...this online world...meat
flesh bodies...pimps and GPS tags shot into bodies...tag those
whores...you always know where they are...But it's a
connection.... Real dolls and bioprinting...online women....
Brutal rape...rape...thousands trafficked...girl...born in
Russia...now in England...girl...born in la Republica
Dominica...now in Boston...girl, born in Brazil...now in
Madrid...what is this new world order, border, disorder...
body dilated...pulsated...videotronic...finding myself in the
webcam repetitions.... The webcam imitations, replication...
Touching you around the world...WHAT? Telepresente
baby...I'm here, I'm there, I'm everywhere...tiny little
thing...born into this world...this social network...take me,
lose me, prove me...brother are you online? Sister can you
connect? NEGATRON...why are you not here??? I know
you exist...brown meat...dark meat.... why can't you read
me? Don't you speak English? Lingua franca...lingua
extendida...Where are you? Where is your fiber optic
presence? WHAT?...online penetration limited bandwidth....
Territorial limits...but wait...WHO? Who is there?...I
know you exist...meat...excluidos...desaparecidos...
WHERE ARE YOU? Internet logics...digital delusions...
moving bodies.... transtime, transspace...transcend time
space...NO: telepresencia...NO: binary coding...infinite
trick...who am I in it...Disaffected? who are you...
Disconnected...am I alone here? Am I alone?*

Acknowledgements

BOT I script was developed with suggestions and comments from Nitza Tenenblat. Figures 6 through 8 are performance stills taken by Cisco at Galeria Studio Cerrillo in San Cristobal de las Casas, Mexico. Figures 9 through 11 are performance stills taken by Rene Garcia at MACLA (Movimiento de Arte y Cultura Latino Americana) in San Jose, California.

Notes

1. Silicon Valley Toxics Coalition (SVTC), *High Tech Trashing.*
2. Dinerstein, "Technology and Its Discontents," 15.
3. Ibid., 16.
4. Ibid., 17.
5. Noble, *Religion of Technology.*
6. Ibid.
7. Wright, "Racism, Technology," 47.
8. Ibid., 53.
9. Marx, *Marx Engels Reader*, 172.
10. Althusser, *Essays on Ideology*, 48.
11. Ibid.
12. Anzaldúa, *Borderlands*, 44.
13. Ibid., 110.
14. Ibid., 109.
15. Ibid., 103.
16. SVTC, *High Tech Trashing.*
17. The performances received extensive media coverage through Radio 2050, KPFA; were written about in www.newmediafix.net and other media sources in Canada, Europe, and the United States; and were featured in lectures, conference presentations, and artist's talks at Mills College, Laney College, UC Davis, SF State, the University of Southern Illinois, SUNY Albany, and others. This resulted in a workshop titled "Technomythologius: Contesting Cyber Hegemony."
18. This work has been exhibited and presented extensively: at the Bioneers conference, at universities around the country, and at museums such as the Oakland Museum. The images were featured in publications throughout the United States, including *ArtWeek* in California.
19. The print version was dispatched to cyberfeminists around the world, reviewed in the feminist art journal *n.paradoxa*, reviewed in the 2007 book *Naked on the Internet* by Audacia Ray, and posted online as a copyleft document.
20. subRosa is a cyberfeminist performance collective that can be visited online at http://www.cyberfeminism.net.

21. SVTC, *High Tech Trashing*, 1.
22. This website, last accessed in 2003, is no longer online.
23. Coalition against Trafficking in Women.

References

AfroGeeks: From Technophobia to Technophilia Conference, University of California, Santa Barbara, May 7–8, 2004.
Althusser, Louis. *Essays on Ideology*. London: Verso, 1984.
Anzaldúa, Gloria. *Borderlands: La Frontera, the New Mestiza*. 3rd ed. San Francisco: Aunt Lute Books, 1999.
Coalition against Trafficking in Women. Accessed July 2002 through January 2006, http://www.catwinternational.org.
Dinerstein, Joel. "Technology and Its Discontents: On the Verge of the Posthuman." In *Rewiring the "Nation": The Place of Technology in American Studies*, edited by Carolyn De la Pena and Siva Vaidhyanathan, 15–41. Baltimore: Johns Hopkins University Press, 2007.
Marx, Karl. *The Marx Engels Reader*. 2nd ed. New York: W.W. Norton, 1978.
Noble, David. *The Religion of Technology: The Divinity of Man and the Spirit of Invention*. New York: Penguin Group, 1999.
Silicon Valley Toxics Coalition and Basel Action Network. "The High Tech Trashing of Asia." Final Report. San Jose, 2002. Accessed October 1, 2010. http://www.ban.org/E-waste/technotrashfinalcomp.pdf.
International Telecommunication Union. "The World in 2010: ICT Facts and Figures." October 19, 2010. http://www.itu.int/ITU-D/ict/material/FactsFigures2010.pdf.
Wright, Michelle M. "Racism, Technology, and the Limits of Western Knowledge." In *Domain Errors!: Cyberfeminist Practices*, edited by Maria Fernandez, Faith Wilding, and Michelle M. Wright, 45–62. Brooklyn, NY: Autonomedia, 2003.

Black Feminist Calculus Meets Nothing to Prove

A Mobile Homecoming Project Ritual toward the Postdigital

Alexis Pauline Gumbs and Julia Roxanne Wallace

There is something to be said for prophecy. We are the future predicted by the careful calculations of our ancestors, their specific choices about when to breathe, when to sleep, who to be, where to go, and for how long. We are the echoes of their scratch work, their sacred carrying, their held lines and ink conclusions. Reading groundbreaking black feminist texts like *Home Girls*, *Some of Us Are Brave*, and *This Bridge Called My Back* published at the same time that we were being born, we know we were an expected audience, a faith-based prophecy come true. We trust the calculations of generations of named and unnamed black feminists. We are proof.

We are Alexis Pauline Gumbs and Julia Roxanne Wallace. Born on the cusp of the 1980s, we have been traveling the United States in a 1988 Winnebago on a journey called the Mobile Homecoming. We go to towns and cities looking for and finding black feminist LGBTQ (lesbian, gay, bisexual, transgender, and questioning) visionaries, making family, and amplifying the brilliance that allows us to exist. We are a digital family reunion on wheels, dancing and offering praise poetry and drumbeats, gathering in circles, replaying past strategies for community building, and generating shareable media to share our practices and the priceless brilliance of our community with the world.

305

To explain this process in the context of the black lesbian feminist and feminist of color genealogies that generate our being, we turn to what we call "black feminist calculus," a process that engages limits, the possibility of equality, and the potential for proof through a poetic practice of being profoundly present to the complexity of our community. This chapter will explain a theory of black feminist calculus and look at how the intergenerational range of very old and very new technologies that we quilt together in our project allows a ritual view of a profoundly connected, spiritually aligned postdigital future.

Black Feminist Calculus: A Primer.
Relevance of Identity, Equality, and Limits

If black women were free, it would mean that everyone else would have to be free since our freedom would necessitate the destruction of all systems of oppression.

—Combahee River Collective[1]

Neither of us was taught calculus, algebra, or any other form of math in school in a way that resonated with the limits, equalities, and imbalances that were most relevant to our survival. Black feminist calculus is based on a method for reading black feminist poetry circa 1979 developed by Alexis Pauline Gumbs.[2] Neither of us are mathematicians, and we suspect that most of our readers are not either, but we want to explain this in a way that is accessible. The way we look at it, the desire to amplify the black feminist brilliance of black LGBTQ people across generations is a polynomial, a problem with many variables to address. And calculus, the study of limits, feels particularly compelling to us because our expansive vision has faced many predictable limits from the very beginning. In fact, the limits that our project faces are historical; they precede us. Our practice of black feminist calculus is an attempt to create balance in the midst of contradictory precedents.

As we explain on our website in our essay about safety on the road as we travel the United States:

We are black and queer, so our histories of travel are not only voluntary, they are compelled and circumscribed by violence, hate and inequality. We hold the legacies of people on the run. We come from travelers who did not choose their journey to this continent. We come from travelers who dare not run out of gas because segregation and racial hatred in the South meant they could not stop without risking their lives. We come from travelers who were pushed off their land with the threat of lynching and the sanction of law. We come from travelers whose neighborhoods got trampled by new highway plans. We come from travelers who were kicked out of their homes for daring to love across boundaries.[3]

The limits we face as black feminist time and space travelers cannot be ignored; they must be addressed and accounted for in our actions and choices. At every step we are challenged to bring our boundless love and our constricted circumstances into balance. For this we use the technology of the equation.

Algebra teaches us that an equation is an equality that is not an identity. In math, identity means $1 = 1$ or $x = x$; in words, it means that the values on either side of the equal sign are the same. Algebra is about the equality of free variables. For example:

$$(x + 1)^2 = x^2 + 2x + 1.$$

This balance will work no matter what integer you plug in for x. The values on each side are the same. So there is no question that the sides of the equation are equal; it can be proven using any number. However, for what some mathematicians would distinguish as a real equation like

$$(x + 1)^2 = 2x^2 + x + 1,$$

the equality is only true if x equals either zero or one. This equation resonates with us, because equality is only maintained for very specific values—zero and one, which also happen to be the numbers that make up the binary code, the basis of contemporary digital technologies.

This problem with forms of equality that only balance out within a binary is an issue that we need black feminist calculus to address. For example, what happens when our community rejects binary gender forms, when we reject validated state forms of recognition, when we don't have access to contemporary digital forms of cultural capital, when the funding in the technology field generally goes to established mainstream organizations controlled by white folks, men, and straight folks, when as organizers of the project we refuse to conform to being either a

501(c)3 nonprofit organization or a traditional documentary film project?

Equations like the one above beg the mathematician to ask the question: Who does the existing relationship work for? *What brings balance on both sides of the equation in the current paradigm?* The answer is that it only works for zero and one. It does not work for two, three, four, or for most of us who do not conform. The queerness of our community and the queerness of our project require a transformative intervention into value. This is what we call black feminist calculus, and it inspires us to introduce new or unlikely variables into the project. For example, this is how we explain the way our use of the Revolutionary Mobile Homecoming Vehicle Sojourner addresses the limits our communities face:

> We come from travelers nonetheless, people who needed to be both mobile and at home, and who often had to choose between the two. So for us the "R" in RV stands for Revolutionary, for Resource, for Road-less-traveled, for Respect, for Re-imagining, for Reality. Thinking about what an RV could have meant for our ancestors and for some of our contemporaries who are running for their lives makes us accountable. We want our journey to be healing for us, and to provide a healing example for others about what movement can mean, where love can live, how home can survive.[4]

Poetic Calculation

The process of addressing limits can be applied to any technology. When you address the interaction of a boundless reality with a limited system through a technology called "language," it is called "poetics." Our process of creating praise poems for the visionaries that we honor and interview as part of the Mobile Homecoming project is an example of poetic calculation. Our love for each of these visionaries exceeds words, deserves new languages, and certainly goes beyond the boundaries of English, a language shaped by the logic of capitalism. However, we continue to create praise poems in English (the primary language of most of our participants). We want to live in a future where everyone chooses their most sacred words to honor the miracle of our elders, and so we enact that practice today, as proof. What follows traces the logic of some of our calculations as we create the Mobile Homecoming through a few selected praise poems for our participants as we journeyed through the desert.

Deciding Where to Start

A crucial step in every calculation is deciding where to start. In the Mobile Homecoming project we start with listening and we start from a place of love. The value of love and presence in our project leads to tangible decisions that prioritize the communities that inspire us. For example, unlike many projects, we made a decision early on that the fate of our project would not be determined by external funding sources and grants but rather by a grassroots community of sustainers who are part of the community the Mobile Homecoming hopes to empower and reflect and with which we are building power.

Placing the financial fate of our community in the hands of our own multiply oppressed community was an act of faith, and the fact that our community donated money to buy a retro RV and to fund the project to travel across the country conducting interviews and hosting events is an affirmation that the work we are doing is valued and needed by our communities. Our interdependence with our beloved community for the basic needs of the project and the basic needs of our lives addresses the limits of a community specifically disempowered by capitalist oppression by valuing contributions and support beyond the financial. We have received blessings, sacred stones, countless meals, places to sleep, names, connections, advice, energy healing, and infinite forms of support that affirm the value of our community members as crucial parts of a whole beyond their individual wealth or lack thereof.

Our values also inform where we start in terms of our methodology. Even though capitalism teaches us to fetishize products, we understand that the deepest value of our project does not come from the media products we create to make our experience and the brilliance of our community shareable. The resounding value of our project is the practice of orienting ourselves and our communities to intergenerationality composed of the practices of sharing time, space, affirmation, and recognition *within* our community. The community itself, created through these acts of trust, faith, and love, is the most important result of our project. This is revolutionary because our calculations, our everyday choices about when to press record and when not to, when to answer our phones, who to partner with, how often to say yes, who to eat with, and where to sleep are governed by the fact that we start from this community that created us, and our ultimate accountability is to the lifecycle of this community, not the values of the dominant class or the goal of gaining recognition and validation from a dominant audience. At the same time, starting with our community gives us access to the brilliance of all communities and the clarity that all oppressed communities have been intentionally fragmented and could benefit from intergenerational rituals and story sharing. The poetic result of our calculations shows us that through black feminist accountability to the intersectionally oppressed visionaries that have made our lives possible, we approach the common needs of a planetary community. Or the Combahee River Collective already taught us that, in order for us to be free, everyone has to be free and all forms of oppression must end. This poem for Alpha Thomas, a powerful elder in the South Dallas community, demonstrates the power of an intentional start:

For Alpha Thomas
Dallas, TX

Elder at the South Dallas Cultural Center
National Public Health Activist and Advocate
and Revolutionary Butch Mother

start here
in the place where
need walks
and answers keep

start here
where self unbound
shares
heart to opening face

start here
in the unsafe
posture of reality stretched
the complexity of your back bone

start right here
out front
where life is hungry
because love is just so visible

i believe a person
could end up anywhere

invent their own omega
but that start
right here
in
alpha

teaches the muscle for
moving through.

Alexis wrote this poem in celebration of Alpha's accomplishment and the achievement of her existence, and we presented it to her the first day we spent with her at the South Dallas cultural center along with a dance and drum affirmation to her name. Alpha later shared her amazing collection of T-shirts, newspaper clippings, and photos of the history of the black LGBTQ community in Dallas and around the country and performed her own poem about surviving breast cancer. Our experience with Alpha proves the value of a good start on many levels.

Choosing an Approach

Another important step in complex math, after deciding where to start or aligning on an order of operations, is to choose an approach. What is the theory that will measure the accountability of our actions? For the Mobile Homecoming a particular understanding of the meaning of intergenerationality governs our actions. As we explain on our website: "We exist because they intended us."

An Ethics of Accountability

This project is about affirming and producing family on the queer terms of choice. Just as much as our biological ancestors and elders have shaped our organs by providing us with their DNA, our chosen ancestors, elders, and mentors have also created us. By being themselves, by refusing to accept the limits imposed on their love, by believing despite everything that love and transformation were possible, and by creating a future worthy of themselves, they have built a world in which it is possible and easier for us to be our wild and growing selves. We know that family doesn't flow in one direction. We know that the past, the present, and the future re-create each other at each moment of encounter. We know that nothing is as natural as it seems. We understand that everything is contingent, so we take nothing for granted. We, therefore, choose our people with as much tenacity as they chose themselves. We choose ourselves with the same force with which they chose us.

We also understand that the choices of our elders to transform the meanings of life, family, and community have come with consequences. Many of our elders have been excluded from institutions such as their birth families, their religious communities, and the healthcare and social services institutions that have traditionally marginalized people of color whose family forms do not conform to any codes. Our elders have often been denied the emotional, spiritual, and financial support that they need. Just as our elders created alternative institutions of mutual support, we know that it is our responsibility to embrace and care for these warriors and to mend and dress any wounds they have incurred along the way. We are responsible for the physical, spiritual, emotional, and financial well-being of our elders. Our heroes and heroines need not become martyrs before they earn our praise. Thus the urgency of our project. They deserve to be lifted up, body, soul, and spirit RIGHT NOW.

Math and all of the social calculations we make depend on a basic theory of how things are related. Every math problem starts from a belief about the relationship between one and two, two and three, n and the nth degree. In our project our basic theory of how we are related to our black LGBTQ community involves a reclamation and celebration of family. We believe that we share not only intersecting oppressions but also a life thread of brilliance that sustains us and connects us. Our encounters with Priscilla Hale, a member of our chosen family who also codirects ALLGO, a visionary LGBTQ people of color organization based in Austin, Texas, exemplify this belief in the everyday organic practice of being family and creating community.

For Priscilla Hale

Codirector of Allgo
Building LGBTQ People of Color Alliances in Texas

heirloom seed
mother of thousands
you are a lesson in roots
and growth
in hands interlocked underground
in fists breaking through soil

you are the answer
to the question
of what happens
when we stay

you are the event
of guerilla gardening
guided and gathering
conditions for growth

the way you convene ceremony
is art
the way you abandon the profane
is elegance

and the way this community flowers
into love
is proof.

At a transformative brunch at the home of Priscilla and her partner
and fellow codirector of ALLGO, Rose Pulliam, we experienced both
the literal garden at their home and the careful nurturing of intergenerational community that they develop through shared meals, laughter,
and collaborative work. Priscilla used and articulated the art of a well-
timed shared meal as a crucial technology for community building and
knowledge sharing.

On Technology. The Necessity of the Digital (Approaching the Limit):

She used her skills not to advance her own status, but to help her fellow slaves, and this under the most difficult circumstances. . . . The
knowledge she conveyed had a politically and materially transforming function, that is, it empowered people to gain freedom.

—Laura Haviland[5]

Driving through a treacherous national park, misguided by GPS technology, using 1980s gas crisis technology in the form of our retro RV to drive,
we finally reached eighty-seven-year-old Vera Martin in Apache Junction,
Arizona, where she lives in a lesbian modular trailer park. The necessity

of the digital and betrayal of the digital converge. After spending the day with Ms. Vera we knew that we needed to share her insights into self-affirmation beyond religious violence, revolution, youth empowerment, and the urgency of our present moment as quickly as possible with all the communities we could reach. It is simply not acceptable to us that the only people able to hear from Ms. Vera would be those with the bad sense to brave Arizona and seek out the lesbian RV park where she is one of two black residents, in a town that is explicitly limited to those over fifty-five (literally, we had to camp forty-five minutes away). The short social media shareable videos that we made almost immediately from key moments in our interview with Ms. Vera demonstrate some of the value of making a digital copy of an irreplaceable in-person experience. Our communities could not be in Ms. Vera's tiny living room with us, but it was important for us to transmit the next best DSLR (digital single-lens reflex) high-resolution thing! As our praise poem emphasizes, Ms. Vera's words are not to be ignored. I wrote this poem about the experience of watching Ms. Vera laugh and count her beliefs on her fingers.

A Catalog of Belief

For Vera Martin
Elder in Black Gay and Lesbian Leadership Forum
and Founder of Old Lesbians Organizing For Change

i believe that laughter is eternal life.

i believe that great grandmothers chosen or given are magical
on gp.

i believe that numbers remember themselves when counted
    in our bodies.

i believe that every mystery is at best only equal to the
    radical unlikeliness
of you
who fled the rule of rape in louisiana
and the reality of boredom in northern california
living
in a lesbian RV park in Arizona
off Rosa Parks street.

and i best believe
that I best better listen
to everything ms. Vera says
and do what she asks
and smile.

i believe in you.

As we alluded to earlier, we find the digital useful as part of an intergenerational range of technologies; however, we are acutely aware of the limits of the binary, both conceptually and experientially. One of the unfortunate things about binary is that it inevitably cuts out some of the data, even though often that data is imperceptible to the average ear or eye. The ones and zeros are a very tiny rounding down of numbers that are more diverse. The tip of the wave is cut off of any digital transmission, prompting the question: What quality do we lose in our access to the ability to make an easier copy? What does it mean to treat our once in a lifetime experience with Ms. Vera as something that can be replicated? Does the binary recoding of our experiences lead us to round down our engagement with each other, treating each other as interchangeable copies and losing the opportunity to honor our irreplaceable differences?

A major question that our use of the digital, our intimate experiences of the limits of the digital, and our work on a project that centers the experiences of oppressed and invalidated people is that the relationship between zero and one resonates with the process of affirming the subjectivity of oppressed people. It is affirming and validating for self-identified LGBTQ people of color to look at Ms. Vera, an eighty-seven-year-old energetic, critical, and laughing elder and to understand that they too might survive to critique and transform a new day. On a larger scale, our project could be understood to play a role in a broader validation project where a whole community of people who are constantly dehumanized by oppression or seen as zeros can affirm that, as Jesse Jackson quipped, we are somebody (one). We understand the civil rights struggles of our intersectionally oppressed communities in this context. In a system where you are either granted the rights of personhood, or not, we are forced to strive for recognition, to prove that we are not nothing, that we exist.

However, before Jesse Jackson said, "I am somebody," Fred Hampton, Chicago leader of the Black Panther Party for Self-Defense, led masses of people in chanting, "I am a revolutionary." The fact is that our project, largely propagated by digital means, has confronted us with the truth that the value of our community and the brilliance of the individuals within it exceed the binary. Who we are is not limited to what the system that recognizes or punishes us can understand. We are nothing and everything. We are both zero and one, where zero is the circle that connects us to each other and one is the unity of our profound connection to each other and all life. And we are every other number too. The truth is that our digital project, because of the accountability of our calculations, leads us to postdigital implications.

Toward the Postdigital

In her articulation of a jazz aesthetic and its relationship to black queerness, performance studies scholar and Mobile Homecoming interviewee Omi Oshun explicitly breaks down the presumptions of binary reality. For her, black queerness means that life is not a choice between "this or that" (i.e., the zero and one that binary code depends on) but rather an understanding of this *and* that, the simultaneity of being that is not mutually exclusive. Black queerness is an experience of being within limiting the self to a binary. Omi Oshun's insight reflects an earlier assertion by black feminist poet Lucille Clifton in her unpublished manuscript on black astrology, which is that black life on the planet is a message that the spiritual and physical, the eternal and the temporal, all of the binaries that we can imagine, do not hold. We are all of these things at once. In our performance for Omi Oshun we presented a poem ritual affirming that "this is that," affirming the unity being and the miracle of being present in the same space as Omi.

For Omi Oshun/Joni Jones

Performance Studies Scholar
Performer
Cofounder of The Austin Project
Coauthor of Experiments in the Jazz Aesthetic

this is that
unspared moment
when we celebrate the truth

when we stand on it
when we look it in the eye and ask it how it got here
when we raise our eyebrows tempting it to leave

this is that
ruthless moment
of truth unsparing
so we wear it
so we pick it up
so we admit we cannot climb over it

this is that
tea-stained moment
when we sit down with the truth
a friend we have been avoiding
a mirror unclothed

this is that
destined moment
when we walk out our warrior
make up our mothering
remember our presence

this is that
this and that
moment when we choose
that this
experience we are calling self
could be anything
and must be now.

Coda

They dreamed dreams that no one knew—not even themselves,
in any coherent fashion—and saw visions no one could understand. . . . They waited for a day when the unknown thing that was
in them would be made known; but guessed somehow in their darkness, that on the day of their revelation they would be long dead.

—Alice Walker[6]

The urgency of our project and the imperative to transform is based on another mathematical principle: that there is such a thing as truth. We believe the interconnected digital reality that we navigate today is ultimately a metaphor. And we have decided that instead of affirming a metaphor that would insist that life imitates code and exists in binary terms, we see circles and oneness. We move beyond yes and no to a more complicated system of divination. We gather in circles and affirm our connection to each other. We invoke alignment where there seemed to be only the possibility of equality. We practice radical presence accountability and love toward a postdigital reality where our alignment is apparent and our access to each other is not limited by space, time, or access to capital. We invite this reality through our use of a relatively old piece of technology, our RV:

> Our RV will not only travel through space, it will travel through time, sitting in the untimely place where this anomaly, this miracle, queer black initiates, media makers, adventurers transmitting history and reframing the future in a mobile home, is possible. We see the RV itself as surrounded in two-way windows, as we take in the lessons that the land and the people have to offer and transmit the insights of our journey out to the world. What would it mean to have a vehicle that is both state of the art and ancient[?] Where wireless streams, and ancestor lessons echo at the same time, where the turning of the wheel is a historical function, fueled by futuristic faith?[7]

We have something to prove and nothing to prove, all at the same time. This is that prophecy. We'll see you there.

Ritual Proof

as in love evidence
check my footwork
watch what it do

Ritual Proof

as in meditation
for clarity for correction

Ritual Proof

as in a path that leads to truth and discovery
as in a measure of power of transcendence of presence
as in an act of resistance of resilience

Ritual Proof

calculus style
as in what is the limit
of this life
this legacy
seen and unseen
echoed in story
hiccupped in common care
reflected through our sanctified soul

How far do we have to go
For our oneness
how still
how silent must we listen
to move, live and thrive forever
as one
as family
with nothing
to prove.

Notes

1. Combahee River Collective Statement (repr. in Hull, Scott, and Smith, *Some of Us Are Brave*), 18.

2. Presented at the Continuing Relevance of the 1970's and published on iTunes U by *Polygraph Journal*, http://www.duke.edu/web/polygraph/events.html.

3. "Safety: Abolitionist Vision," http://www.mobilehomecoming.org/about-2/safety-an-abolitionist-vision.

4. "How We Roll," http://www.mobilehomecoming.org/about-2/revolutionary-vehicle.

5. Laura S. Haviland, "A Woman's Life Work, Labors and Experiences" (repr. in Hull, Scott, and Smith, *Some of Us Are Brave*), xix–xx.

6. Alice Walker, "In Search of Our Mother's Gardens" (repr. in Hull, Scott, and Smith, *Some of Us Are Brave*).

7. "How We Roll," http://www.mobilehomecoming.org/about-2/revolutionary-vehicle.

References

Hull, Gloria, Patricia Bell Scott, and Barbara Smith, eds. *All the Women Are White, All the Blacks Are Men, but Some of Us Are Brave: Black Women's Studies*. New York: Feminist Press, 1982.

About the Contributors

Epifania Amoo-Adare is a researcher, educator, and "renegade" architect with more than twenty-five years' experience working in places like Afghanistan, Armenia, Azerbaijan, Georgia, Ghana, Qatar, the United Kingdom, and the United States. She has a PhD in education from UCLA and is also a Royal Institute of British Architects ([RIBA] part II) qualified architect with diverse and transdisciplinary scholarly interests in areas such as "Third World" feminisms, critical pedagogy, critical social theory, critical spatial literacy, cultural studies, globalization studies, migration studies, urban studies, and international educational development. Currently, Dr. Amoo-Adare lives in Germany, where she works at the Center for Development Research (ZEF), University of Bonn. Here, in collaboration with Crossroads Asia network colleagues, she is responsible for developing space as a synthesizing research perspective for rethinking area studies. Dr. Amoo-Adare is the author of *Spatial Literacy: Contemporary Asante Women's Place-Making* (Palgrave Macmillan, 2013).

Patti Duncan is associate professor and coordinator of Women, Gender, and Sexuality Studies at Oregon State University, where she specializes in women of color feminisms, transnational feminisms, feminist media studies, and motherhood studies. She is the author of *Tell This Silence: Asian American Women Writers and the Politics of Speech* (University of Iowa Press, 2004), coproducer/director of the documentary film *Finding Face* (2009), and coeditor of *Mothering in East Asian Communities: Politics and Practices* (Demeter Press, 2014). Her current research focuses on narratives of rescue, migration, and motherhood in representations of women in the global South.

Susana L. Gallardo holds a PhD in religious studies from Stanford University and a masters in theological studies from Harvard Divinity

School. She is currently a lecturer in the Women, Gender, and Sexuality Studies Program at San Jose State University and in the Program in Chicana/o–Latina/o Studies at Stanford. Susana is a third/fifth generation Chicana from Southern California.

Jessi Gan grew up in the San Francisco Bay Area, where she currently lives with her families. Her writing has appeared in the journals *Amerasia* and *Centro*. She is a doctoral candidate in American culture at the University of Michigan, where she is completing a dissertation about US neurologists' identification of "homosexual" patients in the 1880s.

Alicia Garza is an organizer, writer, and freedom dreamer living and working in Oakland, CA. She is the special projects director for the National Domestic Workers Alliance, the nation's leading voice for dignity and fairness for the millions of domestic workers in the United States, most of whom are women. She is also the cocreator of #BlackLivesMatter, a national organizing project focused on combatting anti-black state sanctioned violence. Alicia's work challenges us to celebrate the contributions of black queer women's work within popular narratives of black movements, and reminds us that the black radical tradition is long, complex and international. Her activism reflects organizational strategies and visions that connect emerging social movements without diminishing the specificity of the structural violence facing black lives.

Alexis Pauline Gumbs is a queer black troublemaker, a black feminist love evangelist, and the instigator of the Eternal Summer of the Black Feminist Mind educational initiative (blackfeministmind.wordpress. com). She and her partner, Julia Roxanne Wallace, are the cocreators of the Mobile Homecoming Project, an experiential archive project amplifying generations of queer black feminist brilliance (mobilehomecoming. org). Alexis holds a PhD in English, African and African American studies, and women's studies from Duke University. Alexis was named one of *UTNE Reader*'s fifty Visionaries Transforming the World in 2009, a Reproductive Health Reality Check Shero, a Black Women Rising nominee in 2010, a recipient of the Too Sexy for 501C-3 trophy in 2011, and one of the *Advocate*'s Top 40 Under 40 in 2012.

Janell Hobson is associate professor of women's, gender, and sexuality studies at the University at Albany. She is the author of *Venus in the Dark: Blackness and Beauty in Popular Culture* (Routledge, 2005) and *Body* as *Evidence: Mediating Race, Globalizing Gender* (SUNY Press, 2012). She also writes and blogs for *Ms.* and other publications, including the online blogs *The Feminist Wire* and *AAIHS (African American Intellectual History Society)*. She has guest edited a special issue on Harriet Tubman for the peer-reviewed journal *Meridians: Feminism, Race, Transnationalism* and is currently researching black women's iconographic histories in transnational perspective.

Gigi Marie Jasper has the great good fortune of having been taught by Jimmy Britton and Nancy Martin at Oxford University, Victor Villanueva at Washington State University, Gordon Pradl at New York University, and Duke Ellington at the University of Wisconsin, Madison. She completed her dissertation, "Educating the Oppressor: Black Teachers, White Students" for New York University and continues to teach Wyoming high school students. Her husband, Steve Shea, is a man of infinite patience and humor.

Ana M. Juárez is an associate professor in the Department of Anthropology at Texas State University. Her publications have appeared in *Chicana/Latina Studies: The Journal of MALCS*, *Frontiers: A Journal of Women Studies*, *The Journal of Latin American Anthropology*, *Human Organization*, *Aztlan: A Journal of Chicano Studies*, *Temas Antropológicos (Revista Científica de Investigaciones Regionales)*, and *Latin American Indian Literatures Journal*. Juárez's research includes issues of race, gender, sexuality, and the effects of globalization in Latin America, especially among Mayas in Quintana Roo, Mexico and among Latinas/os in the United States. She is currently working on an ethnohistory project that uses cemeteries and funerary practices as a lens to understand a Mexican American community in central Texas.

Stella Beatríz Kerl-McClain is a licensed psychologist and an associate professor at Lewis and Clark College in Portland, Oregon. She has worked in many different clinical settings, including women's centers, community mental health agencies, medical settings, and university counseling centers. Her teaching responsibilities include all levels of counseling techniques courses; courses focusing on diagnosis and treatment, practicum, and internship; and courses in diverse populations and counseling theories. Her research interests primarily involve gender, race, and cultural issues in therapy and mental health. She regularly presents at state and national conferences and has publications in several journals, including the *Journal of Multicultural Counseling and Development*, *Counselor Education and Supervision*, *Aztlan: A Journal of Chicano Studies*, and *Rehabilitation Psychology*.

David Leonard is professor and chair in the Department of Critical Culture, Gender and Race Studies at Washington State University, Pullman. He is the author of *After Artest: The NBA and the Assault on Blackness* (SUNY Press, 2012) as well as several other works. He is a regular contributor to *Vitae*, *The Chronicle of Higher Education*, *NewBlackMan*, and *The Feminist Wire*.

Joey Lusk is a writer, feminist gadfly, former sex worker, and Jill-of-all-skills. She draws from an interdisciplinary education in the humanities and sciences, professional experience in the field of mental health, and her own experiences as a woman with an atypical neurological profile. She has been a managing editor of *transcending silence . . .* , the first online undergraduate academic journal in women's studies, at the University at Albany. Most recently, she gave a reading of her short-form memoir, *The Circus of Hagia Sophia*, at the Center for Sex and Culture in San Francisco. Mostly, she argues with people. About everything. All the time.

Darnell L. Moore is a writer based in Brooklyn, New York. He is a managing editor/partner of *The Feminist Wire*, with Tamura Lomax and Monica Casper. He also cocreated YOU Belong, a social good organization, with former NFL player Wade Davis II. In addition, he is a fellow at the Center on African American Religion, Sexuality and Social Justice at Columbia University. And he is part of the Brothers Writing to Live collective along with writers Kiese Laymon, Mychal Denzel Smith, Marlon Peterson, Kai M. Green, Wade Davis, Mark Anthony Neal, and Hashim Pipkin.

Julia Chinyere Oparah, formerly Julia Sudbury, is associate provost and an activist scholar and professor of ethnic studies at Mills College. After a decade of activism in the black women's movement in Britain, Chinyere moved to the United States, where she became involved in racial and gender justice, prison abolition, and birth justice work. She is a cofounder of Critical Resistance and has worked with INCITE! Women of Color Against Violence, Toronto Prisoner Justice Action Committee, Arizona Prison Moratorium Coalition, and other social justice organizations. Chinyere is author of *Other Kinds of Dreams: Black Women's Organisations and the Politics of Transformation* (Routledge, 1998), editor of *Global Lockdown: Race, Gender and the Prison Industrial Complex* (Routledge, 2005), and coeditor of *Activist Scholarship: Antiracism, Feminism and Social Change* (Paradigm 2009), *Outsiders within: Writing on Transracial Adoption* (South End Press, 2006), and *Color of Violence: The INCITE! Anthology* (South End, 2006). Most recently, she coedited with Alicia Bonaparte *Birthing Justice: Black Women, Pregnancy and Childbirth* (Routledge, 2015). She is currently working with Black Women Birthing Justice on a participatory action research project documenting one hundred black women's experiences of childbirth. Chinyere's daughter Onyekachi Georgia was born in 2010.

Suey Park is a graduate of University of Illinois, Urbana-Champaign. She is a board member of Activist Millennials and a member of INCITE! Women of Color Against Violence. She created the viral hashtag #NotYourAsianSidekick and has written for several online publications, including XOJane, Model View Culture, Youngist, as well as her own blog, Critical Spontaneity. Suey is passionate about race, gender, and activism in a digital era.

Praba Pilar is a diasporic Colombian artist keen on disrupting the overwhelmingly passive participation in the contemporary "cult of the technologic." Over the past two decades Pilar has presented cultural productions integrating performance art, street theatre, electronic installations, digital works, video, websites, and writing. These projects have traveled widely to museums, galleries, universities, performance festivals, conferences, public streets, and radio airwaves around the world. Pilar has a PhD in performance studies from the University of California, Davis (2014). Her dissertation, "Latin@s Byte Back: Contestational Performance in the TechnoSphere" explores the work of Latina/o performance artists in the United States who resist, subvert, and contest unethical and destructive aspects of contemporary technological development. She has recently published in the *Lateral Journal of the Cultural Studies Association*, the *Dance Current*, KATALOG, *localflux*, *WEAD Magazine*, and *h+Magazine*.

Hashim Khalil Pipkin is a student in the English PhD program at Vanderbilt University. He studies queer theory, African American literature, and cultures of death. He is also a member of the Brothers Writing to Live collective.

Raquel Z. Rivera is a singer-songwriter, author, and scholar. Her CD *Las 7 salves de La Magdalena/7 Songs of Praise for the Magdalene* (Ojos de Sofia, 2010) weaves together Dominican *salves*, Puerto Rican *jíbaro* music, *bomba*, and other Caribbean roots genres. The album debuted at number 16 in March 2011 on the Top 20 World Music Charts Europe. A founding member of Boricua roots music group Yerbabuena, the Afro-Puerto Rican music ensemble Alma Moyo, and the all-women's percussion and vocal collective Yaya, she has also performed with Grammy-nominated Los Pleneros de la 21, internationally renowned Dominican fusion artists Luis Dias and Xiomara Fortuna, and Pa' lo Monte, Kalunga, Palo Mayor, and various other New York–based Caribbean roots music groups and artists. She has a PhD in sociology and is a visiting scholar at the Sociology Department of the University of New Mexico. She is coeditor of the anthology *Reggaeton* (Duke University Press, 2009) and author of *New York Ricans from the Hip Hop Zone* (Palgrave Macmillan, 2003) as well as numerous articles on Caribbean Latino popular music and culture. Her musical work has earned her artist grants from the National Association of Latino Arts and Cultures (2014), Rockefeller Foundation's NYC Cultural Innovation Fund (2011), Manhattan Community Arts Fund (2010), and the Association of Hispanic Arts (2009). She has received postdoctoral fellowships from the Andrew W. Mellon Foundation (2004–2006) and the Center for Puerto Rican Studies (2007) at Hunter College and a Visiting Library Scholar Award from the University of New Mexico (2011). Born and raised in Puerto Rico, she moved to New York City in 1994 and presently lives in Albuquerque.

Purvi Shah inspires change as a nonprofit consultant, antiviolence advocate, and arts activist. In 2008, during her tenure as executive director of Sakhi for South Asian Women, she won the inaugural SONY Social Service Excellence Award for her leadership fighting violence against women. Alongside her work on gender violence, she has taught underserved youth, organized racial justice convenings, and spearheaded policy change on language access. During the tenth anniversary of 9/11, she directed *Together We Are New York*, a community-based poetry project to highlight Asian American voices. *Terrain Tracks* (New Rivers Press, 2006) is her award-winning book of poetry. *Dark Lip of the Beloved: Sound Your Fiery God-Praise* (Belladonna, 2015) is her new poetry chaplet. She is known for her sparkly eyeshadow and raucous laughter. Discover her work at http://purvipoets.net or @PurviPoets.

Andrea Smith is associate professor of media and cultural studies at UC Riverside and cofounder of INCITE! Women of Color Against Violence. She is the author of *Conquest: Sexual Violence and American Indian Genocide* (South End Press, 2005) and *Native Americans and the Christian Right: The Gendered Politics of Unlikely Alliances* (Duke University Press, 2008).

Gina Athena Ulysse is professor of anthropology at Wesleyan University in Middletown, Connecticut. She is the author of *Downtown Ladies: Informal Commercial Importers, A Haitian Anthropologist and Self-Making in Jamaica* (University of Chicago Press, 2008) and *Why Haiti Needs New Narratives: A Post-Quake Chronicle* (Wesleyan University Press, 2015). She has published numerous articles and creative nonfiction works in refereed journals and anthologies. A poet/performance/multimedia artist, Gina Athena has presented her work in national and international venues. Periodically, she blogs for *Africa Is a Country*, *Huffington Post*, *Ms. Magazine*, and *Tikkun Daily*.

Jamie D. Walker is a journalist, screenwriter, and director who received her BA in drama from San Francisco State University and her PhD in African American literature from Howard. Currently, she teaches documentary making and African American independent film at Santa Clara University.

Julia Roxanne Wallace (Sangodare) is a filmmaker, musician, multimedia artist, priest, and social entrepreneur. Wallace is the founder of Queer Renaissance, a creative multimedia movement based on the belief that *we can create the world anew*, and JRoxMedia, a multimedia consulting business that facilitates and produces media work centered on accountability to queer communities of color and cofounder (with Alexis Pauline Gumbs) of the Mobile Homecoming experiential archive amplifying generations of queer black brilliance. Julia earned a BA from the University of North Carolina, Asheville and an MDiv from Emory University, and she is the cofounder of Black Feminist Film School.

Index

Made in the USA
Coppell, TX
24 September 2020